"Moral failure in church leadership continues to make the news, destroying lives and compromising the witness of the church. In this book, Lance Bacon provides the church with a deliberate and systematic response to sexual misconduct in the church. His scholarly and highly practical treatment of this important topic serves to inoculate ministers against problems that are viral in the church and provides a clear pathway for the restoration of broken ministers."

—JAMES T. FLYNN,
associate dean of instruction and operations,
School of Divinity, Regent University

"All too often, churches are ill-equipped to handle instances of moral failure within the ranks of its pastoral leadership. In many cases, such failure is swept under the proverbial rug of the church or forever held over the head of the guilty. Lance Bacon's work compels us to avoid both extremes by addressing the nature and practice of 'restoration' from a scriptural perspective. This book is a well-researched and biblically informed treatment of one of the most important issues facing the church today. I cannot imagine a timelier and more important work."

—SCOTT ADAMS,
assistant professor, School of Divinity, Regent University

"As we journey through a life of calling, sometimes unfortunate decisions cause heartache and an interruption of ministry. Recovery from spiritual and moral battles comes through a recommitment to the original call and a grateful heart for saving grace."

—TIM HILL,
presiding bishop, Church of God, Cleveland, TN

"Unfortunately, the church has not been on the frontlines of dealing with the issues of sexual immorality in relation to our ministers—until now! Lance Bacon has given the church a scholarly resource that will help us navigate the murky waters of sexual failure. This resource is both academic and practical. Bacon helps us to identify negative behaviors that lead to such moral collapse, as well as sound biblical solutions to restore our brothers and sisters back into the church and their calling."

—MICHAEL A. BALL,
national evangelist, Church of God

"The first step toward recovery is admitting there's a problem. Lance Bacon's work is an apt intervention for the global church, attempting to convince us that there is a problem with a cascade of undeniable evidence. This book is a revealing light or magnifying mirror oriented toward the inner life of the minister. Pastor, do not look away. Reflect on the current clergy carnage, take stock of your soul, and embrace Bacon's lead by committing to work in ministerial recovery and restoration—a work that is no quick fix."

—STEVE HALL,
associate professor of pastoral ministry, Lee University

"How will today's congregation respond after the cyclone of ministerial moral failure wreaks its havoc? In this work, Lance Bacon offers piquant, scripturally sound practical insight on arguably the foremost pitfall facing ecclesial leaders today. Informed by decades of firsthand pastoral experience, Bacon's well-researched, comprehensive guide for restoring the fallen minister presents a compelling, step-by-step roadmap through the wilderness of indiscretion. This book is a must-read for sexually offending clergy, their families, the victims, and fellow congregants immersed in such a storm or weathering through its aftermath."

—PAUL J. PALMA,
author of *Embracing Our Roots: Rediscovering the Value of Faith, Family, and Tradition*

"Today, there are many and varied significant issues in contemporary ministry that result in consequential impact. One issue that is unexpected and brings a myriad of questions is instances of sexual immorality by ministers. The query for information includes why, how, and causal factors. Lance Bacon presents a relevant approach to the magnitude of Galatians 6:1, 'If anyone is caught in any trespass, you who are spiritual, *Restore Such a One* in a spirit of gentleness.' Every ministry leader, pastor, church leader and layperson will find this book filled with theological insight, spiritual guidance, and practical engagement. This is one book to read again and again!"

—MICHAEL L. BAKER,
president, Pentecostal Theological Seminary

Restore Such a One

Restore Such a One

*Holistic Restoration for Ministers, Families,
and Churches Following a Sexual Moral Failure*

LANCE M. BACON

WIPF & STOCK · Eugene, Oregon

RESTORE SUCH A ONE
Holistic Restoration for Ministers, Families, and Churches Following a Sexual Moral Failure

Copyright © 2024 Lance M. Bacon. All rights reserved. Except for brief quotations in critical publications or reviews, no part of this book may be reproduced in any manner without prior written permission from the publisher. Write: Permissions, Wipf and Stock Publishers, 199 W. 8th Ave., Suite 3, Eugene, OR 97401.

Wipf & Stock
An Imprint of Wipf and Stock Publishers
199 W. 8th Ave., Suite 3
Eugene, OR 97401

www.wipfandstock.com

PAPERBACK ISBN: 979-8-3852-2107-3
HARDCOVER ISBN: 979-8-3852-2108-0
EBOOK ISBN: 979-8-3852-2109-7

07/30/24

Scripture quotations taken from the (NASB®) New American Standard Bible®, Copyright © 1960, 1971, 1977, 1995, 2020 by The Lockman Foundation. Used by permission. All rights reserved. lockman.org

Dedicated to my friend, Greg Robinson, who kept me smiling through many challenges inherent to the pastor/theologian call. Though separated by a state, we were united in ministry and, later, pursuing a PhD. You graduated to glory sooner than I would have liked. I celebrate the reward you received. I find comfort as I imagine you walking with Jesus, discussing the deep things of God with which we are left to wrestle. We will continue to do so, though the journey is diminished without you alongside. I shall think of you often as I fulfill this ministry. I eagerly anticipate our reunion. Until that day, my brother . . .

Contents

Illustrations | ix

Acknowledgements | xi

Introduction | xiii

SECTION ONE: HEAVEN, WE HAVE A PROBLEM | 1
1. This Problem Is Worse Than Ever | 3
2. This Problem Is Worse Than We Realize | 25
3. The Biblical Solution | 47
   Section One Summary | 69

SECTION TWO: ELEMENTS OF THE PERFECT STORM | 75
4. Stormfront No. 1—The Flesh (Emotional) | 79
5. Stormfront No. 2—The World (Cultural) | 98
6. Stormfront No. 3—The Devil (Spiritual) | 121
   Section Two Summary | 140

SECTION THREE: WHEN DISASTER STRIKES | 145
7. Assessing the Damage | 150
8. Building the Restoration Team | 173
9. Building the Restoration Plan | 197
   Section Three Summary | 217

SECTION FOUR: RESTORE, REBUILD, AND REINFORCE | 223
10. Restore the Foundation | 227
11. Rebuild the Walls | 245
12. Reinforcing the Structure | 266
    Section Four Summary | 281

Conclusion | 283

Excursus 1: Review of Sexual Morality in Church History | 289

Excursus 2: A Case Study of Pentecostal Pioneers | 301

Excursus 3: The Role of Free Will | 310

Excursus 4: Restoration Resources | 320

Glossary | 332

Bibliography | 339

Illustrations

Figure 1: The Holistic Ministerial Restoration Process | 21

Figure 2: Examples of Christian Worldviews | 105

Figure 3: The Cycle of Temptation | 205

Figure 4: The Holmes-Rahe Life Stress Inventory | 321

Acknowledgements

Above all, I thank God. Such grace is beyond my understanding, and my thanks are beyond words.

I thank my beautiful wife, Crystal, and our four children for their patience and encouragement. You are my greatest blessings.

I thank Dr. Diane Chandler for her wisdom and guidance throughout my journey.

I thank the members of Greater Discipleship Center for their prayerful support and commitment to a kingdom work that often takes their pastor beyond their four walls.

Introduction

"How can you draw close to God when you are far from your own self? Grant, Lord, that I may know myself that I may know thee."

— Augustine of Hippo

If you are reading this, it is with good reason. This book is not the type one peruses on a whim. Perhaps you or someone you care about is a victim of sexual impropriety and doesn't know what to do. Or a congregant looking to rebuild the rubble of a church decimated by scandal. Or a church or denominational leader with the daunting task of confronting a sexually immoral minister. Or a pastor who has succumbed to temptation and wonders if all is lost. Maybe you are nearing a fall, unable to stop, and grasping for deliverance before your world crumbles beneath.

Take heart, my friend. This book will help.

Sadly, though not shockingly, ministerial sexual moral failures are commonplace. Responses vary and often lack a biblical basis. This book presents a holistic restoration model that is applicable in *some* instances. This work neither advocates restoring all offenders nor serves as an arbitrary checklist to ensure due diligence before ministerial reassignment. Restoration to God is available to all, but restoration to ministerial office is limited. Fallen ministers who qualify are in for the fight of their lives, but like Jacob, the touch of God will forever change their walk, identity, and destiny (see Gen 32:24–32).

Let's begin by laying some foundational understanding:

- Though there are many types of moral failures, and the biblical guidance that follows applies to ministerial restoration in each, this book focuses on sexual moral failure as this is the prevalent and arguably most egregious variety.

INTRODUCTION

- Sexual moral failures are rarely a momentary lapse but are often the culmination of spiritual and emotional digression. Under significant ministerial burdens and typically lacking sufficient training in spiritual formation, emotionally isolated pastors sometimes seek relief through learned behaviors through which we avoid pain, cope with struggle, or find happiness and self-worth. Therefore . . .

- Psychology will come into play. Some Christians cringe at the thought, but Scripture has much to say about mental health and thought life. We will explore this in detail, but as we lay foundations, it is essential to note that three powerful forces oppose the spiritual walk: the flesh, the world, and the devil (Eph 2:2–3, cf. Jas 3:15 and 1 John 2:16). The desires we wrestle with are often the product of time and trauma. Rather than work tirelessly to cut away the "bad fruit," we shall look beneath the surface to remove the "bad root" that enables bad fruit to return in due season. Therefore . . .

- This holistic restoration model moves beyond behavior modification to embrace a divine transformation of heart and affections. The goal is to change rather than to cure. Physical, emotional, social, and spiritual formation centers on a "sanctifying psychopathology" that deals with the violator's shame, heals emotional wounds caused by trauma and dysfunctional relationships, reforms neural pathways, and replaces the negative self-image with one's identity in Christ.

- The words "(re)formation" and "(de)formation" appear throughout and deserve an explanation. In this book, "reformation" speaks of an initiated return to what something once was, "formation" is the ongoing creation of something new, and "transformation" speaks to the alteration or redirection of something that exists. Specifically, believers are reformed in the image of God and formed into Christlikeness, resulting in the transformation of thoughts and behaviors. Conversely, "(re)formation" speaks of one's return to one or more of those three actions to resume spiritual and emotional growth and re-form that which was being formed or transformed but was broken amid moral failure. This process similarly seeks to heal (de)formation, the desecration and destruction that results when one deviates from the formative or transformative work.

- Such (re)formation is necessary for ministerial restoration. This process requires the believer to partner with the Spirit and cooperate with crucial ministry figures, including an overseer, mentors, professional Christian mental health providers, and a designated congregation.

INTRODUCTION

Indeed, (re)formation is personal *and* communal. Together, they endeavor to reform the self-oriented patterns of thought and willful behaviors to reconcile with God, family, and possibly ministerial calling.

- Biblical restoration demands the dedicated care of the abused, the violator's family, and the affected congregation. These groups are typically neglected and even shunned; churches retraumatize victims and deny biblical justice when they fail to facilitate the healing of wounds inherent to abuse. This work asserts a biblical justice that requires compassionate support in safe and secure environments.

- The book uses the pronoun "he" when referring to the violating minister, but this neither asserts that males alone can be pastors nor does it deny that some female clergy are guilty of sexual misconduct. The overwhelming majority of violators are males; therefore, this book uses masculine pronouns.

So, why did I write this book? Do I hope to validate my return to ministry after a sexual moral failure? No. I have had no such failure. But I have twice been on staff when a senior pastor fell, have had staff ministers fail, and have counseled dozens of ministers and congregants devastated by this pastoral plague. More times than I can count (or care to admit), I have seen abysmal responses from churches, denominations, and ministry networks. Contemporary restoration models typically build upon secular programs and infuse biblical passages in support. Most are rife with significant deficiencies and are as varied and vast as the opinions that shaped them. Indeed, secular rather than sacred principles typically drive decisions for or against restoration. This disheartening lack of biblical consensus sees one pastor immediately restored, the next banished forever, and others allowed to resume duties after a forced sabbatical or transfer. These approaches neither satisfy the biblical standard nor serve those affected. Such "solutions" only exacerbate the pain of already broken souls and often allow perpetrators to return to the pulpit without spiritual and emotional healing.

There is a better way. It is the biblical way. Rather than include Scripture, this holistic restoration and (re)formation paradigm trusts Scripture to overcome the inadequacies and inconsistencies inherent to most programs.[1] The methodology is straightforward: what, so what, now what? More to the point: what does the Bible say, why does this matter, and what should we do in response?

---

1. This foundation is drawn from 1 Cor 6:12–20; 2 Cor 4:1–2; Gal 6:1–10; 1 Thess 4:3–8; and Jas 5:14–16.

INTRODUCTION

Many readers may want to jump to section 3 and its "now what" guidance. I urge you to ignore this temptation. The preceding chapters identify numerous ways biblical illiteracy, personal preference, and social influence produce poor responses when determining whether and how restoration plays out. Because the individual is a product of nurture and nature, the enemy capitalizes and uses such understanding to his advantage. Holistic formation and (re)formation must do likewise.

HOW WE SHALL APPROACH THE WORD

Psalm 107 is a remarkable song of God's rescue from overwhelming troubles. Its words are remarkably pertinent to this topic. I encourage you to read and meditate upon its promises as you prepare for this journey. In the meantime, let us consider verses 17 through 20:

> Fools, because of their rebellious way,
> And because of their guilty deeds, were afflicted.
> Their souls loathed all kinds of food,
> And they came close to the gates of death.
> Then they cried out to the Lord in their trouble;
> He saved them from their distresses.
> He sent His word and healed them,
> And saved them from their destruction.

God's Word provides healing, deliverance, and salvation. Therefore, a short hermeneutics discussion is necessary to lay a sound foundation.

Any biblical solution requires one to understand and apply God's truth rightly. Exegetical analysis brings cultural and linguistic context to bear. Interpretation presupposes a "theology from above" that views special revelation as normative.[2] Simply put, God speaks into and throughout the restoration process. He speaks through the example of Jesus, the incarnate Word; through the guidance of Scripture, the inspired written Word; through the Spirit's inner witness; and through the living or *rhema* words spoken by the Spirit through individuals.

So what? Why does this matter? How you view Scripture determines how you interpret and apply Scripture. Some view Scripture as predominately (if not exclusively) of human origin, and therefore, its discussions of

---

2. As opposed to a "theology from below" that views the human experience as the norm. This approach emerges from the anthropocentric optimism inherent to Enlightenment thought and presents Scripture as a human record of religious experience void of supernatural influence and inspiration.

INTRODUCTION

sexual behavior and ethics are subject to human interpretation.³ For example, J. Harold Ellens asserts that Scripture "simply assumes that a universal and lively activity of natural sexual play is constantly going on between consenting adults" and rarely addresses the "wide range of normal and healthy sexual play between consenting adults, within and outside of marriage."⁴ He further dismisses Heb 13:4, arguably the primary statement of marital sexual purity, as a "stand-alone statement."⁵ Such a view is in error.

The restoration program situates within the verbal plenary inspiration theory, which asserts the Holy Spirit selected Scripture's content and partnered with human authors who conveyed the revelation in their distinct styles. To ignore the human condition in the formation of the Scripture is hermeneutic Apollinarianism. Conversely, to ignore the divine inspiration of those human writers is hermeneutic Arianism. The inevitable consequence of the latter is that "Scripture does not stand in judgment over us, but we stand over and above Scripture, deciding for ourselves whether Scripture is reasonable."⁶

Scripture is God-breathed, inerrant, and eternal truth. While the conveyance of this prophetic word implies double agency, it does not imply equal agency.⁷ This fallen and fallible creation lacks the language and knowledge to convey, let alone comprehend, the wisdom offered by the infinite and infallible God. This lack necessitates divine accommodation—the universal message does not change, but the Spirit progressively develops our understanding and application of that message amid the ever-evolving contemporary context. The proper understanding of Scripture enables the correct application of Scripture, and the pragmatic application comes in the same way. Just as God and humankind collaborated to form Scripture, they will similarly unite to restore the fallen minister.

Exegetical analyses also employ the "fusion of horizons" central to Hans-Georg Gadamer's hermeneutic. The twentieth-century German philosopher grounds understanding in the linguistically mediated tradition and rejects subjectivism and relativism. Gadamer asserts that our biases and beliefs are the product of our history and, therefore demand a contextual understanding of historical writings to develop contemporary interpretation and application. Analyses also apply social-scientific criticism that

3. Notable examples include Brownson, *Bible, Gender, Sexuality*; Ellens, *Sex in the Bible*; Loader, *Making Sense of Sex*; McCleneghan, *Good Christian Sex*; and Vines, *God and the Gay Christian*.

4. Ellens, *Sex in the Bible*, 12.

5. Ellens, *Sex in the Bible*, 12.

6. Barrett, *God's Word Alone*, 224.

7. Blocher, "God and the Scripture Writers," 505.

INTRODUCTION

considers societal and cultural context through social science paradigms and perspectives.[8] As Bruce Malina asserts, the social system often produces and controls the context from which exegetical meaning emerges.[9] Within that context are hidden and shared meanings that the original reader understands but are lost on today's readers and often replaced by contemporary assumptions.[10] The story of David and Bathsheba illustrates this well. Though they are arguably the quintessential biblical example of moral failure, current scholarship categorizes David as everything from manipulated victim to rapist and Bathsheba as everything from raped to willing participant to manipulative opportunist (a topic we will explore in chapter 1).

By rightly addressing the "what" and "so what," we can determine the "now what." Indeed, *orthodoxy* (right beliefs) enables *orthopraxy* (right affections), leading to *orthopathy* (right actions or behavior), resulting in *orthopathos* (a right and ultimate goal). The teleological goal of the holistic restoration plan is not simply to care for but to cure. The pedagogical and pragmatic *telos* will have a more significant transformative influence on the knowers.[11]

GOALS, OBSTACLES, AND FAIR WARNINGS

Proper restoration is a (re)union with God rather than to vocation. The violator's biblical repentance and submission predicate this (re)union; the failure to effectively demonstrate either suspends the process. Success demands a balance between accountability and action, grace and growth. While fulfilling the ministerial purpose for which the believer remains called and gifted is one mark of success, restoration may not see a return to the previous ministry position. The severity of immorality may require the individual to withdraw from ministry altogether or commit to different ministerial duties. Restoration prioritizes the protection of parishioners from potential victimization and protects the restored minister from future failure. Suppose the fallen minister lacks sufficient victory over disordered desires. In that case, a ministerial role that minimizes emotional triggers may be appropriate. Such individuals may find ways to apply their gifts and

---

8. Elliott, *What Is Social-Scientific Criticism?*, 7.
9. Malina, *Christian Origins and Cultural Anthropology*, 1–9, and *Social World of Jesus and the Gospels*, 7.
10. Richards and O'Brien, *Misreading Scripture with Western Eyes*, 16.
11. Cartledge, *Practical Theology*, 44–45.

callings in administrative functions or even in restorative counseling for those who succumb to the same or similar moral struggles (2 Cor 1:3–5).

The (re)formation inherent to this program addresses common contributors to moral failures, such as the decline of spiritual formation and ministerial burnout. The program also addresses the impact of deformative life events that create emotional wounds and needs through which the flesh, world, and devil draw the individual into illicit behavior. Ultimately, with its demand for grace and discipleship, the (re)formation program presents the violator and Christian community an opportunity to experience growth in a season of decay and godly love in a time of angst and alienation.

So, what should you do if your minister has fallen into moral failure? To quickly forgive and restore is to cheapen grace. To deny any opportunity for restoration is to disregard grace. Let us proceed together and hear what the Spirit says.

What should you do for the violated? Scripture always requires (though the church overwhelmingly neglects) the careful and compassionate restoration of victims, including the minister's family and the affected church. Let us proceed together and hear what the Spirit says.

And what if you are the fallen minister? The victorious and righteous life in Christ enables lasting reconciliation with God, family, and (possibly) ministerial calling. The path is difficult but promises God's remarkable grace and presence. Let us proceed together and hear what the Spirit says.

SECTION ONE
Heaven, We Have a Problem

"Satan also aims at those in office in the church. What better way to infect the whole town than to poison the cistern where they draw their water? He takes special delight in corrupting the heart of a minister. If he can wiggle into a pastor's heart, then he is free to roam among God's flock undetected—a devil in shepherd's clothing. How may the worship of God be discredited? Let the world observe the scandalous conduct of a minister, and many, both good and bad, will reject the truth of the Gospel on the strength of the lie his life tells."

— WILLIAM GURNALL

SEXUAL IMMORALITY IS NOT a new challenge to God's servants. Fallen angels used sex to pollute the gene pool and, in a demonic attempt, to defile humanity (Gen 6:1–7).[1] Noah's son incurred a curse for shaming his naked father (Gen 9:20–25). Lot's daughters violated their father and birthed two cursed tribes (Gen 19:30–38). Reuben lost Jacob's blessing after sleeping with his father's concubine (Gen 35:22; 48:1–6; 49:3–4). Tamar used prostitution to right the wrongs of Judah and his sons (Gen 38). Long could we discuss how Jezebel instituted sexual rituals in worshipping pagan gods and used her sexuality to dominate as queen (1 Kgs 18:1–1; 2 Kgs 9:30; cf. Rev 2:18–29). Or how God ordered Hosea to marry the immoral Gomer to illustrate the people's spiritual adultery and God's promise of restoration. A fuller discussion of womanizing by Samson and Solomon and David's violation of Bathsheba is forthcoming.

The examples are not exclusive to the Old Testament. The New Testament uses the Greek *moicheia* (adultery) and its forms thirty-two times and

---

1. Wright, *Origin of Evil Spirits*, 61–63.

porneia (sexual immorality) and its forms fifty-five times. Notable is John the Baptizer's open attack on adulterers Herod and Herodias, which ends with the prophet's death (Mark 6:17–28). As we shall see, Jesus and Paul also have much to say. Sadly, the lure of sexual immorality will not diminish any time soon.[2]

It is no secret that sexual moral failure is a primary factor in contemporary ministerial failure. Each indiscretion violates the Christian message and its credibility. Each indiscretion leaves wounded souls in its wake. Yet the severity and frequency of moral failures are difficult to ascertain due to the lack of denominational statistics and the tendency of ministers, churches, and denominations to keep such matters private.[3]

What is clear is the church's lackluster and varied response throughout this historic struggle. Torn between anger and empathy, three standard and unbiblical responses toward the fallen minister emerge: destroy, defer, or disregard (explored in chapter 7).

Today, we see significant disparity among pastors, church leaders, and laity regarding ministerial restoration. Some churches do not believe ministerial restoration is necessary. Others do not think it is effective. Some churches do not see themselves as responsible for implementing ministerial restoration, and some believe such restoration is not in their best interest. In the hope of better aligning these differences to biblical truth, the following chapters give reasons why sexual immorality is more prevalent and problematic than many realize, then discuss the biblical guidance for sexual purity and ministerial restoration.

---

2. Consider how Jesus and others point to the days of Noah, Sodom, and Gomorrah when describing the Lord's return (Matt 24:37–39; Luke 17:26–30; 2 Pet 2:4–10; Jude 1:6–7).

3. Grenz and Bell, *Betrayal of Trust*, 18, 27, 115.

1

This Problem Is Worse Than Ever

"When the soul does not direct its efforts to higher things, neglecting itself, it stoops to concern itself with low desires."

— Pope Gregory I

So, how bad is the problem of sexual moral failure? A short compilation of notable examples follows. Suffice it to say the list is the proverbial tip of the iceberg (it is worth noting that roughly 10 percent of an iceberg is visible on the water's surface, but the 90 percent below the surface does most damage). What is above the surface and in full view? The church's increasing acceptance of the LGBTQ+ agenda, the Catholic Church's pedophilia scandals, the moral failures of national ministry figures, and the like. In the hidden depths that lurk below the surface, we find that a remarkable number of churchgoers (including tens of thousands of ministers) frequent pornography sites.[1] Countless numbers participate in hook-up culture or have "friends with benefits." Others are more conservative in their relationships but quick to justify fornication and cohabitation.

Meanwhile, marriage has diminished from the realm of a sacred institution to a temporary contract. The severity of this problem was apparent as I looked upon a church sign when many states voted on same-sex marriage. The sign read, "We are sorry if our gay marriage offends the sanctity of your third marriage." Though misguided, the sign's latter half made a valid point.

Though ministerial sexual misconduct is not new, several dimensions of the problem are new. These include biblical illiteracy, the tendency to place self-preference over sacred truth, unprecedented public acceptance

---

1. For more on this, see chapter 9, subsection 3: Strongholds and the Problem of Pornography.

of immoral leadership behavior, and the prevalence of point-and-click pornography. These challenges can inhibit and devalue the repentance and holistic (re)formation necessary for ministerial restoration. What follows are notable examples from recent years.

CONTEMPORARY EXAMPLES OF SEXUAL MORAL FAILURE

> "When wealth is lost, nothing is lost; when health is lost, something is lost; when character is lost, all is lost."
>
> — Billy Graham

Unfortunately, there are plenty of ministerial moral failures examples from which to choose. Examples include international apologist Ravi Zacharias, who pressured multiple massage therapists for sexual attention.[2] A posthumous review by an outside investigation agreed upon by his ministry substantiated accusations of sexual aggression and acknowledged a repeated sexual activity one woman described as rape. Megachurch pastor, televangelist, and author Robert Morris resigned from Gateway Church in June 2024. Morris had long admitted inappropriate sexual behavior (not intercourse) with a parishioner in the 1980s. He paused ministerial activity at that time to receive counseling. His resignation came more than three decades later when elders learned that the victim was not merely a "young lady," but was 12 years old. An investigation of sexual impropriety led to the resignation on April 3, 2014, of Bob Coy, senior pastor of Calvary Chapel Fort Lauderdale, the megachurch he founded three decades earlier. He admitted to adultery and pornography addiction.[3] An independent advisory group in 2019 found credible the multiple allegations of "sexually inappropriate words and actions" by Willow Creek Community Church Pastor Bill Hybels.[4]

Still, it is impossible to quantify the problem of ministerial moral failure. For every case that is known, there are untold numbers that go unreported. The "typical" church often looks to keep clergy sexual misconduct a secret, and when this fails, they direct their energies "to protecting the church's good name and the pastor's reputation."[5] In addition, this analysis

2. Boorstein, "Evangelist Ravi Zacharias Engaged in Sexual Misconduct."
3. Nolin, "Calvary Chapel Pastor Bob Coy Resigns."
4. Shellnutt, "Willow Creek Investigation."
5. Grenz and Bell, *Betrayal of Trust*, 27.

cannot give a robust reason for any failure nor determine whether restoration is allowable. As explained below, restorative diagnosis and prognosis is a complex process entrusted to key individuals privy to spiritual, emotional, and historical information not available to the public.

However, I provide this list with a purpose. Within these summaries reside telltale indicators, often pointing to causative factors such as emotional woundedness and a pervasive absence of accountability, holistic formation, and resiliency. Beyond the confounding variables and destructive tendencies, some examples demonstrate a remarkable lack of repentance and toxic responses—abuse of power, victim-blaming, and justification of inappropriate behaviors. While each moral failure is unique, these examples reveal common contributors that a successful restoration program will address and overcome.

This subsection will review key aspects of sex scandals in the Catholic Church, Southern Baptist Convention, and Sovereign Grace Churches. Reviews next consider the personal moral failures of television ministry personalities Jim Bakker, Jimmy Swaggart, Perry Stone, and Marcus Lamb. The subsection then considers leaders of national and international ministries and megachurches, including Ted Haggard, Bill Hybels, and Ravi Zacharias. A review of moral failures by emerging leaders follows and addresses Andy Savage, Tullian Tchividjian, Tavner Smith, and Jerry Falwell Jr. The reviews conclude by considering Gordon MacDonald, whose biblical restoration provides a rare success story after ministerial moral failure.

REVIEW: CATHOLIC CHURCH SCANDALS

One cannot address ministerial sexual abuse without acknowledging the scandals that rocked the Catholic Church over the past half-century. The vast majority of violators are pedophiles and thus ineligible for ministerial restoration for reasons addressed in chapter 7. However, the toxic cultures that allowed these predators to flourish are pertinent to any preventative effort consistent with holistic ministerial formation. Cardinal Bernard Law, the highest-ranking American prelate deposed in the sex scandals, is undoubtedly the face of such failure.

Law was the prominent archbishop of Boston and a renowned champion for civil rights and ecumenical unity when accusations emerged that Rev. John J. Geoghan had abused 130 boys over thirty years. An investigation found officials regularly shifted Geoghan among a half-dozen parishes. Law approved one of those moves and later faulted flawed psychiatric assessments for the decision.[6] Geoghan's story spawned similar accusations against eighty other priests. More than two dozen ultimately were removed. Authorities described Law as initially helpful in these investigations but increasingly vague and reticent.

The trial of Rev. Paul R. Shanley soon revealed Law and his predecessor, Cardinal Humberto Medeiros, knew of dozens of pedophilia accusations against the defrocked priest but allowed his continued contact with children. By the end of 2002, it was evident Law had for years transferred abusive priests without telling parishioners or law-enforcement officials. In 2003, the Massachusetts attorney general castigated Law and revealed that 250 priests had sexually abused as many as one thousand children in the Boston archdiocese over forty years. Law knew of the problem before he arrived in 1984 "and had tried to suppress any publicity about it to save the church from disgrace."[7]

A 2018 Pennsylvania grand jury similarly alleged decades of sexual abuse and cover-ups by Roman Catholic officials.[8] The grand jury's 1,356-page report was the culmination of a two-year investigation. The grand jury deemed credible allegations of sexual abuse by more than three hundred priests over seven decades involving thousands of victims in the dioceses of Pittsburgh, Allentown, Erie, Greensburg, Harrisburg, and Scranton.

Pedophilia is not the only sexual moral failure to hit Catholicism. Monsignor Jeffrey Burrill was secretary-general of the United States Conference of Catholic Bishops, making him the top US Catholic Church official when he resigned on July 20, 2021. The abrupt resignation came after his cellphone data allegedly tracked him visiting gay bars, a Las Vegas gay bathhouse, and making regular usage of Grindr, a popular social networking app in the LGBTQ+ community.[9] Sexual misconduct is rampant in other Christian entities as well.

REVIEW: THE SOUTHERN BAPTIST CONVENTION

A bombshell report in 2019 by *The Houston Chronicle* and *San Antonio Express-News* identified 220 pastors, ministers, deacons, volunteers, and Sunday school teachers in the Southern Baptist Convention who were

---

6. McFadden, "Bernard Law."
7. McFadden, "Bernard Law."
8. Lash, "Catholic Church Clergy Sex Abuse."
9. Boorstein et al., "Top U.S. Catholic Church Official Resigns." See also Steinfels, "Deep Strangeness of the Catholic Church's Latest Scandal."

found guilty of sexually abusing churchgoers over twenty years.[10] A total of 380 Southern Baptist leaders and volunteers faced allegations of sexual misconduct involving more than seven hundred victims.

Convention leaders held a service of lament, launched a program to care for abuse survivors, and vowed to release any church that covered up or mishandled abuse. However, the public overwhelmingly viewed SBC as more committed to protecting the institution than the victims. Stories like that of Paige Patterson, former Southwestern Baptist Theological Seminary president, fueled such perspective. Patterson was forced into early retirement in May 2018 after reports emerged that he allegedly told a rape victim to forgive her assailant rather than call the police.[11] In addition, two leaked letters by Ethics & Religious Liberty Commission President Russell Moore in February 2020 and May 2021 accused various SBC leaders of mistreatment of abuse survivors and stonewalling sexual abuse claims.[12] Moore resigned the same month he wrote the second letter.

The most significant backlash came when SBC officials balked at relinquishing attorney-client privilege. Convention officials in the summer of 2021 launched a Sexual Abuse Task Force and hired Guidepost Solutions to conduct an independent investigation into the executive committee's response to abuse survivors. Executive Committee President Ronnie Floyd hesitated to follow Guidepost's recommendation to waive attorney-client privilege in public and written communication.[13] Guidepost cited this as a "best practice" for a relevant and transparent investigation. Floyd cited potential insurance litigation and violation of SBC bylaws. The outcry was swift, as many among SBC's fourteen million members, spread across more than forty-seven thousand congregations, demanded transparency. Leaders conceded and waived the privilege on October 5, 2022.[14] This action came six weeks after the Department of Justice announced it was investigating SBC's handling of the sex abuse cases.[15]

Though arguably the most prevalent, SBC is not the only Christian group to struggle with sexual moral failures in recent years.

---

10. Siemaszko, "Southern Baptist Convention."
11. Pease, "Sin of Silence."
12. Barkley, "Southern Baptist Leaders Respond."
13. Smietana, "Head of SBC Executive Committee Questions Messengers' Resolution."
14. Lea, "SBC Executive Committee Says Yes to Waiving Attorney-Client Privilege."
15. Thornberry, "Justice Department Investigating Southern Baptist Convention."

REVIEW: SOVEREIGN GRACE CHURCHES

Sovereign Grace Churches have faced similar issues and seen varying responses. For example, church officials asked SGC president C.J. Mahaney to step down in 2011 because of "various expressions of pride, unentreatability, deceit, sinful judgment and hypocrisy."[16] The following year, a class-action lawsuit argued that eight SGC pastors, including Mahaney, covered up sexual abuse in the church. A judge dismissed the case due to the statute of limitations, yet Mahaney claimed vindication.

A far more damning indictment came from Al Mohler, president of Southern Baptist Theological Seminary in Louisville, Kentucky. Mohler initially called Mahaney a "friend" and cited his "personal integrity."[17] Mohler later expressed regret for his statement and took responsibility for dismissing the charges and failing to give due regard to victims' claims. "What I did was wrong and caused hurt to the victims and survivors who felt that their experience had been trivialized and dismissed," Mohler said. "And I grieve that, I apologize for that, it was wrong. I would never make such a comment again."[18]

At the time of this writing, Mahaney continued to serve as senior pastor of Sovereign Grace Church in Louisville. He is one of the countless ministers accused of sexual misconduct who remain in pastoral ministry. Many do so without submitting to a biblically restorative program and are unwilling to vacate their pulpit. Jimmy Swaggart is a notable example.

REVIEW: JIM BAKKER AND JIMMY SWAGGART

Sexual moral failure among television ministries tends to carry significant hubris and hypocrisy. The "televangelist wars" of the late 1980s provide a classic example. The episode begins with Jim Bakker's moral failure with twenty-one-year-old Jessica Hahn. Seven years later, Jimmy Swaggart became aware of the tryst and urged the Assemblies of God to investigate. Bakker resigned from Praise the Lord ministries in March 1987. Bakker maintained Hahn seduced him and repeatedly cited betrayal and blackmail as causal factors. Eight days later, Swaggart told a Los Angeles news conference that the PTL scandal was a "cancer" that had to be cut out of

---

16. Pease, "Sin of Silence."
17. Jones, "'What I Did Was Wrong.'"
18. Jones, "'What I Did Was Wrong.'"

the church.[19] So intense were the denunciations that the Rev. Jerry Falwell intervened to urge both parties "cease and desist."[20]

However, another battle was brewing. Swaggart had an ongoing feud with New Orleans minister Marvin Gorman. Defrocked by the Assemblies for immorality, Gorman admitted to one act of moral failure more than a decade earlier and charged Swaggart with defamation.[21] Gorman later contacted Swaggart and made him aware of photos showing Swaggart had visited a New Orleans prostitute in a motel room. Gorman gave Swaggart four months to deal with his moral problem, although he failed to set specific conditions.[22] Gorman released the photos when his deadline passed.

On February 21, 1988, Swaggart tearfully confessed to seven thousand worshipers at his World Faith Center in Baton Rouge, Louisiana. Without naming his offenses, he refused to call his actions a "mistake" and described them as "sin."[23] Swaggart asked God and his wife for forgiveness then declared he would leave the pulpit for an undefined period.

Assemblies of God officials stated Swaggart had confessed with "true humility" to "specific incidents of moral failure."[24] However, the denomination rescinded Swaggart's licensure fewer than two months later. The actions were in response to Swaggart's refusal to submit to church directives requiring him to leave the pulpit for one year and undergo a second year of counseling.[25] Swaggart cited an inability to maintain his $140 million annual ministry and Bible college amid the lengthy departure. However, his lack of contrition and repentance was increasingly evident among ministry leaders. Notably, only one month earlier, Swaggart provided leaders a five-point statement that said "he had never sinned willfully, never lusted after a woman and never made a mistake until being caught at the motel with a prostitute."[26] Such deflections have proven common among television ministers in the early twenty-first century.

19. Dart, "Swaggart Steps Down After Public Confession."
20. Rosenfeld, "Swaggart Tells of Deposition by Hahn."
21. Other ministers and subsequent investigations found Gorman likely participated in numerous affairs. He ultimately filed a $90 million suit against Swaggart, but that was dismissed by a civil district judge.
22. Uncredited, "Day After Marvin Gorman Confronted Jimmy Swaggart."
23. Dart, "Swaggart Steps Down After Public Confession."
24. Dart, "Swaggart Steps Down After Public Confession."
25. Stepp, "Church Defrocks Swaggart."
26. Stepp, "Church Defrocks Swaggart."

SECTION ONE: HEAVEN, WE HAVE A PROBLEM

REVIEW: PERRY STONE

Perry Stone, a Tennessee-based televangelist, was hit in April 2020 with misconduct allegations, including "groping, unwanted kissing and showing women he was aroused."[27] Board directors for Voice of Evangelism, Stone's international evangelistic outreach, received eleven letters that described inappropriate sexual behavior. Nine letters were from women who had worked for Stone and alleged inappropriate touching, kissing, and sexual messaging.[28]

At a private July 2020 event, Stone attributed misconduct to ministry stressors and health problems.[29] He confessed, "At times I've been inappropriate in all this weariness of just non-stop ministry. I let my guard down." Stone said he had asked God and his family to forgive him, and "I very humbly and very sincerely ask those who have been hurt or offended by my actions to, please, also forgive me for those things."

Voice of Evangelism spokesman John Rodriguez described Stone's potential misconduct as "civil in nature and not criminal." He noted the board set forth a restoration plan that included counseling, medical attention, a break from social media, and up to one year away from public ministry.[30]

Reports indicate some ministry members were "outraged" that Stone returned to various duties within weeks and that the board did not thoroughly investigate or involve law enforcement in response.[31] Vocal outbursts at ministry events soon followed. Stone responded with a series of warnings that God would expose and punish people "who were plotting and making war against me and the ministry."[32]

In April 2023, a grand jury declined to file charges against Stone. However, 10th Judicial District Attorney General Stephen Crump expressed concern regarding the allegations and said the case file would remain open.

---

27. Massey, "Women in Perry Stone's Ministry."

28. Martin, "Televangelist Perry Stone Admits He's Not Perfect." One letter claimed Stone locked doors to be alone with women. Others said he "described dreams in which God gave him the okay to pursue other sexual partners besides his wife."

29. Stone later described his actions as hugging, kissing, and rubbing someone's back as common to his Italian heritage and Southern upbringing (Blair, "Televangelist Perry Stone Slams Secular Media").

30. Martin, "Televangelist Perry Stone Admits He's Not Perfect."

31. Massey, "Women in Perry Stone's Ministry Allege Sexual Misconduct."

32. Blair, "Televangelist Perry Stone Slams Secular Media"; Martin, "Televangelist Perry Stone Admits He's Not Perfect."

REVIEW: MARCUS LAMB

Conversely, Marcus Lamb said greed, rather than demonic attack, led to revelations of his extramarital affair. In 2010, the founder of Daystar Television went on air to confess a sexual relationship several years earlier with a human resources employee.[33] Lamb took full responsibility for his moral failure.

Lamb's wife, Joni, described the affair as "an emotional relationship" that became "an improper relationship."[34] The couple entered Christian counseling, established accountability structures in the marriage and ministry, and hoped to keep the adultery private as they reconciled. The duo chose to go public when three "extortionists" allegedly demanded $7.5 million.[35] However, Lamb's example is an exception to the rule. Rather than revealing personal failures to thwart would-be extortionists, most ministers who commit moral failures come clean only after someone airs the dirty laundry. Such is the case for Ted Haggard.

REVIEW: TED HAGGARD

Haggard was president of the thirty-million-member National Association of Evangelicals when he admitted to numerous sexual escapades. He has since publicly wrestled with his sexual struggles.[36] In 2006, a male escort named Mike Jones revealed a three-year relationship with Haggard, who pastored the New Life megachurch in north Colorado Springs. Their meetings involved crystal meth-fueled porn binges, massages, and masturbation. Haggard's actions did not happen in a vacuum. One accuser later described the ministry as an "atmosphere of sexual impropriety."[37]

The church provided an eighteen-month severance package. Haggard agreed to therapy and accountability to his wife and future ministry leaders.

33. Silliman, "Died: Marcus Lamb."

34. Zoll, "TV Evangelist Marcus Lamb Admits Adultery."

35. Zoll, "TV Evangelist Marcus Lamb Admits Adultery."

36. Haggard's resignation letter to New Life states, "I am guilty of sexual immorality, and I take responsibility for the entire problem. I am a deceiver and a liar." With that said, the level of Haggard's admission depends on the source. Haggard first denied but later admitted to masturbation with Mike Jones. The male escort also alleges fumbling attempts at oral sex between the two (Jones, *I Had to Say Something*, 23, 59). Similarly, a New Life volunteer named Grant Haas in 2009 said Haggard masturbated in front of him and offered him drugs on a church trip in 2006, when he was 22. New Life later affirmed it paid Haas $179,000. Haggard denies the drug offer, admits to masturbating, but claims he thought Haas was asleep (Roose, "Last Temptation of Ted").

37. Roose, "Last Temptation of Ted."

SECTION ONE: HEAVEN, WE HAVE A PROBLEM

Haggard and his wife, Gayle, founded Saint James Church in Colorado Springs in 2010. His restoration fell short of the repentance and guided oversight required by Scripture and outlined in chapter 7. Still, his example may provide critical insights into the impact of emotional deformation and the healing found in holistic restoration.

Haggard's therapeutic process played out in numerous public interviews. In 2009, Haggard defined himself to Larry King as a "heterosexual with issues." Later that same year, Haggard characterized himself as an evangelical who "struggles with same-sex attraction."[38] Two years later, he rejected the label "bisexual" not out of inclination but due to his belief system, exclusivity to his wife, and "enforced boundaries" in his life.[39]

Haggard displayed a similar developmental progression when he admitted his struggles with same-sex attraction most likely began with some "same-sex sex play" as a child.[40] Later therapy sessions included eye-movement desensitization and reprocessing (EMDR), which helped trace his same-sex urges to having been molested by one of his father's employees at age seven.[41] Haggard credited therapists with helping him work through these "issues," enabling him to recognize better and reject these illicit impulses.

Notably, Haggard feels his loss of power and influence enabled him to overcome his same-sex attraction. Being fearful of an intolerant response had he revealed his struggles, Haggard chose instead to live in deception—until one defining moment made a choice for him and forever changed his life and ministry. Conversely, the fear church leaders in a prominent Chicago church had for their authoritative pastor facilitated, in part, Bill Hybels's sexual harassment and misconduct.

REVIEW: BILL HYBELS

On April 10, 2018, Hybels declared, "I feel released from this role." That statement sounded his resignation after more than forty years leading the Willow Creek Community Church. However, an increasing chorus of allegations from former members and staff drowned out his sentiments. They accused Hybels of a pattern of sexual harassment and misconduct that included lewd and suggestive remarks, invitations to his hotel rooms, prolonged hugs, and an unwanted kiss.

38. Alexander, "Telling the Truth About Sex," 122.
39. Roose, "Last Temptation of Ted." See also Haggard, *Why I Stayed*.
40. Alexander, "Telling the Truth About Sex," 122.
41. Roose, "Last Temptation of Ted."

Hybels flatly denied wrongdoing and dismissed the allegations as "a calculated and continual attack," a collusion of lies intended to discredit his ministry.[42] Most of his staff and church council initially echoed this response. Subsequent allegations, relentless media coverage, and increasing demand for truth by church members resulted in an independent six-month investigation. By this time, many missteps were evident, and the church's two leading pastors—Heather Larson, who replaced Hybels as lead pastor, and Steve Carter, the lead teaching pastor—resigned in August 2018. The entire board of elders announced at that same time that its members would step down by year's end.

A seventeen-page report completed six months later deemed reliable the "allegations of sexually inappropriate words and actions."[43] The report cited sufficient reason for church discipline had Hybels remained as pastor. Hybels was said to have "verbally and emotionally intimidated both female and male employees."[44] Investigators also noted that neither Hybel's resignation statement nor a two-page personal reflection sent to WCCC elders the following month "acknowledged nor apologized for sexual misconduct allegations."[45]

The report affirmed the ministry's positive impact yet noted a symbiotic relationship to dysfunction. Specifically, the "positive use of power, influence, and management style was a source of growth and global impact of the ministry. The negative use of power, influence, and management style caused dysfunction in these organizations' abilities to consistently implement policies, manage personnel and handle unexpected crisis."[46]

Ultimately, the report blamed Hybels and not the broader church culture, though investigators did cite the need for more robust policies to address inappropriate behavior. For example, the report described Hybels as authoritarian, abrupt, and abrasive and said board members expressed "recurring difficulty in holding Hybels accountable for his leadership and management style."[47]

Still, the most pointed charges against church leaders came from the leaders, many of whom took responsibility for the environment that allowed Hybels's systemic failures. A similar response is found among the

---

42. Pashman and Coen, "After Years of Inquiries."
43. Willow Creek Independent Advisory Group, "Report," 13.
44. Willow Creek Independent Advisory Group, "Report," 13.
45. Willow Creek Independent Advisory Group, "Report," 11.
46. Willow Creek Independent Advisory Group, "Report," 14.
47. Willow Creek Independent Advisory Group, "Report," 6.

leaders of Ravi Zacharias International Ministries, though their admission came after significantly greater struggle and denial.

REVIEW: RAVI ZACHARIAS

Of all examples in this subsection, Zacharias's actions arguably represent the most egregious individual abuse of power. A posthumous independent investigation substantiated accusations of sexual aggression, spiritual abuse, and repeated sexual activity the victim described as rape.[48] Zacharias pressured multiple massage therapists for sexual attention.[49] Zacharias regularly solicited explicit images and did so mere months before his death in May 2020.[50] Investigators found more than two hundred images on retrieved devices.

The report found that Zacharias used overseas travel to hide his abusive sexual behavior. He built trust through spiritual conversations and offered ministerial funds as benevolence offerings to curry favor. One woman said Zacharias "made her pray with him to thank God for the 'opportunity' they both received."[51] Zacharias warned another she would be responsible for millions of souls if she revealed their activities. The international apologist had encounters with multiple women in multiple countries.

Despite such behavior, Zacharias "was able to convince many that not only was he innocent, [but] he was the victim of malicious 'evil'" when the allegations came to light.[52] Inevitably, the independent investigation led the Ravi Zacharias International Ministries' board of directors to describe his actions as "horrendous."[53] The board affirmed its misplaced trust "in Ravi's denial of moral wrongdoing and in his deceptive explanations."[54] Members acknowledged the need "to take an extensive and humbling look at ways that we have fallen short" and adequately diagnose and address "significant

---

48. The rape allegation involved a requirement of sex after Zacharias arranged for his ministry to provide a woman with financial support. See Briggs, "Sexting, Spiritual Abuse, Rape."
49. Boorstein, "Evangelist Ravi Zacharias Engaged in Sexual Misconduct."
50. Silliman and Shellnutt, "Ravi Zacharias Hid Hundreds of Pictures."
51. Barron and Eiselstein, "Report of Independent Investigation," 5.
52. Briggs, "Sexting, Spiritual Abuse, Rape."
53. RZIM, "Open Letter from the International Board of Directors of RZIM," para. 4.
54. RZIM, "Open Letter from the International Board of Directors of RZIM," para. 7.

structural, policy, and cultural problems" that often exist in prolonged abuse—specifically, the failure of accountability.[55]

Zacharias's abuse of power and attitude of entitlement are not exclusive to his generation. Indeed, these are common factors underlying the sexual moral failure of emerging leaders. Tullian Tchividjian is one such example.

REVIEW: TULLIAN TCHIVIDJIAN

In 2015, Tullian Tchividjian, the grandson of Billy Graham, resigned as senior pastor of Coral Ridge Presbyterian Church after admitting to an extramarital affair.[56] Tchividjian remarried five months later and joined the Willow Creek Presbyterian Church ministry team in Winter Springs, Florida. That church released him in early 2016 when another extramarital affair (before the one at Coral Ridge) came to light.[57]

Godly Response to Abuse in the Christian Environment, or GRACE, condemned Tchividjian's actions as a "gross misuse of power."[58] The charge was significant as Tchividjian's brother, Boz, and uncle, Emmanuel Tchividjian, were board members.[59] The sex scandal drove the GRACE board to call for reforms such as more rigorous selection processes and improved training for pastors at seminaries to limit the "continuing transgressions against the vulnerable" in churches.[60]

Not everyone shares their outrage regarding Tchividjian's multiple affairs. In 2018, Fortress Press announced it would republish Tchividjian's book *Jesus + Nothing = Everything*, though the publisher had pulled the book when his affairs went public.[61] In 2019, Tchividjian launched a new non-denominational church called "The Sanctuary" in Jupiter, Florida. It describes itself as a "judgment-free zone where people can come as they are, not as they should be."

---

55. RZIM, "Open Letter from the International Board of Directors of RZIM," paras. 12–13.

56. Lancaster, "Tullian Tchividjian Marries."

57. Jackson, "Tullian Tchividjian's Upside Down Christianity."

58. Blair, "Tullian Tchividjian's Uncle, Brother, GRACE Board." GRACE describes itself as an organization that exists to empower the Christian community through education and training to recognize, prevent, and respond to child abuse.

59. While at GRACE, Boz oversaw high-profile abuse investigations such as the mishandling of sex-abuse allegations at Bob Jones University.

60. Blair, "Tullian Tchividjian's Uncle, Brother, GRACE Board."

61. Jackson, "Tullian Tchividjian's Upside Down Christianity."

Such acceptance is not uncommon in contemporary church culture. Many summarily dismiss offenses and quickly forgive offenders, even when it involves sexual moral failure by ministers. Tchividjian is not alone in this regard. Similar responses met Jesse Jackson's admission of adultery and birthing a child with an aide and Al Sharpton's repeated public engagements with girlfriends during nearly two decades of estrangement from his wife.[62] Yet such acceptance pales to the standing ovation Andy Savage received when he admitted sexual moral failure with an underaged girl.

REVIEW: ANDY SAVAGE

In January 2018, Jules Woodson accused Andy Savage of sexually assaulting her twenty years earlier when she was seventeen and he was a twenty-two-year-old youth minister in Texas. Woodson said Savage offered to drive her home from church but instead took her to a secluded dirt road and had her perform oral sex on him—an event that has caused her lifelong struggle. Woodson said she informed church leaders, but they did not contact the authorities and allowed Savage to resign. Savage acknowledged a "sexual incident" two days after Woodson's public claim. Savage "accepted full responsibility" for his actions. He claimed he apologized to Woodson and sought forgiveness from the Woodson family, the church staff, and the congregation.[63]

Highpoint Church in Memphis, where Savage served as a teaching pastor, responded to his admission with a standing ovation. However, the matter was far from over. A media firestorm led to an investigation into the church's handling of the allegations. Highpoint's senior pastor, Chris Conlee, expressed unwavering support for Savage throughout and declared "total confidence in the redemptive process Andy went through" following the assault.[64] That support would cost Conlee his pastorate.

The investigation concluded in March 2018. Church leaders admitted they handled the situation poorly and were "defensive rather than empathetic in its initial reaction to Ms. Jules Woodson's communication concerning the abuse she experienced, and humbly commits to develop a deeper understanding of an appropriate, more compassionate response to

---

62. Sharpton and Kathy Lee Jordan separated in 2004. He filed for divorce in February 2021.

63. Silva, "Memphis Pastor Admits to 'Sexual Incident.'" See also Johnson, "Tennessee Pastor Andy Savage Resigns" and Blair, "Megachurch Pastor Resigns over Allegations."

64. Blair, "Chris Conlee Resigns from Highpoint Church."

victims of abuse."[65] Savage resigned that month. Conlee, who led the church for sixteen years, left a few months later.

Shortly after his departure, Savage noted that a time of contemplation provided a greater revelation of his responsibility and failures. He said the "inappropriate relationship" with Jules was "not only immoral, but meets the definition of abuse of power since I was her youth pastor; therefore, when our relationship became physical, there could be no claim of mutual consent."[66] He acknowledged the failure to follow due process afterward and said, "Jules deserved, and did not get, a full investigation and proper response twenty years ago."[67]

In October 2019, Savage announced the launch of Grace Valley Church in Memphis. As Savage attempted to rebuild his ministry, a skyrocketing pastor on the other side of Tennessee watched his ministry plummet.

REVIEW: TAVNER SMITH

In 2013, Venue Church launched in Chattanooga, Tennessee. Two years later, it was the nation's seventh fastest-growing church.[68] When 2022 began, the North Georgia campus was empty but far from quiet. Founding Pastor Tavner Smith entered a self-imposed sabbatical after a series of questionable decisions made amid an alleged affair with a married church employee.[69] Allegations, which Smith denies, surfaced in late 2020.[70] In January 2021, the pastor and his wife separated. Divorce proceedings began four months later. In November, Venue volunteers paid their pastor a surprise visit to cheer him up, only to find the pastor in boxer shorts and the employee (now his assistant) wearing a towel. Smith said they'd been cooking chili and spilled food on their clothes.[71]

In late 2021, a video of Smith kissing the employee at a restaurant went viral. Eight staff members resigned in mid-December because the pastor refused to step down and demonstrated a "lack of remorse."[72] Church vol-

65. Blair, "Chris Conlee Resigns from Highpoint Church."
66. Blair, "Pastor Andy Savage Launches New Church."
67. Blair, "Pastor Andy Savage Launches New Church."
68. Outreach Magazine, "2015 Fastest-Growing Churches in America."
69. Martin, "After Pastor's Alleged Affair."

70. Smith's lavish lifestyle and lack of accountability were already in question when rumors of the alleged affair emerged. Staff members spoke of everything from new cars bought every few weeks to Gucci slippers as Christmas gifts.

71. Martin, "After Pastor's Alleged Affair."
72. Martin, "After Pastor's Alleged Affair."

unteers confronted Smith that month. A leaked audio recording allegedly captures the pastor admitting he and the employee had kissed but denying sexual relations. Smith then admits the two intend to pursue a relationship once divorced.[73]

In early January, Smith announced in an Instagram post that he was taking a sabbatical to "fill up, spend time with God, and get some counseling." Conversely, a sabbatical was the last thing on Jerry Falwell Jr.'s mind.

REVIEW: JERRY FALWELL JR.

Upon his forced departure in August 2020 as Liberty University's president and chancellor, Jerry Falwell Jr. joyously recited Martin Luther King Jr.'s famous decree, "free at last, free at last, thank God almighty I'm free at last."[74] That exuberant joy had diminished into uneasy contentment seventeen months later when Falwell told *Vanity Fair* that his myriad of personal and professional challenges left him a believer in Christ but not the church, as "nothing in history has done more to turn people away from Christianity than organized religion. The religious elite has got this idea that somehow their sins aren't as bad as everyone else's."[75]

Falwell's position within Christianity had been one of privilege, and some have long questioned his commitment to Christianity. Such questions came to a head in August 2020 when Giancarlo Granda, whom Jerry and Becki Falwell met while vacationing in Florida, claimed to have had a seven-year sexual relationship with Becki. Granda said Jerry was aware and sometimes watched. On a national media tour, Granda repeatedly described how the Falwells "bought his silence with luxury vacations, rides on Liberty's private jet, and an ownership stake managing a Miami Beach hostel."[76]

The Falwells denied that claim but admitted Becki had an affair with Granda. Jerry claimed to be the real victim—of extortion, to be precise—as Granda allegedly demanded $2 million to keep the affair secret.[77] Then, in early August 2020, as that scandal reached its pinnacle, Falwell posted

---

73. Kumar, "Audio of Venue Church Pastor Tavner Smith."
74. Graham, "Jerry Falwell Jr.'s Departure Brings Relief."
75. Sherman, "Inside Jerry Falwell Jr.'s Unlikely Rise and Precipitous Fall."
76. Sherman, "Inside Jerry Falwell Jr.'s Unlikely Rise and Precipitous Fall."
77. Ironically, Liberty University in April 2021 sued Falwell for allegedly manipulating a new employment agreement, which included a raise and a more favorable severance if he were fired. The board called Falwell's effort a "safety net" in anticipation of fallout for the Granda affair and his support of President Donald Trump. See Smietana, "Liberty Sues Jerry Falwell Jr."

a photo on Instagram with his pants unzipped, a drink in one hand, and his arm wrapped around a pregnant Liberty employee with her belly exposed. Falwell said the woman was his wife's assistant, and the photo was in good fun. Liberty's staff and students were not laughing.

Falwell has long emphasized that he is neither a moral leader nor a minister, but the fundamentalist university he led expected a spiritual example, if not a spiritual leader.[78] Many claimed the departure of the crude-talking, loose-partying president brought relief to the beleaguered campus.

In an ironic twist, a July 2021 lawsuit claimed Liberty staff fined women for violating Liberty's "commitment to Biblical principles of purity and abstinence" even while the Falwells reveled in their debauchery. Worse yet, the women had come forward to report various abuses only to be punished for their role in breaking school rules during the alleged sexual violations. One dozen women filed the federal class-action lawsuit and alleged the university violated Title IX law by discriminating against women who brought sexual assault and harassment allegations and discouraged victims from reporting abuse. The university, in May 2022, settled with those women and eight unfiled claimants who joined equally accused Liberty of creating an environment that increases the likelihood of sexual assault.[79] The settlements were undisclosed but university officials noted related initiatives, including more than $8.5 million in security upgrades, reviews of Title IX policies, and amnesty policy changes that withhold discipline for victims reporting sexual harassment or assault.

While Falwell and the other examples above convey factors common to countless ministerial moral failures, there are exceptions. Notable among them is Gordon MacDonald.

REVIEW: GORDON MACDONALD

MacDonald was a leader among Christian leaders in the 1980s. The best-selling author pastored the large Grace Chapel in Lexington, Massachusetts. He left to run the World Vision Christian relief agency and later became president of InterVarsity Christian Fellowship, one of the nation's largest collegiate missionary organizations. In 1987, anonymous letters made known an adulterous affair that occurred in 1984 and into early 1985. MacDonald publicly admitted his sin and resigned in June.

Where MacDonald's story differs is in his response. There were no victim-blaming or self-imposed sabbaticals. He offered no solutions or

78. Graham, "Jerry Falwell Jr.'s Departure Brings Relief."
79. Guerry, "Liberty University Responds After Lawsuit."

justification for his actions. MacDonald relinquished all rights. He placed the restoration of his soul and family in the hands of God, key ministry leaders, and fellow believers. He believed if God saw fit to restore his ministry, so be it.

A group of Grace Chapel elders comprised MacDonald's restoration team and immediately imposed a year of isolation from the public eye, followed by a second year separated from ministerial function. Spiritual, emotional, and familial counseling and healing consumed this time. This intense struggle provided the basis for MacDonald's classic work, *Rebuilding Your Broken World*. The book centers on "self-inflicted wounds" of sin that result in "unusual consequences of scandal, major loss, or serious long-term pain."[80]

Through his faults and failures, MacDonald came to understand that restoration of a "broken-world person" requires divine grace partnered with ministerial supervision and congregational support. Restoration requires honest and personal reflection, repentance, patience, and submission to God. Each plays out in his six-part program, which includes confession, investigation of events leading or contributing to misbehavior, discipline, comfort, advocacy, and official declaration when accomplished.[81]

MacDonald's controversial return to Grace Chapel in 1993 put his restoration to the test. The elders affirmed MacDonald's successful program completion, and most congregants said the move would be the ultimate expression of forgiveness. Still, a sizeable group argued that MacDonald had forfeited his claim to leadership. Some even left when the church rehired MacDonald by a three-to-one vote.

Five years later, MacDonald was called on to spiritually restore President Bill Clinton after his moral failure with Monica Lewinski. Clinton twice read *Rebuilding Your Broken World* in anticipation.[82] In the following quarter-century, the international speaker penned more than one dozen books, served as interim president and chancellor of Denver Seminary, served as editor-at-large for *Christianity Today*'s *Leadership Journal*, and remains pastor emeritus of Grace Chapel.

---

80. MacDonald, *Rebuilding Your Broken World*, locs. 180, 233.
81. MacDonald, *Rebuilding Your Broken World*, locs. 4147–4207.
82. Fisher, "Clinton's Pastor with a Past."

THIS PROBLEM IS WORSE THAN EVER

LET NOT THIS SICKNESS BE UNTO DEATH

"A wound that goes unacknowledged
and unwept is a wound that cannot heal."

— JOHN ELDREDGE

While MacDonald's example provides hope, this sickness is chronic and comorbid. Society has normalized countless sexual behaviors and justifies illicit sexual responses to emotional trauma. Scripture calls most of these "sins" for reasons we will explore. Sadly, those sexual sins have infected the body of believers. Emergency steps are needed to restore spiritual health and vitality. It is here that the bad news gets worse. To use medical terminology, the diagnosis regarding sexual morality would prescribe pew and pulpit to the latter stages of hospice care.

A quote often attributed to the eighteenth-century philosopher Voltaire (though found in none of his works) defines doctors as those who prescribe medicines of which they know little to cure diseases of which they know less in human beings of whom they know nothing. Western Christianity faces a similar struggle. Many leaders prescribe biblical solutions of which they know little to cure spiritual and emotional disorders of which they know less in people of whom they know nothing. The result often sees vigorous religious activities tinged with an underlying hope that one approach will work. However, ministerial restoration is a deeply personal task without easy solutions.

Do you want a doctor who, after a swift five-minute exam, throws various prescriptions at the problem in the hopes that something will work? Far better is the doctor who knows you as a person, not just a patient, who knows your problems and has a thorough knowledge of potential remedies. Theological doctors need similar competency. As Søren Kierkegaard rightly asserts, "everything essentially Christian must have in its presentation a resemblance to the way a physician speaks at the sickbed."[83]

The doctor's charge is not merely alleviating the symptoms but eradicating the disease. Healing and wholeness require proper diagnosis and prognosis through personal relationships and professional aptitude. What follows is a four-stage recovery plan that moves beyond behavior modification to achieve restoration with God and to ministerial calling. The four steps include:

---

83. Kierkegaard, *Sickness unto Death*, 5.

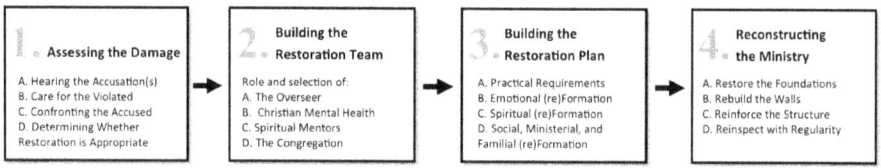

Figure 1: The holistic ministerial restoration process

While it may be tempting to jump to section 3 and search the program for remedy, one would do well to consider the biblical bases that conclude this section and the emotional, social, and spiritual causal factors addressed in section 2. Let's be clear: this restoration plan does not seek to blur the lines between sin and syndrome nor to pathologize moral failure. However, a holistic (re)formation that changes character rather than behavior requires an effective diagnosis that looks beyond symptoms and identifies the often-unseen root causes. As noted above, removing "bad fruit" is a temporary fix; the presence of a "bad root" will enable the continued growth of bad fruit. The goal is to identify and eliminate the bad root. This proper diagnosis enables a proper prognosis, which leads to a sound remedy and recovery plan.

It may seem odd to begin a ministerial restoration discussion with medical jargon, but holistic restoration often describes sin in terms of disease—and with good reason. As a disease evolves, the individual devolves. Still, there is a danger inherent to this metaphor. We have normalized disease and accept its presence as part of life, but there is nothing normal or acceptable regarding sexual moral failure. While medical, social, and psychological agencies often use the language of disease to address sexual immorality, this approach can prove problematic as the "patient" may relinquish responsibility. Similarly, care providers who view the violator as "sick" rather than sinful may rightly prescribe treatment yet omit necessary repentance and sanctification. This approach may lessen guilt but will also discourage maturation and the development of self-control.

A better approach is in the church's historical use of terms such as "sickness." The approach recognizes a symbiosis of sin and sickness that does not excuse the individual from responsibility but warns against spiritual death and eternal consequences. For example, early monastics described the soul's health as *apatheia*, an abiding peace resulting when the individual becomes free from passions and emotional disturbance. Illicit passions hamper spiritual life; the faithful application of discipline (*ascesis*) restores spiritual health. Spiritual exercises strengthen the individual's vitality, purify the passions, and result in charity.[1] As you imagine Rocky Balboa doing one-handed push-ups to his motivating theme song, know that spiritual exercises pay off in a similar fashion. Like that catchy tune, the individual progresses from "trying hard now," to "getting strong now," to "gonna fly now." Recapturing spiritual and emotional health results in growth and strength; whether it is healing emotional woundedness or simply ditching one's stinking thinking, the spiritual exercises increase one's contemplation and relational knowledge of God.[2] This purity of heart brings deep calm and undistracted prayer.[3] The ability to remain calm and peaceful when memories or events stimulate or disorder the passions marks the presence of *apatheia*.[4] In turn, *apatheia* activates *agape*—spiritual health destroys impediments of disease, resulting in self-giving love. Put another way, if you have trouble loving others rightly, it is likely because you do not love yourself rightly. When you lack proper love and affirmation, you will look for love in all the wrong places (to quote another catchy seventies tune).

Purity and peace with God, self, and others are the goals. There is no quick fix or miracle cure. Even when God grants a new heart, as was David's prayer following his moral failure, maintaining emotional health (*apatheia*) requires constant effort because every facet of our being remains exposed to fleshly temptations and demonic attacks. Therefore, the believer must commit to a disciplined training regimen to fully possess his affective faculties and keep disordered desires in check—hence, Paul's preference for athletic analogies (1 Cor 9:24–27; 2 Tim 2:3–6).

Such understanding implies that *apatheia* can be had or lost by degrees. It can. Stop going to the gym for a few years, and then see how easy it is to bench 280 pounds. And therein lies the problem. Christians often stop exercising (physically and spiritually) and instead live in denial. Rather than acknowledge what the mirror reflects, we suck in our gut and squeeze into clothes we have long outgrown in a vain attempt to convince ourselves it's just a few extra pounds. We see ourselves as we were rather than what we have become. The hard truth is, I'm no longer the lean, mean fighting machine I was in my Marine Corps days. Perhaps I don't need to be. After all, I will not likely be required to climb mountains or swim to shore to face the bad guys anytime soon. But does that justify obesity or morbid obesity?

---

1. While contemporary language associates "charity" with benevolence, the monastics used this term to describe godly love.
2. Ponticus, *Praktikos and Chapters on Prayer*, 84.
3. Cassian, *Conferences of Desert Fathers*, 1.4.
4. Evagrius, *Praktikos*, 34, 64–67, 69.

Does my reflection on better days blind me to the unhealthy specimen reflected in the mirror?

Now, apply this to your spiritual exercises. Are you as strong as you once were? It would be best if you were because the spiritual battle is real and rages. Perhaps the Great Physician is prescribing some exercise in godliness (1 Cor 9:25; 1 Tim 4:8). Accept his diagnosis, receive the prescription, and take your medicine.

Christendom has its high and low points when following the doctor's orders. Today, the church is at a low point, arguably its nadir. How do we get back on the right path? It begins with a cry of distress that beckons God's healing word (Ps 107:19–20).

2

This Problem Is Worse Than We Realize

"We need to replace the lies of the enemy with the truth of God;
to do so we need to know the truth of God."

— Christine Caine

Continuing the exercise theme, have you ever seen a gym rat who constantly works on his abs and upper body but always skips leg day? It's an interesting sight. He eventually looks like a boulder resting atop two toothpicks. Would you trust that individual as a personal trainer?

The gym rat's misguided emphasis on the upper body is his boulder to bear. But what if he was your physical therapist who, after a long-awaited knee replacement, had you work exclusively on shoulder exercises? In this scenario, the matter becomes a negligent malpractice that will prove debilitating rather than rehabilitating.

A suitable knee replacement should restore a strong walk. This restoration requires the doctor to identify and repair everything broken and strengthen everything repaired. Restoring a strong spiritual walk is much the same. The problem is that we often don't know what is broken or what it takes to rebuild and restore. And, like the wayward gym rat, we prefer to strengthen the parts others see and admire.

First, let's identify what is broken. When it comes to spiritual health, sexual moral failure shatters the *imago Dei* in which we were formed, the divine covenant and love Jesus provides, and the sacred temple which we become. The following subsections address these three issues.

SECTION ONE: HEAVEN, WE HAVE A PROBLEM

OLD TESTAMENT: SEXUAL IMMORALITY VIOLATES THE IMAGO DEI

> "Nothing teaches us about the preciousness of the Creator as much as when we learn the emptiness of everything else."
>
> — CHARLES SPURGEON

Humankind's story begins with its creation in the *imago Dei*, and that is the best place to start when discussing the cataclysmic effect of sexual moral failure. Such failure involves a willful ignoring of what is right and good as one chooses a lesser good or evil (privation of good) instead. As we will see below, many reasons contribute to these poor choices. No matter the cause, illicit sexual activity violates the grace and image of God.

God created humankind (not a singular man or woman) in the *imago Dei* (Gen 1:26-27). Man and woman is a plurality. Then, the man and woman "become one" (Gen 2:24-25). The *Shema* uses the same Hebrew word (*echad*) to describe the Lord our God as "one" (Deut 6:4). This is unity. In this view, we see the image of God as a plurality in unity, just as God is a plurality in unity. Sexual sins such as fornication, adultery, immorality, and homosexuality desecrate that plurality in unity and thus violate the image of God in which we were formed and are being restored.

Scripture progressively develops such understanding. Levitical Law and prophetic writings explicitly condemn sex outside marriage "in all its forms, both natural and unnatural."[1] The sin and guilt offerings maintain the covenant relationship inaugurated by God by atoning for these and all other transgressions.[2] However, sacrifices don't cover everything, and not all violators qualify.

The unintentional sinner obtains atonement through confession and proper sacrifice.[3] Levitical Law applies this allowance to common individuals, priests, the congregation, and leaders. Intentional sinners obtain atonement through repentance, restitution, and blood sacrifice (Lev 6:1-7).[4] Then there is the deliberate and defiant sinner who despises God's

---

1. Gondreau, "Jesus and Paul," 466. Notable are the sex laws contained in the Holiness Code (Lev 15:18, 24, 33b; 18:1-30; 19:20-22, 29; 20:10-21; 21:9; and Deut 5:18; 21:10-4; 22:13-23:1; 23:17-18; 24:14; 25:5-10; 27:20-23; 28:30).

2. Peterson, *Engaging with God*, 39.

3. Lev 4; 5:15-19; Num 15:22-29; cf. Luke 23:34.

4. The repentance required is described or displayed in 1 Kgs 8:46-50; Ps 51; Hos 3:4-5; 14:2-3.

commands and acts "with a high hand" (Num 15:30–31).⁵ This passage contains the only occurrence of the Hebrew word translated "to affront," which means "to taunt or revile God such as to deny his authority."⁶ This violator knows the action is wrong and doesn't care. He, therefore, is not sacrificially expiable and is "cut off" (*karat*) to protect the people. Such recourse "was reserved for the most heinous or sacrilegious offenses."⁷

One example of deliberate and defiant sin occurs amid Israel's initial assimilation of pagan worship, which often incorporates sexual activity (Num 25:1–2).⁸ As Israel nears its promised land, Moabite women "effectively use sex appeal to lure them to sacrifices honoring Moabite gods."⁹ The *zeba?*-type sacrifices are similar to Israel's sacrifices of well-being (Lev 3; 7). God identifies tribal chiefs as responsible for corrupting Israel with idolatry and harlotry. He unleashes a plague in response and orders the leaders' bodies to be placed on public display. A brokenhearted Moses weeps at the tent of meeting—until an Israelite nonchalantly passes with a Midianite woman in tow.

Zimri was the son of Salu, leader of a Simeonite family (Num 25:14). That he "brought" the Midianite woman is telling. Because the hiphil form of *qarab* used is the usual term for bringing a sacrifice to the sanctuary, "it would be logical for the reader to expect that the Israelite devoutly sets out to make amends with the Lord."¹⁰ But as Roy Gane rightly asserts, Zimri's mission "is not expiation but fornication." Raymond Brown ascribes contempt and defiance in Zimri as his actions break God's commandments without regard for the people's grief or Moses' moral leadership. In Brown's

---

5. The "raised right hand with the outstretched arms was a common symbol of strength and power in ancient Near Eastern literature and iconography" (Zondervan, *NRSV Cultural Backgrounds*, loc. 22269).

6. Zondervan, *NRSV Cultural Backgrounds*, loc. 22269.

7. Zondervan, *NRSV Cultural Backgrounds*, loc. 22269.

8. The digression from intentional into high-handed sin and the subsequent *karat* of the congregation, climaxes in the middle of the eighth century B.C. during the fall of the Northern Kingdom of Israel. Interestingly, God uses illicit sexual activities to demonstrate his grace amid their defiance and directs the prophet Hosea to marry the prostitute Gomer. The spiritual leader was not in error, yet the act illustrates a spiritual principle. God likens Gomer's sexual violations to the spiritual adultery of Israel, a separated people who carry ministerial function (Hos 1:2). The Hebrew word *zanah* is used to decry the infidelity of Israel in Jer 3:8–9; 5:7; 23:14; Ezek 16:32; 23:37; and Hos 1:2; 2:2. For Israel's ministerial function, see Exod 19:5–6; cf. Gen 12:1–3. The metaphor draws significance when God directs Hosea to restore Gomer and offers similar restoration to his wayward nation.

9. Gane, *Leviticus, Numbers*, 717.

10. Gane, *Leviticus, Numbers*, 717–8. E.g., Lev 1:2–3, 10; 4:3, 14.

view, the "provocative insolence" is intolerable.[11] Phinehas, grandson of Aaron, the high priest, would agree.

Zealous for the Lord, Phinehas leaves the assembly with a spear in hand. He enters Zimri's tent and drives the spear through the pair (Num 25:7–8; Ps 106:30). Phinehas's action ends the plague but not before twenty-four thousand are dead (Num 25:9). This marks the highest loss of life the Israelites will suffer during the exodus. Sexual immorality condoned by key leaders proved more devastating than Israel's discontent (Num 11:1–6), jealousy within Moses' family (Num 12:1–2), fear (Num 14:31), rebellion (Num 14:4, 10), disobedience (Num 14:40–45), rivalry (Num 16:1–3), disloyalty (Num 16:41–17:5), quarreling (Num 20:3–5), and irreverence (Num 21:4–5).[12]

God rewards Phinehas's zeal with a permanent priesthood (Num 25:11–13). Phinehas serves as Israel's third high priest for nineteen years, and as chief of the Korahite Levites, he leads the tabernacle gatekeepers (1 Chr 9:19–20).[13] Except for a brief interval when Eli acts as high priest (cf. 1 Sam 1–4, addressed below), Phinehas and his descendants officiate as high priests until the Jerusalem Temple's destruction in AD 70.[14]

Samson will prove equally zealous but not in godly ways. A judge is not necessarily a spiritual leader, but Samson's Nazarite designation places him in this category. Still, the leader "seems concerned only with himself and his immediate wants."[15] Samson is desirous of women, especially the Philistine variety. Samson's demand that his parents arrange a marriage outside the faith community (Judg 14:1–3) was an "unthinkable sin," and disregard of parental guidance was an "open breach of deep-rooted societal norms."[16]

A betrayal by Samson's wife leads to public humiliation and a series of violent and vengeful outbursts (Judg 1:12–2:17). At its conclusion, a depleted and vulnerable Samson, for the first time, turns to God. Samson redefines himself as "Your servant," a designation common to Moses but absent among the judges (Judg 15:18). God responds with a miraculous provision of water, and "thus, by his prayer, he atoned for his vaunting of

---

11. Brown, *Message of Numbers*, 231.
12. Brown, *Message of Numbers*, 227.
13. Youngblood et al., *Nelson's New Illustrated Bible Dictionary*, s.v. "Phinehas."
14. Comfort and Elwell, *Complete Book of Who's Who in the Bible*, 494.
15. Millgram, *Judges and Saviors*, 308.
16. Millgram, *Judges and Saviors*, 328. The author further asserts that the parents' quick compliance indicates Samson's insolence was nothing new and often appeased.

victory."[17] Hillel Milligram similarly defines this as the pinnacle of Samson's life.[18]

Samson's twenty years as a national leader pass with little comment until his eyes light upon a Philistine prostitute in Gaza (Judg 16:1). Isaac of Nineveh posits this moment of sexual immorality, not the cutting of his Nazarite hair, as what severs the divine anointing. Samson, "who was set apart and consecrated to God while still in the womb; whose birth was announced by an angel ... who was granted great power and worked great wonders" defiled himself by union with a harlot. "For this reason God departed from him and surrendered him to his enemies."[19] Indeed, Scripture does not indicate that God's Spirit ever returns to Samson.

Samson once again is betrayed by a Philistine woman and offers a violent response. However, his enemies now recognize the fatal flaw and entreat Delilah. Samson toys with the seductress but eventually reveals the secret of his strength. One revelatory sentence explains this seemingly inexplicable disclosure: Samson told Delilah "all that was in his heart" (Judg 16:17). In bearing his soul, Samson reveals that "he never wanted to be a Nazirite; that this status was imposed upon him, a burden that he has found near impossible to bear."[20] Samson's calling requires that he sacrifice all worldly satisfactions. Samson doesn't want to be a Nazarite or a judge. The man chosen wants to be common. More to the point, Samson wants to be a Philistine. Thus, his revelation to Delilah carries an underlying request: "shave my head and make me normal."[21] It is a desire shared by many burdened by the weight of ministry.

Samson recognizes neither his betrayal nor God's departure. Philistines enter, and he is soon in bondage. In humiliation, Samson turns to God for the second and final time (Judg 16:28–31). Samson fulfills his destiny but destroys himself in the process.

The third example involves the sexual exploitation by Hophni and Phinehas, sons of Eli, the priest and judge (1 Sam 1:9; 4:18). Eli serves at the Shiloh tabernacle that houses the ark of the covenant. His corrupt sons forcibly take for themselves offerings brought to the Lord and have sex with women who serve at the entrance to the tent of meeting (1 Sam 2:12–17, 22). Identifying these women find designations ranging from Nazirites

---

17. Ambrose, *Letter 35*, 157.
18. Millgram, *Judges and Saviors*, 349.
19. Isaac of Nineveh, *Ascetical Homilies 10*, 159.
20. Millgram, *Judges and Saviors*, 359.
21. Millgram, *Judges and Saviors*, 359.

involved in worship service (cf. Exod 38:8; Num 6:2) to cultic prostitutes.[22] Others identify them as "holy women of a strictly ascetic order" and connect the institution to the "serving women" who provided Moses mirrors to make the Bronze Laver (Exod 38:8) and to the prophetess Anna, who served God continually at the temple with fasting and prayers in the time of Christ (Luke 2:36–37).[23] No matter who these women are, the ministers are in the wrong.

Eli rebukes his sons but does little else to correct their sins (1 Sam 2:22–25). God views this as a willful act by which Eli honors his sons over the Lord (1 Sam 2:29). The indictment is notable in that Yahweh repeals a promise he previously stated as eternal, declaring that "those who despise Me will be insignificant" (1 Sam 2:30). The cumulative sins further catalyze the *karat* as God declares he will cut off the sons in a single day (1 Sam 2:31–34, 3:13). There is no opportunity for restoration, and with good reason: the brothers had no regard for the Lord (1 Sam 2:12). Ironically, the brothers' deaths (and that of thirty thousand Israelites) came when they attempted to leverage the power of God whose presence they lacked (1 Sam 4:2–11). The news causes Eli to fall over dead and Phinehas's wife to name her newborn son Ichabod, indicating "the glory has departed" from Israel (1 Sam 4:18–22).

Solomon provides the fourth example. Though a king is not a spiritual leader, per se, Solomon exhibited such a calling in his selection by God to erect the temple (1 Kgs 6), his ministerial function in its dedication (1 Kgs 8), and God twice appearing to him (1 Kgs 11:9). However, the king falls out of favor by way of marriages that violate Levitical law through multiplicity (Deut 17:14–20) and taking wives from non-covenant nations (Exod 34:15–1; Deut 7:3–4), which leads to the worship of false gods (1 Kgs 11:1–8).

Sexual moral failures are a family tradition in Solomon's lineage, a sad reality addressed in the case study of David in chapter 3. Suffice it to say Solomon's escapades are more about power than pleasure. His wives "are princesses and of high political rank; the marriages are matters of political expediency."[24] John Olley further asserts that Solomon's trust in "political alliances, sealed by marriage, rather than wholeheartedly in Yahweh" negates David's dying direction to "be strong, be courageous, and keep the charge of the Lord your God" (1 Kgs 2:2–3).[25] More pointedly, church father

---

22. Bergen, *1, 2 Samuel*, 81.
23. Jamieson, *Joshua-Esther*, 140.
24. Konkel, *1&2 Kings*, 220.
25. Olley, *Message of Kings*, 115.

Augustine posits that Solomon's "libido was not a passing guest; it reigned as a king" as wisdom obtained through spiritual love was lost through carnal love.[26]

The "abominable compromise" sees the one chosen to build God's temple erecting shrines to pagan gods.[27] Solomon incurs God's wrath and judgment. Solomon did not gain the divine gift through merit but lost it through demerit. The king fails to maintain his position by covenant loyalty.[28] Solomon's failure to restore that broken covenant is a willful and deliberate act, evident in the repetitious descriptions of "turn" (1 Kgs 11:2, 4, 9), "follow" (11:5, 6, 10), and "heart" (11:4 three times, 11:9). As August Konkel rightly asserts, "Solomon had wisdom in terms of intellect, but he came to live as a fool. . . . The very man who led in that marvelous prayer at the dedication of the temple did not abide by his own confession."[29] Such willful neglect results in the unprecedented division of God's people.

These four examples demonstrate how willful and unrepented compromise of covenant leads to the *karat*, the cutting off from God. Zimri exhibits the pursuit of fleshly appetites, Samson reveals the inability to overcome brokenness and burden, Hophni and Phinehas act from a sense of entitlement, and Solomon's failure results from his pursuit of power. These stand in stark contrast to the example of Job, who resists sexual immorality (Job 31:1, 9–12).

Notable is Job's declaration that he "made a covenant with [his] eyes" (Job 31:1). His description uses standard Hebrew terminology meaning "cut a covenant."[30] Job places his eyes in the position of the sacrificial animal common to the covenantal ceremony (e.g., Gen 15:10, 18), which "suggests that Job's eyes are being treated as vassals brought under a suzerain's control."[31] More to the point, Job's covenant did not regard infrequent or secret liaisons but stood as an outright rejection of the cultural expectation that one acquires a harem.[32] Indeed, marriage to many women from notable families indicated power and status in Job's world, just as it did in Solomon's world. However, Job's covenant is one of submission in which he views sexual sin as "shameful" (Job 31:11) and to be judged by God's word

---

26. Augustine, *Christian Instruction*, 3.21.31, 72.
27. Konkel, *1 & 2 Kings*, 224.
28. 1 Kgs 3:1–14, 6:11–13, 9:1–9.
29. Konkel, *1 & 2 Kings*, 228.
30. Alden, *Job*, 298.
31. Walton and Vizcaino, *Job*, 321.
32. Walton and Vizcaino, *Job*, 323. This avowal mirrors his statement in Job 31:24–25 that he is not absorbed in the pursuit of wealth.

(cf. Lev 20:10; Deut 22:22–24). Job likens sexual sins to "fire" that spreads and consumes until all is "destruction" (Job 31:12).[33]

Job's understanding is correct and expanded by Jesus' teachings. Therefore, the following subsection considers how this fire progresses to destruction and how Jesus elevates the moral requirement in response. The subsection also considers how Jesus defines the marriage covenant and engages those guilty of illicit sexual behavior.

JESUS: SEXUAL IMMORALITY VIOLATES THE DIVINE COVENANT AND LOVE

"You have heard that it was said, 'You shall not commit adultery,' but I say to you …"

— JESUS OF NAZARETH, MATT 5:27–28

The Gospels advance the biblical sexual ethic despite its lack of "high-handed" sexual violations by ministry leaders. This subsection gives attention to four critical moments of development. These include (1) the Beatitudes, where Jesus redefines the Torah and thus elevates adultery from action to attitude; (2) the theological sanctity of marriage Jesus provides amid the religious leaders' vigorous debate regarding divorce criteria; (3) the unique revelation and commission given by Jesus to a Samaritan woman in admitted sexual sin; (4) and an adulteress's redemption by religious leaders who sought her destruction.

First, in his Sermon on the Mount (Matt 5–7), Jesus redefines the Torah as a gracious divine covenant requiring an obedient and faithful response.[34] He emphasizes the law's moral aspects because religious adherence had become a substitute for moral integrity.[35] In this, Jesus provides "a comprehensive portrait of the right way to live."[36]

Sexual purity is a crucial aspect of Jesus' first discourse. For example, purity of heart (Matt 5:8) carries an association with sexual purity (and specifically, chastity), as "external sexual practices flow from an interior

---

33. This description bears resemblance to the wisdom of Prov 6:27–29 and Song 8:6. Notably, "destruction" is the Hebrew word *abaddon*, a personification of death and the grave (cf. Job 26:6; 28:22; Prov 5:5; 6:32; 7:27).
34. Stassen and Gushee, *Kingdom Ethics*, 91.
35. Cf. 1 Sam 15:22; Isa 1:11–13; Jer 6:20; Amos 5:21–24; Mal 1:6–14.
36. Ratzinger, *Jesus of Nazareth*, 128.

rectitude."[37] As such, the "moral regulation of our sexuality is as much an internal affair as an external one."[38] Indeed, lust originates in the heart, "which is the core of a person's identity and will" (Matt 15:19).[39] In this, Jesus moves past the "bad fruit" to identify and seeks to eradicate the "bad root" of behaviors—a necessary aspect of restoration addressed in the paradigm provided in sections 3 and 4.

In so doing, Jesus elevates the sexual ethic from external avoidance to a holy internal attitude. He does this by equating adultery and lust for sexual relations with a non-spouse (Matt 5:27–30).[40] This escalation is a critical transition in the sexual ethic. As Craig Keener rightly observes, lust "is antithetical to true love: it dehumanizes another person into an object of passion, leading us to act as if the other were a visual or emotional prostitute for our use."[41]

Indeed, Jesus' statement defiantly challenges his day's cultural and religious beliefs. Many men in the ancient Mediterranean (and many in contemporary Western society) thought lust to be healthy and normal. Even devout Jews who lamented lust were deficient in their understanding. They saw lust as leading to defilement, not as revealing impurities of the heart. Here, Jesus places on the desirous individual the responsibility to quell lust and declares guilty not only one who breaks the letter of the law but also one who wants to do so in his heart.

Jesus' subsequent hyperbole to pluck out the right eye and cut off the right hand that causes one to sin is not a call to self-mutilation (Matt 5:29–30).[42] It is quite possible to be blind or crippled and still lust. As Dallas Willard asserts, the "mutilated stump could still have a wicked heart. The deeper question always concerns who you are, not what you did do or can do. What would you do if you could? Eliminating bodily parts will not change that."[43]

---

37. Gondreau, "Jesus and Paul," 473. Cf. Ps 51:10.

38. Gondreau, "Jesus and Paul," 473.

39. Wilkins, *Matthew*, 245.

40. The verb *epithymeō* indicates an activity that moves beyond observation and into contemplation. In equating lust and adultery, Jesus directly quotes the seventh commandment (Exod 20:14; Deut 5:17) and alludes to the tenth concerning covetousness (Exod 20:17; Deut 5:21; cf. Rom 7:7–13).

41. Keener, *Matthew*, s.v. Matt 5:27–30.

42. Some have taken this passage literally. For example, Origen castrated himself to quell the urge of lust. Tertullian took a more biblical approach in advising Christians guard their hearts and remember "the Christian is born masculine for his wife and for no other woman" (Tertullian, *Apology* 46.11–2, loc. 44415).

43. Willard, *Divine Conspiracy*, 167.

SECTION ONE: HEAVEN, WE HAVE A PROBLEM

Christ's pointed message is twofold. First, one must identify willful behaviors and temptations that lead to sexual sins (cf. Col 3:5). The goal turns from literal self-mutilation to self-discipline, a commitment to single-eyed, single-handed, and single-hearted devotion to one's spouse.[44] This discipline requires a radical commitment to "cut out" any avenues through which temptation may enter—for example, Job's covenant with his eyes, as noted above. Second, the individual must recognize that this digression leads to apostasy and judgment if not corrected.[45]

Second, Jesus advances the sanctity of marriage by addressing the Mosaic pronouncement on divorce (Matt 5:31–32; cf. Deut 24:1). This antithesis emerges amid a very public theological debate in which the conservative rabbinic school of Shammai argued divorce was allowable in cases of unchastity. In contrast, the liberal rabbinic school of Hillel held a broad interpretation of the Mosaic "indecency" stipulation and allowed divorce for matters as mundane as a spoiled dinner.[46] Both sides wrongly viewed women as property. In response, Jesus presents marriage as a mutual relationship with reciprocal rights.[47] He identifies sexual immorality as the only justification for divorce, though reconciliation and forgiveness are God's desired outcomes.[48] John Chrysostom's holistic approach further asserts that divorce, like lust, is a heart issue. "For he that is meek, and a peacemaker, and poor in spirit, and merciful, how shall he cast out his wife? He that is used to reconcile others, how shall he be at variance with her who is his own?"[49]

Jesus further decimates the Hillel tradition in a later Pharisaical challenge.[50] The collective synoptic accounts see Jesus expound on the creation story to reveal marriage as a male-female covenant partnership established by God for God's purposes, a joyful companionship in a one-flesh (re) union, and a covenant relationship intended to be faithful and permanent. Again, Jesus declares that one who divorces his wife for any reason other than sexual immorality and marries another commits adultery.[51] According to

---

44. This includes faithfulness to one's future spouse, as well (Deut 22:13–21).
45. Osborne, *Matthew*, 196.
46. Wilkins, *Matthew*, 246.
47. Hays, *Moral Vision of the New Testament*, 352. Cf. Gen 2:24; Mal 2:16.
48. Wilkins, *Matthew*, 262. Cf. Matt 18:15–35.
49. Chrysostom, *Homilies of St. John Chrysostom*, 119.
50. Matt 19:3–9; Mark 10:2–9; Luke 16:18.
51. Sexual immorality (*porneia*) includes any sinful activity that intentionally divides the marital relationship. This concept is explored below. It should be noted that this exception clause is in Matthew's account and is not echoed by Mark or Luke, though Mark's passage adds the important declaration that "what God has joined

Glenn Stassen and David Gushee, Jesus' message was clear: "do God's will for marriage and stop asking when it is permissible to do less."[52]

Third, while Jesus' first discourse elevates the sexual and marital ethic, his discussion with a Samaritan demonstrates the grace extended to a sexual sinner (John 4:7–26). The encounter takes place soon after the imprisonment of John the Baptist for openly attacking the adultery and immorality of Herod and Herodias.[53] Interestingly, Jesus' actions at Jacob's well "invited the accusation of acting in a flirtatious manner."[54] Jewish men did not speak to women in public, especially at wells, which were considered places where a man might find a wife, as did Jewish patriarchs Isaac and Jacob (Gen 24:17, 29:10). If the Samaritan woman initially misinterprets Jesus' intent, her short statement "I have no husband" could be taken "to imply that she was unattached and thus available."[55]

If this depiction is correct, Jesus' response may have proven more shocking to the woman than his willingness to dialogue. Similarly, the Samaritan's history may be more shocking than previously understood. Andreas Köstenberger's exegetical analysis makes possible a greater immorality than found in the consensus. He notes the word ἀνήρ (*aner*) can mean "man" or "husband."[56] Favoring the former definition, he identifies the woman not as a five-time divorcee but as a "serial fornicator."[57] Colin Kruse agrees and posits that "it is possible that she had never been married, but had had a series of affairs with men, culminating in a final adulterous relationship."[58] Köstenberger also notes that rabbis "generally disapproved of more than three legal marriages in a lifetime, even in case of the death of previous husbands."[59] That she gathers water in the noonday heat supports this scenario. Women typically drew water in the cooler morning or evening

---

together, no person is to separate."

52. Stassen and Gushee, *Kingdom Ethics*, 277.

53. Matt 4:12; Mark 1:14; Luke 3:19–20; John 3:24.

54. Köstenberger, *John* (Baker Exegetical Commentary), 148.

55. Köstenberger, *John* (Baker Exegetical Commentary), 152. The misinterpretation gains further support by the fact that the woman already twice misunderstood Jesus' promises of a spiritual blessing and requested immediate satisfaction of physical thirst.

56. Vine et al., *Vine's Complete Expository Dictionary*, s.v. "*aner*," 315. See also Köstenberger, *John* (Baker Exegetical Commentary), 153; and Kruse, *John*, 134.

57. Köstenberger, *John* (Zondervan Illustrated), 46. D. Moody Smith also applies this translation to Jesus' statement that "the one you now have is not your man" (John 4:18). In his view, this moves beyond the charge of living with a man who is not her husband to imply she is living with someone else's man (Smith, *John*, 115).

58. Kruse, *John*, 134.

59. Köstenberger, *John* (Zondervan Illustrated), 46.

hours and in the company of other women. Being alone at an unusual hour suggests other women have shunned her "for what they perceived to be deviant behaviour."[60]

Yet Jesus' words convey invitation rather than condemnation and seemingly liberate the woman from the need to conceal the problematic truth about herself. Kruse further asserts that Jesus' intention was not to create a sense of guilt but to confront the deeper issues of her broken relationships and shattered hopes.[61]

It is to this immoral woman that Jesus gives four immeasurable insights: the opportunity of true forgiveness and a relationship with the living God; the gift of living water, which speaks of the Holy Spirit (John 4:7–10); the true worship sought by the Father (John 4:19–24); and his revelatory affirmation of messiahship.[62] The latter is significant as it is the first of fourteen direct claims to divinity using the phrase "I Am" (*ego eimi*).[63] This occasions Jesus' only self-affirmation of the title "Messiah" before the illegal trial resulting in his crucifixion.[64]

Also of note are the Samaritan woman's responses compared to those of Nicodemus. The latter "is part of the establishment and a member of the Jewish Supreme Court" yet is reduced to incredulity and left speechless by Jesus.[65] The immoral Samaritan woman, on the other hand, "emerges as a dialogue partner who continues to engage Jesus."[66] The pericope concludes with the (once?) immoral Samaritan woman emerging from isolation to evangelize her community (John 4:28–30). What is telling is that she uses her history, once a source of deep shame, to entice others to meet Jesus.

60. Lincoln, *Gospel According to St. John*, 176. See also Köstenberger, *John* (Baker Exegetical Commentary), 148.

61. Kruse, *John*, 134.

62. The word "gift" (*dorea*) is found only here in the Gospels but is used four times in Acts, always in reference to the gift of the Holy Spirit (Acts 2:38; 8:20; 10:45; 11:17).

63. These include seven statements with predicates: I am the bread of life (6:35); I am the Light of the world (8:12); I am the door of the sheep (10:7, 9); I am the good shepherd (10:11, 14); I am the resurrection and the life (11:25); I am the way, the truth, and the life (14:6); and I am the true vine (15:1). Of equal importance are the seven absolute "I Am" statements that stand without a predicate (4:26; 6:20; 8:24; 8:28; 8:58; 13:19; 18:5, 6, 8).

64. Williams, *Renewal Theology . . . Vol. 1*, 328. Cf. Matt 26:63–64; Mark 14:61–62; Luke 22:70. Jesus' preferred self-designation was "Son of Man," a phrase that occurs eighty-two times on more than forty occasions in the Gospels. Specifically, it appears sixty-nine times in the Synoptics and thirteen times in John. The phrase is found only three times outside of the Gospels, all of which speak of Jesus (Acts 7:56; Rev 1:13; 14:14).

65. Köstenberger, *Theology of John's Gospel and Letters*, 201.

66. Köstenberger, *Theology of John's Gospel and Letters*, 201.

Jesus' encounter with a woman caught in adultery soon follows (John 8:1–11). Her story is the final passage considered and provides significant insight into biblical forgiveness and sexual immorality issues.[67]

"Discriminatory action" is evident when the scribes and Pharisees present only the woman with their charges.[68] Levitical law demanded the death of the adulterer and the adulteress (Lev 20:10; Deut 22:22). The man's absence suggests a "patriarchal abuse of what was already a patriarchal legal system."[69] Jesus neither addresses this error nor follows the cultural tendency. Instead, he again elevates the ethic from action to attitude. Levitical law requires witnesses to a capital offense to cast the first stone when the accused is condemned to death (Deut 17:7). Jesus instead directs the one without sin to cast the first stone (John 8:7). None of the accusers are qualified to condemn the woman because sin resides in the heart rather than external action—a core truth Jesus expresses time and again.

One without sin *is* present yet does not bring condemnation. Jesus speaks to the woman as a person (the first to do so in the episode). He discusses her accusers before addressing her actions.[70] This example urges compassion for sinners and caution against hypocritical judgment. Jesus' refusal to condemn the woman does not mean he condones her actions. The pronouncement of merciful pardon carries the potentiality of life free from previous sins. Still, the woman bears the requirement to "not sin any longer" (John 8:11; cf. 5:14). This approach forms the heart of the restoration program presented in section 4.

In conclusion, the Gospels provide a combination of theological discourse and ministerial examples in which Jesus demands an elevated sexual ethic that maintains the sanctity of marriage through self-discipline and commitment to fulfill God's original intent.[71] This demand is tempered by the call for grace and mercy when one falls short of that standard, yet that

---

67. This pericope is not included in the earliest manuscripts. Köstenberger notes that no early church fathers show awareness of this narrative. Its placement disrupts coherence of surrounding passages, differs sharply in Johannine language and style, and features fourteen words not found elsewhere in John's Gospel (Köstenberger, *John* [Zondervan Illustrated], 81). While contemporary theology questions its inclusion in the canon, few question the event's historicity. Andrew Lincoln asserts that the disparity may have resulted when a number of early witnesses "independently decided to omit it" because the story depicted Jesus as too lenient toward adultery (Lincoln, *Gospel According to St. John*, 525). Considering its turbulent history, this passage cannot be ignored, but its inclusion must be tempered.

68. Kruse, *John*, 198.

69. Lincoln, *Gospel According to St. John*, 530.

70. Kruse, *John*, 200.

71. Cf. 1 Tim 3:2, 12; Titus 1:6.

grace carries a greater responsibility for the recipient, as is demonstrated in the next subsection which describes how the Pauline epistles elaborate upon a biblical sexual ethic and identify merciful responses to willful sexual immorality.

PAUL: SEXUAL IMMORALITY DESECRATES THE LIVING TEMPLE

> "Flee sexual immorality. Every other sin that a person commits is outside the body, but the sexually immoral person sins against his own body. Or do you not know that your body is a temple of the Holy Spirit within you, whom you have from God, and that you are not your own? For you have been bought for a price: therefore glorify God in your body."
>
> — PAUL THE APOSTLE, 1 COR 6:18–20

Paul provides no systematic analysis of sexuality but has much to say. The apostle asserts sexual immorality and idolatry are symbiotic (Rom 1:18–32). Purification includes physical and spiritual aspects (2 Cor 7:1). Holiness and sanctification define personal behavior in the pastoral letters.[72]

Similarly, Paul expounds on Jesus' inward demand for moral purity by presenting spiritual formation as a matter of conscience.[73] As noted above, Levitical Law offers no repentance for high-handed sin. Jesus develops the understanding by identifying sin as residing in the heart rather than the action. Paul's writings reveal how high-handed sins progress from the heart into observable action. He then outlines the church's expected response.[74]

This subsection explores the Pauline theology of human sexuality as presented in four key passages: (1) the ouster of one in high-handed sexual immorality (1 Cor 5:1–13); (2) the command to flee sexual immorality, defined as a sin against one's body (1 Cor 6:13–20); (3) sexuality in marital

---

72. Hawthorne et al., *Dictionary of Paul and His Letters*, 401. Notably, 1 Tim 5:22 and Titus 2:5; cf. Rom 13:13–14.

73. Phil 4:8; 1 Tim 1:5; 3:9; 2 Tim 1:3; 2:22. In a bold reversal of his pharisaical tradition, Paul further asserts that ceremonial impurity does not affect moral purity (Rom 14:14; 1 Cor 8:4).

74. Specifically, the new creation is not inherently sinful (Rom 6:6, 2 Cor 5:17). However, habitually offering oneself as "instruments of unrighteousness" (Rom 6:13) sees one begin to live "according to the flesh" (Rom 8:13). Hostile attitude toward God develops and is joined to "evil works" (Col 1:21; cf. Rom 8:27; Eph 4:18–19). Inevitably, the body enslaved to sin indulges in sexual immorality (1 Cor 6:12–20) (Hawthorne et al., *Dictionary of Paul and His Letters*, 772).

relations (1 Cor 7:1–16, Eph 5:21–33); and (4) sexual morality as a ministerial qualification (1 Tim 3:2–7, Titus 1:6–9).

The first passage addresses a Corinth churchgoer (not a ministry leader) who "has his father's wife." The word "has," a euphemism for sexual relations, appears in the present tense infinitive, thus suggesting "an ongoing, habitual relationship, not a one-time affair."[75] The term "father's wife" rather than "mother" indicates she is likely his stepmother. Paul is shocked at this behavior and the church's response. Paul does not specify the reason they are "puffed up." Kenneth Schenck asserts they likely "glory" in this supposed example of freedom in Christ.[76] Craig Blomberg ascribes their attitude to a new "enlightened tolerance" as Christians.[77] While the believers' reasons remain unclear, Paul's response is not. The apostle gives four directives to remove the offender from fellowship.[78] The final quotes the phrase "cast out the evil person from among you," thus connecting Paul's actions to the Levitical requirement to "cut off" the high-handed or intentional sinner.[79]

The notable development is that Paul's intent to "destroy the flesh" is remedial and does not convey the literal "curse/death" application inherent to Old Testament usage. This change is evident when Paul affirms remorse and repentance in a similar (perhaps the same) situation (2 Cor 2:5–11). Paul also uses similar language when correcting Hymenaeus and Alexander (1 Tim 1:19–20). Most telling is that Paul rarely uses σάρξ (*sarx*) in its basic sense, referring to physical flesh, but instead in an extended sense that refers to our fallen humanity and hostility toward God.[80] Thus, Paul recognizes that a more extraordinary dispensation of grace comes with Jesus' elevation of purity from action to attitude. Indeed, where sin abounded, grace abounded all the more (Rom 5:20).

In this understanding, Paul seeks to destroy the sinful orientation to keep the community pure and redeem the sinner.[81] He develops this intent by castigating the Corinthians' participation with prostitutes and explaining the effect sexual immorality has on the body (1 Cor 6:13–20), this subsection's second consideration.

75. Taylor, *1 Corinthians*, 132.
76. Schenck, *1 & 2 Corinthians*, 79. Cf. 1 Cor 6:12.
77. Blomberg, *1 Corinthians*, 105.
78. 1 Cor 5:2, 5, 7, 13; cf. Matt 18:17; 2 Thess 3:14–15.
79. 1 Cor 5:13; cf. Deut 17:7; 19:19; 22:21, 24; 24:7.
80. Fee, *Paul, the Spirit, and the People of God*, 129.
81. Schenck, *1 & 2 Corinthians*, 85. Though unknown, it is possible both intentions were successful and provide Paul's discussion of how the church handled a particular sinner (2 Cor 7:8–13) and the apostle's delight that the discipline led to the individual's repentance (2 Cor 2:5–11).

Paul's syllogism concludes that sexual intercourse with a prostitute unites members of Christ with that prostitute. Therefore, Paul urges each believer to flee πορνεία (*porneia*), or "sexual immorality" (1 Cor 6:18). The noun *porneia* and its related verb are of significant concern and appear thirty-four times in the New Testament.[82] It refers to "any sexual act, whether of an extramarital or unnatural sort, that dishonors marriage in its procreative-unitive nature."[83]

Paul emphasizes the urgency of fleeing by describing sexual immorality as a sin against one's own body. To understand this unique indictment, one must explore Paul's richly articulated concept of "body," or σῶμα (*sōma*). Paul's use of this term unites the physical nature (1 Cor 6:13), the holistic self (1 Cor 6:15, 19), and the church united as Christ's body (1 Cor 12:12–27). Because sexual activity embodies the whole person, sexual immorality desecrates a Christian's union with Christ, self, and others.[84] As Brendan Byrne explains, "[t]he immoral person perverts precisely that faculty within himself that is meant to be the instrument of the most intimate bodily communication between persons."[85]

Indeed, "there are penalties for transgressing the purposes for which God created our bodies, minds, and spirits."[86] Paul's description of *sōma* as a temple reveals the severity of such violations. He uses the Greek word ναός (*naos*), which speaks specifically of the inner sanctuary where God manifested his indwelling, abiding *shekinah* glory.[87]

N. T. Wright expands this understanding by asserting that 1 and 2 Maccabees were prevalent in Paul's mind.[88] In Wright's view, the relationship between idolatry and immorality is central to Paul's theology. Breaking the marriage covenant was akin to breaking the divine covenant.[89] In response,

---

82. Balz and Schneider, *Exegetical Dictionary of the New Testament*, s.v. "*porneia*." This includes five uses in 1 Cor 5–7, which Gondreau describes as "the longest discussion of sexual morality in the formation of Christian identity" (Gondreau, "Jesus and Paul," 480).

83. Gondreau, "Jesus and Paul," 484.

84. Hawthorne et al., *Dictionary of Paul and His Letters*, 872.

85. Byrne, "Sinning against One's Own Body," 613.

86. Rediger, *Fit to Be a Pastor*, 16. Cf. 1 Cor 3:17.

87. Horton, *I & II Corinthians*, 66.

88. Wright, *Paul*, 32–34.

89. Wright, *Paul*, 31. The relationship between marriage and divine covenant is captured in the use of הָנָה (*zānāh*), a verb meaning to fornicate or to prostitute (Baker and Carpenter, *Complete Word Study Dictionary*, 297). The word is used to describe Israel's improper relationships with other nations (Isa 23:17; Ezek 23:30; Nah 3:4), other gods (Exod 34:15, 16; Deut 31:16; Ezek 6:9; Hos 9:1), and Israel's breach of God's covenant relationship (Exod 34:16). Other examples of God's people being described as

the pharisaic tradition held Phinehas's zealous reaction to immorality and idolatry (described above) as its righteous hallmark. That tradition also venerated the zeal of Elijah and, more recently to their day, the Maccabees.[90]

Suppose Paul was rooted in such zealous defense against idolatry and immorality. In that case, his description of the *sōma* as a temple directly links immoral sexual desecration with Antiochus Epiphanes, the infamous "abomination of desolation" and precursor to Antichrist. Antiochus adopted the title "Epiphanes" (the divine manifestation) before desecrating the Jerusalem Temple with a "harsh and utterly grievous . . . onslaught of evil" that included debauchery, prostitution, and intercourse within the sacred precincts (2 Mac 6:3–6). Having sex with prostitutes in the Holy of Holies is shocking, to be sure, and the zeal with which the Temple is purged and purified is an example to follow. But here is the catch: God's Spirit was not in that Temple, having departed in the days of Ezekiel. God's Spirit does reside, however, in the individual and corporate body of believers.[91] Therefore, a Christian's sexual immorality is far more egregious than Antiochus's atrocities.

Such understanding unquestionably elevates the moral standard and responsibility (as Christ's first discourse had), yet the once-legalistic Pharisee remarkably extends restorative grace to violators (as Christ had).[92] Such understanding suggests that sexual immorality, as a violation of the *imago Dei* and desecration of the living temple, is arguably the most serious sin short of blasphemy. Such understanding also brings new and vivid meaning to Paul's commands to flee immorality and to present one's body as a living sacrifice that is holy and acceptable to God (Rom 12:1–2). Similarly, the correlation urges deeper consideration of how believers understand

---

adulterous include Ezek 6:9; 16:32; Hos 4:13; Matt 12:39; 16:4; and Jas 4:4. Paul further develops the divine-human/husband-wife relationship in Eph 5:21–33.

90 Wright, *Paul*, 32–33. The author further asserts that the influence drawn from such role models "explains a good deal of the violent zeal to which Paul later confesses."

91. 1 Cor 3:16–17; 6:13–19; 2 Cor 6:16; Eph 2:21.

92. The battle over circumcision is further evidence of Paul's theological shift. The apostle emphasizes his circumcision (Phil 3:5), which marks the Abrahamic covenant (Gen 17:1–27) and distinguishes the Jewish people. Antiochus prohibited this national identifier and was said to execute circumcised babies and the mothers responsible. Such persecution would surely result in greater commitment by a zealous Pharisee, yet Paul hotly rejects circumcision as a salvific requirement (e.g. Acts 15:1–21; Rom 2:25–29; 3:1, 20; 4:9–12; 15:8; 1 Cor 7:18–20; Gal 2:7–9, 12; 5:1–11; 6:12–15; Phil 3:3–5; Col 2:9–15; 3:10–11; Titus 1:10). Why? The Spirit dwells in this new temple by grace through faith, not observance of Torah (cf. Eph 2:8–9). The new creation in Christ receives a circumcision of the heart. To demand outward circumcision is to neglect the inner temple in which the Spirit dwells. Indeed, Paul remains zealous for the temple's purity.

commands to make no provision for the flesh regarding its lusts (Rom 13:14), to crucify the flesh with its passions and desires (Gal 5:24), and to abstain from sexual immorality and thus fulfill God's desire for sanctification (1 Thess 4:3).

Conversely, biblical marriage symbolizes proper union with Christ, self, and others (1 Cor 7:1–16, Eph 5:21–33). Paul develops this understanding by establishing the need for self-control and submission in marital relations, the third consideration in this subsection.

Paul's seemingly complex approach to sexual relations is presentable in three categories: celibacy, sex within marriage, and sexual immorality (*porneia*).[93] Primarily presented in 1 Cor 7:1–16 and Eph 5:21–33, context is critical when engaging Paul's much-debated instruction.

The passage serves as the apostle's response to a now-lost letter from the Corinthian church, further evidence that sexual issues divided churches from the onset.[94] In this circumstance, the differences emerge from opposite ends of dualistic thought—hedonism or asceticism. While a large contingent of church members visited prostitutes in their newfound Christian "freedom," ascetic believers regarded the body and its pleasures as shameful and therefore urged celibacy. Some ascetics so greatly disdained sexual relations, even within marriage, that they advocated divorce to pursue this virtue.[95]

Paul's masterful response negates the extremes of legalism and liberality yet affirms the blessings inherent to both views. Against the ascetics, he insists sexual relations in marriage are a "good gift from the Creator, to be celebrated."[96] In the same breath, Paul insists that singleness and celibacy are gifts that point to eschatological truths. This dichotomy requires further exploration if one is to create a sexual moral ethic for marriage and ministry.

Paul does not forbid marriage. On the contrary, he later indicts those who do so (1 Tim 4:3; cf. Heb 13:4). Only five verses earlier (1 Cor 6:16), Paul emphasizes the one-flesh union inherent to the creative intent (Gen 2:18, 24). Paul echoes this understanding in connecting spousal roles to God's glory (1 Cor 11:2–16). Similarly, Paul explicitly affirms the marriage relationship as analogous to the relationship between Christ and the church (Eph 5:22–33; cf. Col 3:18–19).

---

93. Ciampa and Rosner, *First Letter to the Corinthians*, 277.
94. Johnson, *1 Corinthians*, 105. The various issues are identifiable in Paul's six-times-repeated phrase *peri de* ("now for," "now about," and "now concerning").
95. Johnson, *1 Corinthians*, 110.
96. Wright, *Paul*, 80.

Paul champions biblical marriage and decimates the hedonistic position by elevating the moral standard. The apostle presents the first clear command for monogamous marriage (1 Cor 7:2; cf. 1 Thess 4:26-28) and restricts sexual activity to the marriage bed. This guidance serves as the clearest indication individuals should remain celibate until marriage (cf. Song 8:4). As Craig Blomberg pointedly asserts, this passage leaves no Christian able to "ever legitimately claim that sex outside of marriage is either a right or is right."[97]

Paul further challenges social mores by calling for mutual submission to and consent of conjugal rights within that union, as each spouse acquires a right over the other and simultaneously alienates a portion of personal independence in the conjugal bond.[98] The apostle allows the spouses to withdraw from sexual relations for a time for spiritual reasons. He couches this as a concession, not a command, yet his approach is rooted in Scripture.[99] Paul's use of the Greek *apostereite* ("deprive") is an especially strong word for defrauding or robbing.[100]

While Paul's theology of marriage eviscerates the ascetic's dualistic notions, it does not deny the virtue of celibacy. On the contrary, Paul identifies celibacy to be ideal.[101] However, Paul does not think most Christians have this gift from God. Recognizing the weak human condition and its propensity for immorality, Paul requires the concession of marriage.

An arguably unintended consequence is that Christians come to view sex as a necessary evil.[102] While more prevalent in early Christendom, the argument against sex for any reason other than procreation still has its adherents. For example, Roy Ciampa and Brian Rosner defend the view by analyzing twenty-five occurrences of the euphemism "to touch" in ancient literature and discussing sexual relations in Roman culture.[103] Mark Taylor refutes this view through systematic analysis of Paul's writing (especially Eph 5:22—6:9) and the understanding that the Song of Solomon idealizes pleasurable sex.[104] In essence, Paul advises marriage not as the lesser of two

---

97. Blomberg, *1 Corinthians*, 141.

98. Prior, *Message of 1 Corinthians*, 116.

99. Exod 19:15; Lev 15:18; 1 Sam 21:4-6; Eccl 3:5; Joel 2:16; Zech 12:12-14.

100. Horton, *I & II Corinthians*, 69.

101. This preference must be tempered by Paul's expectation that Christ would soon return (1 Cor 7:29), which likely put matters such as marriage as secondary or even tertiary to his burden to evangelize the lost. See Schenck, *1 & 2 Corinthians*, 110.

102. Pertinent to this topic, this unhealthy view of sex only amplifies the temptation toward illicit behavior (see chapter 4.)

103. Ciampa and Rosner, *First Letter to the Corinthians*, 267.

104. Taylor, *1 Corinthians*, 163-65.

evils but as a necessary safeguard against evil in a society inundated with temptations.

Simply put, the celibate apostle is not against sex. He is against sexual immorality. While celibacy is ideal, marriage is better than immorality. Therefore, one approaches marriage with the reverence, holiness, and loyalty inherent to God's salvific covenant with the church. Spouses should have regular sexual relations to minimize temptation. Though Christians should not divorce, Paul affirms Jesus' "exception clause" for *porneia* and adds a second allowance for desertion. This addition is in keeping with the foundational biblical definition of marriage—leaving/cleaving and becoming one flesh (Gen 2:24)—as "adultery undermines the unique one-flesh relationship, and desertion makes it impossible to continue cleaving to one's spouse."[105] Paul cautions against but provides an allowance for remarriage after divorce and later for widows and widowers (1 Tim 5:14–15).

In summary, Paul's response to the Corinthian errors demonstrates and draws believers toward God's ideal: spiritual fulfillment within monogamous matrimony. Contrary to accusations of misogyny leveled at Paul throughout the ages, this marital construct neither oppresses nor enslaves but protects and empowers by eliminating the societal double standard and granting husband and wife equal value, rights, and obligations.[106] Still, protection against sexual immorality is a primary factor in Paul's approach to marriage—and one he emphasizes when identifying requirements for prospective spiritual leaders.

Paul's guidance in 1 Tim 3:2–7 and Titus 1:6–9 provides the authoritative criteria for pastoral qualification (cf. 1 Pet 5:1–11). One should not overlook the parallels between ministering to one's family and one's church. Paul uses the terms *episkopos* (overseer, bishop) and *presbyteros* (elder) interchangeably (cf. Acts 20:17, 28). It is worth noting, however, that these words reflect different aspects of ministerial responsibility. The former speaks to one's role as a shepherd over God's flock, while the latter speaks of maturity and dignity.[107] Paul first requires the spiritual leader to be "above reproach"

---

105. Blomberg, *1 Corinthians*, 138–39. The author asserts these behaviors dissolve the marriage, therefore divorce "does nothing but acknowledge legally what has in fact already occurred." As such, other circumstances that prove equally destructive to a marriage can also permit a divorce. Blomberg warns that legitimating divorce runs the risk of "greatly abusing that freedom," but legalistic refusal to consider such exceptions "may do even more physical and emotional damage to an individual."

106. Schenck, *1 & 2 Corinthians*, 109–10; Hawthorne et al., *Dictionary of Paul and His Letters*, 599.

107. Black and McClung, *1 & 2 Timothy, Titus, Philemon*, 224. One must not confuse the office of overseer or bishop with the ecclesiastical office that later developed in the second century. Paul was addressing a pastoral director of the church (1 Tim 5:17),

(1 Tim 3:2). The Greek ἀνεπίλημπτο (*anepilēmpton*) speaks to one who "cannot be taken hold of or criticized."[108] The second directive's opening charge demands one be "blameless" (Titus 1:6). The Greek ἀνέγκλητος (*anegklētos*) speaks of one who cannot be accused. Both concern moral purity and demand the pastor have an untarnished reputation. As noted in the Didache, the oldest surviving manual of church discipline, one must choose "overseers and deacons who are worthy of the Lord."[109]

Paul's guidance to Timothy provides fourteen criteria to determine such worthiness. Guidance to Titus further identifies the blameless character as evident in four areas: an orderly family life; avoidance of vice (pride, temper, drink, power, and money); pursuit of virtue (hospitable, love for what is good, self-control, uprightness, holiness, and discipline); and firm adherence to the truth. These are neither new spiritual principles nor unique to leaders, but "leaders are held to greater accountability in the principles common to us all."[110]

Notable is the command that a pastor is "the husband of one wife" (1 Tim 3:2, Titus 1:6). This direction speaks of fidelity and faithfulness in monogamous marriage.[111] Paul further demands self-control (1 Tim 3:2; Titus 1:8), which reflects the ability to take charge of the mind and control impulses that would otherwise drive one to excessive behavior.[112]

What the self-controlled is within, the respectable is without.[113] Moral deficiency discredits the gospel witness, deafens the unbelievers, and disgraces the ministry and its message.[114] Paul identifies the satanic plot behind such failure.[115] This statement significantly advances Paul's presentation of sexual morality. While marriage protects against *porneia*, one must recognize the spiritual conflict that continues to inflame fleshly appetites.

not a hierarchical office (Lea and Griffin, *1, 2 Timothy, Titus*, 108).

108. Liefeld, *1 and 2 Timothy, Titus*, 312.

109. Twelve Apostles, *Didache*, loc. 133.

110. Black and McClung, *1 & 2 Timothy, Titus, Philemon*, 72.

111. Black and McClung, *1 & 2 Timothy, Titus, Philemon*, 72–3, 223; Lea and Griffin, *1, 2 Timothy, Titus*, 109; Liefeld, *1 and 2 Timothy, Titus*, 118; Stott, *Guard the Truth*, 94; and Towner, *1–2 Timothy & Titus*, s.v. 1 Tim 3:1–7. Some affirm that Paul's instruction could be a prohibition of polygamy, though each argued that this is highly unlikely.

112. Towner, *1–2 Timothy & Titus*, s.v. 1 Tim 3:1–7.

113. Stott, *Guard the Truth*, 95.

114. Lea and Griffin, *1, 2 Timothy, Titus*, 114; Stott, *Guard the Truth*, 99; Towner, *1–2 Timothy & Titus*, s.v. 1 Tim 3:1–7. Maintaining proper reputation with those outside the faith is a significant concern for Paul (1 Cor 10:32; Phil 2:15; Col 4:5; 1 Thess 4:12; 1 Tim 2:2, 5:14, 6:1; Titus 2:5, 8, 10, 3:1–2.) This concern is expressed by others, as well (Acts 22:12; 1 Pet 2:12, 15; 3:1, 16).

115. 1 Tim 3:7; cf. 1 Tim 6:9; 2 Tim 2:26.

As noted above, three powerful forces oppose the spiritual walk: the flesh, the world, and the devil.[116]

Paul takes an uncompromising stance against sexual immorality. He counters the ascetic and hedonistic extremes by presenting monogamous marital sex as consistent with God's creative intent and necessary to avoid temptation. Paul equally argues that all other sexual activity is an ungodly violation of one's union with Christ, self, and others. This moral standard is central to ministerial qualification.

The next chapter considers the biblical guidance for ministerial restoration when an individual fails to meet that requirement.

---

116. Eph 2:2–3; cf. Jas 3:15 and 1 John 2:16.

3

The Biblical Solution

"Truth is so obscure in these times, and falsehood so established, that, unless we love the truth, we cannot know it."

— Blaise Pascal

This chapter closely examines ministerial restoration's biblical and theological foundations. Restoration to Christ following sexual moral failure is possible even when restoration to pastoral ministry is not. Scripture commands restoration to maintain the purity of the church (1 Cor 5:1–13), serve as a warning to others (1 Tim 5:19–20), and restore the repentant and disciplined believer (2 Cor 2:6–8; Phlm 1:10–12). Restoration to ministerial function is more complicated. A systematic analysis of Scripture and theological development, viewed in light of historical application, presents the strict allowance for and careful administration of ministerial restoration after a Christian leader experiences a sexual moral failure.[1] However, sexual moral failures violate a sacred trust with God, the church, and the community. Such failures violate the integrity of Christian ministry and the Christian message; they violate the personhood of the victim and violator alike.

As noted throughout this book and carefully explored in section 3, ministerial restoration is the exception rather than the rule following a sexual moral failure. The following chapter determines allowance and requirements for ministerial restoration by exegetical analysis of six Greek

---

1. This systematic and exegetical approach also validates the fourfold restoration paradigm presented in section 3. Notably, Gal 4—6:10 speaks of a brother who is "severed from Christ" (5:4–7), receives the guidance of a mentor (5:7–26), is restored by the church (6:1–10), and all is done according to Paul's guidance as overseer.

words appearing in the New Testament and translated as "restore" a total of thirteen times. Consideration of biblical repentance follows, which will prove a qualifier and contributor to holistic sanctification in later chapters. Understanding the biblical basis for repentance and restoration enables an in-depth review of David's moral failure, which concludes this chapter. Analysis of the king's actions with Bathsheba engages the familial, social, and spiritual factors further developed in section 2. This analysis presents David's failure as a rape common to monarchs in an honor/shame culture, exacerbated by familial deformation and lack of spiritual discipline, yet atoned for through contrite repentance and submission to God's transformative work.

EXEGESIS: THE SIX GREEK WORDS RENDERED "RESTORE"

> "Most laws condemn the soul and pronounce sentence. The result of the law of my God is perfect. It condemns but forgives. It restores—more than abundantly—what it takes away."
>
> — Jim Elliott

The New Testament uses six Greek words to describe restoration. Exegetical analysis of each word reveals remarkable variance in their applications and provides a full definition of biblical restoration.

Scripture most often translates ἀποκαθίστημι (*apokathístēmi*) as "restore," doing so eight times.[2] The primary particle *apo* notes separation and has a specific connotation to origin. The verb *kathistemi* means "to set, place, or put." When united, the word means "to restore to its former state." Such restoration can be physical, as in the restoration of a withered hand and eyesight.[3] Restoration also can be spiritual, as in the restoration provided by the spirit of Elijah (Matt 17:11; Mark 9:12) and in the Davidic kingdom (Acts 1:6). This word's usage in Heb 13:19 is of considerable worth when developing a ministerial restoration paradigm as the passage notes the desire to return to ministerial origin and function.

Second is the related ἀποκατάστασις (*apokatastasis*), which is used once in Acts 3:19–21. The passage speaks to God's theocracy restoring to

---

2. Louw and Nida, *Greek-English Lexicon*, s.v. "ἀποκαθίστημι," 13.65.

3. For the withered hand, see Matt 12:13, Mark 3:5, and Luke 6:10. For eyesight, Mark 8:25.

perfection all things after repentance and return, removing sin and refreshing through time in the Lord's presence.[4]

Scripture translates the third word, καταρτίζω (*katartizó*), as "restore" only once in its thirteen appearances (Gal 6:1). However, this single occurrence stands as a pillar of biblical restoration: "Brethren, even if anyone is caught in any trespass, you who are spiritual, restore such a one in a spirit of gentleness; each one looking to yourself, so that you too will not be tempted." The fullness of this word, seen through analysis of its complete usage, conveys a far deeper understanding. The word speaks to preparation, arrangement, and adjustment, as in God preparing praise for himself out of the mouths of infants (Matt 21:16) and a body through which he can fulfill the law's sacrificial requirements (Heb 10:5).[5] It also speaks to repairing that which is broken or rent, as in the mending of fishing nets (Matt 4:21, Mark 1:19).[6] When applied in the context of personal formation, *katartizó* describes the strengthening and development that enables one to be what he ought, as in the pupil's training to be like the teacher.[7] This latter definition also presents *katartizó* in the context of believers united in mind and judgment (1 Cor 1:10; 2 Cor 13:11).

The fourth word, ὑγιής (*hugiés*), speaks of one who is sound in body or made whole.[8] The word appears in twelve passages, though only Matthew 15:31 translates this as "restored."[9] This passage describes the crowd as marveling and glorifying God after they saw "the mute speaking, the crippled restored, and the lame walking, and the blind seeing." In Titus 2:7–8, ὑγιής is rendered "sound" and carries a metaphorical meaning of teaching that does not deviate from the truth.[10] This description charges young believers to follow a call for sensibility, a life that serves as an example of good deeds and purity in doctrine. These characteristics ensure every adversary is put to shame and has nothing negative to say about the body of believers.

---

4. Louw and Nida, *Greek-English Lexicon*, s.v. "ἀποκατάστασις," 13.65.

5. Louw and Nida, *Greek-English Lexicon*, s.v. "καταρτίζω," 13.130.

6. Louw and Nida, *Greek-English Lexicon*, s.v. "καταρτίζω," 75.5.

7. Cf. Luke 6:40; 1 Thess 3:9–10; Heb 13:21; 1 Pet 5:10.

8. Louw and Nida, *Greek-English Lexicon*, s.v. "ὑγιής," 23.129.

9. It is worth noting that the words ἀποκαθίστημι and ὑγιής are used in conjunction in Matt 12:13, in which a man stretched out his withered hand "and it was restored (ἀποκαθίστημι) to normal (ὑγιής), like the other." Other passages that speak to the physical restoration captured by the word ὑγιής include Mark 5:34, John 7:23, and Acts 4:10. The word is also used six times in John 5:4–15 when Jesus heals the lame man at the pool of Bethesda.

10. Louw and Nida, *Greek-English Lexicon*, s.v. "ὑγιής," 72.14.

The fifth word, ἀνορθόω (*anorthoó*), notes temple restoration in Acts 15:16, an essential distinction for believers who now comprise the temple in which the Holy Spirit dwells (1 Cor 3:16; 6:19–20).[11] The word appears three times in Scripture and speaks of erecting, rearing again, or building anew. Its use extends beyond the context of structures to the restoration of a deformed person.[12] Such is the case in the Sabbath healing of a woman who, for eighteen years, could not straighten her posture (Luke 13:13). The victim was "made erect" when Jesus removed the demonic infirmity. Hebrews 12:12 also tells the believer to "strengthen (ἀνορθόω) the hands that are weak and the knees that are feeble." This command follows a discussion of God's discipline, described as "given that we may share His holiness," and precedes the imperative that we pursue "sanctification without which no one will see the Lord." Specific warnings against bitterness and immorality ensure "no one comes short of the grace of God." The author explicitly notes Esau, who sold his birthright to satisfy fleshly appetites (Gen 25:29–34).

The sixth and final word translated as "restore" is σῴζω (*sózó*), a verb that means "to rescue from danger and to restore to a former state of safety and well-being; to cause someone to become well again after having been sick; to cause someone to experience divine salvation."[13] While the word commonly speaks of salvation, its use in Jas 5:15 notes that the prayer of faith will "restore the one who is sick, and the Lord will raise him up, and if he has committed sins, they will be forgiven him."

When the words translated as "restore" are considered in their full definition and context, biblical restoration presents a return to a former state and the Lord's presence so that times of spiritual, physical, and emotional refreshing may come. It is healing leading to wholeness that allows the embattled believer to continue in God's perfect plan.

Restoration speaks to mending the torn, repairing the broken, enabling the stricken to stand upright, and strengthening those wounded and weary. As is true when restoring a deficient structure, the biblical paradigm offers no allowance for impurities that weaken the foundations. These must be removed and replaced; only sound doctrine and discipline can build or rebuild a sound believer.

In addition to the examples of sexual moral failure listed above, in which restoration is sometimes offered and sometimes refused, ministers and leaders restored throughout the biblical record provide restorative principles of note. These include God's restoration of Moses and David after

---

11. Louw and Nida, *Greek-English Lexicon*, s.v. "ἀνορθόω," 45.4.
12. Louw and Nida, *Greek-English Lexicon*, s.v. "ἀνορθόω," 17.33.
13. Louw and Nida, *Greek-English Lexicon*, s.v. "σῴζω," 21.18, 21.27, 23.136.

murder and Peter after a thrice-stated betrayal.[14] God also grants restoration to his repentant people (Deut 30), amid the fall and cleansing of the wise (Dan 11:35), and to a disciplined sinner (2 Cor 2:5–11).[15]

Fundamental truths are evident in each instance. For example, God's grace offers healing and (re)formation but does not remove the sufferable consequences inherent to each violation. In addition, God's holiness requires the violator to recognize the severity of his sin and offer an appropriate response through repentance and participation in sanctification. Both are necessary to obtain forgiveness and restoration to God and perhaps ministerial function. However, a word of caution is needed. As noted above, cultural and personal preferences often drive church decisions to allow or refuse ministerial restoration after a sexual moral failure. God's mercy frequently defies such standards and restores some "to positions of prestige, power, and service."[16] Indeed, "there is hope for those ordinarily thought to be a lost cause."[17] Applying the "letter of the law" must not preclude the weightier matters of justice, mercy, and compassion (Matt 23:23). To do so will prove destructive rather than constructive.[18] Therefore, Paul's paradigm for selecting spiritual, gentle, supportive, and self-aware restorers is emphasized (Gal 6:1–10).

The spiritual character stands as the apostle's first qualifier (Gal 6:1). Paul's phrase *hoi pneumatikoi* ("you who have received the Spirit") would seem to be a sweeping congregational qualifier as believers were born from the Spirit (Gal 4:29) and received the Spirit (Gal 3:2, 5). However, Paul's restoration paradigm requires people of the Spirit who markedly depend on and align with the Spirit.[19] The Spirit's fruit is the identifying mark of those who follow the Spirit's direction.[20] Such are guided by divine revela-

---

14. Peter's example is of note. Jesus arguably promotes the disciple from a fisher of men to a shepherd, the role of Jesus in his earthly ministry (John 21:15–17).

15. As noted above, it is likely that the restored sinner of whom Paul speaks is the man who was earlier ousted from the church for having sexual relations with his stepmother (1 Cor 5:1–13).

16. Mosgofian and Ohlschlager, *Sexual Misconduct in Counseling and Ministry*, 250.

17. Green et al., *Dictionary of Jesus and the Gospels*, 867.

18. For example, the Pharisees twice referred to Jesus as a "sinner" (John 9:1–41) not because he was immoral or idolatrous but rather because he failed to keep the Sabbath the way the Pharisees thought it should be kept. Self-righteousness blinded these religious leaders. They rejected the signs that affirmed Jesus as Messiah and displayed God's merciful intent because these actions did not align with their expectations. For this reason, Jesus, who was called a "sinner" by the religious leaders, defines them as such in Gethsemane (Matt 26:45; Mark 14:41).

19. Barton et al., *Galatians*, 199; Keener, *Galatians*, 528, 530; Stott, *Message of Galatians*, 161; Wright, *Galatians*, 346.

20. Gal 5:16–25; cf. 1 Cor 2:14–3:4, Heb 5:13–14.

tion rather than humanistic reasoning and hold a trialectic tension between Scripture, the Holy Spirit, and the contemporary community.[21] This quality is necessary because any corrective or directive solution must be rooted in Scripture, relating to the individual's experience through understanding (not just explanation), and allow the Spirit to unite and operate in both.[22]

Participation by mature, fruit-bearing believers enables interdependence to overcome individualism as "personal responsibility before God is surrounded by a mutual accountability."[23] Mutual accountability requires the spiritual to speak the truth in love and restore in a spirit of gentleness, Paul's second criterion for restoration (Gal 6:1).[24] The verb *katartizó* (restore) well conveys the demand for attentive gentleness. As noted above, ancient writers used this word to describe the setting of a broken bone and the mending of torn fishing nets. In displaying similar care, the spiritual mentor is to neither neglect nor reject the broken.[25] Humiliation and gossip are forbidden (1 Cor 12:23).[26] Biblical discipline should be remedial "and not merely or even primarily punitive."[27] Instead, the gentle response leading to repentance is nonjudgmental and forgiving.[28]

To walk in gentle nonjudgment and forgiveness requires careful self-evaluation, Paul's third criterion for restoration (Gal 6:1). Holistic restoration demands unconditional love but not unconditional acceptance. Conversely, while understanding and correcting ungodly behavior requires the spiritual to judge the actions rightly, one should not judge the actor.[29] A willingness to believe the worst about others only brings out the worst in oneself. As Augustine rightly asserts, "there is no surer test of the spiritual

---

21. Browning et al., *From Culture Wars to Common Ground*, 337; Hayford, *Restoring Fallen Leaders*, 55; Nipkow, "Empirical Research Within Practical Theology," 54.

22. Browning et al. *From Culture Wars to Common Ground*, 335; Cartledge, *Mediation of the Spirit*, 3; Crabb, *Connecting*, xvi.

23. McKnight, *Galatians*, 290.

24. As Keener notes, 2 Cor 12:20–13:3 may be instructive amid the combination of firmness and regret at needing to be firm (Keener, *Galatians*, 528). See also 1 Cor 4:21; 5:5–7.

25. Barton et al., *Galatians*, 200; Stott, *Message of Galatians*, 160. Indeed, the tenderness of Christ refuses to crush even the smallest hope. See Foster, *Celebration of Discipline*, 188. Cf. Isa 42:3, Matt 12:20.

26. Bonhoeffer, *Life Together*, 92. Cf. Eph 4:29, 2 Tim 2:24–26, Jas 4:11–12.

27. Blomberg, *1 Corinthians*, 109. See also Johnson and VanVonderen, *Subtle Power Spiritual Abuse*, 97.

28. Hession, *Forgotten Factors of Sexual Sin*, loc. 983. Matt 5:12; 7:1–5; 18:15–35; Luke 17:1–4; 2 Cor 2:6–8; Gal 6:1–2; Eph 4:32; Col 3:12–15; Jas 5:19–20.

29. Laaser, *Healing the Wounds*, 93; Murray, *Saving Truth*, 129. Cf. Matt 7:1–5, Titus 3:1–2.

person than his treatment of another's sin. Note how he takes care to deliver the sinner rather than triumph over him, to help him rather than punish him and, so far as lies in his capacity, to support him."[30] Therefore, the spiritual restorer must guard against pride, indifference, and feelings of superiority, as these eviscerate the humility required for gentle restoration.[31] This standard requires genuine self-knowledge and honest appraisal of how the experience affects the one offering counsel.[32]

Paul's fourth criterion identifies the need for practical support that centers on bearing another's burden and thus fulfilling the law of Christ (Gal 6:2). Indeed, Jesus took into his body every aspect of evil and overcame that darkness by his light and love (2 Cor 5:21, 2 Pet 2:24). The church is now the body of Christ and must do likewise.[33] Thus, C. S. Lewis considers the "load, or weight, or burden of my neighbour's glory" the holiest object next to the blessed sacrament and "should be laid daily on my back."[34] In doing so, "every sin of every member burdens and indicts the whole community [yet] the congregation rejoices, in the midst of all the pain and the burden the brother's sin inflicts, that it has the privilege of burying and forgiving."[35]

In essence, "those who are spiritual" know that to be better *than* sinners, one must be better *to* sinners (Luke 6:27–36). This understanding is central to any restoration theology. Jesus was more critical of those who dismissed sinners than of the sinners themselves.[36] Furthermore, Jesus' approach to repentance and restoration is eschatological. Jesus' repeated and reputed engagement with sinners foreshadows the celebratory messianic banquet to come; those with whom he fellowships reveal who will receive vindication in the renewed Kingdom.[37] The selection of banquet partners

---

30. Augustine, *Epistle to the Galatians Letter 56* [1b.6.1], as quoted in Edwards, *Galatians, Ephesians, Philippians*, 93.

31. Bonhoeffer, *Life Together*, 102; Stott, *Message of Galatians*, 162; Wright, *Galatians*, 355. See also 1 Cor 10:12–13; Eph 4:30–32; Col 3:12–15; 1 John 1:7–9.

32. Oden, *Pastoral Counsel*, 7; Willimon, *Pastor*, 217.

33. Wright, *Galatians*, 354. Cf. Jas 5:19–20.

34. Lewis, *Weight of Glory*, 45–46. The "glory" of which Lewis speaks is the eternal glory received when the believer finishes the race of faith and hears Jesus declare "well done, good and faithful servant." The obligation of fellow believers is to ensure the individual finishes well.

35. Bonhoeffer, *Life Together*, 103. The Lutheran pastor further asserts that the failure to extend "help, encouragement, and forgiveness" is "unchristian" (p. 105). See also Barton et al., *Galatians*, 198. Cf. 1 Cor 12:12–27, esp. v. 26.

36. Dunn, *Jesus Remembered*, 532.

37. Green et al., *Dictionary of Jesus and the Gospels*, 868. This assertion centers on Matt 21:31.

further asserts neither condemnation nor exclusion but the restoration of repentant sinners as God's chief intention.[38]

Again, while restoration to God is available to all, restoration to ministry is available to some. The following subsection presents repentance as the inceptive act for those to whom God extends such grace. The following chapters explain that this includes a proper understanding of sin's destructive nature and the sanctification required to overcome sin's stain and control.

THEOLOGICAL CONSIDERATIONS OF REPENTANCE

"We are not called to be burden-bearers, but cross bearers and light-bearers. We must cast our burdens on the Lord."

— Corrie ten Boom

Scripture contains no stated prohibition against the restoration to calling after any sinful behavior. On the contrary, a return to relational right standing with God is arguably the primary purpose of Scripture, and the resumption/completion of divine purpose continually marks this relational restoration. Notable is Peter's restoration after having denied Christ—a restoration that saw him not simply return to the position of a "fisher of men" but promoted to the role of a shepherd (John 21:15–17). With that said, ministerial restoration is neither a right nor a guarantee.[39] Restoration to calling depends on circumstances and requires contrition, repentance, and submission to God's transformative work.

This understanding begins early in God's journey with Israel. Though Israelites do not fulfill a ministerial role commensurate with the fivefold ministry (Eph 4:11), individual Israelites comprise a holy people anointed and called to illuminate God's light and love. This status is a ministerial function—a critical understanding when considering many passages that speak of restoration following the nation's spiritual adultery. For example, the era of the Judges enters its sin cycle time and again due to the assimilation of religious observance that results in a progressive religious decline from monotheism to syncretism to polytheism to outright apostasy. Such behavior only worsens when the kingdom splits after Solomon's death,

---

38. Green et al., *Dictionary of Jesus and the Gospels*, 867.

39. Contrary to numerous examples of restorations that quickly (and wrongly) cite God's gifts and callings as irrevocable (Rom 11:29). The passage's context speaks of God's call of Israel, not a minister guilty of egregious behaviors.

THE BIBLICAL SOLUTION

leading to Jeremiah's repeated cry of *shuv* ("return") and the charge of Israel's unfaithfulness (Ezek 16; Isa 5). Still, God demonstrates his unending love for this unfaithful bride by restoring Israel to relationship and purpose, as depicted in Hosea's example. A return to ministry to and for God predicates these examples of relational restoration. Regarding restoration after the literal act of adultery, David is arguably the example par excellence as he maintains his kingship and prophetic role after his multifaceted moral failure. A case study follows.

Suffice it to say there is no sin so great that it is beyond God's grace but no sin so small that it does not require God's grace. And that undeserved grace requires humankind's unreserved repentance. This healing takes considerable time and effort and often begins "with the prophetic act of truth-telling."[40] Such truth emerges from a broken spirit and contrite heart (Ps 51:17). As demonstrated below, many apologies accompanying ministerial moral failure confessions fall short of this measure. Instead, the typically shallow apologies seek to maintain positive public relations, though, as Jon Coutts rightly asserts, such apologies "tend to be concerned neither with the public nor with relations, but with amplification and vindication of the self."[41]

Indeed, genuine confession is necessary to find compassion (Prov 28:13), yet "actionable admission" better defines biblical repentance. The Hebrew שוב (*shuv*) and the Greek μετάνοια (*metanoia*) present repentance as a reorientation toward God and away from ungodly behavior, thus changing one's thinking and behavior.[42] Such change is evident in the sinful woman's submissive and generous worship of Jesus (Luke 7:36–50), the prodigal who "comes to his senses" and returns to the father's house (Luke 15:17–18), and the sinful tax collector who demonstrates humility and genuine contrition (Luke 18:9–14).

Though not synonymous with sorrow or remorse, godly mourning should accompany repentance (2 Cor 7:10). David's lament provides a strong example (Ps 51). The Greek πενθέω (*pentheó*) also develops this truth when addressing genuine anguish over sin.[43] In fact, "Judaism regarded the sacrifice of the unrepentant as 'an abomination to the Lord.'"[44] In later

---

40. DeGroat, *When Narcissism Comes to Church*, loc. 1635.

41. Coutts, *Shared Mercy*, 145.

42. Green et al., *Dictionary of Jesus and the Gospels*, 771. Notably, the Greek word is a compound of *meta*, meaning "change," and *nous*, meaning "mind."

43. Taylor, *1 Corinthians*, 134. Cf. Matt 5:4, Mark 16:10, 1 Cor 5:2, 2 Cor 12:21, Jas 4:9.

44. Peterson, *Engaging with God*, 39. Cf. Prov 15:8; 21:27; Sirach 34:18–19. The author adds that the Mishna tractate on the Day of Atonement says, "If a man say, I will

Christian tradition, compunction views "holy tears as part of a pedagogical strategy to bring therapy to the soul," an essential aspect of sanctification addressed below.[45]

Biblical repentance seeks relational restoration, not pardon from punishment.[46] This understanding is evident in Zacchaeus's newfound generosity and unsolicited commitment to recompense those he had defrauded (Luke 19:1–10).[47] Indeed, repentance recognizes and corrects abuses inflicted on God, others, and oneself.[48] For this reason, one must not offer irreverent or formulaic repentance. As John Stott rightly observes, believers must not presume on God, approach atonement too quickly, or assume sin does not provoke God's wrath simply because it does not provoke our own.[49]

Conversely, biblical repentance admits sin and moral weakness. David provides a telling example. Confronted by God's prophet, the king confesses his sin.[50] Nathan immediately responds that the Lord "also has put away your sin" (2 Sam 12:13). David changes his thinking, God reciprocates, and repentance restores the right relationship.

In addition, biblical repentance takes responsibility, is open to feedback, values community over self, is rooted in humility, and is committed to correction. This approach includes a rejection of one's autonomy and control (John 12:25). When Jesus bids his followers lose their lives, the Greek word ἀπόλλυμι (*apollumi*) does not speak of misplacing or modifying but rather destroying that old life.[51] Such repentance is contrite and continuous, as the violator repents not just of an act but a condition.[52] Indeed, repentance moves beyond simple confessions of lust and impurity to seek an end of willful continuation in sin.[53]

---

sin and repent, I will sin again and repent, he will be given no chance to repent. If he say, I will sin and the Day of Atonement will clear me, the Day of Atonement will effect no atonement" (*Yoma* 8.9).

45. Coulter, "Introduction," 18.

46. Zondervan, *NRSV Cultural Backgrounds*, s.v. Lev 4:35; loc. 17325; cf. Num 14:9–24; Gal 6:7–8.

47. It is notable that the religious leaders refer to Zacchaeus as a "notorious sinner" while Jesus calls him a "son of Abraham."

48. Hession, *Forgotten Factors*, locs. 126–28.

49. Stott, *Cross of Christ*, 110.

50. Note the difference in Saul's response when he was confronted by the prophet Samuel. The insincerity of the king's confession "I have sinned" is captured in his subsequent supplication "but please honor me now before the elders of my people" (1 Sam 15:30).

51. Vine et al., *Vine's Complete Expository Dictionary*, s.v. "apollumi," 164.

52. London and Wiseman, *Pastors at Risk*, 81–85.

53. This truth is captured in John's first epistle, though the apostle's explanation can

Repentance initiates the divine effort to bridge the infinite gulf caused by sin's threefold alienation from God, others, and oneself. The violator surrenders self-preservation in the hope of restoration with God and others.[54] God's response is forgiveness, defined less by "a static, juridical concept of expunging a record of transgression than a dynamic, social-psychological experience of being released from the deleterious effects of guilt and sinful behavior and restoring broken relations between human beings and God and among themselves."[55]

In summary, repentance is the proper response to God's grace, which results in a rejection of sin, a return to obedience, and the right attitude toward God, self, and others. God's response of forgiveness enables restoration with each. Until one repents, "the situation which we have created for ourselves is our responsibility. But from the moment when we humble ourselves in repentance and confession, the situation becomes God's."[56] Once in God's hands, the work of sanctification begins. The following subsection addresses this reformative and restorative work.

A CASE STUDY OF DAVID AND BATHSHEBA

"When you turn to God you discover He has been facing you all the time."

— Zig Ziglar

David survives an angry giant, a jealous king, and a disgruntled army, yet his sexual impulses nearly topple the king. David amasses three wives and ten concubines despite a divine prohibition (Deut 17:14–17). Though this is a cultural commonality among kings of his day, it violates God's Law,

---

be confusing, and even appear contradictory, apart from exegetical analysis. Specifically, 1 John 2:1 speaks of helping believers not sin, while 1 John 3:9 says no one born of God will sin. The former is in the Greek aortist tense, which presents the sin as a one-time (rather than continuing) event. In this case, the believer has an advocate with the Father, Jesus Christ. The latter verse presents sin in the Greek present tense, which would note continuing action. Therefore, "it is clear that John is by no means teaching that the regenerate person never commits a sin, only that it is not natural to him" (Williams, *Renewal Theology . . . Vol. 2*, 89).

54. This is a necessary aspect of restoration in the *imago Dei*. See Hoekema, *Created in God's Image*.

55. Green et al., *Dictionary of Jesus and the Gospels*, 284. The authors note this level of divine forgiveness is closely associated with the terms *aphiēmi*, *aphesis*, and *apolyō*, which relate to "freedom, release, letting go."

56. Hession, *Forgotten Factors*, loc. 837.

which David is prone to keep.⁵⁷ His disobedience here might be consequential were it not for other mitigating factors. For example, David's penitent repentance following Nathan's indictment includes an affirmation that he was "brought forth in iniquity, and in sin my mother conceived me" (Ps 51:5). Thus, David affirms the far-reaching influence of a longstanding sinful nature, which contextually centers on sexual immorality.⁵⁸ Similarly, John Goldingay argues David's selection of the yiqtol rather than qatal pronoun "*yāda*" in Ps 51:4 speaks to his nature and "makes explicit that this acknowledgement is more than a past event or onetime recognition."⁵⁹ David's subsequent comment on birth and conception further indicates his "waywardness and failure go back to the very beginning of the suppliant's life, whether one identifies that as birth (the first colon) or conception (the second colon)."⁶⁰

Notable is the fact that David does not punish Amnon for the rape of Tamar, perhaps because this is a crime David himself committed with Bathsheba (explained below). This omission results in Amnon's murder by Absalom and the latter's subsequent rebellion, which provides "an obvious link between David's casual attitude toward sexual liaison and human life."⁶¹ Even in his old age, the people who know David best believe a naked virgin will enliven their dying king (1 Kgs 1:1–4). Nothing in the text indicates that David desired a naked virgin for sexual activity, but it begs the question: why would the king's advisors take this action? Why would they not seek one of David's wives or concubines for this duty?

There can be no doubt that David fell prey to sexual malfeasance. Conversely, his response to moral failure with Bathsheba stands as the epitome of restoration. That David is guilty of sexual moral failure is evident. The anointed king covets a married woman, commits adultery (possibly rape), and premeditates Uriah's murder. As noted above, these sins separate the violator from God and defile the people, the land, and God's dwelling place.⁶²

Because contemporary theology often justifies David and vilifies Bathsheba (a common tendency in ministerial moral failures), this subsection

---

57. Note what one might call the "asterisk of I Kings 15:5," which states that "David did what was right in the sight of the LORD, and had not turned aside from anything that He commanded him all the days of his life, except in the case of Uriah the Hittite."

58. Wilson, *Psalms*, 774.

59. Goldingay, *Psalms Vol. 2*, 128.

60. Goldingay, *Psalms Vol. 2*, 129. The author adds that David's is a "personal statement about the suppliant's particular life, and it is not clear that this personal statement is assumed to apply to everyone."

61. Wright, *Paul*, 173.

62. Lev 18:24–30; Num 35:30–34; cf. Ezek 23:37–38; Isa 59:2–3.

first establishes David's culpability. Considerations that follow identify David's failure to subdue the three opposing forces: the flesh, notably illicit passions resulting from deformative and traumatic life events; the world, especially adverse cultural, familial, and societal influence; and the devil. Analysis reveals five internal and external formative factors that contribute to David's unexpected and ungodly behaviors. First, David is emotionally malformed by dysfunctional family relationships and experiences. Second, David's "advisors" are enablers who fail to provide spiritual accountability. Third, David's relaxation of spiritual disciplines gives him an opportunity to sin. Fourth, the adverse influence of culture produces an attitude of entitlement. Fifth, David abuses his position and authority, taking Bathsheba for his sexual desire and enlisting complicit acolytes.

David's moral failure demonstrates lust that births sin, which brings death (cf. Jas 1:15). Consequences include the deaths of four children and exile amid a son's betrayal. Yet God spares David, though adultery and murder are capital crimes.[63] God allows David to remain king, an anointed position that includes the ministerial function of shepherding God's people, and even blesses David's remaining years. Repentance is the key that unlocks this grace. Therefore, the following analysis considers David's culpability, emotional malformation, lack of accountability, relaxation of spiritual disciplines, attitude of entitlement, abuse of position and authority, and repentance.

David's Culpability Considered

Contemporary scholarship categorizes David as everything from manipulated victim to rapist. The latter, more severe charge includes Richard Davidson's assertion of "power rape"[64] and Walter Brueggemann's charge that Nathan's parabolic lamb lying with the poor man but taken by the rich man carries an accusation of rape.[65]

Others vindicate David by claiming Bathsheba's complicity and identify her as everything from a willing participant to a political provocateur motivated by social standing.[66] Commentators describe Bathsheba's bathing—a ritual purification concluding her menstrual period—as everything

---

63. Exod 21:12–14; Lev 20:10; 24:17, 21; Deut 22:22.
64. Davidson, "Did David Rape Bathsheba?," 89.
65. Brueggemann, *First and Second Samuel*, 280.
66. For example, Tamber-Rosenau, "Biblical Bathing Beauties," 56, and Bailey, *David in Love and War*, 85.

from "feminine flirtation,"[67] to a "contributing factor" lacking modesty,[68] to a deliberate and provocative provocation.[69] Robert Bergen affirms that Scripture says nothing of Bathsheba's motivation (or lack thereof), yet he ascribes her actions to anything from naivety to personal desire.[70] In truth, her commitment to keeping the Law ends with the violation of Bathsheba and the Law by the one anointed to be the highest upholder of God's Law.[71]

As Kyle Worley rightly observes, "Christians have historically been willing to slut-shame Bathsheba to keep any stink (beyond adultery) off of David."[72] She is villainized as a "sex kitten who bewitched a divinely chosen king" and a conniving vixen "coquettishly parading around naked" to seduce God's chosen.[73] Because it is difficult and undesirous to imagine the godly David "could sin without some tantalizing temptress making him do it . . . we need someone to blame for our hero's fall."[74]

Exegetical analysis portrays David as anything but heroic. Conversely, Scripture views Bathsheba as the victim, most directly by Nathan's parabolic description of the exploited lamb (2 Sam 12:1–4). Equally significant is Bathsheba's diminishing identity as she is increasingly objectified. The story introduces Bathsheba by name but soon distinguishes her as the daughter of Eliam, then as Uriah's wife, and simply as "the woman" once David satisfies his lust (2 Sam 11:3–5).[75] That Scripture never describes Bathsheba as loving David reinforces Bathsheba's victimization. This omission starkly contrasts Michal, David's first wife, who is twice said to love David (1 Sam 18:20, 28) and even risks her life to protect David from her father's wrath (1 Sam 19:12).

Scripture neither accuses nor maligns Bathsheba but affirms "the thing that David had done was evil in the sight of the Lord" (2 Sam 11:27).[76] God's severe reaction closely parallels the divine response to Onan's sexual

---

67. Hertzberg, *I & II Samuel*, 309.
68. McGee, *History of Israel*, 230.
69. Nicol, "Bathsheba, A Clever Woman," 360.
70. Bergen, *1, 2 Samuel*, 364.
71. Grey, "Prophetic Call to Repentance," 15.
72. Worley, "Why It's Easier to Accept David as a Murderer than a Rapist," para. 22.
73. Garland and Garland, *Flawed Families of the Bible*, 154.
74. Garland and Garland, *Flawed Families of the Bible*, 154.
75. Even Jesus' genealogy identifies by name Tamar (who seduced her father-in-law), Rahab (a prostitute) and Ruth (a gentile) yet refers to Bathsheba as "the wife of Uriah" (Matt 1:3–6).
76. Nathan's prophetic indictment omits Bathsheba, as well (2 Sam 12:7–12).

misconduct (Gen 38:10). Onan died for his misbehavior. David's penalty "could be expected to be equally severe."[77]

Before identifying why God commutes the sentence, consider why David departs from God's heart and Law. David's actions result from neither a lapse of reason nor a moment of weakness. David acts upon illicit passions resulting from emotional malformation and exacerbated by ungodly cultural influence, an attitude of entitlement, and abuse of power.

David's Emotional Formation

As explained in section 2, holistic restoration requires one to recognize the factors that contribute to illicit behaviors to disarm triggers and circumvent conditioned responses. Some individuals cope with or numb such struggles through learned and conditioned behaviors. It is reasonable to question whether any connection exists between David's emotional formation and apparent tendencies toward sexual gratification. In this regard, analysis of David's moral failure is impossible, as event and emotional details are limited, making proper diagnosis implausible. One can only speculate concerning the significance various events play in David's emotional formation. While Scripture rightly identifies David as a man after God's heart (1 Sam 13:14), it also conveys several key events in David's life worth considering when seeking to understand the conducive environment and destructive actions resulting in Bathsheba's violation and Uriah's murder.

For example, personal distress, depressive episodes, and feelings of rejection are evident at various junctures throughout David's life.[78] David interacts with God throughout these challenging circumstances and grows in character and calling. He also voices repeated and significant emotional struggles.[79] While it is impossible to quantify these and other events' specific impacts on David's emotional formation, adverse effects may have affected his overall formation.

Jonathan's death may be a factor in David's emotional formation. The duo demonstrates mutual respect and care throughout their friendship. This bond is perhaps most evident when David falls on his face at an earlier parting and bows three times before his loyal friend, confidant, and

---

77. Bergen, *1, 2 Samuel*, 368.

78. For indications of depression, see 1 Sam 26:24; 30:6; 2 Sam 3:35; 22:7; 24:14; 1 Chr 21:13. David also deals with rejection by his father (1 Sam 16:13), brother (1 Sam 16:28), father-in-law (1 Sam 18:8–9), wife (2 Sam 6:20), and son (2 Sam 15:13). In fact, God rejects David's dream of building the temple (1 Chr 22:8).

79. For example, Pss 13; 22; 52; 56; 59; 60.

righteous advisor (1 Sam 20:41). They wept together, and David "wept immeasurably." News of Jonathan's death years later sees David overcome with sorrow. His song of mourning speaks of his beloved and delightful brother, a close friend whose love was more wonderful than the love of women (2 Sam 1:11–27).[80] Indeed, the tragic loss of his closest friend and confidant may have contributed to David's sin with Bathsheba—meaning that David lost his personal support and accountability partner. While it is unclear whether Jonathan's death contributed to or triggered David's depressive episode discussed below, the lack of Jonathan's counsel may have left a gap in David's emotional support system. While David rightly affirms that he alone is responsible for those decisions (Ps 51:2–4, 9), one must consider whether the king's lack of accountability contributes to his unfortunate choices and actions.

David's Lack of Accountability

It is reasonable to question whether David would have abandoned the battlefield, let alone commit adultery and murder, if Jonathan were at his side. Indeed, Jonathan is a man of discernment (1 Sam 14:6) and integrity (1 Sam 14:43; 20:12–13). Jonathan is courageous in expressing his convictions; he does not hesitate to speak the truth to a king who wants none of it (1 Sam 14:43; 19:4–6; 20:32) and brings reconciliation when the king demands revenge (1 Sam 19:7). When it comes to David, Jonathan is a loyal friend (1 Sam 18:1–3; 19:2–3; 20:4–11, 18–29), confidant (1 Sam 20:1–3), and an encourager in times of distress (1 Sam 23:16). Though the prince of Israel, Jonathan's commitment to David's kingship is evident (1 Sam 18:4; 20:30–31; 23:17).

Now Jonathan is dead, and in his place stands Joab—a valiant warrior on the battlefield but a vicious manipulator in state affairs. The general supports the king when it serves Joab's interests. Notably, Joab remains in David's good graces by carrying out (without question or hesitation) the execution of Uriah, a brave and valuable soldier (2 Sam 11:14–25). Conversely, Joab conspires against the king when a command does not serve his interest, such as in the killings of Absalom (2 Sam 18:9–17) and Amasa (2 Sam 20:9–12).[81] Rather than encourage his complacent king during David's wartime absence (2 Sam 11:1–2), Joab takes swift command of Israel's

---

80. David's commitment to Jonathan is further evident in his committed care of Mephibosheth, Jonathan's disabled son (2 Sam 9).

81. Notably, David's list of heroes and valiant men omits the flawed Joab yet concludes with Uriah the Hittite (2 Sam 23:8–39).

army—and leaves David to wander about the palace. Alone in the palace, the relaxation of spiritual disciplines renders David more susceptible to temptation.

David's Relaxation of Spiritual Disciplines

The cause of David's willful abdication of spiritual disciplines and responsibilities is not explicit. His actions follow a series of triumphant campaigns that brought unprecedented success and popularity. Yet the king sets aside his armor as Israel's soldiers carry the ark of the covenant into battle.

David soon manifests "the works of the flesh" (Gal 5:19–21). Indeed, David's focus shifts from his relationship with God to his desire for a bathing woman. The word "saw" derives from the Qal imperfect of רָאָה (ra'ah), indicating David was staring. The lustful look dehumanizes the woman into an object for sexual gratification. David's failure to turn away marks a turning point in his life and ministry. The look evokes a desire that develops into intentional pursuit and self-centered exploitation.

David's devolving character ethic is evident in subsequent demands, as he lies to satisfy his lust and greed. As Diane Chandler notes, ethical leaders perceive and are sensitive to moral issues and the impact of their choices on others. In contrast, unethical leaders "use personal power to advance self-interest and personal goals at the expense of followers."[82] David exhibits "four by-products of success—loss of strategic focus, privileged access, control of resources, and inflated belief in [one's] ability to manipulate outcomes."[83] David's attitude of entitlement further exacerbates these factors.

David's Attitude of Entitlement

David's privileged access and attitude of entitlement become apparent. A servant identifies Bathsheba as the daughter of Eliam, one of David's valiant warriors (2 Sam 23:34); granddaughter of David's close advisor, Ahitophel (2 Sam 16:23); and married to Uriah, one of David's "mighty men" (1 Chr 11:41). None of this deters David. Scripture is concise in its description: the king saw, sent, inquired, took, and lay (2 Sam 11:2–4). The quick action presents David's inability to wield power rightly.[84] Instead of serving, David

---

82. Chandler, "Perfect Storm of Leaders' Unethical Behavior," 77.
83. Ludwig and Longenecker, "Bathsheba Syndrome," 268–69.
84. Arnold, *1 & 2 Samuel*, 540.

exercises his royal power by sending and taking. Instead of defending, he exploits the vulnerable.

Similarly, David's cold and self-oriented exploitation further evidences the adverse influence of cultural norms and secular principles. Neighboring monarchs took what they wanted because everything belonged to the king.[85] Taking without responsibility or appropriate accountability is evident in the lack of conversation and comfort. David does not call Bathsheba by name.[86] David does not entice "with seductive words; rather, he uses his status and authority as a king to get what he wants."[87] The calling of Bathsheba is the first of numerous actions that illustrate David's abuse of position and authority.

David's Abuse of Position and Authority

David's egregious abuse of power finds him taking "simply because he can."[88] The ease of David's actions reveals a "power imbalance" that Bathsheba cannot withstand.[89] As Jacqueline Grey rightly asserts, Bathsheba "is the female subordinate in an honor-shame culture who most likely perceives herself powerless to reject the behavior of those in authority."[90] Bathsheba's concluding action further illustrates this power imbalance. She neither affirms David nor seeks a subsequent liaison; she neither voices accusations nor complaints. Bathsheba simply and quietly returns "to a place of safety and forgetfulness, her home."[91]

David's taking, seemingly at its conclusion, takes an unexpected turn with the news that Bathsheba is pregnant (2 Sam 11:5). The king, much like contemporary ministers ensnared by sexual moral failure, turns to manipulation in a vain effort to maintain reputation and position. Uriah's religious conviction and loyalty to fellow soldiers thwart David's plan to conceal his

---

85. David twice took a wife for himself—Abigail, the widow of a man David threatened to kill (1 Sam 25), and Michal, the wife whom David abandoned then demanded back though she had married another (2 Sam 3:14–16). The king's efforts to entice Uriah to sleep with the impregnated Bathsheba may indicate David's initial intent is to bed rather than wed Bathsheba.

86. Scripture identifies her only as "the woman" when the episode concludes (2 Sam 11:5).

87. Abasili, "Was It Rape?," 9.

88. Brueggemann, *First and Second Samuel*, 274. It is worth noting that Samuel had warned that kings are takers (1 Sam 8:11–19).

89. Worley, "Why It's Easier," para 16.

90. Grey, "Prophetic Call to Repentance," 15.

91. Grey, "Prophetic Call to Repentance," 15.

illicit liaison (2 Sam 11:11). Being a Hittite, Uriah "is not even a child of the Torah. But he is faithful."[92] The dichotomy of king and subject runs deeper still. Uriah, a principled man of godly character, refuses to sleep with his wife. David, in comparison, sleeps with a venerated soldier's wife—a soldier who is risking his life on a battlefield the king has vacated.

David has grossly underestimated Uriah and now employs "a scandalous but uncomplicated tactic" with the expectation that drunkenness will drive Uriah to appease his passions.[93] The failure of David's "pathetic attempts to manipulate and control Uriah" brings an order of execution and further reveals the king's pitiful dependence on human power structures.[94] Notably, David shows neither a hint of sorrow nor remorse. "It seems justifiable in David's eyes that this good man should die in order to conceal the king's sin."[95]

David's manipulation and preservation of reputation may even drive his decision to take Bathsheba as his wife. Robert Bergen questions whether David assumes the *gō' ēl* responsibility and commits to the lifelong care of Uriah's widow to display a nobility of character.[96] While one can only speculate, the possibility is not beyond a man who "did not act out of love for anybody but himself."[97] Yet David's selfish violation of others is not the final word in his story. David's rule and relationship with God may have ended poorly, as had his predecessor's, were it not for his heartfelt repentance in response to a prophetic voice of correction.

David's Repentance

David gives no indication of wrongdoing in the year that follows. The cognitive dissonance on display is not uncommon and often sees unethical behavior rationalized; suppression or reconstruction of events are as common as unbridled narcissism leads to self-deception.[98] Indeed, "power tends to corrupt, and absolute power corrupts absolutely."[99] The depth of David's

---

92. Brueggemann, *First and Second Samuel*, 275.

93. Bergen, *1, 2 Samuel*, 366. The author notes that David likely learned this technique from the origin of the Ammonites, the very people Uriah was now fighting (cf. Gen 19:30–38).

94. Arnold, *1 & 2 Samuel*, 528–9.

95. Arnold, *1 & 2 Samuel*, 530.

96. Bergen, *1, 2 Samuel*, 368. Cf. Gen 38:8; Deut 25:5–6; Ruth 4:5.

97. Hession, *Forgotten Factors*, locs. 332–57.

98. Chandler, "Perfect Storm of Leaders' Unethical Behavior," 75.

99. Dalberg-Acton, "Letter to Mandell Creighton," 364.

SECTION ONE: HEAVEN, WE HAVE A PROBLEM

corruption is evident in his instruction that Joab "not let this thing be evil in your sight" (2 Sam 11:25). Unlike David, God did see Uriah's death as evil. In a critical narrative shift, God sends a prophet to declare divine power and purpose to the king who had sent people to declare his worldly power and purpose (2 Sam 12:1–15).

The severity of David's self-absorption is evident in Nathan's cautious approach, which indicates the "narrative struggles with how truth shall speak to power."[100] Simply put, kings can have prophets put to death. Such authority is evident in David's condemnation of the rich man in Nathan's parable. Notably, David's Torah violation does not negate his responsibility to impose Torah requirements on others.[101] God's authority remains on the king; David's response to God's correction will determine whether that authority remains.

David rightly responds to God's correction. The king does not blame others, justify his actions, or offer obligatory self-serving repentance as did his predecessor (1 Sam 15:20–24). David does not attempt to eliminate the prophet, as did Jehoiakim (Jer 26:21) and Jezebel (1 Kgs 17:1). Instead, David confesses and describes his actions as "evil," noting deliberate defiance of God's expectations (Ps 51:4).[102] Such understanding drives David to beg forgiveness and seek spiritual and ministerial restoration.

Though Levitical Law provides no sacrifice to cover such sins, David's petition begins by invoking terms of ritualistic cleansing: blot out, wash away, and cleanse (Ps 51:1–2).[103] The king affirms his need for inner transformation and seeks a new and clean heart, a "steadfast spirit," and a "willing spirit" to overcome his wayward passions and their causative factors (Ps 51:5–6, 10–17). This internal transformation must precede external ministry. Acutely aware of the Spirit's departure from King Saul, David affirms his need for the divine presence to work in him and through him (Ps 51:11, cf. 1 Sam 16:14). David promises to use this restoration to help restore others (Ps 51:12–13) and testify of God's deliverance (Ps 51:13–17).

God "put away" David's sin in response, "refusing to let it be an obstacle to the fulfillment of God's purpose with Israel through David."[104] David's penitent prayer in Ps 51 reflects how sin gives way to God. Words for "sin" appear one dozen times in the first nine verses but only twice in the following verses, while God is named once in the first nine verses but six times

---

100. Brueggemann, *First and Second Samuel*, 280.
101. Bergen, *1, 2 Samuel*, 370. Cf. 1 Chr 16:22.
102. Goldingay, *Psalms Vol. 2*, 127. See also McKnight, *Psalms Vol. 1*, 242.
103. Lennox, *Psalms*, 166.
104. Goldingay, *1 and 2 Samuel for Everyone*, 146; 2 Sam 12:13.

in the following verses.[105] "The poet literally and literarily is emptied of sin and filled with grace."[106] Without question, David will endure significant consequences for his actions.[107] Still, God restores David's relationship, and his service unto God continues.

Though contemporary ministers will never carry King David's far-reaching authority, each wields commensurate power in the lives of their congregants. People seeking emotional and spiritual help are vulnerable, especially in imbalanced power relationships.[108] Dysfunctional settings have conditioned some women to comply with men in authority. Others let their guard down in relationships of trust. Some are readily compliant and have not learned to set firm boundaries or rightly respond to boundary violations. God's anointed minister must not follow David's lead in such examples.

Many factors contribute to David's moral failure, but Bathsheba herself is the least among them. As noted above, mutual consent is impossible amid the significant power gap between the king and the subject. Even if Bathsheba were complicit, Scripture places the blame squarely on the king. David's desires are his seductress, and he alone is responsible for his actions.

David's failure and those of contemporary ministers carry many other similarities. Desires often originate within unresolved deformative life events. The neglect of spiritual disciplines and responsibilities exacerbates the ungodly tendencies inherent to one's malformation. The position of power can enable the individual to act upon an attitude of entitlement often birthed in personal success and shaped by cultural standards.

David appeases his fleshly desires without hesitation and protects his reputation with vigor. When an unwanted pregnancy threatens the façade of godly character, David resorts to "multiplied duplicities" to hide what he has done and is still doing.[109] The king goes so far as to offer "an innocent man upon the altar of his own reputation."[110] This perpetuation of

---

105. Goldingay, *Psalms Vol. 2*, 140.

106. Goldingay, *Psalms Vol. 2*, 140. The author is quoting Schaefer, *Psalms* in *Berit Olam*, 129.

107. All told, four of David's sons would experience premature death—an unnamed son (cf. 12:18), Amnon (cf. 13:29), Absalom (cf. 18:14–15), and Adonijah (cf. 1 Kgs 2:25). More pointedly, George McKnight describes David as having "infected all of his children with the sins of violence and lust" (McKnight, *Psalms Vol. 1*, 243).

108. Mosgofian and Ohlschlager, *Sexual Misconduct in Counseling and Ministry*, 25.

109. Hession, *Forgotten Factors*, loc. 365.

110. Hession, *Forgotten Factors*, loc. 355.

one transgression after another, or "adding sin to sin" (Isa 30:1), remains a typical response to sexual misbehavior.[111]

Ministers guilty of sexual moral failure should note how David responds to the prophetic indictment with immediate confession void of denial or excuse. The Lord's forgiveness "was equally direct and unrestrained."[112] Though David's sin carries the death penalty, God responds to David's repentance with forgiveness, thus ensuring life. God offers this remarkable grace in response to genuine penitence. This extension of restorative grace "may be the hardest part for today's readers to accept."[113]

In summary, grace offers restoration to God and, in some cases, restoration to ministry. Two defining factors are evident in David's reclamation: Nathan's prophetic word of correction and David's biblical repentance in response. Repentance includes the rejection of sin, a return to obedience, and the right attitude toward God, self, and others. Such repentance is the critical catalyst to restoration but is insufficient. Gradual holistic sanctification follows as the repentant minister participates in God's forgiving and empowering grace. Enabling grace, true repentance, and crucifixion of the flesh enable the forsaking of illicit desires and entrusting oneself in God's loving presence. Such understanding is centuries in the making, as theological queries and temptation repeatedly have tested and refined these truths.

---

111. Grey, "Prophetic Call to Repentance," 15.
112. Bergen, *1, 2 Samuel*, 373.
113. Arnold, *1 & 2 Samuel*, 551.

Section One Summary

"Life can only be understood by looking backward;
but it must be lived looking forward."

— Søren Kierkegaard

SEXUAL MORAL FAILURE IS a persistent struggle throughout Christian history. Leaders have offered varied and repeated calls for holiness, but these typically focus on avoidance rather than emotional and spiritual formation or ministerial development. The church is left to deal with everything from authoritarian leadership to twisted theologies. The prevalence of this problem, especially among church leaders, has proven past solutions inadequate.

Any number of personal behaviors and toxic cultures contribute to ministerial moral failure. These include personal destructive tendencies, emotional and spiritual malformation, narcissistic tendencies, abuse of power, and failure of appropriate organizational intervention and oversight—worse yet, conducive environments and institutional protectionism foster many of these examples. The reviews above address only a few high-profile examples, which are rife with causative factors and commonly deficient responses. Unfortunately, the severity of ministerial sexual moral failure and its fallout expressed in those examples are likely worse than imagined.

Reliable data regarding the prevalence of ministerial moral failure is challenging because of the nature of self-report surveys, lack of transparency, and social desirability predisposition of participants.[1] Yet some

---

1. A standardized restoration program would reduce ambiguity and increase accountability. The program would provide a national database through which the public can access information without violating laws pertaining to personally identifiable information, the publication of private facts, or the Privacy Act of 1974. Denominational leaders would have limited access to verify individuals seeking licensure or assignment had no previous violations. In the rare cases of ministerial restoration, designated leaders would use the database to record individual plans and progress.

SECTION ONE: HEAVEN, WE HAVE A PROBLEM

researchers have probed this issue. For example, an assessment started in 1989 and adopted in 1998 by the Francis A. Schaeffer Institute of Church Leadership Development found that 30 percent of 1,050 pastors polled had been in an ongoing affair or had a one-time sexual encounter with a parishioner.[2] Another study found that 12 percent to 15 percent of clergy have committed sexual boundary violations.[3] An analysis of more than five hundred churches found that nearly one in four experienced a "pastor-congregation disruption due to a pastor's sexual activity."[4] The Hartford Institute for Religion Research found that sexual misconduct caused division between pastor and congregation in 23 percent of 532 congregations from fourteen denominations over the past forty years.[5] Research among evangelicals and Seventh-day Adventists shows that approximately 12 percent of their pastors commit adultery.[6] About two hundred pastors were fired from Southern Baptist churches each month from 1984 to 1996. While moral failure was not the leading cause, it was among the top ten.[7] The Presbyterian Church (U.S.A.) estimates about fifty clergy sexual misconduct cases every year.[8]

Louis Selzer reports that upwards of 39 percent of clergy admit to some form of sexual misconduct in ministry, roughly one in ten have committed adultery with members of their churches, and between one-quarter and one-third of ministers have engaged in other sexually inappropriate conduct with parishioners.[9] Much of Selzer's data is drawn from the late-1980s to the mid-1990s and could seem too dated. Notably, he gathered the statistics before the prevalence of point-and-click pornography and the effect that industry has had on moral failure.

Still, there are significant difficulties in quantifying this epidemic. The problems are evident in a commonly referenced 2007 study that shows the three largest insurers of churches and Christian nonprofits receive about 260 claims of sexual abuse against a minor each year. However, those figures exclude groups covered by other insurers, victims older than eighteen, cases undisclosed to insurance companies, and victims who never came forward.[10]

---

2. Krejcir, "Statistics on Pastors."
3. Thomas et al., "Clergy Apologies Following Abuse," 16.
4. Sutton et al., "Does Gender Matter?," 647.
5. Pop et al., "Restoring Pastors Following a Moral Failure," 278.
6. Bissell, "Restoring Fallen Pastors," ii.
7. Hicks, "Study of the Conflicts Within Churches," 78–79.
8. Smith, "When Mentor Becomes Molester."
9. Selzer, "Integrated Mentoring Model," 5.
10. Pease, "Sin of Silence." The insurance report to which the author refers is

SECTION ONE SUMMARY

So, how bad is the problem? Boz Tchividjian, founder of GRACE and a former Florida assistant state attorney, said sexual abuse in evangelicalism rivals the Catholic Church scandal of the early 2000s.[11]

While catastrophic in numerous ways, sexual moral failure does not necessarily disqualify one from ministerial service. Some would disagree. For example, R. Kent Hughes and John H. Armstrong in 1995 differentiated between restoration to the church and restoration to ministry, arguing that clergy who have committed adultery should not be restored to pastoral leadership, as this would prove "profoundly harmful to the well-being of the fallen pastor, his marriage, and the church of Jesus Christ."[12] A 2015 reprint of the article on the *Christianity Today* website reaffirmed that position. John MacArthur argues that sexual sins "irreparably shatter a man's reputation and disqualify him from a ministry of leadership forever because he can no longer be above reproach."[13]

Others, such as John Stott, argue that to be above reproach and blameless does not mean faultless "or no child of Adam would ever qualify for a share in the oversight."[14] Similarly, Jay Smith posits that "no believer lives perfectly above reproach," so past sins cannot permanently disqualify from leadership.[15] John Armstrong notes that past sins might influence one's present life, but "character is not set in cement."[16] Indeed, none would be worthy of ordination if the propensity for falling into sin was sufficient for disqualification.[17] As Jack Hayford rightly posits, would not Jesus equating lust and adultery require everyone to withdraw from ministerial leadership?[18]

Paul's qualifiers instead require the pastor to be a person of unquestioned integrity, a status that centers on present, observable behavior. Such assessment requires a lengthy period of formation and examination leading to ordination and after sexual moral failure if restoration is permitted. If so, this long and scrutinizing process is necessary to determine whether the fallen minister remains dominated by sinful tendencies or displays unity and faithful commitment to God and family. Even if the latter holds,

---

French, "Report: Protestant Church Insurers Handle 260 Sex Abuse Cases a Year."
11. Pease, "Sin of Silence."
12. Hughes and Armstrong, "Why Adulterous Pastors," 33.
13. MacArthur, *Master's Plan for the Church*, 256.
14. Stott, *Guard the Truth*, 92.
15. Smith, "Can Fallen Leaders Be Restored to Leadership?," 463.
16. Armstrong, *Can Fallen Pastors Be Restored?*, 81–82.
17. Grenz and Bell, *Betrayal of Trust*, 132.
18. Hayford, *Restoring Fallen Leaders*, 30–31.

one does not easily mend broken reputations. Therefore, any effort toward ministerial restoration should anticipate significant difficulty in regaining respect from those inside and outside the church.

While the grace of restoration gives reason to rejoice, this blessing must never become a conduit of "cheap grace." God's word warns sternly against sexual sins such as lust, fornication, adultery, immorality, and homosexuality. These are arguably among the most grievous sins—and with good reason. The severity of sexual immorality extends well beyond one's rejection of God and proves more grievous than all other sins. Echoing the Pauline theology above, immorality and idolatry are symbiotic, if not synonymous. As Martin Luther asserts, "Whatever your heart clings to and relies upon, that is your God; trust and faith of the heart alone make both God and idol." This insight is significant because immorality is idolatry, and idolatry is formative. One's loyalty and commitment ignite new thoughts that form habits and develop character (Rom 8:5; cf. Ps 1). Every individual continually transforms into the image of the object worshipped, be that God or idol.[19] As G. K. Beale pointedly observes, "we resemble what we revere, either for ruin or restoration."[20]

In matters of sexual immorality, this deformation not only separates the violator from God but violates the *imago Dei* in which he was created—one that sees male and female complement and complete each other in a one-flesh union to be fruitful, multiply, and form a new social unit (Gen 1:26–2:24). Sexual moral failure also violates the divine covenant and desecrates the living temple.

The effects of violating this plurality in unity are far-reaching. Sexuality is not only procreative but existentially unitive. Indeed, the sex act is a powerful theological statement (1 Cor 6:16–20). Sexual morality directly connects to "our incompleteness as embodied creatures [and] lies behind the human quest for completeness, expressed through the drive toward bonding."[21] Thus, sexuality can disclose its true meaning only within the proper context of marriage and amid the proper intent to express covenantal love in mutual commitment and submission.[22] Conversely, any unbiblical sexuality that defines one's identity simultaneously distorts the correct view of God. Where the plurality in unity produces biblical sexuality, identity in plurality produces sensuality.

19. Hos 9:10; Rom 1:24–32; 2 Cor 3:18.
20. Beale, *We Become What We Worship*, 22.
21. Grenz and Bell, *Betrayal of Trust*, 67.

22. The plurality in unity shared by husband and wife is symbolic of the spiritual plurality in unity shared by Christ and the church. Cf. Matt 19:5–6; Mark 10:8; Eph 5:21–33.

SECTION ONE SUMMARY

As such, purity is the corrective solution to the immoral idolatry Paul contests because sexual holiness "is part of what it means to turn from idols and serve the true and living God. It is part of being a genuine, image-bearing human being."[23] Conversely, sexual immorality sets the individual as a false god, thus perpetuating a false humanity. The shattering of the *imago Dei* demands biblical repentance that looks beyond confession and forgiveness to reform the plurality in unity once shared with God and others.

Holistic restoration offers a return to a former state and the Lord's presence so that times of spiritual, physical, and emotional refreshing may come. Repentance is the inceptive act for those to whom God extends such grace. Holistic healing allows the embattled believer to continue in God's perfect plan. This participative work sees the internal work of sanctification precede the external empowerment for ministry. Forgiveness, acceptance, and self-worth found in God quell the illicit passions. Growth in God's grace and knowledge restores the *imago Dei*, thus enabling the individual to love God, others, and self rightly. This lifelong development—upward, inward, and outward—is evident in Jesus' repeated engagement with the repentant and demonstrated in David's restoration.

However, the allowance does not equal assurance. Many unique factors contribute to failure, and many unique factors affect the outcome. Much like salvation, narrow is the way to restoration, and few will find it.

As noted above, success requires the removal of bad roots, not just bad fruits. This elimination is no easy task. There is no "typical" path that leads to sexual moral failure. Poor choices result from countless confounding variables that emerge for several reasons.[24] Yet, recent scholarship has identified common variables that seem to facilitate, if not foster, ethical failures among leaders. Notables are Art Padilla's "toxic triangle" and Diane Chandler's "perfect storm."[25] Both identify three characteristics that culminate in unethical behaviors: the confluence of destructive tendencies within the leader, susceptible followers, and conducive environments/situational context.

This triad is consistent with the three powerful forces Scripture presents as opposing the spiritual walk: the flesh, the world, and the devil. As such, the next section will present intrapersonal considerations underlying moral failure, social and cultural considerations underlying moral failure, and spiritual considerations underlying moral failure. Such understanding

---

23. Wright, *Paul*, 218.

24. Yarhouse and Tan, *Sexuality and Sex Therapy*, 252. See also Ward and Beech, "Integrated Theory of Sexual Offending," 21–36.

25. Padilla et al., "Toxic Triangle," 176–94; Chandler, "Perfect Storm of Leaders' Unethical Behavior," 69–93.

is foundational to a holistic restoration program that will form and reform godly character while restoring the right relationship with God, self, and others. Because holistic formation equally inhabits emotional, physical, and social constructs, restoration demands one identify and rectify deformative emotional, psychological, social, and theological factors that form and contribute to unbiblical behaviors.

SECTION TWO
Elements of the Perfect Storm

> "One of the frightening things about the wilderness is how many voices you hear in it. It is hard to discern between the voices—which ones are truthful and worthy of our attention and which ones are dangerous and should be ignored."
>
> — N. T. Wright

In the fall of 1991, the seventy-foot longliner *Andrea Gail* left Gloucester, Massachusetts, and headed 575 miles into the North Atlantic in search of swordfish. The ship was well-equipped to land a big catch and weather nearly any storm, but nothing could prepare the six-man crew for the tempest forming on the horizon. Their rough outing had ended well, and the crew was three days into the voyage home when three deadly weather fronts converged—a hurricane, a nor'easter, and an anticyclone. No one had seen anything like this. Winds nearing one hundred miles per hour and one-hundred-foot waves battered the vessel. Strength and abilities, equipping and experience—all was for naught. The crew didn't stand a chance.

This tragedy spawned a 1997 bestselling book and a 2000 movie of the same name. It also provides a descriptive analogy for the convergence of emotional, social/cultural, and spiritual forces opposing Christian life and ministry—in biblical parlance, the flesh, the world, and the devil.

I anticipate resistance as our discussion of ministerial restoration shifts to emotional and psychological matters. More times than I care to remember, I have heard the chide that "you can't counsel out a demon!" I fully agree. But it is equally valid that one cannot cast out a deformative life event. You can't "pray away" the trauma of abuse, rape, or violence

SECTION TWO: ELEMENTS OF THE PERFECT STORM

that has adversely impacted and shaped someone's emotional health. The traumatic event(s) happened and has changed how s/he views and lives in this world. Emotional brokenness leaves emptiness to fill and wounds to heal. Worse yet, the victim has likely built protective walls that are not easily toppled and finds some measure of resolution through behaviors that typically are void of godly influence. Put another way, we learn to cope. Some coping mechanisms seem reasonable, even righteous but ultimately fail because they seek infinity within the finite and legitimacy from the illegitimate (which is very much in keeping with Augustine's definition of original sin). We return to and rely on these learned behaviors to numb the pain or provide some sense of worth. This reliance increasingly separates the individual from God's calling and standard. What is needed is a new approach to stress and struggle—a renewal of the mind (Rom 12:2). Such renewal requires psychological analysis of cognitive and behavioral factors. Understanding what factors influence the moral responses of people to immoral acts or scandalous behavior can be an early step toward developing a stronger sense of moral integrity.[1]

Holistic formation develops and maintains the integrity of the heart (Ps 24:4), mind (Rom 12:2), spirit (1 Thess 5:23), body (1 Cor 6:19–20), and emotions (Gal 5:22). Because these factors are symbiotic, holistic formation and (re)formation demands that one rightly identify deformative events, especially those from formative years—primarily to age five and during puberty—as well as traumatic life events. The impact of nurture over and above nature is often the primary factor in shaping one's worldview, self-identity, and self-worth. While contemporary Christian ministry tends to omit social and psychological considerations from Christian formation, identifying causal factors improves one's understanding of inappropriate and illicit behaviors. Such understanding enables the violator to move beyond repeated repentance for "bad fruit" to recognize and remove the "bad root." Then, he can bear abundant good fruit upon being fully grafted into the True Vine.

If you struggle to see the connection and believe "psychobabble" has no place in a discussion of spiritual matters, allow two points of consideration. First, humankind is in a fallen condition. That means Jesus is the only "real" human (what God intended humans to be). Jesus was no stranger to emotions. He was well acquainted with grief and joy. At times, Jesus was compassionate. At other times, angry. He wept at Lazarus's tomb, was overcome with sorrow in the garden of Gethsemane, and agonized on the cross. He expressed exhaustion, frustration, sympathy, and empathy. In Jesus, we

---

1. Pop et al., "Restoring Pastors Following a Moral Failure," 276.

see "a picture of the complete human who reflects God's own image in a way that no sinful human has . . . Jesus was fully emotional, but in a way that was always harmonious, not imbalanced, inappropriate or disorders. . . . [Jesus' emotions] never master him or function wrongly."[2] Ergo, healthy emotions are a necessary component of the Christlikeness to which we are called.

Second, consider how the devil seems to know exactly how to tempt you in ways that so often succeed. How is this possible? Satan knows the hurt you have endured. He knows what you lack. He knows where you find rest. He knows what you desire. The tribulations and temptations that follow are a product of the perfect storm—the collusion of flesh, world, and devil that sees each draws its strength from the woundings that took place in your life, especially in formative years; the identifiable and measurable events that have shaped your views of self and world, which have left parts of you broken and empty. Their enticements promise to satisfy the ego, fill the emptiness, and heal the brokenness but only drag you into the depths.

The solution is a sanctifying psychopathology or a sanctifying homeostasis that enables holistic formation and (re)formation.[3] Formation and (re)formation require a renewal of the mind. Failure to address all factors of the perfect storm is why many Christians continually struggle and fail. Such believers, including ministers, desire to fight the good fight of faith but fail to don the whole armor of God. The helmet of salvation is often missing as believers fail to take every thought captive and develop the mind of Christ. This omission proves disastrous since most spiritual warfare occurs in the six inches between the ears. When ill-prepared for battle, the remaining armor merely covers (or is used to hide) the dirty garments of illicit behaviors learned long ago and developed over time.

Indeed, humans trust their learned behaviors to provide protection and meet emotional needs. Scripture repeatedly warns against this approach.[4] Still, many will justify their behaviors rather than renew their mind. Some will cheapen grace with the expectation that a simple prayer of obligatory repentance will suffice. Some even believe they are entitled to behave in such a way. This approach fails to see sin for what it is. This approach

---

2. Pennington, *Jesus the Great Philosopher*, 110–11.

3. Psychopathology is the study of mental and social disorders. Homeostasis is a self-regulating process by which biological systems regulate physiological processes, thus allowing aggregate components to bring strength and balance to any part of the system that is out of balance. The pragmatic approach of a sanctifying psychopathology is strengthened by the shift in psychology in recent years from a Bio-psychosocial (BPS) to a Bio-psychosocial-spiritual (BPSS) model.

4. For example, Ps 139:23–24; Prov 3:5–6; 14:12; 28:26; Jer 17:9; Matt 15:19; Phil 4:6–7.

fails to see the Savior for who he is—one who desires to heal brokenness and deliver from bondage (Isa 61:1–2, Luke 4:18–19).

From this approach, one can see 2 Cor 10:3–5 (spoken in the context of correction) in a different light. Instead of attempting to modify behavior or continuously cut away bad fruit, one would do better to recognize that most strongholds are founded on experiential emptiness and brokenness and built using false promises of fulfillment. There is a better way.

The psalmist speaks comfort to those tossed about by this perfect storm. It tells of those who "cried out to the Lord in their trouble, And He brought them out of their distresses. He caused the storm to be still, So that the waves of the sea were hushed. Then they were glad because they were quiet, So He guided them to their desired harbor" (Ps 107:28–30). Reaching this desired and safe harbor requires looking beyond behaviors to consider the root of those behaviors. The individual must rightly recognize the holes in his heart that allowed the planting and growth of deadly sins. Therefore, the subsections that follow explore the synergistic relationship between the three elements of the perfect storm: (1) the causative psychological, psychological, and emotional factors to include the adverse effects of emotional woundings; (2) social and cultural considerations such as worldview, ethics, and norms; and (3) spiritual considerations such as the lack of spiritual formation and the resulting power of temptation.

A warning before we cast off: bad roots reside beneath the surface. Uprooting the flesh, world, and devil will be painful, as it reveals long-buried pains, but this allows God's love and grace to fill one's emptiness and mend one's brokenness. No longer ignorant of Satan's schemes (2 Cor 2:11), this believer can weather the storm.

Shall we set sail?

4

Stormfront No. 1—
The Flesh (Emotional)

"The best way to keep a prisoner from escaping is to make sure he never knows he's in prison."

— Fyodor Dostoevsky

THE APOSTLE PAUL POINTEDLY warns against making provision for the flesh regarding its lusts (Rom 13:14). He urges the crucifixion of the flesh with its passions and desires (Gal 5:24). Those lusts, passions, and desires speak to our emotions. Often, the wrong satisfaction of each originates in behaviors learned in our efforts to heal brokenness.

We all suffer from some measure of brokenness. Because it is so common, some believe brokenness to be normal. It is not. Others see themselves as broken beyond use or repair. They are not. Some turn to illicit behaviors in a misguided attempt to escape shame or find loving approval, a survival strategy by which violators wrongly medicate the wounds of childhood to survive unspeakable pain. As Mark Laaser notes, "[it] is not that they are terrible, sinful, immoral people . . . they can't give up the coping strategies they believe have kept them alive for years."[1]

That is not to say that every moral failure is the result of emotional trauma. There are numerous contributing factors and variables. But

---

1. Laaser, *Healing the Wounds*, 113. That is not to diminish no dismiss the severity of illicit behaviors. The violator's immorality is sinful and destructive. Sin can never be a solution. Therefore, those who willfully and continually relies on ungodly solutions to mitigate or medicate brokenness, or those who placate rather than eliminate brokenness, is a rebel rather than a victim. Holistic restoration recognizes the effect of emotional brokenness, but places responsibility on the violator in its attempt to overcome.

analyses demonstrate that most sexual moral failures are rooted in one or more of the following four categories: (1) an outplay of trauma from a time when innocence was misused or abused; (2) misshapen views of self-worth and sexuality; (3) coping mechanisms for excessive stress; or (4) from an illegitimate attitude of entitlement fostered by an abuse of power.

Physical, sexual, and emotional abuse are the primary causes of cognitive deformation that could develop into illicit behaviors later in life.[2] Physical abuse refers to acts of aggression intended to cause pain or injury to another or acts of negligence that result in bodily injury. Sexual abuse connotes any form of sexual activity—verbal, visual, or physical—performed without consent.[3] It is an exploitation of the victim to satisfy an abuser's needs. Emotional abuse can be verbal (e.g., angry outbursts, insults, threats, belittling, and criticizing) and nonverbal (e.g., withdrawal or abandonment, failure to affirm, and withholding love). Intention aside, these actions are hurtful. Emotional abuse is an "ongoing process in which one individual systematically diminishes and destroys the inner self of another."[4]

Chronic emotional abuse and neglect are just as devastating as physical and sexual abuse.[5] Emotional trauma falls into two kinds of abuse: invasion and abandonment.[6] The former occurs when boundaries become too loose and someone crosses the line. The latter happens when boundaries become too rigid and restrict the love and care, attentive listening, nurturing, and guidance the individual needs to thrive. Therefore, anything from losing a loved one to losing innocence can initiate emotional trauma. These wounds often morph into emotional patterns of negative feelings that relate to persistent anger, shame, fear, anxiety, adequacy, insecurity, self-rejection, self-doubt, self-condemnation, pessimism, cynicism, and despair. Unfortunately, ministerial pressures only increase the number and severity of these underlying issues.

I live just outside of Langley Air Force Base in southeastern Virginia. On any given day, one can watch the F-22 Raptors roar into the wild blue yonder. Such feats are not difficult when propelled by two Pratt & Whitney F119 engines that enable the aircraft to hit 1,500 mph (nearly two and a

---

2. It should be noted that while those who have experienced traumatic abuse are statistically more susceptible to sexual disorders, some illicit sexual behaviors result from injury rather than incurment. For example, traumatic brain injuries may initiate or increase sexually deviant behaviors. See Clinton and Laaser, *Quick Reference Guide*, 32.

3. Langberg, *Counseling Survivors of Sexual Abuse*, 80.

4. Lorin, *Emotional Abuse*, 1.

5. Walsh et al., "Resiliency Factors," 4.

6. Laaser, *Healing the Wounds*, 94–95.

half times the speed of sound). Long could we talk about its state-of-the-art avionics and weaponry. Indeed, the enemy is no match for these formidable fighter jets. But imagine something happened during early production that left a microscopic flaw deep within one of those engines. The defect may not be apparent and may not cause problems during routine operations, but the continuous surge of heat and pressure that is common to aerial combat will cause that flaw to expand. Eventually, there will be a catastrophic failure.

Ministers are much like the F-22 Raptor. Unfortunately, ministerial selection and training programs are not very good at inspecting their engines. Many programs focus on talent and charismatic qualities that can attract a large congregation.[7] However, programs that substitute skill-based training for spiritual formation fail to identify brokenness and prepare ministers for the many stresses that will exacerbate their emotional struggles.[8]

Frankly, ministers are not eager to address the issues, either. To do so evokes shame and perceptions of weakness seen as detrimental to good ministerial standing. This critical omission ignores or underestimates the significant role that emotional experiences play in developing personal and social values. Emotional experiences shape who we are; therefore, we must rightly view and manage emotional experiences to become who we desire to be.

A good engine inspection begins with the understanding that most actions and attitudes are established in our formative years, which means the roots of brokenness run deeper than you might imagine. As John Bowlby's classic attachment theory, Erik Erikson's eight stages of life, and more recently, neurobiological attachment rightly assert, the pattern of relating to others rarely originates in adulthood; rather, childhood experiences imprint these behaviors.[9] Therefore, the individual is as much a product of nurture as nature.[10] That means the family unit is predominant when building your engine. The family is so powerful that emotional withdrawal by a

---

7. This is akin to the effect the 1984 movie *Top Gun* had on Navy recruiting. It only takes the right leading man and the right soundtrack to build a following.

8. Flynn, "Firewall," 309–24.

9. Bowlby, *Attachment and Loss: Vol. 3*; Erikson, *Identity and the Life Cycle*. See also Grenz and Bell, *Betrayal of Trust*, 50. For example, shame can take root as early as fifteen to eighteen months of age in response to nonverbal cues of disapproval (Thompson, *Soul of Shame*, 62).

10. Notably, in the view of Kay Marshall Strom, "abusers are made, not born" (Strom, *In the Name of Submission*, 67). See also Boa, *Conformed to His Image*, 108; Harvard University, "Serve and Return," paras. 1–3; van der Kolk, *Body Keeps the Score*; Ripley and Worthington, *Couple Therapy*, 25; Yarhouse and Tan, *Sexuality and Sex Therapy*, 251–52.

mother has a more profound and long-lasting impact on mental stability than hostile and intrusive behavior.[11]

So, a strong family will build a strong engine. Unfortunately, nearly all families have some level of dysfunction, which is how those fatal flaws find their way into your engine. Physical, sexual, and emotional abuse diminish self-worth. Persistent feelings of inferiority often provoke a repertoire of attempts to earn significance. In Kenneth Boa's view, "a person is incomplete without a sense of belonging and a belief that someone genuinely cares that he or she exists. The problem is that in our experiences this need to belong is at best only imperfectly met, and in many cases, almost completely unmet."[12]

No matter the cause, the emotional brain seeks to restore what was lost, denied, or stolen—the critical issue is how one fills such voids. It is here that illicit and ungodly coping mechanisms form. These learned responses may temporarily provide what is lacking or soothe what is hurting but ultimately prove destructive.

It gets worse. Behaviors learned in formative years are not easily unlearned. That means the illicit responses (like the brokenness they seek to cover) expand over time. How does one overcome? As Peter Scazzero rightly notes, Christian formation requires one first go backward to move forward.[13] In other words, one must return to the (de)formative life events that have adversely affected self-identity, self-worth, and worldview and reform this brokenness through God's truth, healing, and power. Only when the minister is restored to his divine design can the ministry be restored to its divine intent. Therefore, we must disassemble the engine and rebuild or replace the defective parts. What follows is a troubleshooting manual that identifies the predominant causative factors that contribute to ministerial moral failure, such as dysfunctional family relations, the effect of trauma and shame, and the adverse influence of narcissism and entitlement.

A BEGINNER'S GUIDE TO COGNITIVE CONDITIONING

"Nothing fixes a thing so intensely in the memory as the wish to forget it."

— MICHEL DE MONTAIGNE

The apostle Paul presents quite a quandary in Rom 7. He desperately desires to do right but does not. Instead, he finds himself returning to loathsome behaviors. Does this sound familiar?

11. van der Kolk, *Body Keeps the Score*, 120.
12. Boa, *Conformed to His Image*, 108.
13. Scazzero, *Emotionally Healthy Spirituality*, 71.

Paul's predicament is not uncommon, and his struggle is as much physiological as it is spiritual. Like the apostle, the battlefield on which we fight is a small part of the brain known as the limbic system. Primary components include the hippocampus, which plays a major role in learning and memory, and the amygdala, which attaches emotional content to those memories. Thus, our actions and attitudes develop as we form and give meaning to episodic memories.

The problem is that our emotions are much like wet cement. Anything that falls upon them will leave its imprint. These imprints, whether positive or negative, are critical factors in one's development of neural pathways that govern how we think, feel, and act. The connections between brain cells that form our behaviors and responses strengthen as they communicate more frequently and faster in response to repeated experiences or repeatedly omitted experiences. Eventually, behavior becomes automatic. Neural pathways deepen over time, much like a path in the woods becomes more defined with each successive hiker.[14]

For this reason, emotions prime our actions; the things done to us greatly govern the things we do. Here is a simple illustration: anger and fear activate the amygdala and stimulate the hypothalamus. However, the physiological response to anger will increase blood flow to the arms and hands, while the response to fear increases blood flow to the legs. Individual and collective experiences condition our responses.

Because our emotions are like wet cement, those imprints are most easily formed in the early stages when cement is solidifying. As noted above, patterns of relating to others rarely originate in adulthood but are imprinted through childhood experiences. Ample research supports this claim. Among the findings: [15]

- A parent's positive response to a newborn's cry builds and strengthens neural connections and aids in his or her development.

- The brain lays out basic circuitry during the first two years of life. The baby's brain has hundreds of millions more neurons than an eight-year-old's. Those neurons are highly responsive to experience. A

---

14. Struthers, *Wired for Intimacy*, 85.

15. This list is compiled from Bowlby, *Attachment and Loss*; Boyce and Erkert, "Spiritual and Relational Formation," 20; Bowlby, *Attachment and Loss*; Erikson, *Identity and the Life Cycle*; Gingrich, *Restoring the Shattered Self*, 27–36; Gunnoe, *Person in Psychology and Christianity*, 82; Harvard University, "Serve and Return," paras. 1–3; Jennings, *God-Shaped Brain*, 49–54; Keating, *Open Mind, Open Heart*, 146; Thompson, *Soul of Shame*, 52–54.

two-year-old's brain is as active as an adult's; within a year, it will be twice as active and stay that way for a decade.

- Early human attachments with primary caregivers teach the immature infant brain to organize and regulate itself. Secure attachment sees a premium placed on empathy, attunement, validation, and the proper setting of boundaries.

- Ninety percent of a child's brain development happens before age five. These are formative years. It will take significant time and effort to overcome the damage done by the lack of proper development. Conversely, children who receive warm, responsive nurturing in their early years are less likely to respond poorly to stress later in life.

- The lack of stable and caring communication can impair physical, mental, and emotional health and flood the developing brain with potentially harmful stress hormones. High-stress and low-nurturing or abusive environments will overdevelop the fear and emotion centers (amygdala) and impair the growth of the reason, love, and judgment centers (prefrontal cortex). If not corrected, traumatic responses can become "hardwired."

- Exposure to adverse psychosocial experiences such as physical or sexual abuse, neglect, and socioeconomic deprivation may result in emotional, immune, and metabolic abnormalities. These individuals will demonstrate difficulty with empathy, compassion, patience, trust, altruistic love, and sympathy.

- The lack of nurturing love due to persistent parental rejection or unavailability renders individuals unable to show or receive affection and often corrupts their social and moral sensibilities.

- The need for relational connection finds the traumatized individual creating and continually developing a false persona to cope and relate meaningfully with others.

- Repeated trauma often results in a psychological defense called dissociation, a disconnection of aspects of self or experience that can result in a significant struggle with identity.

- People learn to function in their dysfunction, but one can unlearn faulty psychological mechanisms and develop new ones. Without a redemptive relationship or positive therapeutic intervention, these dysfunctions will perpetuate into future generations because wounded children become wounded parents who are unable to establish healthy relationships with their children and, worse yet, instill their dysfunctional patterns through repeated behaviors.

While abuse and trauma can happen at any age, children are far more likely to form destructive pathways for three reasons. First, their rational thought is not fully developed until much later—typically in the late teen years for women and the mid-twenties for men. As a result, the cognitive response to emotional wounds becomes ingrained over the years to the point that "the rational brain is basically impotent to talk the emotional brain out of its own reality."[16] Though new ways of acting and reacting may seem right and reasonable, the emotional brain knows what it likes and gets to cast the deciding vote. Put another way, the spirit is willing, but the flesh is weak.

The second reason children are more likely to form destructive pathways is that they (and many adults) find it difficult to affirm a parent or guardian's shortfalls. We may voice anger regarding boundaries they set or mistakes they made but characterizing parents as "bad" diminishes the source of stability, protection, and nurture so desperately desired and needed for emotional development. Children instinctively feel safer being the "bad" one and soon assume that identity.

The third factor reinforces this assumption: children view the world through "magical thinking."[17] Though adults (with the benefit of rational development) couch this as "pretending" or "fantasy," children live in a world in which make-believe is reality—and perceive themselves as having the power to cause the events they observe. For example, did you ever believe how you wore your rally cap would determine whether your team would win or lose? Kids genuinely do. This magical thinking is why kids believe they are the cause of their parents' divorce, even when told otherwise. More pertinent to our topic, magical thinking is why kids commonly believe they are responsible for the abuse they endure, be it passive or aggressive. A child who sees himself as culpable will typically adopt an "existence guilt" in which he believes himself deserving of disrespectful or dehumanizing treatment.[18]

A child's traumatized and unformed brain equates emotion with hurt and subsequently suppresses natural emotion to ensure safety and survival. Feelings become viewed as "wrong and not to be trusted or too dangerous to access, let alone express."[19] Such tendencies continue into adulthood and

---

16. van der Kolk, *Body Keeps the Score*, 48.
17. Wilson, *Released from Shame*, 29.
18. Wilson, *Released from Shame*, 29, 76.
19. Hands and Fehr, *Spiritual Wholeness for Clergy*, locs. 286–91.

result in individuals being unable to express emotion or relate to others meaningfully.

Malformed neural pathways become dominant as they are traveled time and again. Eventually, the individual will process every event through these ill-formed paths. As a result, traumatized people tend to superimpose their trauma on everything around them until the very event that caused so much pain becomes their sole source of meaning. This change fundamentally reorganizes the brain's ability to perceive and think, inevitably shaping and solidifying ill-formed perceptions, thoughts, and actions. As Bessel van der Kolk notes, "behaviors are not the result of moral failings or signs of lack of willpower or bad character—they are caused by actual changes in the brain."[20] Trauma will see natural boundaries become neural walls. Within those walls reside emotionally malformed individuals who grow to be "empty, dependent, and needy, tending toward behaviors designed to placate and please others."[21] The individual inevitably contends with driving impulses to prevent, protect, and provide—to prevent anything that might evoke negative reaction by others, protect one's physical and emotional self, and provide the behaviors by which one may obtain affection or affirmation that is lacking. The variations are many. The brain will sometimes suppress memories and emotionally painful experiences. Some pathways create an emotional numbness called "dissociation." Others employ "displacement" to transfer suffering onto another individual or object (e.g. someone frustrated at work takes their anger out on the family).

Similarly, twisted views of sexuality often result from sexual abuse endured in childhood. If exposed at a time when the unformed brain cannot begin to comprehend the emotional complexities inherent to such activity, some abused children will grow to view sex and love as synonymous, and some will project their anger in the forms of gender hatred. In contrast, others will view "right" sex as necessarily mysterious, uncomfortable, and dangerous—that sex must be bad to be good. [22]

Trauma also adversely affects the brain's physiology and disengages critical brain areas necessary for integrating the past.[23] Thus, when triggered, the individual does not simply *remember* the event but *relives* the event. It is difficult to rationalize with the triggered individual as the emotional brain takes control, and protection/provision is its primary goal. This

---

20. van der Kolk, *Body Keeps the Score*, 3.
21. Hands and Fehr, *Spiritual Wholeness for Clergy*, loc. 281.
22. Laaser, *Healing the Wounds*, 56–7.
23. van der Kolk, *Body Keeps the Score*, 220–21.

response is undesirable and typically unexpected. Each episode increases shame and struggle and drives the individual into deeper isolation.

As Aristotle rightly asserts, the habits formed in youth make no small difference but make "a very great difference, or rather all the difference."[24] Let's consider one more example. Suppose a child lacks attunement, attachment, and affirmation.[25] This child will likely struggle with low self-worth, mistrust his perceptions, automatically assume he is wrong or deficient, and therefore seek validation of every decision.[26] If validation is lacking—and especially when deep-seated insecurities, low self-esteem, or unresolved questions about sexuality compound the issue—the individual will seek their solution elsewhere, typically within the coping mechanisms learned in response to trauma. As Stanley J. Grenz and Roy D. Bell observe, "the lure of forbidden sex may be a symptom of his search for healing for his own wounded sense of self."[27] In light of learned behaviors, many see illicit sexual activity as the only way to meet their need for love and nurture.

So, why do we keep doing what we don't want to do? Why are these coping mechanisms so difficult to discard? Because our minds "have been previously programmed to live independently of God and that is the chief characteristic of our flesh."[28] Your emotional brain learned long ago that it could find relief, if not respite, by tapping into your neurotransmitters. These chemical messengers, which include norepinephrine, epinephrine, and serotonin, influence brain efficiency and function. The neurotransmitter most associated with pleasure and reward is dopamine. Its release, which can come by substance or experience, effectively shuts down one's emotional center, called the amygdala.

This shutdown brings brief moments of bliss absent of fear and shame, "a transcendent freedom from all worry."[29] Orgasm releases dopamine, but the stimulus demanded is ever-increasing. Repeated activity results in a reinforced neurological habit; intense cravings occur when one deprives the brain of dopamine. If acted upon, the behavioral response takes on a salvific quality as the "solution" becomes a false idol. This false idol's worship is

---

24. Aristotle, *Nicomachean Ethics*, 45.

25. Attunement is the matching of affect between child and parent or caregiver by which the child feels recognized, accepted, and known. Attachment is the deep bonding by which the child has emotional needs met and experiences security. Affirmation is the acknowledgment of worth.

26. Wilson, *Released from Shame*, 42.

27. Grenz and Bell, *Betrayal of Trust*, 136.

28. Anderson, *Steps to Freedom in Christ*, 6.

29 Struthers, *Wired for Intimacy*, 98.

commonly called "addiction," which Dennis Okholm categorizes as "unhealthy ways of experiencing the neuro-rewards."[30]

Most experts define addictions as the compulsion to use a substance or activity to cope with everyday life and categorize addictions as either substance or behavioral (sometimes referred to as physical and psychological). The former speaks to materials such as alcohol and drugs, and the latter to actions such as sex, gambling, or shopping. Addictions do not emerge in a vacuum but exist along a continuum, which means that "even the most physiological of the addictions have behavioral components, and chemical changes in the brain characterize even the most behavioral of the addictions. Addiction is always a whole-person disorder."[31] As Mark Laaser notes, the seeds of addiction are sown "in the deep and fertile ground of chaos, dysfunction, silence, and abuse."[32] While addictive behaviors manifest in personal ways to mitigate learned rules and roles and medicate specific trauma, families frequently use addiction as a stress management strategy.

Scott Sullender presents five standard features of addiction: they produce a positive and pleasurable mood change, the habits lead to tolerance, obsessive thinking soon dominates, there is a loss of control and willpower, leading to self-destructive behaviors.[33] Tim Clinton and Mark Laaser similarly classify sex addiction as "the misuse of sexual behavior that becomes habitual to change (ostensibly for improving) one's mood or psychological state."[34] They further emphasize how the use and abuse inevitably increase physical dependence, leading to withdrawals, which creates further stress and perpetuates negative cycles.

Patrick Carnes organizes this in a four-step cycle of preoccupation, ritualization, compulsive sexual behavior, and despair.[35] Notable is how each stage displays striking similarities to alcoholism and drug dependency and that each cycle intensifies with each repetition.

Poly-addiction, a commonality found in behavioral and substance addicts alike, adds momentum to this downward spiral. The inherent tendency is to replace the behavior or substance that is overcome with another behavior or substance to ease the pain and anxiety. One who gives up drinking may start smoking like a freight train. Another may break an addiction

---

30. Okholm, *Dangerous Passions Deadly Sins*, 46.
31. Sullender, *Ancient Sins*, 4.
32. Laaser, *Healing the Wounds*, 88.
33. Sullender, *Ancient Sins*, 7–20.
34. Clinton and Laaser, *Quick Reference Guide*, 150–51.
35. Carnes, *Out of the Shadows*, 19–20.

to pornography only to become a compulsive gambler or overeater. While the switch may help end an illicit behavior, it fails to address the root causes.

Holistic (re)formation seeks character transformation over behavioral modification.[36] For this reason, Paul finds his solution in Christ and a reformed mind (Rom 12:2). Still, many opt to function within dysfunction.

FUNCTIONAL DYSFUNCTIONS

"It is those we live with and love and should know who elude us."

— Norman Maclean

As noted above, families are the primary force in emotional formation. That is not to say that Mom and Dad are to blame for bad behaviors. However, familial relationships significantly influence one's strengths and weaknesses of character and help construct the coping mechanisms to overcome the latter (which often become what Scripture calls "generational curses").

Everyone desires to belong, be seen, and be loved. Lack in these areas will twist one's understanding of identity and worth. As noted above, children have only the emotional brain on which to rely, so they learn to perform, achieve, or behave in ways that minimize trauma and maximize reward. Some take responsibility for dysfunction, and the constant charge that "you are" becomes internalized as an "I am" identity. Others endeavor to meet unrealistic expectations in the hope of obtaining a moment of affection or affirmation. Some find cooperation the only way to please others and protect themselves amid boundary violations. These and other responses are the fertile feeding grounds for our great adversary, shame.[37]

Jesus despised shame as he endured the cross (Heb 12:2) and with good reason. Though there are healthy forms, shame was the first adverse emotion felt by fallen humankind (Gen 2:25; 3:7–10). Shame caused Adam and Eve to cover the consequence of their sin and elicited responses of victimization and blame. Shame also drove Adam and Eve to hide from God. Not much has changed.

Shame has rendered humankind the only self-loathing species on earth. Just ask those who struggle with malformed or broken emotions—unhealthy

---

36. And with good reason. Behavior modification asserts that human actions are products of our environment (like Pavlov's dogs). Such thought leads to operant conditioning, a method that claims to control behavior by applying appropriate stimulus (rewarding good behavior and punishing bad behavior).

37. It should be noted that shame and guilt are not synonymous. Guilt recognizes "I have done a bad thing." Shame is the belief that "I am a bad person."

shame is prevalent among those abused and wounded in childhood.[38] They typically view themselves as unworthy, undesirable, and flawed to the point that no one can love them. Worse yet, many choose the wrong covering when dealing with sin and shame. Some are like Adam and Eve and hide behind fig leaves. Some are like Jacob and don a goatskin covering (Gen 27). And some cover themselves with an abundance of seemingly righteous works (Isa 64:6). Allow me to explain.

Like Adam and Eve, some use the fruit of God's creation to hide their sin and shame. They hide behind approval and achievement. For this reason, Peter Scazzero warns against three powerful temptations: I am what I do (performance), I am what I have (possessions), and I am what others think (popularity).[39] Robert McGee presents the tendency as the "satanic formula," which states Self-Worth = Performance + Others' Opinions.[40] In this formula, the individual finds his identity in personal achievements and what (he thinks) people think about him.

Perfectionism is a tell-tale sign of inadequate covering and shame. Pertinent to our topic, the perfectionist minister appears intelligent, driven, and organized. Such qualities are desirous, inspirational, and even viewed as evidence of God's anointing. Often, these qualities belie a persona created by an unhealthy family structure that could not cope with and did not allow or accept failure. The perfectionist who focuses on performance views love as something one must earn—and, by extension, the perfectionist views God as more concerned with how one acts than who one is.[41] Achievement and acceptance define self-identity. Therefore, perfectionists cannot admit mistakes and will exhibit anger when not in control. Unable to meet his stringent standards, let alone the expectations of others (be they real or perceived), the perfectionist is increasingly critical and indifferent to others. Feelings of failure and frustration devolve into depressive episodes. He overcomes inadequacies by working harder, for "perfectionism, at its core, is protectionism."[42] Ministers preoccupied with spiritual performance

---

38. Laaser, *Healing the Wounds*, 107–8; Thompson, *Soul of Shame*, 62; Wilson, *Released from Shame*, 25.

39. Scazzero, *Emotionally Healthy Spirituality*, 50–53.

40. McGee, *Search for Significance*, 21. See also Mosgofian and Ohlschlager, *Sexual Misconduct in Counseling and Ministry*, 19.

41. Johnson and VanVonderen, *Subtle Power Spiritual Abuse*, 56.

42. Briggs, *Fail*, 82.

STORMFRONT NO. 1—THE FLESH (EMOTIONAL)

often hide behind false confidence.[43] For this reason, "many times the more prideful a person is the more inferior he or she feels."[44]

Some forego fig leaves and choose goat skin to cover their shame. Such was the case for Jacob. He was not the favored son, so this deceiver pretended to be someone he was not to obtain the father's blessing. Narcissists are much the same. These master manipulators tug on heartstrings with the gentle caress of a master harpist yet are equally skilled in pointing fingers and shirking responsibility.

Narcissist ministers are commonly "described as charismatic, gifted, confident, smart, strategic, agile, and compelling."[45] Yet to baptize narcissism as spiritual giftedness "does a great disservice to them and ignores deep wells of shame and fragility lurking within."[46] Narcissism often develops amid brokenness and, like Jacob donning the goat hair, sees the individual disguise emotional insecurities with seemingly strong character and bravado. Isaac is duped (not unlike many contemporary churches) and confers the blessing upon the imposter. This is despite Isaac being uneasy since the son sounded like Jacob but felt like Esau. It is a lesson churches would do well to learn—when identifying and blessing the one chosen by God, we should be led by what we hear rather than what we feel. Why? Because many, and perhaps a majority of ministers, are narcissists.[47] As Thomas Manton rightly asserts, ministry is "an attractive evil; it suits pride and self-love and feeds conceit."[48]

The narcissist's deception often goes unnoticed or unaddressed because the broken minister, who craves success and superiority, populates his leadership team with admirers and sycophants.[49] Within this leadership team, the pastor's approval becomes the gold standard that some view as synonymous with divine approval. The perpetual fear of status degradation and removal is equally powerful as status enhancement. Indeed, this

---

43. DeGroat, *When Narcissism Comes to Church*, locs. 934–37; Hetzendorfer, *Pastoral Counseling Handbook*, 73.

44. Minirth and Meier, *Happiness Is a Choice*, 186.

45. DeGroat, *When Narcissism Comes to Church*, loc. 117.

46. DeGroat, *When Narcissism Comes to Church*, loc. 152.

47. Cluster B DSM-V personality disorders feature narcissistic traits most prominently—and is the spectrum on which most ministerial candidates score in personality tests. See DeGroat, *When Narcissism Comes to Church*, loc. 298.

48. Manton, *Exposition on the Epistle of James*. Manton's comment reflects upon Jas 3:1.

49. McKnight and Barringer, *Church Called Tov*, 27. The authors further warn that "independent churches are especially conducive to leaders who want to be unsupervised and unchecked."

was a primary factor in Ravi Zacharias International Ministries' failure to properly investigate allegations of sexual misconduct by its founder. In their acknowledgment of wrongdoing after years of denial, the board affirmed that "in situations of prolonged abuse, there often exist significant structural, policy, and cultural problems. It is imperative that where these things exist in our organization, we take focused steps to ensure they are properly diagnosed and addressed. . . . We regret that we allowed our misplaced trust in Ravi to result in him having less oversight and accountability than would have been wise and loving."[50]

Good works provide the third covering for shame. Many who struggle with emotional wounds will use the "three unholy rules of dysfunctional families" to weave this covering—don't think, don't feel, don't talk."[51] This approach may prevent immediate conflict, but failing to hear or accept someone's feelings proves destructive in the long run since individuals are created and yearn for intimacy and acceptance. A family in which feelings are neither allowed nor modeled also renders the individual unable to rightly express or consider others' feelings. In this scenario, rules and roles eventually replace relationships.

Rules of conduct maintain some measure of control. A person ill-equipped to deal with emotions will use rules to control others' behaviors and prevent the adverse scenarios that would poke the proverbial bear. On the other hand, roles provide clear expectations of how individuals act within the family to hide or avoid unhealthy tendencies, project a healthy structure, and maintain harmony—even if "harmony" is merely the temporary absence or careful prevention of hostilities.

Roles are "learned early and played well at great sacrifice to emotional well-being."[52] More than one person can play the same role in a family, and individuals may fulfill multiple roles. Notably, many ministers describe the qualities of a "rescuer" when discussing family history. This individual is expected to "fix" everything and everyone and assumes the full and exhausting responsibility for doing so. Does this sound familiar? Here are other typical family roles:

- The hero or "golden child" is the favorite who can do no wrong. Caregivers expect this child to excel. Other children exist in comparison with this child.

- The saint is a hero who excels in a religious or spiritual manner.

50. RZIM, "Open Letter from the International Board of Directors," paras. 11 and 14.
51. Mosgofian and Ohlschlager, *Sexual Misconduct in Counseling and Ministry*, 121.
52. Laaser, *Healing the Wounds*, 85.

- The lost child receives less attention and feels left behind. This child learns to stay out of the way, be seen and not heard, and bury feelings. Later in life, the lost child may appear strong and silent.
- The scapegoat or "black sheep" is expected to fail or be wrong. This child is often ostracized and blamed when things go wrong.
- Mascots are family comedians adept at using humor to bury or suppress feelings.
- The doer is the family member who gets things done and keeps the household operating. The doer often becomes a workaholic.
- The enabler tolerates inappropriate behavior and works to save other family members from the consequences. They like to give the impression their family is "normal."
- The martyr wants everyone to know how much s/he sacrifices for the family. As such, complaints are a constant communication tool.

Many individuals learn to function within the rules and roles, but this does not present a functional family in the proper sense. Most families operate in a state of malfunction, which occurs when the system is damaged but continues to function at a diminished capacity, or dysfunction, which occurs when the system stops working or works incorrectly. Still, the rules and roles become familiar, and humans crave the comfort found in familiarity (which is why many transfer rules and roles into future relationships). Usually maintained in the name of family loyalty or love, unhealthy rules and roles leave broken and untreated souls strewn among the wreckage. Such dysfunction can sow the seeds of sexual addiction.

Sexual addicts generally emerge from rigid and emotionally disengaged families. For example, those for whom intimacy was not provided or modeled in childhood become adults who often view sexuality as a powerful counterfeit of interpersonal intimacy.[53] The individual seeks satisfaction in everything from fantasizing to sexting, sporadic hook-ups or prolonged affairs, and engagement with pornography or prostitutes. In such cases, the sex act is a penultimate goal; the ultimate goal is the blissful numbness that results. Countless ministers who wrestle with these realities inevitably turn to sexual activity to medicate old wounds, find meaning, and find love. Though the "love" may be disordered, many experience more kindness and nurturing from a prostitute than a parishioner—primarily because their

---

53. Hands and Fehr, *Spiritual Wholeness for Clergy*, loc. 245.

malformation has presented "love" as a self-affirming or self-satisfying act detached from intimacy and emotion.[54]

God's solution is far different and sees believers conform to the image of his Son (Rom 8:29). Section 4 addresses ways to overcome shame and dysfunction sans fig leaves, goat skins, and righteous works. Such deliverance is non-negotiable: you cannot clothe yourself with Christ until you have discarded the old coverings (Eph 4:22–24). The removal of all ungodly coverings allows reunion with God and others.

THE NEED TO PLOT A NEW COURSE

"What is past is prologue."

— WILLIAM SHAKESPEARE

In summary, illicit sexual behavior among ministers is not a simple matter of willful disregard in the pursuit of personal pleasure. Such behaviors often result from various factors, including psychological, physiological, and emotional wounding. Everyone seeks a haven to escape pain and shame or find loving approval and affirmation. But like a ship that lacks rudders and sails, the individual whose emotional formation included little or no example of building a healthy identity and coping with struggle can do little to steer toward the desired haven when storms arise. The prevailing forces will control this vessel as it struggles to stay afloat.

Over time, the embattled mariner learns strategies and techniques to survive rather than avoid or conquer the storms. What helps you stay afloat amid the ministerial maelstrom? Where do you find worth and affirmation, reward, or relief? What is your escape? What is your excuse?

Illicit sexual behavior is the unfortunate choice for a sizeable number of ministers. Ironically, some of those individuals entered the ministry to obtain what sex now provides. Perhaps you or someone you know entered pastoral ministry hoping to obtain the long-denied affection and approval. Ministers driven by unmet emotional needs may be blind to their motivation. Thinking he is solely concerned with what will bring praise and honor to the Lord, he may make decisions based on what makes him feel accepted, acknowledged, and appreciated.[55] Unfortunately, the ministry cannot meet such needs. In fact, ministry often repays the minister with everything but the affection, attention, and approval he desperately desires.

---

54. Laaser, *Healing the Wounds*, 39, 56–57.
55. Grenz and Bell, *Betrayal of Trust*, 51.

STORMFRONT NO. 1—THE FLESH (EMOTIONAL)

The ensuing frustration is a remarkable contributor to sexual moral failure, a consequence we will explore in chapter 6.

Suffice it to say in many respects, illicit sexual behaviors are the result of shame as much as they are its cause. Because the individual seeks to fill the void or numb the pain caused in formative years, these adverse actions create and perpetuate one's weaknesses and inadequacies. Dysfunctional families often produce dysfunctional love. Without redemptive healing and renunciation, dysfunctional love can devolve into sexual addiction. Not everyone who endures emotional malformation or sexual violation will follow this pattern. However, those who have fallen prey often demonstrate compulsive and consuming behaviors, an inability to control intrusive thoughts or behaviors, and denial evidenced by minimization, self-justification, and blame-projection.[56]

Malformation can manifest in low self-esteem, persistent dissatisfaction, the capacity for rationalizing harmful actions or attitudes, fear of failure, poor impulse control, and a sense of entitlement. Any threat to one's sense of personal worth and purpose can lead to feelings of inferiority and attempts to earn significance. As Pope Gregory I rightly notes, the "disturbed heart has lost the satisfaction of joy within" and "seeks for sources of consolation without."[57]

From this perspective, sinful actions are seen not as acts of selfish rebellion but as misdirected attempts to fulfill emptiness, find worth, or heal the brokenness that grows in complexity and scope over the years. If left untreated, most individuals have only the detrimental behaviors ingrained by formative experiences to escape the pain or meet the need. Indeed, the best predictor of future behavior is past behavior.[58] Patrick Carnes illustrates this in a study of one thousand sex addicts that found 81 percent were sexually abused, 74 percent physically abused, and 97 percent emotionally abused.[59] Mark Laaser further notes that the "secret sin of sexual addiction grows from seeds planted in childhood, and symptoms may go undetected for

---

56. Mosgofian and Ohlschlager, *Sexual Misconduct in Counseling and Ministry*, 16. Laaser notes that many sex addicts are poly-addicts who will simply transition to another vice if they fail to address emotional and spiritual issues in healthy ways. Attention deficit disorders, depression, and anxiety are the three most common mental health conditions addicts suffer (Laaser, *Healing the Wounds*, 58–59).

57. Gregory the Great, *Morals on the Book of Job*, 39:25.

58. This assertion is readily dismissed by Christians who contend that as new creations in Christ, old tendencies are washed away by the blood of Christ. Yet, history demonstrates that Christians rarely experience an immediate and complete transformation of their inner lives. In fact, many remain broken despite a lifetime of committed spirituality. Sins are washed away but Christlike character must be formed.

59. Carnes, *Don't Call It Love*, 109.

years. In adolescence, the indicators of this disease [sexual addiction] may be confused with normal sexual development. In adulthood, the disease grows progressively worse. Ultimately, if untreated, its victims will die."[60]

Ministers are not immune but at significant risk, as unhealed dysfunction and deficient formation "leaves a pastor essentially addicted to reaching for emotional highs, such as those experienced in infatuation."[61] Many who struggle with sexual malfeasance have poor self-images, which often go unnoticed because the individuals hide their struggle by overachieving and appearing self-confident. Rather than an attempt to convince others, this often is a subconscious attempt to convince themselves. Indeed, their duplicitous behavior frustrates friends and family, who are well aware of the depression behind the mask.[62]

Alas, there is hope! The Lord will bring the weary sailor out of the storm and guide him to the desired harbor (Ps 107:28–30). Emotional health is just as powerful as emotional hurt. How we receive and respond to help is equally formative as our reception of and response to hurt.[63] In much the same way that malformed emotional health contributes to illicit behaviors in the hopes of medicating unspeakable pains, a rightly reformed emotional health will help the minister forego destructive coping mechanisms and instead pursue the development of Christlikeness. Therefore, holistic formation and ministerial restoration give emotional health significant attention by identifying and overcoming undeveloped and wounded emotions, correcting malformed perceptions and behaviors, and helping the minister find his true identity in Christ. Success sees the (re)formed and restored minister transformed by a renewed mind; he casts off old ways of thinking to allow the attitudes of Christ to guide (Rom 12:2; Phil 2:4–5).

Section 4 will help us plot a course toward that desired haven. Before setting sail, remember that the emotional tempest is only one component of this perfect storm. To overcome this triad's destructive synergy, chapter 5 will consider the ways culture affirms self-orientation and unbiblical coping

---

60. Laaser, *Healing the Wounds*, 15.

61. Thoburn and Balswick, "Prevention Approach to Infidelity," 46.

62. As Briggs rightly notes, masks are "nothing more than emotional armor" that are to be removed, as we are called to bear God's image, not keep up our own (Briggs, *Fail*, 90).

63. One's image of God and self-image draw heavily on one's perception of and experience with other people, particularly parents or primary caregivers. Fortunately, these views can change over time based on subsequent loving relationships. "Thus, the goal of the emotional formation relates to reconciling one's self-image with the way that God views us, as being worthy recipients of God's love" (Chandler, *Christian Spiritual Formation*, 93).

mechanisms, and chapter 6 will address the very personal satanic strategy to entice, give life to sin, and progressively destroy life in Christ (Jas 1:14–15).

5

Stormfront No. 2—The World (Cultural)

"A belief is not merely an idea the mind possesses.
It is an idea that possesses the mind."

— Robert Oxton Bolton

History has long presented Christianity as a sacred church ministering to a secular world. The contemporary reality arguably sees a secular church ministering to a pagan world. Though sacred by Christ's sanctification, the Western church is secular in the sense that many leaders and congregations push socially accepted, though biblically prohibited, behaviors through a progressive path that demands recognition leading to tolerance, then acceptance leading to approval, and ultimately conformity leading to advocacy (or persecution, if resisted). Failure to acquiesce is deemed intolerant and even hateful.

Some churchgoers who push a preferred agenda fail to see that their definitions of "truth," "good," and "right" are rooted in secular rather than sacred ideologies. Others urge acceptance to keep people in the pews and maintain popularity within the community. Many ministries fear social rejection; Scripture warns against social acceptance. For these and other reasons, secular thought has invaded the sacred and exerts far more significant influence than Christians realize.[1]

---

1. Such failure is not unique. The influence of Greek dualism is evident in the early Roman Catholic Church, as is the Enlightenment in the emergence of liberal theology. Culture's adverse influence on the church is evident in the Crusades, the defense (by some) of slavery, and the church's deafening silence in Germany during World War II. Today, homosexual marriage and ministers (and some other aspects inherent to the sexual revolution) have torn apart hundreds of churches and even denominations.

STORMFRONT NO. 2—THE WORLD (CULTURAL)

At the time of this writing, cultural forces are working hard to "deconstruct" numerous long-standing social institutions. Two agencies under vehement attack are those through which God primarily relates to his people: the family, which God institutes in Gen 1, and the church, which God institutes in Acts 2.

Such actions are the consequence of society's rejection of "positive freedom" (the freedom through self-mastery to pursue a greater good) in favor of "negative freedom" (liberation from external restraints, freedom of choice without limits). Contemporary culture calls courageous the one who lives without regard for social norms. The true human is s/he who expressively explores one's passions sans inhibitions and social prohibitions. Conversely, those who define right living and pursue mastery of desires in service to a greater good are inhuman. The refusal to live out their passions is a cowardly rejection or denial of the true self.

Before we delve into the error and influence inherent to such assertions, it should be noted that the apostle Paul ended this debate for all who would call themselves Christians. Paul repeatedly endorsed the transformed character that enables positive freedom. Furthermore, he showed negative freedom to be an illusion (Rom 6:15–23). As Paul rightly asserted, we are all slaves. The question is, To what will we be enslaved: sin leading to death or the Spirit leading to life?

Indeed, overcoming immorality and developing moral integrity requires the fallen minister to understand the adverse influence of society and culture.[2] Illicit sexual behaviors are difficult to discard when they have long served as coping mechanisms to deal with pain and lack. Abstention becomes more complicated when the world tolerates and even celebrates such behaviors. Everything from government to education to entertainment declares these actions to be not only acceptable but deserved.

Simply put, we have power over what we believe but fail to understand the power those beliefs hold over us. Social media influencers provide a good illustration. These individuals build a reputation, often an empire, by sharing knowledge and opinions and holding sway over an impressionable audience. They influence tens of millions with one short social media post. For good or bad, these individuals shape public opinion, affect buying trends, and can elevate or decimate people and causes with the touch of a button. The typical boomer or Gen X may be unable to name the top ten influencers, but millennials and Gen Z certainly can.

Similarly, cultural worldviews serve as powerful influencers of individual and group thought. For example, we now know that gender

---

2. Pop et al., "Restoring Pastors Following a Moral Failure," 276.

dysphoria results not only from emotional distress but also from societal conditioning. More relevant to this book's topic, the evolving opinions toward pornography provide a strong example. In ranking "bad things," teens and young adults ranked the failure to recycle and significant consumption of electricity or water as more immoral than viewing porn.[3] A related social opinion argues that the meaning of sex is dependent on context, though an increasing number of psychologists reject this position and warn that uncommitted sex is dehumanizing.[4] How does our culture carry such influence? Social identity theory provides telling answers. The theory asserts that the social structure defines the individual's self-worth. Therefore, one's place in that structure is paramount. Individuals strive to achieve and maintain distinctiveness within a tribal context. Granted, the approach sounds counterintuitive (a matter we will explore in the chapter's second subsection), but the narrative forms the individual's identity, and the group provides mutual affirmation.

Moralistic therapeutic deism is a notable cultural worldview thriving in such social construct. The term, coined by sociologist Christian Smith, speaks of three predominate social beliefs. "Moral" speaks to moral relativity, a postmodern concept that views truth as relative. The idea is that what is true for me may not be true for you. Furthermore, whatever satisfies my needs is true, and that truth can change as circumstances change. Therefore, there is no eternal truth or moral absolutes. "Therapeutic" speaks to the priority of personal happiness, typically defined as maximizing pleasure and minimizing pain. "Deism" speaks to an element of spirituality in which many believe that some god or ultimate good exists and created the world but does not relationally engage with individuals or become directly involved with state affairs. This god only desires that people be congenial and kind. Therefore, good works (as defined by the individual in point 1) will surely bring good things back to you and secure your place in heaven (again, as defined by the individual).

Perhaps you agree with some of the points just described. God does not. However, most Americans do, and as discussed below, Christians are not immune. Therefore, this chapter considers the predominant influences contributing to the acceptance of illicit behaviors among contemporary Christian ministers: self-identification misshapen by worldview and self-worth misshapen by idolatrous worship. The chapter concludes by discussing the necessary renovation of the structure that allows these problems to flourish.

---

3. Barna Group, *Porn Phenomenon*, 81.
4. Hettlinger, *Sex Isn't That Simple*, 80.

STORMFRONT NO. 2—THE WORLD (CULTURAL)
SELF-IDENTIFICATION MISSHAPEN BY WORLDVIEW

"Know that we must serve not the times, but God."

— Athanasius

Have you ever had a discussion devolve into debate, only to find yourself insisting that rejection of someone's beliefs or actions is not a rejection of the person? Chances are you have. How did that go? Chances are it did not go well. The emerging generations see the world very differently. Individualism is the highest notion, and they equate personal beliefs with personhood. Therefore, to reject their beliefs or behaviors is to reject them. How did this dramatic shift occur in such a short span? Well, the shift was subtle and was not short.

Selfhood is the eye of this storm. Selfhood is how individuals understand their self-identity, worth, purpose, happiness, and relation to others. A radical shift in how selfhood is determined and defined began more than two hundred years ago and has seen unprecedented progression (or digression, as it were) in the past sixty years. Personal happiness is the goal, and truth (determined by the individual) is the only guide.

Indeed, this perfect storm has generated a tsunami of change, altering the landscape. Tsunamis and tidal waves are not synonymous. Balance governs the latter, specifically, the gravitational interactions of the sun, moon, and earth. Contrary to popular opinion, waves do not form in the unseen depths as a movement of water but on the surface as a transfer of the wind's energy. The orbital motion creates a concentration of kinetic energy that passes through the water. When the seafloor disrupts this unification of forces, the wave breaks the surface to rise above its obstacle. Beachgoers experience an awesome crash of power. Most waves are beautiful to behold, fun to play in, and can propel people and objects to desired destinations.

Tsunamis are quite different. Most tsunamis begin with an earthquake below or near the ocean floor. The breaking and shifting of foundational tectonic plates causes instability and the sudden displacement of ocean waters—the water thrusts with incredible force, traveling as much as 500 mph. Tsunamis come in a train of waves that boast a wavelength (the distance between the waves) of hundreds of miles.[5] The resultant wall of water can rise 50 to 100 feet, but some tsunamis are much larger. Indonesia measured a 167-foot wave in the 2004 Indian Ocean tsunami that killed more than 230,000 in eighteen countries. The largest recorded tsunami hit

---

5. National Oceanic and Atmospheric Administration, "Tsunamis."

SECTION TWO: ELEMENTS OF THE PERFECT STORM

Lituya Bay, Alaska, on July 9, 1958. Its wave topped 1,700 feet, some 450 feet taller than the Empire State Building. That is the kind of force that has hit contemporary culture.

Psychological sociologist Philip Rieff outlines this surge of self-orientation in his sweeping yet informative four-point classification of self-identity. For over two millennia, people found self-identity and centered morality in service to others—family and friends, community and country.[6] Rieff exemplifies this understanding in his first three stages: the "political man" of the Greeks, the "religious man" of the Hebrews and Christians, and the "economic man" of eighteenth-century Europe. In each, the individual finds worth and purpose within the communal context; society structures itself on morality derived from a transcendent source, and the individual conforms and contributes to that order. This transcendent source progressed from Hellenistic fate to Christian faith and arguably reached its apex with Aquinas's moral edifice, which centers on God's character. The resultant cultural stability was maintained even when religious views waned amid the rise of Enlightenment—a period in which the "economic man" found his sense of self in the ways he provided for family and contributed to society—because social order and morals remained grounded in the sacred.[7]

However, Romanticism shook that stability as it gave rise to the "psychological man" and his inward-focused selfhood (that sound in the distance is the tsunami alarm). His is an "expressive individualism" in which self-meaning, defined through autonomous feelings, is satisfied by personal happiness.[8] Ethics thus became increasingly subjective, a function of feeling with no common authority by which morals and behavior could be justified or judged. In short, the individual became the arbiter of truth and the justifier of behavior. The individual determines what is right and true and lives in light of that truth.

Carl Trueman sees in this a societal transition from the mimetic view, in which humans discover and conform to the world's given order and meaning, to one of *poiesis*, in which the world is "raw material" to be manipulated by the individual who creates meaning by his power and for his

---

6. Rieff, *Triumph of the Therapeutic*, 4. Also worthy of consideration is Charles Taylor's notion of the "buffered self," in which truth and identity are self-contained, as compared to the "open and porous self," which connects people to God and relegates truth and identify under the influence of external forces (Taylor, *Secular Age*).

7. Trueman, *Rise and Triumph of the Modern Self*, 75.

8. Trueman, *Rise and Triumph of the Modern Self*, 79–80. While the Aristotelian-Thomist view of human nature and moral action is teleological and centered in (differently defined) categories of happiness, it must be noted that this individualistic variation is absent of social structure and lacks appeal to tradition.

purpose.[9] Trueman believes such individualism echoes Nietzsche's philosophical call for humans to transcend themselves "to take the place of God as self-creators and the inventors, not the discoverers, of meaning."

This transcendence necessitates disestablishing social, historical, and cultural orders now viewed as oppressive to authentic humanity. Adherents repurpose institutions such as schools and churches to be servants of the individual's inner well-being, places where one goes to perform rather than be formed or transformed.[10] Conversely, many view any sacred ethic that challenges immorality as oppressive, hateful, ignorant, "and even a sign of serious mental or moral deficiency."[11] With increasing volume came the calls to deconstruct anyone and anything that would deny one's pursuit of self-defined happiness.[12] As a result, many ministers, especially millennials and younger, have emerged from a social paradigm that deems a vast array of illicit sexual behaviors acceptable and seeks to destroy the biblical ethic that says otherwise. The source of happiness and truth is not God but man. To place teleological purpose and possibilities within the individual is nothing new. Listen close, and you will hear Satan's assurance that "you will be like God" (Gen. 3:5) recast in the closing words of B. F. Skinner's book *Beyond Freedom and Dignity*: "we have not yet seen what man can make of man."[13]

This tsunami has hit with unimaginable force. The destructive waves created a widening chasm between the generations and changed how we view ourselves, others, and God. Such worldviews include the beliefs and practices that shape an individual's priorities and relationships to God and

---

9. Trueman, *Rise and Triumph of the Modern Self*, 39–42. Conversely, the Aristotelian-Thomist view is not commensurate with this or the related consequentialist and utilitarian views that determine the "good" by its effect. The mimetic view "enables individuals to distinguish between what they are and what they should be" (p. 82).

10. Trueman, *Rise and Triumph of the Modern Self*, 49.

11. Trueman, *Rise and Triumph of the Modern Self*, 21.

12. Jean-Jacques Rousseau, Karl Marx, and Friedrich Nietzsche were primary voices in this belief, which argued that the authentic self was misshapen and corrupted by social conventions that must be overthrown if humanity was to reach its full potential. Conversely, C. S. Lewis rightly asserts that "if they say that all thoughts are thus tainted, then, of course, we must remind them that Freudianism and Marxism are as much systems of thought as Christian theology. . . . The Freudian and the Marxian are in the same boat with all the rest of us and cannot criticize us from the outside. They have sawn off the branch they are sitting on. If, on the other hand, they say that the taint need not invalidate their thinking, then neither need it invalidate ours. In which case they have saved their own branch, but also saved ours along with it." (Lewis, *God in the Dock*, 272).

13. Skinner, *Beyond Freedom and Dignity*, 215.

others, assess the meaning of events, and justify our actions.[14] Worldview informs how we answer life's core questions regarding origin, purpose, and ultimate truth.[15] In the tsunami's wake we find significant changes to worldview, even within the church. For example, is God your everything and the lens through which you view all aspects of life? Perhaps not as much as you think.

Christian researcher George Barna defines a Christian worldview as one that views everything through Scripture, understood as absolute moral truth, and accepts six core biblical beliefs: the accuracy of biblical teaching, the sinless nature of Jesus, the literal existence of Satan, the omnipotence and omniscience of God, salvation by grace alone, and the personal responsibility to evangelize.[16] A 2009 national study by Barna's research institute found that only half of Protestant pastors and one in ten professing Christians agree with each statement.[17] The latter number dropped significantly by 2020 when the American Worldview Inventory 2020 found that only 6 percent of Americans hold a biblical worldview—down from 12 percent just twenty-five years prior.[18]

If a shrinking number holds a Christian worldview, through what lens do they view life? Our pluralistic post-Christian culture is rife with competing worldviews, including deism, naturalism, atheism, humanism, nihilism, pantheism, universalism, Eastern philosophies, New Age philosophy, and postmodernism. It is a kaleidoscope, to be sure, but these views share one commonality: the refusal to recognize Christian Scripture as authoritative. Each marginalizes Christian truth and its ethical standards and offers an alluring substitute at every turn.[19] This "secular/sacred split," as described by Nancy Pearcey, is unrecognized and unopposed mainly because Christians are biblically illiterate.[20] As a result, countless ministers and Christians who

---

14. Palmer, *Elements of a Christian Worldview*, 22–3.

15. Pearcey, *Total Truth*, 51.

16. Barna Group, "Barna Survey Examines Changes in Worldview Among Christians," para. 2.

17. Barna Group, "Barna Survey Examines Changes in Worldview Among Christians," para. 4.

18. Arizona Christian University, "Is the Bible True?," para. 2. The American Worldview Inventory 2020 is a nationally representative sample of 2,000 adults conducted by George Barna in conjunction with the Cultural Research Center at Arizona Christian University.

19. Pearcey, *Total Truth*, 17.

20. For example, the American Bible Association and Barna Group found that no US city had a majority of residents who are "Bible-minded," defined as those who read the Bible weekly and strongly assert the Bible is accurate in the principles it teaches. Chattanooga, Tennessee topped the list at 50 percent in the rating. Only 25 percent

lack a biblical worldview have come to accept social constructs that wrongly define and apply truth and identify the individual as the arbiter of right and wrong. The American Worldview Inventory's results are telling:

Biblical Teaching	% in agreement			
	E	P	M	C
Believes there is an absolute moral truth	48%	31%	42%	31%
Believes the Bible is the primary source of moral guidance	58%	62%	29%	23%
Believes God is the basis of all truth	72%	70%	37%	43%
Believes the Bible is the word of God, and trustworthy and reliable	74%	67%	37%	47%
Believes a person who is good enough or does enough good works can earn eternal salvation	42%	51%	39%	15%

Key: E = Evangelicals, P = Pentecostals, M = Mainline, C = Catholic
Source: *American Worldview Inventory 2020*; N=2,000 adults, 18 or older; conducted by the Cultural Research Center at Arizona Christian University.

Figure 2: Examples of Christian Worldviews[21]

A separate Barna national study found that 61 percent of practicing Christians agree with ideas rooted in new spirituality, 54 percent resonate with postmodernist views, 36 percent accept ideas associated with Marxism, and 29 percent believe in ideas rooted in secularism.[22]

This tendency toward postmodern individualism is rooted in the utilitarian philosophies of Thomas Hobbes and John Locke. Though each approached individualism differently, both defined society as a conglomeration of contracts that individuals enter for protection and to advance their self-interest. German philosopher Immanuel Kant further developed this concept by recasting the Aristotelian nature and freedom espoused by Thomas Aquinas within Newtonian physics' deterministic machine. His resultant "freedom" is better defined as "autonomy," as the determination of moral law—traditionally the function of God alone—is relegated to individual human rational will.[23] Essentially, the individual is subject only to

---

of the nation is considered Bible-minded. (Barna Group, "America's Most [and Least] Bible-Minded Cities," para. 2.). Researchers analyzed the Bible reading habits and beliefs of 76,505 nationwide adult respondents over a ten-year period to calculate each city's ranking.

21. Arizona Christian University, "AWVI 2020 Results," 5.

22. Barna Group, "Competing Worldviews Influence Today's Christians," para. 3.

23. The word "autonomy" is comprised of the Greek root words *autos*, meaning "self," and *nomos*, meaning "law."

ethical standards determined by and imposed on oneself, and thus, "Kant has made reason into God."[24]

This ethical self-enterprise gained further strength in the moral relativity that dominated the latter twentieth century and shaped the postmodern concept of *zeitgeist* from which most contemporary ministers emerged. Karl Barth serves as an unfortunate example. Barth is arguably one of the most influential theologians of the past century, and his insights continue to inform Christian thought. Throughout his influential and massive *Church Dogmatics*, Barth supports his pointed, determined, and demanding views with an abundance of Scripture and theological thought . . . but wavers on the issues of fidelity in marriage. He questions whether marriage is an exclusive and irrevocable covenant.[25] Barth further posits that "marriage has no divine basis and is thus dissoluble."[26] How can one capable of navigating the most difficult theological issues run aground when traversing this basic tenant of the faith? Herein lay the power and influence of autonomy. Barth's "theological partner," Charlotte von Kirschbaum, was far more than a coworker. She was a life partner with whom Barth spent research summers. The theologian later invited von Kirschbaum to move into the Barth home, much to the dismay of his wife, Nelly, and their children. Barth's example bears witness to the fact that our preferences skew our perceptions.

Autonomy tears apart the tectonic plates; relevant to this topic, the biblical foundations for truth and life. The resultant tsunami usurps God's authority and allows the individual to justify sinful behaviors—a right reserved for God alone.[27] Like the Barth household, the fabric of society (and the church) has been torn asunder by the baseless belief that truth is relative to the individual. And this tsunami shows no sign of receding, even after modernity failed to deliver the goods. Rather than admit that humankind's preferences, biases, and inadequacies render the individual incapable of rightly defining truth, Western culture is replacing relative truth with a post-truth mindset that acknowledges objective truth but views such truth as optional and subordinate to personal preference."[28] In other words, accepted truths are those that align with individual purposes and opinions. The subsequent tendency is one of "confirmation bias," in which the individual

---

24. Pearcey, *Total Truth*, 105. Though this work does not afford a fuller discussion, it should be noted that the two sides in Kant's dichotomy were not only independent but outright contradictory, for if nature really is the deterministic machine of Newtonian physics, then how is freedom possible?

25. Barth, *Church Dogmatics*, 207.

26. Barth, *Church Dogmatics*, 211.

27. Rom 5:8–10; 8:33; Gal 2:16.

28. Murray, *Saving Truth*, 14–17.

gathers information that reinforces what s/he wants to be true (not what is true) and discards the rest. Hence, the "answers to life's questions no longer need to correspond to reality. They need only cater to our desires."[29]

Remember, tsunamis come in a train of waves, so brace for another impact.

The post-truth approach emphasizes rights over responsibilities. Such attitude is prevalent among "legacy Christians" for whom Christianity is a "background noise that can safely be ignored."[30] Within this willful ignorance, there echoes Ivan's nihilistic affirmation that without God, everything is lawful.[31] The contemporary minister may not proclaim this with the boldness displayed by the brother Karamazov or with the vigor common to contemporary worldviews that declare "we make the rules. We are responsible for nothing outside ourselves. We are the kingdom, and the power, and the glory."[32] Yet, the oft-unspoken attitude that dominates Christian thought is one in which the individual identifies himself as the arbiter of truth and the proverbial center of his universe.

Such belief allows and often manifests in different standards of conduct. One justifies personal behaviors that s/he expects others to avoid. Ron Sider affirms this tendency through numerous national polls, statistics, and social studies. He concludes that one of the greatest scandals of this age is that "evangelical Christians are as likely to embrace lifestyles every bit as hedonistic, materialistic, self-centered and sexually immoral as the world in general."[33] As noted in Alan Wolfe's painful yet pointed assertion, "in every aspect of the religious life, American faith has met American culture—and American culture has triumphed."[34]

While the influence of a secular worldview is evident, to varying degrees, in numerous examples, this reality proves to be a double-edged sword in holistic restoration. Secular worldviews not only influence illicit behaviors but can influence denominational and congregational responses. Jack Hayford notes, "if humanism governs the resolution of this problem, the authority of Christ and His Word will have been supplanted."[35]

---

29. Murray, *Saving Truth*, 23.
30. Kinnamon and Lyons, *Good Faith*, 27.
31. Dostoyevsky, *Brothers Karamazov*, 310.
32. Rifkin, *Algeny*, 244. Such declaration echoes the primary mean by which Satan seeks to exert human sovereignty toward autonomy from God (Gen 3:1–7).
33. Sider, *Scandal of the Evangelical Conscience*, 13.
34. Wolfe, *Transformation of American Religion*, 3.
35. Hayford, *Restoring Fallen Leaders*, 20.

We will discuss the responsibilities of churches and denominations in section 3. Suffice it to say, "our lives are shaped by the 'god' we worship—whether the God of the Bible or some substitute deity."[36] Therefore, Scripture will not be free to redeem unless the minister, members, and church leaders view Scripture as the ultimate truth, effective for "teaching, for rebuke, for correction, for training in righteousness" (2 Tim 3:16). Biblical renewal is transformative by nature and reiterates the demand for holistic (re)formation of the repentant violator and the afflicted congregation. Unfortunately, the god worshiped in the secular worldview is remarkably difficult to dethrone.

SELF-WORTH MISSHAPEN BY THE MOST DANGEROUS IDOL

"It is not paradoxical or absurd that God becomes and is man ... but it is certainly paradoxical and absurd that man wants to be as God."

— Karl Barth

What is the most dangerous idol we can worship? The one who stares back at you from the mirror every morning. And if you buy into the belief that the individual determines what is right and true, and the goal is personal happiness, you will soon bow at that altar. Many already do. Some seek to please the idol by maximizing pleasure and minimizing pain. Others justify and rationalize sexual misconduct as a viable, even necessary, solution to overcome emotional woundings and feelings of loneliness and isolation. And what's that sound we hear? That is the chorus of culture singing the praises of sexual "freedom" and affirming the sense of entitlement that typically follows.[37]

Scripture contains an episode of idol worship like the one described. Aaron is anxious, and the people persuade the high priest to fashion a golden calf (Exod 32:1–10). They call the golden calf "Elohim" and "Jehovah." Aaron even declares "this is your god, O Israel, that brought you out of the land of Egypt!"

Did you catch that? They didn't set out to create a new or false God. When God did not provide what they wanted in the manner they expected and within their timeline, the people made God into what they wanted him

---

36. Pearcey, *Total Truth*, 23.

37. The irony is this: being created in God's image, to elevate anything above him is to demean ourselves.

to be. Heavily influenced by their Egyptian worldview, they formed a golden calf that placed no requirements on them and was blind and indifferent to their sin. A powerful worship service erupted, but God was nowhere near. He was on the mountain inscribing the Torah.

Ministers and churches repeatedly attempt to form God into their image or what they want him to be. Their prayers echo the cries of Veruca Salt during her visit to Willy Wonka's chocolate factory. They want the whole works, the prizes of all shapes and sizes, and no matter how they want it now! Indeed, bratty Veruca was a bad egg, but her sense of entitlement is not unique. Such spoiled demand speaks to a problem beyond poor impulse control—it is a problem of deficient ethics.

The Trappist monk Thomas Merton rightly notes that bad habits result from bad ethics. "Unintentionally and unknowingly, or without having the power to do otherwise," individuals with poor personal ethical standards will inevitably fall back into imperfections and natural desires.[38] Merton describes these bad habits as "living roots from which, in spite of our best intentions, we constantly suffer a regrowth of bitter, tenacious offshoots of imperfections." So we tirelessly try to cut away bad fruit before anyone takes note, but this misses the point: the real problem is the bad root that produces the bad fruit. The only solution is to uproot and clear these bad habits from the garden of one's soul.

That garden ground is where you make your stand. Let us not forget where Satan makes his first appearance and Jesus claims his first atoning victory. The believer who tilts toward self-preference follows the path of Adam and Eve and will inevitably neglect his walks with God in the cool of the day. This journey leads away from that solid and level ground; when demands and stresses increase, the minister does not know where to turn. Ill-equipped to handle the common yet significant pressures, old struggles with self-worth and identity return and open old wounds. He is now on very shaky ground. The deceiver, whom we will address in the next chapter, makes his move. He subtly asks, "did God really say?" as he promises peace and purpose within the coping mechanisms learned in times of brokenness. The minister is likely isolated and has no one to urge a different course. Such help will certainly not emerge from society, which accepts and embraces the individualism and autonomy that awaits. The shaky ground now becomes quicksand. The minister struggles to find footing in a fleeting attempt to overcome this entente, but the harder he fights, the deeper he sinks. Then he sees it: a moral high ground that declares his actions reasonable and him deserving of the tasty fruit. His ascension ends the quicksand struggle,

---

38. Merton, *Ascent to Truth*, 188–89.

but the minister fails to see his moral high ground is in enemy territory. The ethics, methods, and justifications used to end his struggle are secular rather than sacred.

Put another way, many Christians believe they are men of character and can withstand the temptation of illicit behaviors. They think themselves ethical and in some ways are—but not necessarily in the right ways. Case in point: how do you know the right thing to do? Sin renders us spiritually dead, worldly-minded, disobedient children driven by demons and the desires of our flesh (Eph 2:1–3). And don't follow your heart—that thing is deceitful above all things and desperately wicked (Jer 17:9) and is killing you from within (Matt 15:18–19).

Remember all that talk of individualism and identity in the previous subsection? Here is where the rubber meets the road. The rise of individualism inherent to "psychological man" sees an arguable digression of selfhood and social morals and the embrace of secular ethics to justify the "good" one defines and does. But secular ethics are, by definition, void of godly truth and godly *telos*, the end goal and purpose of one's life. Secular ethics produce deficient Christian character, at best.

The philosophies of Ayn Rand provide a telling example of rational self-interest and its inevitable consequence. Though vocal regarding the need for a moral code to guide one's life, the objectivist argued that the "first right on earth is the right of the ego. Man's first duty is to himself. His moral law is never to place his prime goal within the persons of others."[39] Ergo, society and self-will function best when driven by self-interest. Rand thus rejected any transcendent source for ethics and knowledge; she strongly rejected altruism and went so far as to describe the man who attempts to live for others as "a dependent. He is a parasite in motive and makes parasites of those he serves. The relationship produces nothing but mutual corruption."[40]

In loose regard to this book's subject, Rand's sexual ethic distinguished "errors of knowledge" from "breaches of morality."[41] One makes allowances for the former, which is unintentional, results from insufficient knowledge, and is willingly corrected. The latter is "a conscious choice of an action you know to be evil, or a willful evasion of knowledge, a suspension of sight and of thought" that should not be forgiven or accepted. Although the need to acquire and rightly act upon knowledge seems commendable, the lack of

---

39. Rand, *For the New Intellectual*, 80.

40. Rand, *For the New Intellectual*, 82. The Christian ethic would counter that authentic humanity is not parasitic but centered in God's decree of mutuality (Gen 2:18) in which the individual rejects autonomy and embraces community with God, true self, and others.

41. Rand, *Atlas Shrugged*, 1059.

inherent grace and forgiveness is troublesome. Furthermore, being rooted in rational self-interest provides considerable flexibility when applying the ethic. How does one define "evil"? And if it is not evil, is it allowable? By this twisted thought, Rand convinced two betrayed spouses that her fourteen-year affair with colleague Nathaniel Branden was a rational expression of their intellectual communion. She minimized evil and justified her behavior, and she is not alone.

The "enlightened" culture imbued by New Age optimism flatly rejects the assertion of an evil impulse within and "does not like to face the fact that humans have a tremendous capacity for evil."[42] One cannot overstate the prevalence of such thought and its challenge to holistic (re)formation. Contemporary society vests itself in the therapeutic psychology model that incessantly declares, "you are a good person!" This model defines help as feeling good about oneself and happiness as avoidance of pain, discomfort, and sacrifice. Our struggles are considered the fault of others, genetics, or external circumstances. Therefore, it is acceptable to depart from unfulfilling relationships and forego altruism. As psychologist Albert Ellis wrote, "The emotionally healthy individual should primarily be true to himself and not masochistically sacrifice himself for others."[43] Jesus flatly disagrees (e.g., John 15:13).

Such thinking resulted in humankind's fall and alienation from God. Similarly, our autonomous desires cause us to fall out of God and into ourselves—and what a terrible fall that is. Still, the prevalence of autonomy and self-orientation is the dominant force in shaping personal ethics, and many who celebrated the tectonic shift are unaware of the dangers heading their way. The desire for autonomy over eternal truth has accelerated the atrophy of individual and social morality. Contemporary culture's increasing rejection of the *imago Dei* (with accountability to God) in favor of *Deus Homo* (with accountability to no one) has lost what it means to be human and to value other human beings.[44] As Abdu Murray rightly asserts, in the "confused quest to elevate ourselves to deities, we actually have become devils."

Sadly, this expressive individualism provides an enticing solution to ministers who have long sought affirmation and battled with self-identity. This secular ethic has consumed the church. Extensive borrowing from these and other secular ethics has resulted in the "detheologizing" of seminary

---

42. Nystrom, *James*, 82.

43. Ellis, *Case Against Religion*, 3. See also McMinn, *Psychology, Theology, and Spirituality in Christian Counseling*, 34. Cf. Rom 12:10; 14:9; 15:2; Phil 2:4; 1 Thess 5:11.

44. Murray, *Saving Truth*, 63, 65.

and sanctuary.[45] Rather than embrace theological ethics—which seeks to develop ethical norms, standards, principles, and virtues—moral guidance often draws from philosophical ethics rooted in a deficient or even counter-Christian framework of beliefs.[46] This tendency has left many ill-equipped to remain afloat, let alone save those swept away in the tsunami's waters.

While ministerial practice is ever-evolving and must adapt to the emerging culture, the significant and eternal consequences of this sacred trust demand ministers recognize and overcome the influence of secular reasoning in the ethical decision-making process. Such formation is critical because "at crucial moments of choice, most of the business of choosing is already over."[47]

With so many choices, what ethics should one pursue? Dennis Hollinger analyzes five predominant approaches to forming and applying a Christian ethic.[48] These include:

- **The ethic of consequences, or teleological ethics**. This approach holds that results all humans can calculate and assess will determine right and wrong. The challenge to Christian ethics resides in the analysis used to determine worth—who determines the consequences considered, and how is that choice made?

- **Ethical egoism.** This approach is rooted in liberalism and centers on the individual moral actor—personal pleasure is the highest good and the primary goal of life. Therefore, one should do whatever will produce one's highest good.[49] The challenge is that this self-defeating enterprise contradicts the biblical demand for self-giving and self-sacrificing *agape* love.

---

45. Sensing, *Qualitative Research*, locs. 141–49. For example, Christians have sometimes found Kant's emphasis on universal moral absolutes to be compatible, but Dennis Hollinger rightly warns that a Christian ethic can never be purely rational because "doing the good is never divorced from the ultimate good, God, in both motivation and content" (Hollinger, *Choosing the Good*, 41).

46. Hollinger, *Choosing the Good*, 15–16. These include everything from the utilitarian approach that believes morality is rooted in the desire for happiness to the Kantian view that morality is a rational matter. Moral behavior (or lack thereof) is shaped by economic circumstances for the Marxist, repressed sexual instincts for the Freudian, and stimulus-response mechanisms for the behavioral psychologist.

47. Murdoch, *Sovereignty of Good*, 37.

48. Hollinger, *Choosing the Good*, 27–48.

49. Ethical egoism, first articulated by Epicurus (341–270 BC), should not be viewed as selfish impulse but a rational ethic of hedonism (the pleasure principle) in which pleasure is pursued through self-restraint and moderation. It is worth noting that Adam Smith, "the father of modern capitalism," centered his influential work *The Wealth of Nations* on economic autonomy and self-interest centered in ethical egoism.

- **Utilitarianism.** This Enlightenment approach determines moral right in the benefit(s) a majority receives (the greatest good for the greatest number of people). With little to no reliance on a priori notions of morality, it determines ethical behavior through scientific calculation of maximized pleasure and minimized pain. The challenges reside in the inability to determine and objectively weigh those consequences. Specifically, who decides what is good? Furthermore, willingly omitting the minority not included in the "greatest number" contradicts biblical precepts that demand provision and deliverance for such.

- **Principle or deontological ethics.** This approach is of significant worth to the Christian ethic as it asserts certain acts are inherently right or wrong and known as such through moral principles or rules.[50] The challenge is that principle ethics focuses on actions and minimizes moral character. While principles enable the minister to know the good and the right, obedience alone does not make one moral.

- **Character or virtue ethics.** Rather than judge what a person does, this approach centers on the individual's character development. The key is not what one should *do* but what one should *be*. Accurate assessment of moral character is determined not by adherence or abstinence but by the Christian community's witness that partners with the Spirit's transformative power to develop moral virtue. This formation will result in natural adherence or abstinence from the moral actor.

Ministerial restoration demands the rejection of self-justifying ethics and acceptance of a virtue ethic to serve as the governing paradigm for ministry and life. The approach provided in section 4 aims to build moral character and reinforce that character through a virtue ethic that assesses choices. This approach centers on sound theology drawn from biblical hermeneutics interpreted by the faith community. Legitimate sources of authority for Christian ethics include Scripture (the magisterial authority), direct divine guidance, an informed and sanctified moral conscience, Christian tradition, and the wise input of church leaders. These weave together to create the "rich tapestry of Christian moral conviction."[51] As such, the restoration ethic builds from the foundations of Jesus' teachings and example, draws understanding from Israel's prophetic tradition, and anticipates continued growth that will culminate in the eschaton. This ethic

---

50. Deonotological ethics make strong use of self-examination as presented in the Socratic method. It posits that knowledge is the key to a moral life; people are not willingly immoral but will choose the good when presented (a hallmark of Thomas Aquinas's theology).

51. Stassen and Gushee, *Kingdom Ethics*, 82.

seeks moral good through the Spirit's leading, sanctified reasoning and the church's collective wisdom from past and present. Because proper Christian ethics center around who one is rather than what one does, ethical development requires repentance, the practice of the corrective patterns, and participation in the transformative initiative. Proper thought and action will emerge from the transformed character that results. Such transformation is inseparable from grace because the Christian's moral obligation is not a demand but a gift, and the Christian is incapable of knowing or doing good apart from God.[52]

A word of warning as we head for higher ground: be wary of idealism as God works all things together for good. To believe your good works are indicative of your goodness is the antithesis of holistic formation. This approach leads to legalism, self-righteousness, and ultimately guilt and frustration. Idealism fails to perceive the depths of evil and wrongly believes the purity of will and principle can oppose the power of evil.[53] As Rebecca Pippert rightly asserts, we "can't reach in and straighten a twisted nature. Though we are responsible for our condition of sin, we are powerless to change it. Can we overcome our addiction to ourselves by sheer willpower? What self-improvement course will give us the power to stop ourselves from being self-centered and self-absorbed?"[54]

Restoration after moral failure requires the minister to reject self-orientation and to stop relying on secular morals to justify worldly behaviors. What is needed is an ethic that blends Christian principles with the development of Christian character, emphasizing the latter. Simply put, the Christian ethic must follow the example of Christ, who proved the Jewish reliance on spiritual discipline and the Greeks' dependence on education to be morally insufficient.[55] Jesus instead displayed "an almost exaggerated accent on the inward aspects in root causes of the religious action."[56] His point was clear: a transformation of heart and character is required. One experiences such transformation through *agape* love rather than legalism or loyalty (Rom 13:8–10; Gal 5:14). This requires the minister to imitate, assimilate, and ultimately emulate Christ.

---

52. Hollinger, *Choosing the Good*, 41.

53. Bonhoeffer, *Ethics*, 67–68.

54. Pippert, *Out of the Saltshaker and Into the World*, 173. See also McMinn, *Psychology, Theology, and Spirituality in Christian Counseling*, 185.

55. Rae, *Moral Choices*, 46–47.

56. Vermes, *Religion of Jesus the Jew*, 195.

STORMFRONT NO. 2—THE WORLD (CULTURAL)

Glen Stassen and David Gushee emphasize four critical dimensions that may prove helpful in developing this Christian character ethic.[57] See if you can discern the path to avert the perfect storm (flesh, world, and devil) within these dimensions:

- The **"basic convictions dimension."** Foundational convictions centered on God's character, activity, and will; "the ultimate source for morality is not God's commands but God's character."[58] Human nature as participants in God's will also receive careful consideration, which develops convictions regarding forgiveness, discipleship, justice, ministry, and mission.

- The **"way of reasoning dimension."** This dimension recognizes that character is shaped in the community and thus ensures consistent development and application of the Christian ethic through holistic training and communal practice. Moral reasoning does not function autonomously. Rather, habits of mind and heart hone moral reasoning. Therefore, virtues "need a community where they are engendered, fostered and refined."[59]

- The **"passions/loyalties dimension."** Seeks to understand the causal history of our emotions and change the negative and destructive emotions accordingly. Rather than adopt a stoic or monastic approach to abstinence, the holistic Christian ethic argues that to deny the place of passions in human life is to succumb to a vast illusion. As noted by Simon Harak, "The autonomous mind was an Enlightenment myth, launched by Descartes and now thoroughly discredited. Instead, we are embodied persons, with characteristic passions seized by fear, stricken by jealousy, falling in love, surprised by joy, moved with compassion."[60]

---

57. Stassen and Gushee, *Kingdom Ethics*, 59–68.

58. Rae, *Moral Choices*, 24.

59. Hauerwas, *Community of Character*, 115. Again, the Thomist influence is evident in this paradigm. In his attempt to reconcile Aristotle's philosophy with Christian theology, Thomas Aquinas held the primacy of reason and knowledge over the will and argued that the will follows what reason presents as the highest good. This contrasts with Bonaventure's commitment to Augustine's Christianized Platonism and deontological ethics, from which he argued that human free will is voluntary and spontaneous yet subject to sin unless changed by grace, and John Duns Scotus's view that human will holds primacy over reason. The latter's assertion that choice is random proved especially influential to Cartesian thought and liberal Christian theology.

60. Harak, *Virtuous Passions*, 2.

- The **"perceptions dimension."** Recognizes the need to be self-aware and self-critical about loyalties and presuppositions that shape our way of seeing (Matt 6:21–22). Additionally, perception of the context powerfully shapes one's response.[61]

In summary, the self-oriented secular ethic that dominates social thought is rooted in expressive individualism that celebrates self-justification and is insufficient to meet the Christian moral standard. The moral posturing inherent in secular ethics is an illusion, even when united to religious or benevolent insight and action. Self-determined and self-achieved good works fall short of the godly standard.[62]

Instead, the Christian minister must find grace and contentment in God alone (Phil 4:10–13) and his identity in Christ alone (Eph 2:10).[63] Section 4 fully develops this endeavor. Unfortunately, the secular opinions and expectations of congregants and denominations alike often contribute to the pressures that contribute to moral failure and deserve our attention.

THE NEED TO BUILD A BETTER HOUSE

"Those who love to be feared fear to be loved, and they themselves are more afraid than anyone, for whereas other men fear only them, they fear everyone."

— Saint Francis de Sales

Seafarers and mariners are not the only ones who need protection against perfect storms. Hurricanes caused $2.6 trillion in property damage from 1980 to August 2023 in the United States alone.[64] This analogy certainly lends itself to the homes and families destroyed by acts of sexual immorality,

---

61. For example, in the context of ministerial moral failure, an overseer, mentor, or church that reduces sin to a set of behaviors tends to be judgmental while those who recognize sin as a state of brokenness, "a shared condition that influences all humanity," will see the violator as an equal in need of grace (McMinn, *Psychology, Theology, and Spirituality in Christian Counseling*, 216).

62. Paul Freston goes so far as to cite this tendency as why evangelicals often gain political power only to slide into various scandals. He observes, "The legalist who depends on rules, when he enters a sphere for which his church has not elaborated rules, becomes literally unruly. . . . they are legalists and therefore people without principles" (Freston, "Evangelicals and Politics in the Third World," 125–26).

63. To find this requires one emerge from the darkness that hinders relationship with God; to abandon one's selfish and lustful desires to know and love God and find true happiness in Him alone (see Pascal, *Pensées*, 46).

64. National Oceanic and Atmospheric Administration, "Hurricane Costs," figure 1.

STORMFRONT NO. 2—THE WORLD (CULTURAL)

and we will have much to say on that issue. For now, let us turn our attention to the church home that must also protect against these cataclysmic effects. The sad truth is most are ill-prepared to weather the storm.

Perhaps you are familiar with Jesus' parable of the wise and foolish builders (Matt 7:24–27). The story describes two storm-ravaged houses built on very different foundations. What was the cause for the difference? Many will say the solid rock represents God's Word, but that is incorrect. Both builders received the Word. Obedience to that Word provided the solid foundation (and subsequent survival).[65]

The contemporary church has significant cracks in its foundation. These include selective literalism (adhering to Scriptures one is willing or able to accept while discarding the rest), biblical illiteracy, and the intrusion of secular worldviews and ideologies. Narcissistic power structures, egoism, and personal preferences have seeped through the cracks. Pertinent to this book's topic, many churches find themselves submerged in a "moral revolution" that sees increasing numbers accepting divorce culture, the liberation of sex from reproduction, openness to divergent sexualities, the prevalence of heterosexual cohabitation, and the normalization of homosexuality.[66]

The church is to be in the world but not of the world (John 17:11–16). Cracked foundations allow the world to be in the church but not of the church.

That is not to lay blame for moral failures on broken church structures alone. Causal factors of ministerial sexual failure are as unique as the individuals who fall prey. Indeed, this is the perfect storm of which we speak. But sometimes, churches fail to provide a safe harbor to weather the storm. The cracks in their foundations give the stormwaters access, and the minister and church are soon over their heads.

Recent scholarship has identified common cracks that facilitate if not foster, ethical failures among leaders. Notables are Art Padilla's "toxic triangle" and Diane Chandler's "perfect storm."[67] Both identify three characteristics that culminate in unethical behaviors: the confluence of destructive tendencies within the leader, susceptible followers, and conducive environments/situational context. The bottom line is that many churches

---

65. Indeed, foundations are everything. It is notable that righteousness and justice are the foundation of God's throne (Ps 89:14), the church was founded on Peter's confession that Jesus is the Christ and the Son of God (Matt 16:13–18), and expansion of that church is founded on Jesus (Isa 28:16, 1 Cor 3:9–11).

66. See Mohler, *We Cannot Be Silent*.

67. Padilla, et. al., "Toxic Triangle," 176–94; Chandler, "Perfect Storm of Leaders' Unethical Behavior," 69–93.

have professing Christians who either do not know, care, or believe these illicit sexual behaviors are wrong.

While Padilla notes the role of "susceptible followers," Chandler more pointedly identifies the "lack of effective accountability and viable support systems" by categorizing followers as conforming, colluding, or conspiring.[68] Indeed, spiritual empowerment that lacks accountability provides fertile ground for narcissistic personality disorders. Whether agreeable acolytes or supportive sycophants, these enablers elevate the minister, subordinate others, and demand accountability to the structure rather than the scriptural standard.[69] Unquestioned and uncorrected narcissistic tendencies (often initially viewed as strong leadership qualities) inevitably devolve into grandiosity, entitlement, and a lack of empathy.[70] The scenario typically results in abusive behaviors; the minister becomes predatory, and the enablers become protective.

Referenced earlier, Ravi Zacharias provides a telling example. The international apologist was interested in Eastern treatment, a therapeutic approach that harmonizes the body's chemistry and strengthens physical and emotional systems. He invested in two spas, Touch of Eden and Jivan Wellness, in Alpharetta, Georgia. He intended to use the spas as a conduit for Ayurvedic massage to support his philanthropic ministry. A personal masseuse soon became part of his travel entourage.

While ministers who accompanied Zacharias said they never witnessed inappropriate behavior, one high-level staff member urged Zacharias not to bring the masseuse "not because they feared actual impropriety but because they feared the appearance of impropriety."[71] Zacharias "grew angry and barely spoke to this staff member for a long period of time," who was effectively "sent to Siberia."[72] Zacharias ultimately sexually harassed three women at the two spas he co-owned and had inappropriate relationships with other women. At the same time, his electronic devices contained more than two hundred "selfie"-style photographs of women.[73]

In response to the independent investigation, the Ravi Zacharias International Ministries board of directors described the victimization perpetrated by its founder as "horrendous."[74] The board affirmed its mis-

---

68. Chandler, "Perfect Storm of Leaders' Unethical Behavior," 78–79.
69. McKnight and Barringer, *Church Called Tov*, 27.
70. DeGroat, *When Narcissism Comes to Church*, locs. 237, 294.
71. Barron and Eiselstein, "Report of Independent Investigation," 7.
72. Barron and Eiselstein, "Report of Independent Investigation," 6.
73. Barron and Eiselstein, "Report of Independent Investigation," 2.
74. RZIM, "Open Letter from the International Board of Directors," para. 4.

placed trust "in Ravi's denial of moral wrongdoing and in his deceptive explanations."[75] The board acknowledged the need "to take an extensive and humbling look at ways that we have fallen short" and adequately diagnose and address "significant structural, policy, and cultural problems" that often exist in prolonged abuse—specifically, the failure of accountability.[76] While the contributing factors to Zacharias's moral failures are not uncommon, the board's confession and contrite apology certainly are. While preceded by numerous defenses and official rejections of abuse claims that "lacked compassion and concern,"[77] the repentance demonstrated runs contrary to the self-justifying morality that has come to dominate Western culture and Christianity.

Suffice it to say, we not only have a problem in the church—in many cases, the church is part of the problem. What can we do? David struggled under a similar burden when he asked, "If the foundations are destroyed, What can the righteous do?" (Ps 11:3). The answer is in Ps 12:

> Help, Lord, for the godly person has come to an end,
> For the faithful have disappeared from the sons of mankind.
> They speak lies to one another;
> They speak with flattering lips and a double heart.
> May the Lord cut off all flattering lips,
> The tongue that speaks great things;
> Who have said, "With our tongue we will prevail;
> Our lips are our own; who is lord over us?"
> "Because of the devastation of the poor, because of the groaning of the needy,
> Now I will arise," says the Lord; "I will put him in the safety for which he longs."
> The words of the Lord are pure words;
> Like silver refined in a furnace on the ground, filtered seven times.
> You, Lord, will keep them;
> You will protect him from this generation forever.
> The wicked strut about on every side
> When vileness is exalted among the sons of mankind.

Indeed, we pray you to help, Lord, and bring us into the haven where the foundations are sure and the harbor is safe. Only the truth of God's pure words can seal the foundation's expanding cracks and flush out the stagnant

---

75. RZIM, "Open Letter from the International Board of Directors," para. 7.
76. RZIM, "Open Letter from the International Board of Directors," para. 12–13.
77. RZIM, "Open Letter from the International Board of Directors," para. 14.

secularism. How might one discern this sacred truth? Here is a simple way to test the waters. Any "truth" comprised of worldly wisdom and accepted by worldly people is not of God. Divine truth is confirmed by Scripture, accepted by the godly, and resisted by the worldly.[78] As A. W. Tozer rightly asserts, "You can always test the quality of religious teaching by the enthusiastic reception it receives from unsaved men. If the natural man receives it enthusiastically, it is not of the Spirit of God."[79] If worldly people find life lessons in the minister's book, affirmation in his podcast, or are comfortable in the sanctuary, but there is no conviction of sin and urgency to run to Jesus, then roll up your pant legs. There are cracks in that foundation and a storm on the horizon.

Such understanding provides a sound and timely segue as we prepare to battle the third element of the perfect storm. Brace yourself, for this one is the most dangerous of all.

Once more into the abyss . . .

---

78. 1 John 4:1–6. See also 1 Cor 2:14, 2 Cor 11:14–15, 1 Thess 5:21, Jas 3:15.
79. Tozer, *The Crucified Life*, 61.

6

Stormfront No. 3—The Devil (Spiritual)

"Like a good chess player, Satan is always trying to maneuver you into a position where you can save your castle only by losing your bishop."

— C. S. Lewis

OUR EVALUATION HAS CONSIDERED two elements of the perfect storm: the flesh/emotions and the world/culture. If one defines culture as the people's collective thinking, then whoever controls the mind controls culture. Here, we meet this terrible triad's final and most powerful element—the spiritual forces that align against you. If unopposed, these spiritual forces will become a "master of disaster."

Again, this perfect storm is a convergence. Its inception is often negligible and unnoticed. Perhaps someone or something exposes a long-buried hurt. The manufactured smile belies the truth addressed in chapter 4: the triggered individual does not simply *remember* the event but *relives* the event. Your thoughts go round and round, and like a tropical storm that gains strength from the warm ocean waters, your storm soon reaches hurricane strength. Your mood darkens.

Here, the devils join the fight. They antagonize. They amplify. Then, they offer a way out, a way to calm your storm. As noted above, these spiritual entities know exactly what bait will lure you from God's safe harbor. These watchful devils know your strengths and weaknesses, your wishes and wants. They know your tendencies and tempers. What you like and what you lack. They know who you love, what you love, and how you love.

They know *you*.

And this is how they are able to carry you away, enticed by your own lust (Jas 1:14). No need to endure such pain and pressure, they say. Out on that horizon awaits everything you desire ... everything you *deserve*! The world's influence soon floods in, beckoning you on. They justify and encourage a little pleasure cruise. You soon raise the anchor and cast off, determined to venture just a little way out. Indeed, "no man chooses evil because it is evil; he only mistakes it for happiness, the good he seeks."[1]

The journey begins well—after all, sin is pleasurable for a season (Heb 11:25). Driven by various winds, you sail farther out, enjoying the ride and confident you can keep the ship afloat. Eventually, you spot trouble on the horizon. Ominous clouds foretell danger to come. Perhaps you can get to the harbor before being hit by the coming storm. Perhaps you have before. Perhaps disciplined devotion to your faith and sacred office enabled a white-knuckled turnaround before past storms battered your vessel. Perhaps. But this storm intensifies beyond your abilities. You desperately look toward the safe harbor, but the whisper of doubt rolls like thunder: "You are too far gone. No one will help you. No one can help you. And no one would let you return if they knew what you had done. Not even God." You decide that your best hope is to ride the storm out. But you can neither navigate nor escape this storm. You are taking on water and sinking fast.

Keep a life raft in proximity if you do not buy into all this talk about devilish deceptions. After all, "the greatest trick the devil ever pulled was convincing the world he didn't exist."[2] Such threat is why a holistic restoration plan must give special attention to the spiritual deceptions that lead ministers into the snare of sexual sins and then seek to deny their rescue and possible restoration. Failure to provide spiritual credence would be catastrophic in the eyes of C. S. Lewis, who rightly notes that "there are two equal and opposite errors into which our race can fall about the devils. One is to disbelieve in their existence. The other is to believe, and to feel an excessive and unhealthy interest in them. They themselves are equally pleased by both errors."[3]

Holistic restoration demands one understand how sin entices and enslaves if one is ever to overcome that temptation. The progression of sin from thought to inclination to action is well-expressed in Scripture

---

1. Though often attributed to *Frankenstein* author Mary Shelley, this quote originates with her mother, Mary Wollstonecraft, in "A Vindication of the Rights of Men, in a Letter to the Right Honourable Edmund Burke; Occasioned by his Reflections on the Revolution in France," printed in 1790.

2. Though some readers may attribute this quote to Keyser Söze, played by Kevin Spacey in the 1995 thriller *The Usual Suspects*, Charles Baudelaire deserves credit for coining the phrase in "The Generous Gambler," a short story printed in the Paris newspaper *Le Figaro* in 1864.

3. Lewis, *Screwtape Letters*, ix.

and notably in Jesus' Sermon on the Mount (Matt 5–7). Most pertinent to this book is the insightful analysis of Jerusalem's first pastor regarding sin's conception, birth, and the death sin ultimately brings (Jas 1:14–16). Specifically, this tactic sees the individual tempted when carried away and enticed by his desire (*epithymia*). This Greek word conveys a negative application common to matters such as lust, selfish ambition, or evil desire.

Furthermore, the temptation (*peirasmos*) "is clearly restricted in origin to the internal, to its source lodged within us."[4] Such temptation encourages the individual to accept self-oriented solutions to satisfy the needs caused by emotional wounding(s). Because the evil desire is of the individual's making and choosing, it is equally the individual's responsibility. James warns that failure to take responsibility will bring forth death. This death is not to be understood as one possible or unfortunate consequence, as his use of the verb form *apotelestheisa* indicates spiritual death is the completion of sin's goal. Therefore, this chapter will address the pressures imposed by unbiblical ministerial standards, temptation, the seven deadly sins, and the critical need for divine guidance.

MINISTERING AT CRUSH DEPTH

> "Behold, I have found only this, that God made men upright,
> but they have sought out many devices."
>
> — KING SOLOMON, ECCL 7:29

Getting you in too deep is a favorite tactic of the spiritual forces. When taking a deep dive, we find a great example in the Virginia-class submarines, half of which are built not far from the church I serve. As a journalist covering our nation's military, I had the privilege of touring a number of these remarkable vessels. The $2.5 billion sub comes in at 337 feet and 7,800 tons (longer but lighter than the Seawolf class), can hit speeds greater than twenty-five knots, stay submerged for three months, and operate for thirty-three years without refueling. But that is not what gives the enemy pause. The Block V and later variants boast unmatched stealth and can launch everything from torpedoes and unmanned undersea vehicles to SEAL teams and forty Tomahawk missiles.

Indeed, these attack subs rule the depths but are limited by "crush depth." Officially, the Virginia-class operates around eight hundred feet. In truth, the subs can submerge twice and perhaps thrice as deep. But once

---

4. Nystrom, *James*, 74.

they pass the classified crush depth, things go very bad very fast (they call it "crush depth" for a reason).

The issue is pressure. A vessel at two thousand feet experiences more than nine hundred pounds of force exerted on every square inch. Every thirty-three feet of depth adds 14.7 psi. That means *Titanic*, which rests 12,400 feet below the ocean's surface, experiences 5,500 pounds of force on every square inch of its surface. That's a lot of pressure.

Ministers also experience remarkable pressures as they navigate unseen depths to rebuff any enemy infiltrator. Like a submarine on patrol, some pressures are common to the task. Others, not so much.

The devil's chief mission is to exert sufficient pressure to crush the minister and ministry. Three tactics are remarkably efficient: unfair, unbiblical, and ungodly expectations. Let's pop the periscope and look at each.

First, we have unfair expectations. By this, I mean unfair demands placed on the minister by the congregation. To illustrate, I offer the following email shared by a fellow minister who likes to poke bears:

> The perfect pastor preaches for exactly fifteen minutes. He condemns sin but never upsets anyone. He works from 8 am to midnight and is also the janitor. He makes fifty dollars a week, wears good clothes, buys good books, drives a good car, and gives about fifty dollars weekly in the offering. He is twenty-eight years old and has been preaching for thirty years. He has a burning desire to work with teenagers and spends all his time with senior citizens. He makes fifteen calls daily to church families, shut-ins, and the hospitalized. He spends all his time door-knocking but is always in his office when needed. The perfect pastor has a perfect wife and perfect children, and their perfect family will make every birthday party, recital and church function. The perfect pastor will bless every wedding, provide any counseling, and preach every funeral. He will bring a covered dish to every chicken dinner. He will fix your car when its broken, mow your lawn when needed, and babysit your kids every weekend. And he will do all this and preach a power-packed sermon every Sunday . . . which lasts only fifteen minutes.

While good for a laugh (though hitting a bit close to home), I would define the perfect pastor as one intimate with God and committed to the primary purpose of that calling.[5] God anoints and instructs the pastor for

---

5. To be clear, the pastor's primary purpose is to equip the saints for the work of ministry, build the body of Christ until all attain unity in and of the faith, and enable believers through instruction in the knowledge of God's Son until each reaches maturity and stature found only in the fullness of Christ (see Eph 4:11–13).

STORMFRONT NO. 3—THE DEVIL (SPIRITUAL)

every task, and s/he obeys these ordained steps. The perfect pastor is, first and foremost, a servant of God and, therefore, a servant of God's people but not a slave to their demands. S/he is consumed by the fire of God and passionate to see it spread. S/he can come boldly to the throne of grace, has faith to move mountains, offers effectual and fervent prayers that avail much, is humble in reflection and committed to growth, and is determined to see others flourish.

To which does your ministry more closely align?

Whether you love to serve, love to help, or just want to keep the peace, unbiblical demands quickly bring you dangerously close to crush depth. As William Willimon warns, the great ethical danger is not ministers might burn out, but black out, "that is lose consciousness as to why we are here and who we are called to be for Christ and his church."[6]

Most ministers are stretched too thin and tend to live on the edge of physical and emotional limits, which is a dangerous place to reside. Demands placed on clergy put pastors at significantly greater risk for depression than any other occupation, military and emergency services included. The depression rate among clergy is slightly more than double the national rate of 5.5 percent. Anxiety rates among the clergy are 13.5 percent and more than 7 percent simultaneously experienced depression and anxiety.[7] Seventy percent of pastors regularly consider leaving the ministry. Roughly 40 percent do, most after only five years.[8]

While some ministers evade the pressures of unbiblical demands, the pressures of unbiblical expectations crush many. This second satanic strategy sees church or denominational leaders cast secular, rather than sacred, ministerial vision. The unspoken emphasis is on building a larger congregation, often at the expense of building a better and biblical congregation. Because pastors and church members often equate size with success or attendance with anointing, church growth has become the force that often drives preaching and priorities. Under pressure to increase nickels and noses, formulaic programs and seminars present church growth in ways designed to maximize capacity and contributions. Business rather than biblical models provide the standard measures determining whether a ministry is "successful." Numeric and financial growth validates the ministerial

---

6. Willimon, *Calling and Character*, 21.

7. Duke Divinity School, "Clergy More Likely to Suffer from Depression, Anxiety."

8. Krejcir, "Statistics on Pastors."

vision and personal value. Image takes precedent over impact and charisma over cruciformity.[9]

In this construct, ministerial success and ministerial formation are rarely compatible. As a result, many ministerial ordination and training programs have abandoned holistic formation and concentrated instead on marketing and skills-based training.[10] The emphasis on management over maturation renders many ill-equipped to handle ministerial stress rightly. The inability to manage or mitigate such challenges exacerbates the tendency to find self-worth and identity in personal performance. It leads some to abuse ministerial authority and act inappropriately toward vulnerable followers. The analysis of wreckage finds sexual malfeasance among four prevalent disorders that result. The other three are depression, post-traumatic stress disorder, and substance abuse.[11] While all four will see the vessel slowly descend into the depths, self-appeasing actions that are sexual are especially devastating. Sexual impropriety violates the sacred trust of ministry, shatters victims' emotional and spiritual wellness, destroys unity within the church, and hinders the reception of God's grace and message in the community.

Ungodly expectations are the third and final satanic strategy to crush the minister and ministry. While the previous were external to the minister, these pressures are self-inflicted by those seeking power or popularity.

Henri Nouwen captures this tendency well by correlating contemporary ministry and Jesus' wilderness temptations. Nouwen posits that Satan urged Jesus to be relevant by turning the stones into bread, to be spectacular by leaping from the temple in demonstration of God's power and favor, and to be powerful by receiving a kingdom without having to bear a cross (Matt 4:1–11, Luke 4:1–13).[12]

Be relevant! Be spectacular! Be powerful!

Be careful.

Such demands are unbiblical and arguably satanic. The acclaimed priest and psychologist goes on to say:

---

9. "Cruciformity" refers to a formative process oriented toward the selfless death of flesh that is inherent to Jesus' crucifixion and central to Paul's theology, expressed most notably in Gal 2:20. Notably, Kenneth Boa identifies six distortions of the church foster manipulation rather than ministry: human agendas of power, institutionalism, a quest for significance, repackaging cultural agendas in spiritual language, diminished diversity and commitment, and the imposition of marketing, management, and entertainment models (Boa, *Conformed to His Image*, 428).

10. DeGroat, *When Narcissism Comes to Church*, loc. 323; Flynn, "Firewall," 309–24.

11. Rediger, *Fit to be a Pastor*, 124.

12. Nouwen, *In the Name of Jesus*.

STORMFRONT NO. 3 — THE DEVIL (SPIRITUAL)

> The long painful history of the Church is the history of people ever and again tempted to choose power over love, control over the cross, being a leader over being led. Those who resisted this temptation to the end and thereby give us hope are the true saints. One thing is clear to me: the temptation of power is greatest when intimacy is a threat. Much Christian leadership is exercised by people who do not know how to develop healthy, intimate relationships and have opted for power and control instead. Many Christian empire-builders have been people unable to give and receive love.[13]

Nouwen is not the only one to recognize the contemporary tendency to measure worth by secular (satanic?) means. As noted in chapter 4, Scazzero warns against three powerful temptations: I am what I do (performance), I am what I have (possessions), and I am what others think (popularity), and Robert McGee presents the "satanic formula" which states Self-Worth = Performance + Others' Opinions. In addition, Kenneth Boa agrees that many "seek to validate their worth and find fulfillment through achievement and performance" and warns that feelings of competence and fulfillment can be "thwarted by direct and indirect experiences of performance rejection that can lead to feelings of personal inadequacy."[14]

Brace for impact.

Ministers who strive to be relevant, spectacular, or powerful will find the authority or anointing alluring. Cravings for plaudits and popularity will form them into ever-affirming charmers who espouse self-help sermons and turn sanctuaries into social clubs. They do this in the name of God but introduce few to the God they name. Such ministers feed off the honor, respect, admiration, and affirmation that ministry (seemingly) affords.

Inevitably, the pressures become too much to bear. The relevant, spectacular, and powerful pastor is ill-equipped to handle conspiring church bosses or bring biblical correction to an influential member or big giver who might leave. The minister will buckle under the undeserved criticism from unfaithful members, the heartbreak that follows every departure, and the weightiness of every hospital visit and funeral. Equally crushing are the months that end with more need than money. Let us not forget the unending struggles with the spiritually immature and the super-spiritual alike, the drain caused by the overly needy and the uncaring, the countless counseling sessions that fall on deaf ears, and the countless hours of study and

---

13. Nouwen, *In the Name of Jesus*, 60.
14. Boa, *Conformed to His Image*, 108.

SECTION TWO: ELEMENTS OF THE PERFECT STORM

preparation for sermons soon forgotten. Oh yeah, and there are demonic attacks leveled against you and your family throughout.

Here, a shepherd will stand while a hireling will seek a bigger or better church.

I am not saying that one should avoid ministry. I am saying that unless you are absolutely sure of ministerial calling, do something else. Ministry—biblical ministry—is not sugar and spice and everything nice. Real ministry is difficult and draining. Real ministry can be vicious. Real ministry is a battleship, not a cruise ship. Just ask Moses, Elijah, Job, Jeremiah, and Jonah. Real ministry drove each to the brink of crush depth and left each wishing they were dead or had never been born.[15]

Such stress beckons the beleaguered to find respite, but malformation often points them in the wrong direction. Michael Todd Wilson and Brad Hoffman give a powerful insight. With the premise that "great ministers don't just happen" and "great falls from ministry don't just happen either," the duo discovered seven consistent contributors to all ministerial failures: (1) lack of genuine intimacy in relationships with God, spouse, and others; (2) a distorted sense of calling; (3) inadequate stress-management skills; (4) lack of appropriate boundaries; (5) failure to prioritize recreation; (6) insufficient people skills; and (7) underdeveloped leadership skills.[16]

How close are we to crush depth? Dangerously close. According to various studies, between 75 percent and 90 percent of pastors felt unqualified or inadequately trained to cope with ministry. Half said they are unable to meet the demands, 71 percent said they battle depression weekly, and 81 percent felt ill-equipped to disciple/mentor others in Christian formation. Eighty percent of pastors said ministry affects their families negatively, with 33 percent calling it an outright hazard. Seventy-seven percent said they do not have a good marriage. Sadly, 38 percent were divorced or currently in a divorce process, and 30 percent had an ongoing affair or a one-time sexual encounter with a parishioner. Perhaps most telling is that only 23 percent of pastors said they "felt happy and content on a regular basis with who they are in Christ, in their church, and in their home."[17]

---

15. For Moses, Num 11:13–15; for Elijah, 1 Kgs 19:4; for Job, Job 3:11; for Jeremiah, Jer 20:14; for Jonah, Jonah 4:8.

16. Wilson and Hoffmann, *Preventing Ministry Failure*, 9. While commendable, this list lacks a critical factor to (re)formation: the effect of negative trauma that proves deformative in developing self-identity, self-worth, and worldview as addressed in chapter 4.

17. These statistics are compiled from Fuller Institute of Church Growth, "1991 Survey of Pastors"; Krejcir, "Statistics on Pastors"; London and Wiseman, *Pastors at Greater Risk*, 20.

A national survey of fourteen thousand pastors found that roughly one-quarter face significant marital problems.[18] Jack Balswick and John Thoburn argue that such numbers are critical because marital dissatisfaction, coupled with work boredom, is a top contributor to sexual liaisons.[19] According to Thoburn and D. M. Whitman, marital stress negatively affects marital satisfaction, and marital dissatisfaction is a primary factor in pastoral infidelity.[20] Conversely, a healthy and sexually satisfying relationship with one's wife and an open, accountable relationship with at least one other minister has been the two most important factors in preventing male ministers' moral failure.[21] More than one-fourth of male pastors cite their relationship with their wives as the most important reason for sexual fidelity.[22]

If you have or will accept the call, don't set sail until you know your crush depth and are well-trained in the godly strategies that will relieve any pressures that may threaten your vessel. And know this: even when you win this battle, your enemy will not easily surrender. If Satan cannot crush you, he will try to entice you.

HAVING CONCEIVED, DESIRES GIVE BIRTH

> "People caught in addictive and immoral patterns of behavior are subjected to some of the cruelest harassment of the enemy. First, Satan temps them into sin and then mercilessly condemns them for sinning."
>
> — NEIL ANDERSON

Jerusalem's first pastor gave fair warning regarding sin's conception, birth, and the death it ultimately brings (Jas 1:14–16). How are we so naïve as to take the bait time and again? Before considering the enemy's enticing tactics, let us rightly understand this deadly weapon called "sin." After all, you cannot defeat what you do not define.

Scripture uses various passive and active words to describe that sin. For example, the Hebrew רָשָׁע (rāšāʾ) describes a wicked and impious person who lived without respect for God's Law.[23] Similarly, the Greek words ἀδικί (adikia) and πονηρία (ponéria) capture inward corruption or

---

18. Barna and Kinnamon, *State of Pastors*, 36.
19. Balswick and Thoburn, "How Ministers Deal with Sexual Temptation," 277.
20. Thoburn and Whitman, "Clergy Affairs," 492.
21. Thoburn, "Predictive Factors," 108.
22. Balswick and Thoburn, "How Ministers Deal with Sexual Temptation," 277.
23. Green et al., *Dictionary of Jesus and the Gospels*, 863. E.g., Ps 1:1.

perversion of character. The former denotes irreverence and unrighteousness.[24] The latter speaks of vicious or degenerate wickedness.[25] Trespass or transgression, specifically when one goes beyond a known boundary, is conveyed by the Hebrew עָבַר (*'abar*) and the Greek παράβασις (*parabasis*).[26] The Greek ἀνομία (*anomia*) describes lawlessness or the disregard for a known law.[27] The Hebrew terms פָּשַׁע (*pasha'*) and סָרַר (*sarar*), as well as the Greek words ἀπείθεια (*apeitheia*), ἀφίστημι (*aphistémi*), and ἀποστασία (*apostasia*), speak of rebellious disobedience.[28] However, the most common words used to depict sin are the Hebrew חָטָא (*chata'*) and the Greek ἁμαρτάνω (*hamartanō*).[29] Both words denote missing the target; *chata'* suggests a deliberate and culpable decision to fail, while *hamartanō* indicates the violator is aiming at the wrong target.[30]

Sin is not only defiance and disobedience but also deviation—a willful or uncorrected departure resulting in liable failure to fulfill God's intent. We aim to please ourselves rather than God, and thus, we miss the mark. The deviation causes immediate alienation from God, others, and oneself.[31] Alienation from God creates what the existentialist philosopher Søren Kierkegaard describes as an "infinite gulf" that God alone can bridge.[32] Alienated from God, everything begins to fall apart.[33] Athanasius describes this as dissolution of physical, spiritual, and psychological integrity resulting in corruption.[34] Such refusal of God "constitutes a radical denial of oneself that

---

24. Erickson, *Christian Theology*, 521–52.

25. Stott, *Cross of Christ*, 91.

26. Erickson, *Christian Theology*, 522–23.

27. Erickson, *Christian Theology*, 522.

28. Erickson, *Christian Theology*, 523–24.

29. Erickson, *Christian Theology*, 519–21.

30. Erickson, *Christian Theology*, 520. See also Green et al., *Dictionary of Jesus and the Gospels*, 863.

31. This alienation is immediately evident in Eden as Adam and Even hide from God, are ashamed, and confrontational (Gen 3:8–16). The subsequent worship of self, based on a fractured view of self, often leads to fractured relations with God and others and abuse or neglect of calling. The Old Testament expresses such understanding in describing sin as defiling the name of God (Lev 20:3; Ezek 43:8), the people of God (Jer 2:23; Ezek 20:43; Hos 5:3; 6:10), and the place of God (Lev 18:24–30; 20:2; Num 19:20; Deut 21:23; 2 Chr 36:14; Ps 106:38; Isa 24:5; Jer 2:7; 3:1–2, 9).

32. Lane, *Concise History of Christian Thought*, 268.

33. Namely, the body (Rom 6:6, 12; 7:24; 8:10, 13), the mind (Rom 1:21; 2 Cor 3:14–15; 4:4), and the emotions (Rom 1:26–27; Gal 5:24; 2 Tim 3:2–4).

34. Athanasius, *On the Incarnation*, 113. Because God created everything from nothing, it is necessary to recognize that everything remains suspended over the void of nothingness, held by the God who sustains and gives meaning to all things.

threatens one's own reason for being."[35] Similarly, the German pastor and theologian Dietrich Bonhoeffer describes this as "the process of disunion."[36] In his view, humanity can know good and evil only apart from God. Because this knowledge comes through estrangement from the origin, the individual defines good and evil in relationship to self rather than God. Worse, this self-oriented disunion places the individual in enmity with God.[37]

Augustine's theology of original sin offers valuable insight. His persistent renunciation presents sin as neither created by nor co-eternal with God, who is unchangeably good and the creator of all that is good. Instead, evil is the absence or "privation of good until at last a thing ceases altogether to be."[38] Indeed, human nature "has a tremendous capacity for self-deception and evil in the guise of good."[39] Thus, inordinate love of a lesser good, typically perceived as a greater good, arises from misusing free will and renders the individual responsible.[40]

Many church fathers rely on Augustine's Christianized Platonism to bridge that gulf and sequester the sinful nature. Unfortunately, the modified dualism inherent to Augustine's theology leads them to emphasize asceticism to "avoid, suppress, and ultimately escape" what they perceive as an inherently inferior physical world along with its sinful bodily functions.[41] This approach is not conducive to a holistic restoration, which views the human dilemma as moral rather than metaphysical. Pertinent to this book's topic, Josh Harris rightly asserts that "part of the challenge Christians face in a lust-filled world is remembering that neither sex nor sexuality is our enemy."[42] Nothing is unclean in itself (Rom 14:14). "It becomes unclean only when sinners use it to express their rebellion against God. The line between good and evil is not drawn between one part of creation and another

---

Therefore, to turn from God is to cast oneself into that abyss; to turn toward non-being and thus become corrupt.

35. Macchia, *Justified in the Spirit*, 422.

36. Bonhoeffer, *Ethics*, 22–29.

37. Isa 59:2; Rom 8:7–10; 1 Cor 2:14; Eph 2:15–16.

38. Augustine, *Confessions of St. Augustine*, 37.

39. Trull and Carter, *Ministerial Ethics*, 50. The authors cite as central to this assertion Niebuhr, *Nature and Destiny of Man*.

40. Wogaman, *Christian Ethics*, 54.

41. Pearcey, *Total Truth*, 76–77. Notably, Bonhoeffer's review of monasticism reveals the "fatal error" of this approach. This "living protest against the . . . cheapening of grace" soon transformed humble discipleship into meritorious achievement, and the "monk's attempt to flee from the world turned out to be a subtle form of love for the world" (Bonhoeffer, *Cost of Discipleship*, 46–47).

42. Harris, *Not Even a Hint*, 26.

part but runs through the human heart itself—in our own disposition to use the creation for good or for evil."[43]

This understanding of sin is critical in addressing sexual immorality, as "the heart always provides for what it values."[44] The propensity to provide (and, therefore, pursue evil) resides in one's pride, defined as self-exaltation amid the depreciation of others and denial of one's need for God's help.[45] Pride accentuates the error and evil of others while giving unmerited weight to one's unrealistic good; it entails narcissism and self-glorification, "being in love with [one's] idealized image."[46]

Indeed, sin is the target and pride the weapon—but how does the enemy get one to pull the trigger? In truth, we've known this tactic for quite some time.

Catholic theology identifies pride as commanding seven deadly or capital sins. These, in turn, employ all other sins in the privation of good.[47] Indeed, "like cancer, sin kills because it reproduces."[48]

John of the Cross expounds Aquinas's theology in telling terms. Though more than four centuries old, his definition of capital sins closely resembles the tendencies common to today's sexually immoral ministers and the toxic church cultures that enable sexual sins to flourish.[49] The approach by John of the Cross provides valuable insight into how each capital sin works to lead the believer astray. Obsessive negative thoughts or

---

43. Pearcey, *Total Truth*, 84. This approach displays the theological distinction between structure and direction. Structure refers to the created character of the world, which is still good even after the Fall. Direction refers to the way we "direct" those structures to serve either God or idols.

44. Boa, *Conformed to His Image*, 47. Cf. Matt 6:19–34.

45. Okholm, *Dangerous Passions Deadly Sins*, 162–63.

46. Katz, "Self-Esteem," 310.

47. Capital sins understood as the source of all sins that contradict Christian holiness. Whether these sins are mortal (a rejection resulting in spiritual death) or venial (one that may lead to damnation but does not sever union with God) depends on the degree to which they oppose God's love and grace.

48. Plantinga, *Not the Way It's Supposed to Be*, 55.

49. John of the Cross, *Dark Night of the Soul*, 36–90. Specifically, he defines pride as an unteachable tendency to condemn others and become impatient with their faults. Avarice is discontentment with God-given spirituality. Those who struggle in this way strive to learn rather than grow in poverty of spirit and interior life. Lust finds more pleasure in the spiritual blessings of God than God himself. Wrath easily evokes irritation, lacks sweetness, and has little patience to wait on God. Gluttony resists the cross and chooses pleasures as do children. Envy constantly compares and is unhappy when others do well; it not only wants what others have but does not want them to have the same. Sloth pursues spiritual sweetness and good feelings and will run from difficult challenges or appraisal.

judgments typically digress from sinful attitude to sinful action.[50] Thus, sexual immorality "stems from the sinfulness of the heart and a reluctance to be in a passionate, dependent relationship with God."[51]

The Christian's formative response, sixteen centuries in the making, recognizes and engages the seven deadly sins: vainglory, avarice, lust, envy, gluttony, wrath, and sloth.[52] The deadly sins, arguably lost in Protestant thought, is a theological paradigm by which Christians can rightly recognize and respond to spiritual conflicts initiated by personal temptations.

The seven deadly sins are rooted in virtues and vices—acquired moral qualities cultivated (or conquered) through habit and gradually internalized through years of formation. Repeated activity increases one's proficiency and gradually forms one's character. Evagrius of Pontus first identified the deadly sins as eight evil thoughts or demons (*logismoi*) employed to deceive and deter the Christian believer.[53] This understanding emerged when Evagrius, along with the desert fathers of the Eastern Orthodox tradition, had withdrawn into the wilderness to cultivate a contemplative spirit by which they could face and overcome temptation.

Evagrius's disciple John Cassian introduced this theology to the Western church and grouped the vices into three alliances that form against the believer.[54] Gluttony and lust involve the body and the soul; therefore, one should conquer these first. Along with avarice, they comprise the concupiscible or the strong desire of fleshly appetites. Cassian's emotional category included anger, sadness, and despondency, while he placed vainglory and pride in the category of rational thought.

Pope Gregory I honed Cassian's list to seven and presented these in the context of spiritual warfare. Pride serves as commander-in-chief, while the seven deadly sins work in tandem as generals. All other sins are soldiers deployed by these generals to achieve the overall strategy of destruction. Catholic moral theology came to view the seven as mortal sins because they cause spiritual death, having "cut us off from God's grace when we reject the source of our spiritual life, the indwelling of the Holy Spirit."[55]

---

50. Smith, *Bible Doctrine of Sin*, 36. Cf. Jas 1:14–16.

51. Schaumburg, *False Intimacy*, 21–22.

52. This book works from the seven deadly sins first enumerated by Pope Gregory I in the sixth century and elaborated by Thomas Aquinas in the thirteenth century. Furthermore, there is agreement with Aquinas's assertion that vainglory and pride are not synonymous and that the latter is the source of all sin.

53. DeYoung, *Glittering Vices*, 27.

54. Okholm, *Dangerous Passions, Deadly Sins*, 4.

55. DeYoung, *Glittering Vices*, 35.

Thomas Aquinas accepted such notions when he further developed these seven's disastrous effects on spiritual formation and life. However, Aquinas preferred to identify the seven as "capital vices," a term that noted these seven as the source of all subsequent sin. The word "capital" derives from the Latin *caput*, meaning "head," a status defended by Aquinas when he addressed whether lust is a capital vice. In response, he defined capital vices as "that which has an exceedingly desirable end so that in his desire for it, a man goes on to the commission of many sins, all of which are said to originate in that vice as their chief source."[56] In doing so, Aquinas underscored the cataclysmic effect these seven have on spiritual formation and the dispositions and habits that incline the individual to sin.

In this view, vices are "subtle and deceptive imitations of the fullness of the human good."[57] The vices promise something good (e.g., love, happiness, comfort, affirmation, protection, pleasure, and self-worth) but provide this apart from the ultimate good, which is God. In Augustinian terms, such loves are "disordered."[58] As such, the individual seeks these genuinely good things "in a misguided or even idolatrous manner: in the wrong way, at the wrong times and wrong places, too intensely, or at the expense of other things of greater value."[59]

The initial surrender to temptation may begin as an impulsive response but inevitably gives way to a willful preference for pleasure and forms a habit. Augustine's famous prayer as a "miserable young man" captured this truth. He implored God to "grant me chastity and continency, but not yet."[60] An older and wiser Augustine would admit that he feared God would soon hear and deliver "from the disease of concupiscence, which I desired to have satisfied rather than extinguished." Yet when Augustine truly desired to end his lustful ways, he found they had become habituated; his "old mistresses enthralled me, shook my fleshly garment, and whispered softly, 'Dost thou part with us?'"[61] The vice never produced what it promised, yet habitual reliance further delayed Augustine, who was hesitant "to burst and shake

---

56. Aquinas, *Summa Theologiae*, II-II, 153–4.
57. DeYoung, *Glittering Vices*, 38.
58. Augustine, *On Christian Doctrine*, I.27. cf. Augustine, *City of God* 15.22, 25.23. Dante similarly conveys such understanding in *Purgatorio*, the second part of his classic *Divine Comedy*, in which he presented the seven deadly sins in terms of disordered love: The proud, envious, and wrathful were guilty of misdirected love; the slothful were guilty of deficient love; and the avaricious, gluttonous, and lustful were guilty of excessive love.
59. DeYoung, *Glittering Vices*, 39.
60. Augustine, *Confessions*, 17.
61. Augustine, *Confessions*, 26.

myself free from them, and to leap over whither I was called." Indeed, the deeply rooted behavior patterns evident in Augustine's example are echoed throughout the ages and offer strong testimony that the habituated individual prefers pursuing sin (and whatever "good" it promises) over a relationship with the ultimate good. Because these patterns rarely remain confined to a single act, they soon permeate all conduct and ultimately assail all character.

Scott Sullender further develops this adverse effect on character in his assertion that the historical meaning of "deadly" is best captured by the contemporary word "addictive."[62] In his view, the seven sins are addictive in nature and "begin in the mind with addictive or obsessive thinking. Then, once acted out, they have a way of driving us to sin again and again and again; they are repetitive or compulsive behaviors." As such, they are "quite capable of enslaving the human spirit and killing our psychological and spiritual freedom as children of God."[63]

In short, satanic forces target actual and perceived needs that result from emotional wounding(s) and deficient moral development to design specific temptations that promise to satisfy the desires. The minister who succumbs will experience momentary but addictive satisfaction, while desire gives way to demand as habitual behaviors increasingly reform character. Therefore, a holistic ministerial restoration plan requires the individual to recognize personal weaknesses to anticipate and eliminate temptations. By taking every thought captive and obeying Christ, the individual will ultimately destroy satanic strongholds, arguments, and all arrogance raised against the knowledge of God (2 Cor 10:4–5). However, the individual cannot do this alone. While moral and intellectual virtues are acquired, theological virtues are "infused" yet not fully formed in us (2 Pet 1:3).[64] Instead, God's sanctifying grace works in partnership with the individual's submission and obedience to replace vices with virtues and form new habits that build Christian character in the process of sanctification.

Through sanctification and holistic formation, the believer takes hold of a moral compass by which s/he can navigate the perfect storm.

---

62. Sullender, *Ancient Sins*, locs. 175–77.
63. Sullender, *Ancient Sins*, locs. 175–77.
64. Palmer, "Ethical Formation," 111.

SECTION TWO: ELEMENTS OF THE PERFECT STORM

THE NEED FOR A COMPASS THAT POINTS NORTH

"Why fight when you can negotiate?"

— CAPTAIN JACK SPARROW

The scenario is reminiscent of the compass carried ever-so-close by Captain Jack Sparrow in Disney's *Pirates of the Caribbean* movie series. Though seemingly broken, the compass is cherished by the unlikely protagonist— and with good reason. Captain Jack knows the compass does not point to true north but to what you most desire. However, the carefree pirate fails to realize that the compass can point to his desire but cannot deliver on the promise. As a result, Captain Jack continually chases the horizon in a vain effort to satisfy his insatiable desire for position, possession, pleasure, and ultimately, eternal freedom. Temptation works much the same way. Rather than point to true north, desires guide the self-oriented individual. This immoral compass may deliver the minister to his desire, but that desire rarely delivers on its promise. Instead, the adventure brings great peril and comes with unexpected costs. Just ask Captain Jack and his crew.

Reforming character requires far more than a legalistic commitment to the right behavior. As noted above, deformative life events skew the minister's determination of "right," and secular norms unduly influence him. Even an individual who rightly identifies the right behavior is incapable of meeting that standard. The human heart is so desperately wicked that one cannot come to God even if desired—and the sinful nature has no desire to do so.[65] Prevenient grace enables that turn to God, but more is involved if one is to remain on the path. Progression from ill-conceived "right" behavior requires the minister to recognize God for who he truly is, recognize himself for who he truly is, and acknowledge sin for what it truly is. Our "doing (our actions) should flow out of being (our identity); the better we grasp our identity in Christ, the more our actions should reflect Christlike character."[66]

One cannot overstate the resistance the flesh and spiritual forces offer in response. The selection of Greek words used in key spiritual formation pericopes captures this conflict well. Notable is the biblical writers' use of *agō*, *agōn*, and *agōnía*. The former means "to lead" and appears sixty-five

---

65. Isa 64:6; Jer 17:9; Matt 7:3; John 1:5; 3:19–21; Rom 1:21–22; 3:10; Eph 4:17; 1 John 1:8; cf. 2 Sam 12:1–15. This does not mean that we are void in matters of conscience. Scripture clearly teaches that we all have knowledge of right and wrong (e.g., Rom 2:15).

66. Boa, *Conformed to His Image*, 36.

STORMFRONT NO. 3 — THE DEVIL (SPIRITUAL)

times in the New Testament.[67] A pertinent example is Paul's use of the word when declaring that all whom the Spirit of God leads are sons of God (Rom 8:14). The word *agō* is the root for *agōn*, which describes an intense conflict or contest, typically of the human will. Scripture often illustrates this principle through athletic analogies.[68] Indeed, the Spirit's leading into truth and godliness starkly contrasts the human will that wants to go its own way and thus evokes an intense response from the latter. The result is *agōnia*, which speaks to the agonizing struggle and pain of the "soul conflict."[69] This word describes the anguish experienced by Christ in the garden of Gethsemane (Luke 22:44), resulting in a physical, emotional, and spiritual struggle.[70]

Victory in this struggle is possible only when the individual draws upon the grace of God in the exchange of the human will for Christ's empowering Spirit within, which allows the development of Christlike character through Spirit-led spiritual disciplines. The conferment of a new nature free of sin's domination demands a discussion of free will. Though far from settled, free will is critical to developing a holistic program of ministerial restoration and (re)formation. Therefore, the reader is encouraged to read "Excursus 3: The Role of Free Will."

For a biblical example of the exchange of the human will for Christ's empowering Spirit, one needs to look no further than Paul's actions when caught in a tempest of his own (Acts 27). The apostle was a prisoner bound for Rome. The Augustan cohort transferred Paul and other prisoners from ship to ship as they pressed forward (and pressed their luck). The winds were increasingly contrary. Progress was slow and difficult. They came to a port called Fair Haven; the sea was now dangerous, and Paul warned of disastrous consequences if they set sail. But the small fishing village was not an ideal harbor, and Phoenix, one of the best harbors in this part of Crete, was fewer than fifty miles away. The pilot and the ship's captain proved more persuasive than Paul. An apparent break in the weather sealed the deal and the ship set sail.

The centurion likely did not know that mountains immediately north of Fair Havens obscured the visibility of storms that swept down the Cretan mountains. The centurion and crew were also unaware that a storm was brewing: an east wind (*Euros*) and north wind (*Aquilo*), what Scripture calls a Euroclydon. The ship was soon in the grips of this cyclonic tempest. Having done everything else they knew to do, the crew dropped four anchors

---

67. Newman, *Concise Greek-English Dictionary*, s.v. "ἄγω."
68. Unger, *New Unger's Bible Dictionary*, s.v. "agony."
69. Pratt, "Agony," s.v. "agony," 71–72.
70. Matt 26:36–46; Mark 14:32–42; Luke 22:39–46; cf. Heb 5:7–8.

and held on for dear life. Here, Paul gave a remarkable direction: cut the anchors and forfeit the ship.

An anchor is a heavy object that holds a person or vessel secure, a weight that keeps them fixed. We all have anchors that keep us secure. They prevent us from drifting and help us survive the storms. But anchors wrongly used can keep us from where we need to be. Such was the case for Paul and his shipmates. They were storm-battered for two weeks. So violent was the storm that seasoned sailors were seasick and refused to eat. Storm clouds veiled the sun and stars for many days, which meant that they could determine neither their position nor the direction they should go. The crew dropped the anchors in a last-ditch effort to ride the storm out, but God had revealed to Paul their only hope: they needed to find a firm foundation. And it was not the storm that stopped them. It was the anchors.

The fact that there were four anchors is intriguing. I am not purporting to uncover some mystical hidden meaning here. Still, in this story, we see four significant mistakes made by the crew, and each is pertinent to our discussion of a perfect storm culminating in a ministerial moral failure.

- **Mistake No. 1: They were not content.** Fair Havens was small and "not suitable to winter in." The crew was unhappy where they were and set sail. Interestingly, they headed for Crete, a word that means "fleshly, carnal."

- **Mistake No. 2: The refusal to correct bad decisions.** This voyage was all wrong. Adverse weather was typical this season, and the dangers were well-known.[71] Conditions worsened with each port, yet the crew repeatedly pressed ahead. Even when the man of God flatly warned of disaster and much loss.

- **Mistake No. 3: They put their faith in the wrong things.** Specifically in their vessel and abilities. They secured the skiff with difficulty and undergirded the ship with cables. They were trying to keep everything together. They thought the ship was their only hope.

- **Mistake No. 4: They sacrificed much to stay afloat.** First was the cargo, then the ship's tackle. Notably, they jettisoned some of their sustenance and means to obtain more.

In summary, flesh drove these sailors, who proved unwilling to adjust course, placed trust in the wrong things, and sacrificed much to stay afloat.

---

71. More than one thousand known shipwreck remains from antiquity in this region bear witness.

STORMFRONT NO. 3—THE DEVIL (SPIRITUAL)

Indeed, "there is a way that seems right to a man, but its end is the way of death" (Prov 14:12, 16:25).

And then there is God's way.

Paul was the most experienced traveler on board that ship.[72] Rather than direct damage control, the apostle directed them to eat some bread. A word of hope followed: God would spare these wayward sailors and all their passengers, 276 in total, because the man of God had asked for them. Like a good mentor, Paul prayed for them throughout (hold that thought!). Now, God would make a way of escape, but there was something they had to do.

It was time to cut the anchors.

---

72. The apostle had eleven voyages on the Mediterranean under his belt and had travelled at least 3,500 miles by sea. In those travels, he had been shipwrecked three times and had spent a night and a day in the open sea (2 Cor 11:25). Paul had sea legs and was what the US sea services would call "salty."

Section Two Summary

"Each new generation and each new person reaps what others have sown and sow what others will reap."

— Cornelius Plantinga Jr.

This section considered the synergistic relationship between the three elements of the perfect storm. Specifically, the flesh, presented as the causative psychological, psychological, and emotional factors to include the adverse effects of emotional woundings; the world, presented as social and cultural influences such as worldview, ethics, and norms; and the devil, presented as spiritual considerations such as the lack of spiritual formation and the resulting power of temptation. While the "perfect storm" analogy draws from a rare convergence of three natural storms, all pastors struggle to withstand some (if not all) storms mentioned above. These ministers battle in various ways and varying degrees—and many pastors are not faring well.

As George Barna rightly notes, the Christian community in North America does not need stronger leaders. It needs more resilient leaders.[1] In Stanley Grenz's view, the Christian community needs more moral leaders.[2] Both are necessary. The resilient minister can resist temptation and manage ministerial, psychological, and physical pressures. Moral formation will sanctify that minister and develop divine character. This formation is central to the ministerial call but is neither automatic nor easy to achieve. The reason it is difficult is this: people don't want to change who they are. They want to feel better about who they are. The resulting lack of formation is evident in the numerous cases of ministerial moral failure over the past half century; each failure stands as a violation of sacred trust, power, sexual trust, the pure image of God, the integrity of the pastorate, and the personal identity of the minister.

1. Barna and Kinnamon, *State of Pastors*, 9.
2. Grenz, "We Dare Not Fall," 38.

SECTION TWO SUMMARY

Indeed, holistic formation, including emotional and moral aspects, is essential to ministerial calling. As Gregory Koukl asserts, "Morality protects us from the brutality of living in a world where people act out their natural impulses. Animals always do what comes naturally."[3] Illicit behaviors are often natural to those who emerge from broken homes with wounded emotions and warped views of sexuality. An exponential movement away from God marks the subsequent outplay. As a result, divine grace and presence are sought "only in situations that extend beyond our control or where our knowledge does not reach . . . [and thus] God becomes 'the God of the gaps,' the *Deus ex machina*, present only where we have not yet learned how to cope."[4] The diminishing reliance on sacred moral codes increasingly renders individuals "profoundly volatile, subject to confusion, and liable to collapse."[5]

Such tendencies can be overcome only by strong theological perspectives drawn from sound hermeneutics, teamed with a genuine search for "the moral good through the Spirit's leading, sanctified reasoning, and the collective wisdom of the church, both past and present."[6] It is to this endeavor our attention soon turns.

The restoration paradigm presented in sections 3 and 4 does not seek only to quell the tempests of the flesh, world, and devil. Indeed, those storms must be stilled, but a once-stilled storm may return. The development of Christlike character gives the minister an ability to rise above. The storms faced by Christ's disciples provide a good example.

Scripture describes two storms that threatened the disciples' lives. Remember that many disciples in those boats were seasoned fishermen who had seen everything the Sea of Galilee had to offer. They could recognize a storm's severity and knew how to respond. But these two instances caught them unaware. Though undoubtedly confident in their skills, they soon fought and feared for their lives.

Jesus slept in the boat during the first storm, but not for long. Frightened and somewhat angered disciples awakened him. "Do you not care that we are perishing?" they asked. I'm sure you know the answer and how the

---

3. Koukl, *Tactics*, 185. Koukl builds this upon Thomas Hobbes's assertion that life in an unregulated state of nature is "solitary, poor, nasty, brutish, and short." (Hobbes, *Leviathan*, loc. 1629). Humankind is neither God nor animal. Yet we try to remove the identifying boundaries in both categories—we want to be God to justify our pleasures and desires and we want to be animalistic to serve our pleasures and desires.

4. Stassen and Gushee, *Kingdom Ethics*, 33.

5. Trueman, *Rise and Triumph of the Modern Self*, 78.

6. Hollinger, *Choosing the Good*, 153–62.

SECTION TWO: ELEMENTS OF THE PERFECT STORM

story ends. Jesus rebuked the storm; peace and still tranquility followed. For the Sea of Galilee, at least. The disciples were bewildered.[7]

The second storm found the disciples once again fighting against a storm.[8] They saw a figure walking on the water and believed it was an omen of impending doom. Instead, it was Jesus who was strolling past. Notice that Jesus didn't calm the storm this time. I imagine the disciples were hoping, perhaps even expecting, that he would. But Jesus offered little more than words of encouragement.[9] To Peter's credit, he did not cry, "Deliver us! Calm this storm!" Peter said, "If it's you, bid me come!"

When you feel like you are about to sink, do not grow frustrated that Jesus hasn't calmed your storm. Jesus invites you to walk in authority over your storm, upon the very thing that would otherwise destroy you. Such a victory requires faith and formation. Let us not forget that Peter begins to sink the moment he focuses on the threatening waves. But with eyes fixed on Jesus, Peter (and you) can walk in the miraculous. Jesus took Peter by the hand, and together, they walked to the boat and proceeded to their destination. Similarly, no storm can sink you when you accept Jesus' hand and walk in faith.[10]

One final note from this second event is worth consideration. Mark's Gospel describes the disciples in the boat as utterly astonished. They still did not know what to make of Jesus or what to do in response. Mark gives the reason for their struggle and seeming inability to join Peter's walk on the water: they had hard hearts. Indeed, a hard heart will cause you to miss Jesus as he passes by. A hard heart will prevent you from deliverance and the opportunity to walk in the miraculous.

A Christian character ethic breaks up that hard heart as it centers on the understanding that the "Holy Spirit does not simply affirm what we always believed but dynamically engages us in a process of continuous learning and correction."[11] The development of Christian character is neither an immediate nor simple event. An honest appraisal of oneself is the initial and most basic necessity in developing and ultimately exhibiting inward

---

7. Matt 8:23–27; Mark 4:35–41; Luke 8:22–25.

8. Matt 14:22–36; Mark 6:45–56; John 6:16–20.

9. In truth, Jesus' statement is far more than encouragement. In the truest translation, he declares "Fear not, I Am!" Jesus' statement uses the Greek phrase *ego eimi*, which is used in the Septuagint to capture God's self-revelation and identity (Exod 3:14; Deut 32:39; Isa 41:4; 43:10; note also the double *ego eimi ego eimi* in Isa 43:25; 45:18, 46:4; 51:12).

10. E.g., Pss 37:24; 91:5–10; Isa 54:17; 59:19; Luke 10:19; Rom 8:28.

11. Stassen and Gushee, *Kingdom Ethics*, 118. This is what Thomas Aquinas calls "participation in divinity." Cf. Ezek 36:26–27.

truth. This ethic is, therefore, a communal activity in which faith relates to others, a formative activity in which faith shapes identity, a practical activity in which faith seeks understanding for the proper application, and a public activity in which faith expresses itself in society.[12] Society clamors to accept the individual's ever-changing identities. Truth demands identity to be found in Christ, the only place true happiness can be found.

Ultimately, everything comes down to the pursuit of happiness. As Blaise Pascal rightly asserts, "all men seek happiness. This is without exception. Whatever different means they employ, they all tend to this end. . . . This is the motive of every action of every man, even of those who hang themselves."[13] Despite its many deficiencies, secular ethics rightly identifies happiness as *telos*. However, the happiness derived from secular ethics is a myriad of self-oriented options concerned with living and faring well, which is absent of any divine sustaining grace. Pursuing wrongly defined happiness through unbounded autonomy (disguised as freedom) results in emotional and spiritual enslavement.[14] Like a storm passing over warm ocean water, the wrong pursuit of happiness escalates the inner storms, which soon hit us with hurricane-force intensity.

The Christian ethic similarly identifies happiness as the end goal but necessarily reduces this to God alone.[15] True freedom resides in the realization that there is only one choice. Because true happiness is found only in God, the restored minister must be found in Christ. This positioning is so essential that Paul uses the phrase ninety-two times in his letters.[16] Being in Christ is relational; in the truest sense in Greek, the individual is in Christ's control and embrace.[17] This proximity demands a (re)formation program

---

12. Sensing, *Qualitative Research*, 160.

13. Pascal, *Pensées*, 47–8.

14. Murray, *Saving Truth*, 80.

15. Notably, Augustine identifies God as the *summum bonum* (the highest good) and argues that "there is a joy that is not given to those who do not love you, but only to those who love you for your own sake. You yourself are their joy. Happiness is to rejoice in you and for you and because of you. This is happiness and there is no other. Those who think that there is another kind of happiness look for joy elsewhere, but theirs is not true joy" (Augustine, *Confessions*, 10.22). The works of Thomas Aquinas advance such understanding. Two works stand out: *The Manual against the Heathen* presents in three books arguments based on reason and philosophy, with Scripture and church tradition invoked only to confirm conclusions already reached by reason. Aquinas uses the fourth book to present doctrines which cannot be reached without Christian revelation. Second is *Summa Theologiae*, a massive work of more than two million words that takes Augustine's neoplatonist theology and restates it in Aristotelian terms.

16. Paul also uses the phrase "in Him" twenty-three times and "in the Lord" forty-five times.

17. Porter, *Idioms of the Greek New Testament*, 159.

that resists acceptance of or adherence to secular worldviews and ethics that define self-worth through personal achievement and social affirmation.

Therefore, we must adjust course and shift from storm avoidance to storm response. Specifically, section 3 considers what ministers, congregations, and leaders can do when hit by a disaster of ministerial moral failure. The chapters lay the foundation for a holistic ministerial restoration program by addressing (1) immediate actions to take after accusations or evidence come to light, (2) the development of the restoration team, and (3) the construction of the restoration plan.

SECTION THREE
When Disaster Strikes

"What does the world need: gifted men and women outwardly empowered? Or individuals who are broken, inwardly transformed?"

— GENE EDWARDS

THE PERFECT STORM HAS hit. The vessel founders. Now, the church sets out to seek and save those who are otherwise lost. Unfortunately, many neglect this search and rescue mission for several reasons. To illustrate, let us consider a famous sinking with which many are familiar, if not through the study of history, then through the movie magic of Hollywood. It is the tragic story of *Titanic*.

The luxurious passenger ship struck an iceberg a few miles off the coast of Newfoundland on the night of April 14, 1912, during her maiden voyage from Queenstown, Ireland, to New York City. Fewer than four hours later, the ship that had been declared "unsinkable" was swallowed by the North Atlantic's frigid, black waters. More than 2,200 souls were aboard *Titanic*. Fewer than one-third survived.

There was another ship in the North Atlantic that fateful night. *Californian* radio operator Cyril Evans sent an ice warning to *Titanic* at 10:55 p.m. *Titanic*'s Jack Phillips told Evans to "Keep out! Shut up! You're jamming my signal. I'm busy. I'm working Cape Race." Unlike the simple *Californian*, the majestic *Titanic* carried some of society's elite—wealthy business leaders, presidential aides, former congressmen, and some of the world's leading architects, editors, and entrepreneurs. Phillips was too busy sending their messages and meeting their needs to be bothered by common ice warnings. Besides, no harm would befall the mighty *Titanic*. She was the best built, aided by the latest and greatest technologies, and crewed by the best and brightest minds. The tiny *Californian* didn't even deserve to share the same waters! *Californian* would do well to mind her business and weather her own storms.

Evans obliged. He shut off his wireless radio and went to bed as *Titanic* steamed toward a seventy-eight-mile ice field. Forty minutes later, *Titanic* Lookout Frederick Fleet spotted an iceberg from his perch in the crow's nest. First Officer William Murdoch responded well. He ordered *Titanic* "hard-a-port" (to the left), and the engines reversed. He also ordered the crew to close doors to the (supposedly) watertight compartments. But *Titanic* was too big to make the necessary turn. No doubt, hearts beat with increasing intensity, and breaths became trapped in tight throats as the massive ice island grew larger. Five minutes after Fleet's warning, *Titanic*'s starboard side scraped along the iceberg, and icy water poured into the forward compartments.

Not long after, *Californian* crewmembers saw the massive *Titanic* brilliantly lit by dazzling lights that danced on a black horizon. Something didn't look right; some thought she seemed to list. Several of her lights went dark just before eight illuminating lights shot into the night sky. *Californian* crewmembers determined *Titanic* was having a party. They had no idea she was sinking—the lights were not fireworks; they were flares signaling the need for help. Similar calls filled the radio: "We are sinking fast . . . cannot last much longer." Distant ships heard the distress signals, but *Californian* was no longer listening.

At this moment, James Cameron's 1997 film depicts a priest surrounded by praying passengers. The scene is anchored in truth. There were eight ministers aboard *Titanic*. All sailed as second-class passengers. None survived.

- Reverend Robert James Bateman was a Baptist minister returning to Florida after visiting his mother's grave in England. He helped his sister-in-law into a lifeboat, gave her his coat, then returned to the sinking ship.
- Survivors recounted how Father Thomas Byles urged calm as he gave absolution and blessings, leading others to the lifeboats with comfort and encouragement.
- Father Ernest Courtney Carter, an Anglican priest, and his wife, Lillian, were offered lifeboat seats. Both refused, encouraging others to go in their places.

SECTION TWO SUMMARY

- Reverend John Harper's six-year-old daughter survived, but the Baptist preacher spent his last minutes in the cold water, where he comforted and converted numerous victims.
- Free Will Baptist minister and evangelist Reverend Charles Leonard Kirkland had buried his wife and some of their children in the years before setting sail. That night, he spent his last moments comforting those who were perishing.
- Reverend William Lahtinen pastored the Apostolic Lutheran Church in Cokato, Minnesota. His wife Anna entered a lifeboat, then chose to remain with him on the sinking ship.
- Father Juozas Montvila turned down a seat in a lifeboat to stay onboard and provide solace, consolation, and absolution. At age 27, Montvila was the youngest of *Titanic*'s clergymen.
- Father Josef Peruschitz was a Benedictine monk and a teacher. He declined a lifeboat seat and was last seen ministering aboard the doomed ship.

Before we resign *Titanic* to her fate, let us consider another boat of interest that navigated those frigid waters that fateful night—a tiny vessel known as Lifeboat Number 14. Captain Edward Smith ordered the lifeboats to launch just twenty minutes after the collision. *Titanic* carried twenty lifeboats with a combined capacity of 1,178 people, slightly more than half of the embarked passengers and crew. One might think people would fight for a spot or cram into the lifeboats. On the contrary, the crew launched only seventeen lifeboats, most half-empty. Congressional testimonies revealed that many passengers didn't believe they were in danger. Boarding the lifeboats was something between a precaution and a pesky intrusion. But everyone soon realized the impossible yet inevitable truth: the unsinkable *Titanic* was sinking fast.

Lifeboats frantically paddled away from *Titanic* for fear of getting sucked down by the massive ship as she succumbed to her watery grave. Only Lifeboat 14 returned to seek and save the lost.

Passengers and crew in other lifeboats thought about going back. Some were too afraid. Some assumed it was too late. Some expected ships to arrive soon—vessels better equipped and responsible for such rescue. But it was nearly two hours before *Carpathia* arrived. That crew pulled 705 survivors from lifeboats but none from the water. It was too late.

Lifeboat 14 was the exception. Fifth Officer Harold Lowe commanded the craft, which launched at 1:30 a.m. with sixty of sixty-five seats occupied. After *Titanic* sank, Lowe gathered Lifeboats 4, 10, 12, and Collapsible D. He

SECTION THREE: WHEN DISASTER STRIKES

distributed his passengers among the four boats, then returned to the area where *Titanic* went under. Lifeboat 14 saved four in the water and rescued the survivors of a swamped lifeboat.

One of the men saved by Lifeboat 14 later testified that in the icy waters, while clinging to debris, Reverend John Harper swam up to him and challenged him with the invitation to "believe in the Lord Jesus Christ and thou shalt be saved." He rejected the offer. Harper gave the man his lifejacket and said, "You need this more than I do." Harper continued to offer comfort to those around him. The waves soon brought him and the man together again. The persistent Harper gave a second invitation, and with miles of water beneath his feet, the man gave his life to Christ. Harper soon succumbed to his watery grave. Four years later, at the Ontario meeting of survivors, the unnamed man identified himself as "the last convert of John Harper."

Where are you in this story? Some are like the proud and powerful *Titanic*. You may even believe that you and your ministry are unsinkable. But there is an iceberg on your horizon, and like *Titanic*, your inevitable collision with things that reside in unseen depths will sink you.

Some of you are like the passengers strewn among the wreckage. You were part of a great ministerial journey when the vessel struck an iceberg. Neither you nor the staff expected let alone prepared for such a disaster. Now, you cling to anything you can find to stay afloat, praying and waiting for someone to pull you to safety.

Some resemble *Californian*. You have issued your warning, only to be ignored. Offended, you have turned off the radio and misinterpreted the calls for help. *Titanic* survivors testified that they could see *Californian* in the distance, perhaps as close as six miles, and could not understand why she did not come to their rescue.

To watch the depths swallow a once-mighty ministry raises many painful questions. Why did no one heed the warnings? Why did competent people miss or misinterpret the distress signals? What more could have been done to avoid the disaster? These are fair questions that we will address in due time. Right now, people are perishing—the violator and his victim(s), family, and church members. Right now, we must seek and save those who will otherwise perish. Lifeboat 14 is the vessel committed to that godly task. The following section invites you aboard, whether for deliverance or duty.

The following chapters address three actions essential to this rescue mission. Chapter 7 presents steps to determine whether a violator is eligible for ministerial restoration. Topics include the proper assessment of charges and ways to approach an accused minister. Chapter 8 describes the necessary actions for building a restoration team for cases where restoration is deemed appropriate. In such cases, God's truth and grace redirects rather than removes. In addition, restoration demands accountability through the Christian community and is an act to which the community of grace is obligated.[1] Therefore, this step moves beyond administrative matters such as duration and location to define the roles and responsibilities of the overseer, mental health professionals, spiritual mentors, and laity. Chapter 9 outlines steps for building the individual restoration plan. This process includes emotional and spiritual (re)formation and deliverance from illicit tendencies that threaten the violator's restoration to God, even if not to ministry.

Welcome aboard, now let's get underway!

---

1. Thomas and Sutton, "Religious Leadership Failure," 308–27, Wright, *Galatians*, 354. Cf. 1 Cor 12:11; Eph 2:19.

7

Assessing the Damage

"The starting point for the early church was this awareness of the abyss of sin inside each person, the murky depths of which only the top few inches are visible. God, who is all clarity and light, wants to make us perfect as he is perfect, shot through with his radiance. The first step in our healing, then, is not being comforted. It is taking a hard look at the cleansing that needs to be done."

— FREDERICA MATHEWES-GREEN

THE STORM HAS HIT and left severe devastation in its wake. It is time to assess that damage, clear the debris, and rebuild. Nehemiah provides a worthy analogy for biblical restoration (Neh 1–6). While Nehemiah was neither guilty of moral failure nor in need of ministerial restoration, the nation and the people of Israel were both.[1] Their harlotry resulted in a seventy-year Babylonian exile. A small remnant returned to Jerusalem to rebuild the city's walls and temple and to restore Torah living and worship. It crushed Nehemiah to learn that things were not going well. He used his position as the cupbearer to petition King Artaxerxes. The request to help the remnant rebuild his family's homeland was bold since the king had shut down the rebuilding program not long before (Ezra 4:18–21). However, Artaxerxes granted his approval and added considerable support.

Nehemiah was responsible for rebuilding Jerusalem's walls.[2] This considerable task required thoroughly inspecting the wall, removing tons of

---

1. See Ps 106; Jer 3:1–15; Ezek 16:15–52; 23:1–49; cf. Hos 1–14.

2. Ezra was responsible for the reconstruction of the community and its commitment to God's covenant (Ezra 7–10; Neh 8:1–12). Earlier, Zerubbabel was responsible for temple reconstruction (Ezra 1:5—6:22; Hag 1–2; Zech 4:6–10).

rubbish, and repairing sizeable breeches. Nehemiah wisely divided the responsibilities among people who had a mind to work (Neh 4:6). Not people with a mind to criticize and complain, sit back and watch others work, or build personal kingdoms and reputations. Instead, a people determined to rebuild God's temple and restore their covenant with God.

This "mind to work" is a crucial designation. Ministerial restoration often meets unbiblical responses that range "from a *laissez-faire* indifference about restoration to a pharisaical rush to permanent retirement."[3] Three standard and unbiblical responses toward the fallen minister emerge: destroy, defer, or disregard. Each result in the spiritual (de)formation of many individuals, fails to help the minister and victims, and damages the church, sometimes beyond repair.

- **An attitude to destroy** speaks of the tendency to remove or accept the resignation of the fallen minister without consideration of restoration. Exacerbated by "cancel culture," the need to maintain a perceived holy standard and protect the church's good name are the primary reasons many opt for this seemingly quick and clean solution. Yet in this effort to protect its self-interest, the institution fails to realize "its self-interest to be the same as the interests of the people it is supposed to serve."[4] Furthermore, demand for permanent removal ignores the Savior's ability "to renew, re-create, and restore."[5]

- **An attitude to defer** speaks of pseudo-restorative programs that require suspension from ministerial duties for a designated, rather than situationally determined, period. Temporary removal serves more as a "penalty box" as it focuses on remediation rather than restoration. Required counseling is general in scope, and accountability is minimal. What typically follows is a relocation that lacks full disclosure—a familiar yet catastrophic error. "In the church we sometimes think that hiding the truth somehow serves a higher purpose. The Bible refuses to expunge the errors of its heroes from the history it narrates."[6] Such misguided approaches and expectations have "merely deadened our humanity, instead of setting it free to develop richly, in all its capacities, under the influence of grace."[7]

---

3. Hayford, *Restoring Fallen Leaders*, 24.
4. Fortune, *Is Nothing Sacred?*, xiv.
5. Hayford, *Restoring Fallen Leaders*, 22. Cf. John 8:1–12; 2 Cor 5:17; Phil 1:6.
6. Grenz and Bell, *Betrayal of Trust*, 115.
7. Merton, *Thoughts in Solitude*, 13.

- **An attitude of disregard** speaks of the desire to forgive and move forward quickly. Laden with typical clichés such as "the pastor is only human" and descriptions of a momentary weakness by a minister who otherwise demonstrates a strength of character. This approach may be rooted in love for the pastor or fear that the church may collapse. Regardless of the reason, quick reinstatement sacrifices the fallen minister "on a self-serving altar" that fails to maintain the tension between forgiveness and the fruits of repentance.[8] This unwillingness to endure sound doctrine adversely affects the person, the pulpit, and church polity.[9]

Many churches address restoration on a sliding scale, even within these three categories. For example, the laity is more inclined to restore a pastor addicted to internet pornography than one who has committed adultery, and both violators are more likely to receive congregational support than a minister guilty of homosexual liaisons, though biblical prohibitions give both equal regard. Respondents split on whether a rehabilitated minister should not be able to return to active pastoral ministry, but 74 percent support the restoration of the sexually offending clergy to a ministerial role that provides no access to victims.[10]

Indeed, one can expect significant opposition within and without, as seen in Nehemiah's example. Many enemies were angry that God's people had united for this great work. Notable among them were Sanballat and Tobiah. The former is a Babylonian name meaning "sin has given life," and the latter is a Hebrew name meaning "the Lord is very good." Indeed, one can expect opposition from the devilish and the religious alike when restoring service to and worship of God. Such forces prefer God's people remain in a place of captivity. In Nehemiah's example, these angry adversaries united to ridicule and ultimately threaten violence (Neh 4:1–17).

It is not surprising that God's people soon grew weary. Rebuilding a wall is a tough job, but it is more difficult when one must remove the piles

---

8. Hayford, *Restoring Fallen Leaders*, 24.

9. Cf. 2 Tim 4:1–5. Notably, many mistakenly point to the example of King David for biblical support for quick resumption of calling (Hayford, *Restoring Fallen Leaders*, 44). While David's example is of critical importance, and is explored in chapter 3, this approach fails to recognize his year-long struggle, contrite repentance, and the consequences that remained throughout his life and ministry.

10. 1 Cor 6:9; 1 Tim 1:10. See also Barna Group, *Porn Phenomenon*, 118; Bissell, "Restoring Fallen Pastors," ii; Shipley, "Increasing the Knowledge of Pastors and Church Leaders," 59–86, 206–10; Sutton et al., "Does Gender Matter?," 647; Sutton and Jordan, "Evaluating Attitudes Toward Clergy Restoration," 865; Sutton and Thomas, "Can Derailed Pastors be Restored?," 583–99; Wells, "Needs Assessment," 201–17.

of debris left by the collapse and perform guard duty to protect the families from attack. Amid this struggle, the enemy planned a massive attack to encircle and destroy God's people. Nehemiah urged the weary to fight for their families and reminded them that God fights on their behalf. Each member of this united team held a tool in one hand and a sword in the other, committed to building while battling. God's people repelled repeated attacks and built a robust new wall atop the existing foundation. It is an example the ministerial restoration team would do well to follow. Therefore, the following chapter considers the individuals and spiritual skills necessary to "rebuild the wall." Specifically, this includes guidelines for hearing the accusation(s), determining eligibility for ministerial restoration, and concludes with a discussion of ministerial support provided to victim(s), family members, and the affected congregation.

HEARING THE ACCUSATION AND ACCUSED

"Tolerance is the last virtue of a depraved society. When you have an immoral society that has blatantly, proudly, violated all of the commandments of God, there is one last virtue they insist upon: tolerance for their immorality."

— D. JAMES KENNEDY

A deliberate and systematic response to allegations of ministerial sexual abuse begins by properly hearing the accusation, confronting the accused minister (which may include a formal hearing), and assessing eligibility for ministerial restoration. How church leaders confront an accused minister with credible charges follows. This engagement will prove critical when church leaders determine whether and to what extent a ministerial restoration plan is in order.

Hearing an accusation, especially against a beloved minister or colleague, is difficult. Most would rather not, and many do not. Countless churches have voiced ill-informed calls to "judge not" and unworthiness to "cast the first stone." Such examples display the consistent failure to differentiate between forgiveness and restoration as well as the tendency to misappropriate passages that address the former to substantiate the latter. Jesus' command to "judge not" speaks of judging one's heart or standing with God, not one's actions. Immediately following this command is the description of removing a log from one's eye to see well enough to remove the speck from another's (Matt 7:1–5). The identification of the speck and its removal are acts of judgment.[11] Indeed, we judge actions to correct and improve, not to condemn others. Conversely, in the contention that no one has the right to judge another's actions, we have judged ourselves worthy to determine that we should judge no actions. Why would we trust our judgment over God's?

Nonjudgmental tolerance is not an option. Scripture requires the church to judge immoral behaviors and provide a biblical response.[12] Therefore, accusations must be heard and investigated for understanding and healing, not blaming and condemning. Indeed, "when we are so eager to believe the worst about others, we bring out the worst in ourselves."[13]

To rightly assess any accusation requires an exact description of the alleged offense(s). An allegation of sexual impropriety certainly includes but is not limited to sexual activity outside a marriage covenant.[14] Impropriety includes sexual activity with consenting adults, children, and incapacitated persons. Investigators should also be mindful of "authority rape." Malfeasance also includes unwanted or inappropriate physical touch, sexually explicit or implicit comments, indecent exposure, inappropriate physical actions, and the use of pornography.

Though Scripture requires the violated to confront the offender (Matt 5:23–24), it is "morally inexcusable and psychologically violent" to require a sexually abused woman or child to meet with the perpetrator.[15] In addition, strict reliance on Paul's guidance to "not accept an accusation against an elder except on the basis of two or three witnesses" may prove insufficient (1 Tim 5:19). Sexual harassment and abuse do not "typically happen in the presence of witnesses."[16] Therefore, the church is morally obliged to immediately respond to credible sexual misconduct allegations, even if only

---

11. Similarly, a tree is known by its fruit and differentiating good fruit from bad is an act of judgement (Luke 6:43–45). Pertinent to this topic, Paul asks the church why it had failed to judge a matter of sexual immorality—a matter he had judged despite being absent (1 Cor 5:1–3). He goes on to explain that God judges those outside, but the believers judge those within (1 Cor 5:12–13). See also John 7:24; 1 Cor 6:1–6; 11:13, 31.

12. For example, consider Paul's response to the Corinthian church that failed to properly judge and address sexual sin (1 Cor 5).

13. Murray, *Saving Truth*, 42.

14. This list draws heavily from Rediger, "Clergy Moral Malfeasance," 37–38.

15. McKnight and Barringer, *Church Called Tov*, 49.

16. McKnight and Barringer, *Church Called Tov*, 50. This legalistic application of Scripture neglects the weightier matters of the Law: justice, mercy, and faithfulness (Matt 23:23). Conversely, as noted above, many contemporary examples of ministerial moral failure include testimony of multiple victims (witnesses) who were not believed despite similarity in their stories.

one individual brings an accusation.[17] Furthermore, investigators must be especially attentive to the violated. The distressed congregant may be in shock, self-condemnation, or concerned that investigators will not take her seriously—and may even be repudiated.[18]

Instead, congregational and regional or state denominational leaders should assemble an investigative committee of both genders to hear the accusation(s) and confront the accused on the victim's behalf. Properly assessing charges requires disqualifying committee members with angry, judgmental, or punitive feelings.[19] No matter how marred the image, the fallen minister still bears the image of God and must be viewed in this light. Investigators should also be mindful of presumed guilt. There is merit to such caution in a "cancel culture" fueled by countless sexual ethic violations by ministerial and secular leaders. Codependent relationships, defined as a need for professional or emotional approval from the accused, also render one ineligible as this individual may lack objectivity. The investigation team aims to discern the truth, not diagnose the problem or offer corrective counsel.

Once heard, the victim is entitled to an explanation of the ensuing process. The investigative team should inform her of ministerial support available, as described below. Accusations deemed credible precipitate further inquiry and action. In that case, the church should tell the victim of its intent to investigate the case even if she does not desire to press the allegation.

Next, congregational and denominational leaders must take a difficult but necessary step and confront the accused minister.[20] The accused minister should receive written allegations, time to prepare himself spiritually and emotionally, and be allowed to respond. The confrontation should begin privately and, if necessary, proceed by biblical guidance (Matt 18:15–18; 1 Tim 5:19–20). The next step moves to present the allegations

---

17. Grenz and Bell, *Betrayal of Trust*, 156, 162–63; Trull and Carter, *Ministerial Ethics*, 180.

18. Notably, the Canadian Mental Health Association found that only twenty-four of eighty-two victims of professional abuse reported the situation to police or other professionals. Only four were convinced that their complaints had been taken seriously. See Fieguth, "After All These Years," 29, quoted in Grenz and Bell, *Betrayal of Trust*, 22.

19. Laaser, *Healing the Wounds*, 140.

20. If the sexual violation involves criminal activity, the overseer should immediately notify law enforcement. Ministerial restoration is highly unlikely in such cases. However, church polity must be followed to remove the minister properly and officially from his pastoral position. In addition, the overseer should initiate efforts to restore the fallen minister to God and family.

and investigation procedures again in the presence of two or three witnesses, which should be the church's governing body (the church council, board of elders, deacons, etc.). Suppose the alleged violator refuses or does not confess despite sufficient reason to suspect sexual impropriety. In that case, the investigation team should call a formal hearing to present charges before the church's governing body or the congregation. Denominational or congregational polity guides this formal hearing. If the alleged violator still refuses to participate in the investigative process, the fellowship disassociates the alleged violator.[21]

Investigators should prepare for a possible unpleasant reaction, replete with anxiety and spiritual conflict. Avoid judgmental comments and restrict questions to known behaviors and accusations to quell this tension. An investigation is not a debate but a dialogue. The goal of the former is to win the argument. The latter aims to build bridges where people can retreat from hardline positions and recognize errors. Though an accused minister may enter with an anticipation or intent for conflict, it takes two to debate. Deny the debate, and a conversation may commence.

Still, conversations do not come easy and sometimes do not come at all. Prepare for responses ranging from disbelief to denial, anger to anxiety, and evasion to confession. In addition, the Christian who has succumbed to willful sin is probably very good at rationalizing his illicit behaviors. He will likely attempt to prove himself right because, at this point, affirmation is more important than truth. Thus, some ministers try to spin the facts to their advantage (and even portray themselves as victims). One may "use all the means in his power to deflect or deny the charges and to intimidate, delay and even harass those who dare to question" him and manipulate congregational supporters to oppose any action taken against him.[22] No matter the response, investigators must follow the code of ethics adopted by the church or denomination and comply with legal imperatives and statutes.

Leaders should exonerate a wrongly accused minister before the church to protect his reputation and ministry. Similarly, leaders should immediately remove the minister if sexual misconduct is substantiated. That minister is no longer blameless, of good reputation, or temperate, but instead is self-willed and disqualified from ministerial service.[23]

---

21. Matt 18:17, 1 Cor 5:1–13. This excommunication from fellowship is neither permanent nor irrevocable but remedial in its intent (cf. 1 Tim 1:20).

22. Grenz and Bell, *Betrayal of Trust*, 166–67. Jack Hayford notes that a spiritual manipulator of this sort lacks the spirit of submission that is "at the foundation of all true spiritual authority" (Hayford, *Restoring Fallen Leaders*, 52).

23. 1 Tim 3:1–13; Titus 1:6–9. Removal from ministerial function will often meet resistance for any number of reasons such as financial instability, protection of

Confession and repentance do not grant immediate return to ministerial function. The investigative team must give an initial assessment of that possibility. As noted above, many violators are disqualified from ministerial restoration regardless of repentance.[24] If deemed eligible for a restoration program, the violator enters a period of intense spiritual, emotional, and familial counsel, usually one to three years. This time is necessary to begin the proper reformation of each aspect. It allows church leaders to validate the genuineness of the violator's repentance and his commitment to restoration. Progress is a crucial factor in determining ministerial restoration. Therefore, the decision for ministerial restoration cannot rest on a single moment. Notifying victims and church members is required once church leaders decide whether ministerial restoration will be considered or denied.

PROPER ASSESSMENT OF CHARGES AND RESTORATION

"Be so preoccupied with good will that you haven't room for ill will."

— E. Stanley Jones

As noted above, restoration to ministry is the exception rather than the rule. "Because of Christ, the church should assume restoration is possible, but because of sin and the dismal record of recovery, it should expect that full recovery and restoration to ministry will be rare."[25] Still, it is worth noting that Nathan honored the adulterous David enough to seek his restoration. This paradigm proceeds in the same spirit and understanding that not every violator is a predator.

Critical care offered in the local hospital provides a good analogy. Qualified first responders are the first to arrive after a life-threatening event. They take full advantage of that precious "golden hour" to assess vital signs and initiate four life-saving steps: start breathing, stop bleeding, protect the

---

reputation, and struggle with self-worth and identity. In addition, "many pastors are afraid of silence" (Briggs, *Fail*, 83). The busyness and affirmation inherent to ministerial service provides a powerful conduit to avoid and even negate one's struggle with self-worth. Church leaders should recognize that the violator's removal from ministry, though necessary, will induce considerable struggle.

24. Yet even in this case, repentance is necessary for spiritual restoration. Thus, the emotional and spiritual reformation addressed below remains beneficial to the repentant but disqualified violator.

25. Mosgofian and Ohlschlager, *Sexual Misconduct in Counseling and Ministry*, 252.

wound, and treat shock. Regarding ministerial restoration, first responders ensure the breath of life can freely flow, prevent the loss of Christ's life-giving blood, start holistic treatment of woundedness, and stabilize the emotional trauma. First responders also deliver the critically wounded to a dedicated place of healing when more intricate and specialized care is required. The emergency room is well-designed to receive and treat the injured. Proficient doctors and nurses skilled in general and specialized care spring into action. The triage determines the severity of the wounds; the diagnosis identifies the necessary treatment, while the prognosis outlines the path to achieving the best possible outcome. Even when emergency care and surgeries are successful, full recovery will require a critical patient to endure prolonged care, including time in an intensive care unit, a rehabilitation center, and physical and psychological therapy. It is necessary but not enough to stop the bleeding (or behaviors).

Repentance is the first vital sign to check. Chapter 8 explores this topic in detail. Suffice it to say the absence of repentance makes the restoration question moot. God does not reform an autonomous being in his image. Because pastors who fall into sexual sin are often master manipulators, the evaluator must receive the violator's explanation but not allow it to become an excuse. For this, Chuck DeGroat offers helpful distinctions between "vulnerability and fauxnerability," the latter being "a twisted form of vulnerability [that] has the appearance of transparency but serves only to conceal one's deepest struggles."[26] Watch for contradictions, inconsistent character, disclosures that focus on the past rather than the present moment, an end to empathy when not on the platform, passive-aggressive tendencies, a "victim mentality," an oversharing or "emotional dump" to engender sympathy, excessive self-referencing, power-posturing, and a preoccupation with performance and reputation.

Conversely, biblical repentance provides evidence that the individual recognizes his error and desires change, and that God has provided the grace to make that change. Such repentance requires confession by the violator to spiritual leaders and possibly in public.[27] Indeed, "lies are the death of community," a truth affirmed when Peter holds truth-telling as superior to protective paternalism and empathetic care (Acts 5:1–11).[28]

---

26. DeGroat, *When Narcissism Comes to Church*, loc. 1206; see also Mosgofian and Ohlschlager, *Sexual Misconduct in Counseling and Ministry*, 248.

27. 2 Sam 12:13; Matt 3:6; Acts 19:18; Jas 5:16.

28. Willimon, *Pastor*, 350. Notably, this is Luke's first use of the word "church" the book of Acts. See also Bonhoeffer, *Life Together*, 89, 113–14; DeYoung, *Glittering Vices*, 177.

Humble and full-hearted repentance will include submission to God and accountability to spiritually mature overseers.[29] Repentance requires confession based upon godly sorrow, along with self-knowledge. Manipulative predators and narcissists bury self-knowledge beneath self-defense and self-deception. Therefore, the evaluator must carefully and prayerfully apply spiritual discernment.

That there is "no stereotypical perpetrator of sexual misconduct" adds to this difficulty.[30] The minister whose sexual indiscretion is a one-time occurrence is far different from one whose indiscretions are a recurring pattern of life. Both are far different from the violator who exhibits predatory behaviors. Therefore, professional psychological help is required to establish a formal diagnosis.[31] This diagnosis is not counseling. Instead, the comprehensive assessment will provide valuable insight when determining restoration qualification and whether recidivism is likely.

A mental health professional, preferably one who is distinctly Christian in life and practice, can identify severe and often longstanding emotional and spiritual issues associated with sexual malfeasance. Professionals are familiar with deceptive tendencies and skilled at thwarting attempts to evade answers or excuse behaviors. Furthermore, they know when and when not to push an issue. For example, many who struggle with emotional trauma develop mastery in trigger avoidance. Well-meaning Christian counselors who press into an intrusive reexperiencing may unintentionally retraumatize the individual.

The overseer must ensure each mental health professional has informed consent and signed releases to talk to anyone he deems necessary. In addition, the fallen minister should provide a signed acknowledgment that the evaluator is a mandatory reporter, and the report could have significant consequences, including loss of employment. Evaluators thoroughly review the violator's life history, including sexual and marital history, past treatment, and personnel records, in preparation for in-person analysis. The evaluator shares pertinent findings with the overseer after the violator consents to release these findings.

---

29. This is a critical need as pastors "probably have less peer supervision than any other profession"(Willimon, *Pastor*, 399).

30. Grenz and Bell, *Betrayal of Trust*, 42.

31. Tan, *Counseling and Psychotherapy*, 371–72. See also Coe and Hall, "Transformational Psychology View," 215; DeGroat, *When Narcissism Comes to Church*, locs. 669–80; Hathaway and Yarhouse, *Integration of Psychology & Christianity*, 8, 22–24; Laaser, *Healing the Wounds*, 148, 151–52; Mosgofian and Ohlschlager, *Sexual Misconduct in Counseling and Ministry*, 125, 238, 241; Roberts and Watson, "Christian Psychology View," 149–75.

SECTION THREE: WHEN DISASTER STRIKES

Suffice it to say, the overseer must allow time for the mental health professional to administer psychological assessments such as the Minnesota Multiphasic Personality Inventory (MMPI), the California Psychological Inventory (CPI), the Rorschach, and the Enneagram to assess sexual typology and recidivism. The diagnosis's inherent details will inform whether an attempt toward ministerial restoration should continue and, if so, what emotional, behavioral, and marital treatment is appropriate. Overseers may retain the mental health professional for further consultation and additional meetings with the violator.

It is necessary to state that psychotic disorders, predatory psychopathy, and paraphilia automatically disqualify the offender from ministerial restoration.[32] Offenders in these categories often display chronic personality disorders, have significant sexual or impulse control disorders, and consistently demonstrate a poor prognosis for change. Such understanding automatically disqualifies pedophiles. Beyond the stigma associated with a return to pastoral oversight, the treatment is too complex, recovery is unproven, and recidivism rates are high.

Also disqualified are those diagnosed with a narcissistic personality disorder. The narcissist has an inflated sense of self-importance, an excessive need for admiration, and lacks empathy. Extreme confidence often hides a "fragile self-esteem that's vulnerable to the slightest criticism."[33] They are experts at seducing and are deliberate, sophisticated, and cunning. "Remorse is often superficial and manipulative. They are not good candidates for change because they fundamentally deny that their behavior is wrong."[34]

Cluster B DSM-V personality disorders feature narcissistic traits most prominently—and is the spectrum on which most ministerial candidates score in personality tests.[35] Indeed, there are too many Elmer Gantrys populating the pulpits.[36] This cluster also includes borderline personality disorder, antisocial personality disorder, and histrionic personality disorder.

---

32. Trull and Carter, *Ministerial Ethics*, 241, 257. See also Gabbard, "Psychotherapists Who Transgress Sexual Boundaries with Patients," 1–17; Grenz and Bell, *Betrayal of Trust*, 62; Laaser, *Healing the Wounds*, 94; Trull and Carter, *Ministerial Ethics*, 86; and Yarhouse and Tan, *Sexuality and Sex Therapy*, 243–50. Paraphilia refers to sexual deviations including pedophilia, voyeurism, fetishism, exhibitionism, masochism and sadism, and transvestism.

33. Mayo Clinic, "Symptoms and Causes," para. 1. See also McKnight and Barringer, *Church Called Tov*, 33; Useem, "Power Causes Brain Damage."

34. Mosgofian and Ohlschlager, *Sexual Misconduct in Counseling and Ministry*, 257.

35. DeGroat, *When Narcissism Comes to Church*, loc. 298.

36. The classic novel sees its namesake confuse his craving for popularity and profit with a calling to ministry. Addicted to "the drug of oratory," Gantry finds his fix

Conversely, borderline personality disorder renders one vulnerable and insecure and "features an interpersonal instability that makes consistent, healthy relating difficult." [37] These behaviors are due to a pervasive inner sense of emptiness and shame, while fear of abandonment presents a constant need for reassurance. Those with antisocial personality disorder (sociopathy) are shameless and believe themselves above accountability. These individuals are prone to callous indifference, manipulation, and rule-breaking. This behavior often appears among "pastoral predators who use and abuse their power to exploit others."

Violators who succumb to uncontrolled lust, the illicit search for emotional acceptance amid unrequited love (lovesickness) or masochistic surrender show "a greater likelihood" of rehabilitation.[38] Peter Mosgofian and George Ohlschlager offer a threefold approach that differentiates the predatory violator, the mixed violator (who demonstrates traits and dynamics from both ends), and the vulnerable violator.[39] The vulnerable and mixed violators are less dangerous and are "more likely to repudiate and control sexual abuse. Some of these can even be restored to moral living and ministry."[40] Sexual misconduct in these categories usually results from a failure to realistically evaluate one's vulnerability and minimize one's potential for misconduct.

Similarly, Stanley Grenz and Roy Bell identify the "wanderer" and the "lover" categories.[41] The wanderer is not premeditative and would typically never contemplate a sexual liaison with a congregant. Rather than step over the boundary, he falls into sexual misconduct. However, an overwhelming crisis, loneliness, or struggle may "tip the balance" for this vulnerable person who typically struggles with inadequacies. On the other hand, the lover truly feels in love and succumbs to his affections. This individual is the "normal neurotic."[42] In both cases, violations typically include a regretted return to learned behaviors that once eased unresolved brokenness. Such violations may consist of pornography or prostitution or could involve a consenting partner.

---

among enthusiastic and unaware congregations (Lewis, *Elmer Gantry*, 228).

37. DeGroat, *When Narcissism Comes to Church*, locs. 593–606.

38. Mosgofian and Ohlschlager, *Sexual Misconduct in Counseling and Ministry*, 242.

39. Mosgofian and Ohlschlager, *Sexual Misconduct in Counseling and Ministry*, 53.

40. Mosgofian and Ohlschlager, *Sexual Misconduct in Counseling and Ministry*, 53.

41. Grenz and Bell, *Betrayal of Trust*, 42–45.

42. Lebacqz and Barton, *Sex in the Parish*, 129.

The biblical allowance for such restoration is evident in the exegetical analysis of Gal 6:1. For example, Craig Keener defines the offender as "caught unaware" or "overtaken by surprise," which suggests the sin was not premeditated and perhaps committed in the passion of the moment.[43] Even here, investigators must tread carefully. For example, the question of consent may arise. Though the congregant or counselee may affirm a willingness to participate, the struggles for which she sought counsel—lack of intimacy, woundedness, vulnerability, or emotional abuse, for example—are often tied to her sexuality and may include sexual or emotional traumas dating to childhood. Acting upon her emotional needs and illicit tendencies is predatory and unethical and re-victimizes the counselee as it deepens rather than delivers her unhealthy patterns.

No matter the degree of indiscretion, a minister found guilty of sexual misconduct is biblically disqualified from serving. The overseer must attend to the violator's spiritual restoration and determine whether ministerial restoration is allowed and recommended. This determination begins by assessing the degree to which the violator is repentant and is open to psychological evaluation, counseling, and a guided restoration process.

Because sexual offense involves "a wide range of people with a great range of problems," decision-makers will use interviews and personality assessments to determine spiritual and emotional disposition.[44] Professional mental health evaluations are valuable when diagnosing core offender typology and determining whether restoration is efficacious. For example, the Sexual Addiction Screening Test and the Sexual Addiction Inventory are competent diagnostic tests for diagnosing sexual addiction.

Decision makers should remove other factors that dominate restoration decisions from consideration. These include the pastor's popularity and the threat of church splits if the overseer ignores the congregation's preference. Congregational preference carries strong influence and can demand anything from immediate restoration to permanent removal from ministry—and either choice can prove erroneous.[45]

Similarly, the perceived need for a minister's skill and experience often drives denominational decisions. Such attitudes are in error, in the view of A. W. Tozer, as it "is inconceivable that a sovereign and holy God should

---

43. Keener, *Galatians*, 531. In support, Keener cites Martinus de Boer, Chrysostom, Gordon Fee, Ronald Fung, Don Garlington, Martin Luther, and Josephus. Furthermore, note the difference between inadvertent and deliberate sins in Num 15:22–31. See also Barton et al., *Galatians*, 198.

44. Mosgofian and Ohlschlager, *Sexual Misconduct in Counseling and Ministry*, 249.

45. Pop et al., "Restoring Pastors Following a Moral Failure," 282.

be so hard up for workers that he would press into service anyone who had been empowered regardless of his moral qualifications. . . . Gifts and power for service the Spirit surely desires to impart; but holiness and spiritual worship come first."[46]

When is ministerial restoration proper and possible? John Armstrong offers three practical questions in making this determination.[47] First, does the leader exhibit the fruits of true repentance? Second, is the leader's sin resulting from a momentary moral lapse or part of a habitual, cunning, and deceptive sin that reflects a seriously flawed character? Third, will the leader be accountable to others as he works through the restoration process?

An overseer who deems ministerial restoration appropriate is responsible for providing the proper time and guidance to ensure its success. Armstrong describes three common approaches to the restoration timeline: immediate, ultimate, and spiritual.[48] Immediate restoration involves minimal time as it wrongly asserts that to be forgiven is to be qualified. Spiritual restoration requires no time as it offers personal restoration but no restoration to the office.

For this reason, Armstrong offers the second option, which includes restoration to the pastoral office after some time (generally one to three years) to allow for intense spiritual, emotional, and familial counsel.[49] Jack Hayford extends that range by an additional year with the understanding that sin "isn't the fruit of a moment; neither is restoration."[50] Hayford believes this "discipline of time" is about healing and mending, not punishment. Mosgofian and Ohlschlager present restoration in more pointed terms and state that when "we do not discipline in a serious manner, we reject justice; by not heeding the real harm of these activities, we undermine genuine healing grace."[51]

Such restoration comes neither quickly nor easily. Public confession by the violator marks the initiation and public affirmation by the restorer is the culmination of this process. Periodic review by the overseer during this time of personal restoration is a primary factor in determining whether ministerial restoration will continue.

---

46. Tozer, *That Incredible Christian*, 37.
47. Armstrong, *Can Fallen Pastors Be Restored?*, 42.
48. Armstrong, *Can Fallen Pastors be Restored?*, 32, 92.
49. Armstrong, *Can Fallen Pastors be Restored?*, 32; see also Briggs, *Fail*, 141.
50. Hayford, *Restoring Fallen Leaders*, 38.
51. Mosgofian and Ohlschlager, *Sexual Misconduct in Counseling and Ministry*, 250.

Regardless of the decision to allow or deny ministerial restoration, church leaders and congregants are obligated to hear the victim(s) and provide holistic healing, as the following subsection addresses.

HEARING AND HEALING THE VICTIM(S)

> "It seems easier to be God than to love God, easier to control people than to love people, easier to own life than to love life."
>
> — Henry Nouwen

In addition to initiating the spiritual and emotional care necessary for the violator's holistic restoration, the overseer is equally responsible for ensuring those adversely impacted by the minister's illicit behavior receive similar support. This subsection summarizes the care and challenges typically facing three groups: the abused, the violator's family, and the minister's congregation. Victims in these three groups require personalized care that is as unique as the individuals themselves. Compassionate support in safe, secure, and open environments is vital. Ultimately, holistic ministry to the victims "will be challenging, exhausting and probably even expensive."[52]

Churches retraumatize victims and deny biblical justice when they fail to hear the victim and facilitate the healing of wounds inherent to abuse. As Peter Levine rightly asserts, "Trauma is not what happens to us, but what we hold inside in the absence of an empathetic witness."[53] Thus, neither the church leaders nor the congregation decides whether the victim has been heard and helped. This determination resides with the victim alone (Matt 18:15–19).

The Spirit is an empathetic witness, but this requires intimacy with God—and intimacy is something many victims come to fear. Betrayal by one who professes to represent God often sees victims project feelings of betrayal upon God himself.[54] Therefore, pastors, Christian counselors, and spiritual mentors must be competent and committed to engaging all four

---

52. Grenz and Bell, *Betrayal of Trust*, 129.

53. Levine, *In an Unspoken Voice*, xii. See also DeGroat, *When Narcissism Comes to Church*, loc. 1800; Trull and Carter, *Ministerial Ethics*, 180.

54. Chandler, *Christian Spiritual Formation*, 52; Cooper-White, "Soul Stealing," 197; Grenz and Bell, *Betrayal of Trust*, 35; Johnson and Van Vonderen, *Subtle Power Spiritual Abuse*, 41. For example, a 2006 national survey by Baylor University found that 23 percent of people viewed God as benevolent or loving, while 32 percent saw him as authoritarian, 24 percent as distant, and 16 percent as critical. Five percent claimed to be atheist (Jennings, *God-Shaped Brain*, 27).

historical functions of ministerial care—healing, sustaining, reconciling, and guiding.[55]

Much harm can come within the congregational setting, as well. Preventing further harm begins with the prohibition of victim-blaming. While some women involved in seemingly consensual though illicit behaviors may bear some responsibility, pastoral influence and power paradigms, as well as his commission to maintain the sacred trust, must remain the preeminent factor. Christians are not allowed to vilify those with whom they disagree or depict as disloyal. It is also necessary to dismantle narcissistic structures that inflict further trauma through humiliation, criticism, exclusion, and the like.[56] Instead, Christians should extend loving inclusion, which is an intentional act that:

- Aims to negate self-imposed blame by the victim, who often believes herself responsible for or deserving of the abuse suffered.
- Works with the victim to overcome shame. As Ann-Janine Morey powerfully asserts, "sexual abuse by pastors exhibits the same dynamic as incestuous abuse, which takes place within the context of an intimate relationship (family, church, counseling) between an authoritative and powerful person (a relative or minister) and a person who is vulnerable to and trusting of that power (a child or counselee)."[57]
- Extends patience as the victim reclaims herself—perhaps a lifetime of patience. Emotional, spiritual, and professional counseling support can ease heavy burdens and enable the victim to press forward.[58]
- Brings justice to open her prison door. Justice-making is a process that demands truth-telling, acknowledging the violation, compassion, protecting the vulnerable (further harm to the victim and others who may be at risk of harm), accountability, restitution (such as payment for therapy), and vindication.[59]

The example of Lori Anne Thompson, a victim of online sexual abuse by Ravi Zacharias, highlights right and wrong approaches to victim support. In the latter category, a Christian counselor advised her at the time of the abuse not to tell anyone, especially her husband, as "the kingdom

55. Benner, *Strategic Pastoral Counseling*, 15; Willimon, *Pastor*, 208.

56. For a fuller and descriptive list, see Out of the FOG, "Top 100 Traits of People Who Suffer from Personality Disorders."

57. Morey, "Blaming Women for the Sexually Abusive Male Pastor," 866.

58. Though Scripture does not directly address the issue, the relief to Bathsheba's secret and silent struggle when Nathan arose as God's advocate is worth consideration.

59. Fortune and Poling, *Sexual Abuse by Clergy*, 9–10.

of God would be irreparably damaged."⁶⁰ Thompson was already suicidal when her husband became aware of the sexting. Their family soon disintegrated in shame and blame. Zacharias's ministry added to this burden by filing lawsuits and bringing accusations to "publicly and falsely crucify" them. The restoration of family structure and individual self-worth eventually saw progress after years of trauma-informed therapy.

Like Thompson, some victims will need professional and possibly long-term psychiatric care.⁶¹ Sexualization and objectification undermine self-confidence, and many victims see themselves as flawed and defective.⁶² This struggle includes extended victims such as family members. As Thompson explains regarding her husband, the "lack of any cognitive framework for clergy sexual abuse mixed with deep attachment wounds of his own [left] my husband drowning in shame and excruciating pain."⁶³ Some participants, both willing and coerced, may suffer from emotional brokenness and the resulting struggle with "learned powerlessness" (i.e., they have not learned the skills needed not to be victimized) and are unable to advocate for themselves.

In contrast, others believe it would be disloyal to do so. Discussing the violation may become overwhelming as emotions of repulsion, self-doubt, shock, confusion, and terror flood the victim. Shame and fear of abandonment render it difficult for many victims to speak. Some even experience emotional or physical stasis, as revisiting abuse often causes the victim to relive (rather than remember) the sensory and emotional trauma.⁶⁴

Successful Christian and psychiatric counseling offers loving acceptance, validates pain and experience, and endeavors to understand the pain. This care builds trust through which the partnership, led and enabled by the Spirit, heals broken hearts, rebuilds self-identity, urges unconditional forgiveness, establishes healthy actions and attitudes, and restores hope.

---

60. Thompson, "Victim Impact Statement."

61. Such need is well expressed by Ruth Hetzendorfer, a Christian counselor and professor who flatly states,. "When I first started counseling, I was amazed at how many women had been sexually abused. I soon realized that all my education did not prepare me adequately to deal with this issue" (Hetzendorfer, *Pastoral Counseling Handbook*, 7).

62. Sexualization is linked with the three most common disorders diagnosed in females: eating disorders, low self-esteem, and depression (Yarhouse and Tan, *Sexuality and Sex Therapy*, 52).

63. Thompson, "Victim Impact Statement," para. 12.

64. This freeze response "might be the most toxic to our souls" as it leads the victim to emotionally dissociate to avoid further harm (DeGroat, *When Narcissism Comes to Church*, loc. 2012(. See also van der Kolk, *Body Keeps the Score*, 219; Thompson, *Soul of Shame*, 66–8.

Yet, such counsel is not exclusive to the victim. The violator's family also requires intense spiritual and psychological care.

The violator's wife should enter personal, professional counseling as soon as possible, as her husband's sexual misconduct can devastate every facet of her being. His unfaithful behavior may cause her to question her adequacy as a woman and wife and her role as an adequate "pastor's wife." His illicit lifestyle may further cause her to forfeit her lifestyle—her position in the church, the friends she needs now more than ever, and possibly her job and home. In this desperate hour of isolation comes the harsh realization that "if she were able to stay within the marriage relationship, her only companion would be the man who hurt her."[65]

As if the scenario weren't bad enough, some wives must face this daunting reality while tending to their wounded children, burdened by betrayal, embarrassment, and fear of an uncertain future. While such effects are common to children of divorce, minister's children also see their father "transformed from a much loved and admired pastor to a public pariah."[66] The sudden force with which this happens leaves emotional scars that may never heal. In addition, the children—especially those in their formative years—may enter into depression, develop unhealthy views of sexuality, and never develop an ability to trust.

The healing of a betrayed wife begins with an allowance to grieve.[67] This normal process often starts with shock and denial, a natural protective response. Emotions soon progress to anger, a natural redirection of pain and suffering. Mourning and possibly depression follow, which are natural ways to grieve the seeming death of the relationship amid the struggle between what was and what will be. "Bargaining" is a common but unhealthy tendency at this stage. To avoid further pain, the wife may falsely accept blame for "driving" the husband into unfaithfulness and offer to change her behavior.[68] Such instances demonstrate the critical need for the wisdom and guidance of "those who are spiritual" and professional counselors. Ultimately, the betrayed spouse will come to a place of acceptance, which does not mean she condones her spouse's actions but has accepted and is ready to move forward in this new reality.

---

65. Bryce, "After the Affair," 64.

66. Grenz and Bell, *Betrayal of Trust*, 127.

67. Grief stages can be experienced within hours or (more normally) in days or months. In addition, the wife may repeat the stages several times. See Clinton and Laaser, *Quick Reference Guide*, 138–39.

68. Though not responsible for her husband's behavior, it should be noted that the wife and husband are mutually responsible for their future relationship.

In anticipation of the significant challenges, the couple should permit a period of separation to allow both individuals time and emotional space to process feelings and perhaps prevent negative responses such as "flooding, flying, and fighting."[69] A safe, protected distance may also be necessary for the wife's emotional and physical protection. The reunion may not be peaceful and could be awkward and contentious. Sound counsel helps reason overcome emotion so that communication can take place. Still, the lack of communication that contributed to marital problems may prove a point of contention in marital restoration. Emotional malformation renders many violators unable to share their feelings in healthy ways. Some violators are emotionally closed and unable to feel, let alone share how they feel.[70] For others, feelings are painful reminders to be avoided at all costs. Still, others find non-attached conversation far easier, as it does not require vulnerability and thus erases the fear of abandonment that might occur if the "true me" becomes known. Of course, these tendencies prove incredibly frustrating for spouses who desire close connections. Here, counselors must first construct communication techniques to rebuild trust through truth-telling.[71] This effort will eventually address the need for personal responsibility and accountability and replace the tendency to isolate with a commitment to participate.

The violating minister's congregation is the third victim that requires spiritual and emotional restoration.[72] This responsibility may be the most neglected aspect of sexual misconduct.[73] The overseer or designated denominational leader can expect to find a myriad of emotions and responses strewn among the wreckage. These include shocked disbelief, anger, or denial; feelings of failure, betrayal, and helplessness; avoidance of the issue; fear about the future; suspicion of leadership; and victim-blaming. Some parishioners will unite in solidarity, while others wish to speak in

---

69. Ripley and Worthington, *Couple Therapy*, 52; see also Clinton and Laaser, *Quick Reference Guide*, 139.

70. This is a strong example of why professional psychiatric care is necessary, as "we cannot heal what we cannot feel" (Bradshaw, *Healing the Shame That Binds You*, 54).

71. For example, the need to identify and discuss things that are or are not helpful to the individual or relationship may begin as a written exercise and progress to verbal comment toward full discussion. In this approach, the couple learns healthy communication skills while correcting unhealthy beliefs and behaviors.

72. This is in keeping with Christ's compassionate care for sheep that are hurt and helpless, and without a shepherd (Matt 9:36; Mark 6:34; cf. Acts 20:28; Eph 4:1–16).

73. Mosgofian and Ohlschlager, *Sexual Misconduct in Counseling and Ministry*, 181.

privacy. Careful observation of all responses will reveal whether the church is healthy or toxic.[74]

While each church is unique, ministerial moral failure requires counsel for congregants in four common areas: unity with God, unity with one another, acceptance of responsibility, and commitment to persevere. The overseer must balance the pastoral mission (mercy) and the prophetic mission (justice).[75] Balance is achieved through truth-telling, acknowledging the violation (and thus breaking its power to continue to harm), demonstrating deliberate and sustained compassion for victims, accountability of wrongdoing by the violator, restitution made to the victim(s), and exoneration of victim(s) to sever any associated guilt or shame and enable the victim(s) to identify as an accepted and unstained member of the community. As Jacqueline Grey rightly asserts, "the reputation of individuals or institutions is not to be prioritized over truth-telling" as this undermines the justice of God.[76]

Overseers, mentors, and church members should expect unity to prove elusive and fragile. This challenge is especially true when toxic leadership dominates the church. The hierarchy, patriarchy, and power in which narcissistic systems thrive undermine the church's "cruciform humility" and "kenotic configuration."[77] Such structures allow illicit behaviors to flourish and fail to develop the biblical discipleship that enables individual and corporate perseverance. Yet even a spiritually strong church should anticipate polarization within and a possible loss of confidence among congregants and community alike.

A congregation's holistic restoration requires overseers or designated leaders to dismantle the toxic church systems that often form around and enable the minister's illicit activities. Ideally, this would take place before the leader devolves into immoral behavior. Still, such proactive measures are uncommon because it is difficult to identify, let alone "confront, systemic narcissism in churches that are seen as successful, special, blessed, Spirit-led, and anointed."[78]

---

74. Healthy churches demonstrate commitment to finding the truth, healing the hurting, and extending God's grace. The toxic church responds (at least initially) with denial and defense and seeks to protect image over function.

75. Fortune, *Is Nothing Sacred?*, 114–18; Mosgofian and Ohlschlager, *Sexual Misconduct in Counseling and Ministry*, 186.

76. Grey, "Prophetic Call to Repentance," 24–25. Indeed, David's legacy might have ended were it not for Nathan's obedient application of this principle (2 Sam 12:1–15).

77. DeGroat, *When Narcissism Comes to Church*, loc. 323.

78. DeGroat, *When Narcissism Comes to Church*, loc. 119.

SECTION THREE: WHEN DISASTER STRIKES

Accusations of pastoral misconduct make toxic church cultures far easier to identify. Church leaders typically try to preserve the secret of pastoral misconduct in such systems. When this fails, they try to protect the church's good name and the pastor's reputation. As Scot McKnight and Laura McKnight Barringer note, eight telltale signs emerge as church leaders seek to protect the minister and ministry: [79]

1. Discredit accusers and critics through character assassination, questioning motives, or alleging collusion.
2. Demonize accusers and critics as evildoers trying to do harm.
3. Spin the story with an alternative version or false narrative. Strong denials from the pastor and other leaders often precede this approach.
4. Gaslight critics by making them question their memory, perception, or judgment.
5. Present the perpetrator as the victim.
6. Silence the truth through nondisclosure agreements and membership covenants.
7. Suppress the truth through shaming, intimidation, or the threat of consequences.
8. Issue a fake apology, one void of confession or repentance, designed to appease the audience. It commonly offers excuses and justification for inappropriate behavior.

Even when rightly identified, removing a toxic leader does not necessarily eradicate a toxic church culture. Narcissism, by nature, demands complete allegiance. When its toxic tendencies metastasize within the collective, it produces powerful systems that "hide invisible forces that work below the surface."[80] Dismantling these systems is difficult, requiring personal and organizational honesty and a willingness to take intentional steps toward systemic healing. This correction is no easy feat. "Grandiose systems often resist change, however. They resist because grandiosity works. Integrity gives way to pragmatism; honesty gives way to illusion. The status quo is much easier than the work of becoming self-aware."[81] In addition to the actions of Ravi Zacharias previously mentioned, other notable examples include:

---

79. McKnight and Barringer, *Church Called Tov*, 56–72.
80. DeGroat, *When Narcissism Comes to Church*, loc. 1502.
81. DeGroat, *When Narcissism Comes to Church*, loc. 1560.

- Mark Driscoll's 2014 removal from the Acts 29 church planting network for an abusive leadership style that displayed "arrogance, responding to conflict with a quick temper and harsh speech, and leading the staff and elders in a domineering manner."[82] The board also noted "ungodly and disqualifying behavior" related to heavy criticism of various groups made under the pseudonym "William Wallace II."[83]
- The 2018 removal of Bill Hybels as Willow Creek's pastor after forty-five years. In addition to confirming "sexually inappropriate words and actions," an independent investigation noted "denigrating verbal abuse" and the repeated description that Hybels would "power up" when he disagreed with others.[84]
- The 2019 removal and "public rebuke" of founding pastor James MacDonald from Harvest Bible Chapel after decades of "insulting, belittling, and verbally bullying others," improperly exercising positional and spiritual authority over others to his advantage, and "extravagant spending utilizing church resources resulting in personal benefit."[85]

Designated leaders will face deep and sometimes visceral responses ranging from anger to empathy. Some believers may reject the possibility of wrongdoing on the pastor's part. Others may demand swift forgiveness and restoration—if not on the pastor's behalf, perhaps to maintain a good reputation or financial stability for the church's sake. Others may be confused and cautious, unsure of what has happened or how best to proceed. Still, others may feel the church is too slow or soft in response; feelings of betrayal or commitment to a righteous standard drive the demand for a swift and strong response. The necessary call for solidarity with victims and the potential emergence of past victims is likely to add fuel to this proverbial fire.

Like a fallen minister, restoring a broken church requires honesty, transparency, and submission to the Spirit's transformative and healing works. Some cases also require corrective measures. As asserted in chapter 5, secular culture may adversely influence an individual's actions and attitudes. Similarly, churches have their own cultures, and their influence is profound. Unhealthy church cultures often fail to hear or heal the victim or restore (to God and perhaps ministry) the violator. Before this failure,

82. Lee, "Story of Mark Driscoll and Mars Hill."
83. Bailey, "Mark Driscoll Removed."
84. Miller, "Misconduct Allegations Against Willow Creek Founder."
85. Buckley, "Harvest Bible Chapel Elders Issue 'Public Rebuke.'"

usually years prior, the unhealthy system may have placed unreasonable demands on the pastor, resulting in emotional depletion and increasing vulnerability. Unhealthy systems sometimes fail to maintain pastoral accountability and development. Still, others see a symbiotic bond form between narcissistic leaders and sycophants. No matter the scenario, the dysfunctional church comes to be led by an increasingly dysfunctional pastor. Toxic systems create an atmosphere where violators can thrive and victims are susceptible. The repentant church unifies with the Spirit and designated restoration team to dismantle the dysfunctional structure and restore or create a healthy Christian community (e.g., 1 Cor 5:1–13).

With the broken victims and dysfunctional church structures addressed, the following chapter addresses the necessary steps for building the restoration team.

8

Building the Restoration Team

"Think of me as a fellow patient in the same hospital who, having been admitted a little earlier, could give some advice."

— C. S. Lewis

I HAVE ENDURED AND provided disaster relief after many hurricanes, but none compare to Hurricane Katrina. I was part of a team that arrived in New Orleans the day after Katrina hit in August 2005. The sight of floodwaters and leveled forests one hundred miles inland provided ominous warning of disasters unimagined. Indeed, the catastrophe grew in severity with each passing mile. The storm claimed more than 1,800 lives, left millions homeless, and caused approximately $161 billion in property damage.

Some might say our comparatively small team contributed little to the grand scheme. The families we served might say otherwise. Our team gutted and rebuilt a church facility that served a large and newly homeless population. Elsewhere, we restored an abandoned pavilion from which we operated a sizeable distribution center that supplied hundreds of families daily. Medical teams and relief agencies soon joined. Through it all, we offered spiritual and emotional support. We saturated the survivors with our prayers and God's promise that he would not abandon them in their time of need.

Imagine if all the countless relief teams had set up soup kitchens and nothing more. Survivors certainly need sustenance, but that is not all they need. Victims of natural disasters need medical and psychological care. They need clean water and clothing, shelter and sanitation. Storm-ravaged individuals have little, if any, hope of meeting these and other needs on their own. Instead, they must rely on multiple agencies to restore what was lost.

Ministerial restoration following a perfect storm is no different. A moral failure will cause many victims to incur various damages. Chapter 7 addressed this disaster response as it pertains to the abused, the violator's family, and the affected congregation. The following chapter details the specialized restoration team needed to restore the fallen minister to God and his calling.

Indeed, biblical restoration is a team effort. Though Lazarus committed no moral failure of which we know, the raising of Jesus' friend provides a good analogy (John 11:1–44). Lazarus was dead for four days. As Mary pointedly observed, Jesus did nothing to change the situation. It might have been cause for celebration when Jesus ordered the gravestone removed, but Martha instead challenged the command. "By now, he stinks," she said. In other words, don't go there. Perhaps you could have done something sooner, but you're too late. Now, the matter is dead and buried. And frankly, it stinks. Just leave it alone.

That's how many followers of Christ view a fallen minister. He is dead to us. This whole situation stinks. Just bury him away where no one can see, and let us get about our business.

Undeterred, Jesus told the people to roll away the stone. What a beautiful moment! Granted, the men tasked with this duty were probably not thrilled. Gravestones weighed between one and two tons and, once in place, would likely require an uphill push to open the sepulcher. But that is the beauty of it—Jesus' spoken command could have caused the stone to vacate, yet he directed Lazarus's friends and family to remove the massive object that stood between Lazarus and the Lord. Then, having commanded Lazarus to come out of his dark tomb, Jesus told the onlookers to loose him and let him go, to cut away everything that kept Lazarus bound. Only then could he walk free and with the Lord. Jesus still expects his followers to remove the grave clothes so the restored can put on "grace clothes."[1]

Get ready to roll away those heavy stones and cut away the grave clothes. The following subsections describe such restoration teams. Each team is personalized, tailored to the individual violator and circumstances, and comprises specialized participants uniquely contributing to success. These include a denominational leader responsible for selecting and leading the team; professional Christian mental health counselors who provide emotional, behavioral, and marital treatment; spiritual mentors who hold the violator accountable for holistic growth and set boundaries that will

---

1. Cf. Isa 61:10; Zech 3:1–5; Rom 13:12–14; Eph 4:22–32; 6:10–18; Col 3; 1 Pet 5:5, Rev 3:18.

protect the violator and others; and a designated congregation whose community provides space for relational interaction and holistic (re)formation.

THE ROLE OF THE OVERSEER

"From the first commencement of my episcopacy, I made up my mind to do nothing on my own private opinion, without your [his fellow clergy's] advice and without the consent of the people."

— Cyprian of Carthage

Cyprian was the bishop of Carthage in modern Tunisia during the brutal Decian persecution (AD 249–250). The church viewed martyrdom as discipleship to this point, but the edict marked the first coordinated Empire-wide persecution of Christians. Rome eliminated numerous senior bishops and leaders. Notably, Pope Fabian in Rome; Babylas, the bishop of Antioch; and Alexander, the bishop of Jerusalem, were tortured and died in prison. Rome also imprisoned and tortured Origen when he refused to recant his faith. The church father was released when the edict ended but died from his injuries soon after.

Some leaders and laity pointed to these martyrs as examples to follow. Others lapsed under the threat of torture and death. Many "lapsi" later sought reconciliation through repentance, but some who stood in faith (and bore gruesome scars as testimony) demanded the church excommunicate all apostates. Cyprian opted for a middle ground and restored lapsed believers if they demonstrated contrition and completed a rigorous battery of penance.[2]

Such context makes the quote above all the more remarkable. Cyprian's emphasis on the role of bishops arguably diminished the priesthood of all believers. Still, his approach affirmed the role of fellow ministers and laity in ecumenical decisions up to and including restoration. Such restoration remains a partnership between ministers and the laity.

Unfortunately, contemporary denominational leaders have a dismal track record when addressing sexual misconduct. A typical response

---

2. It should be noted that Cyprian went into hiding as the aforementioned bishops were martyred. Though he faced harsh criticism, Cyprian's reasons were rooted in function rather than fear. Cyprian essentially established the belief that salvation was impossible apart from the church, which meant the people were heavily dependent on the ministers. Therefore, rather than allow see the church lose the function, wisdom, and experience of its leaders, he advocated his survival strategy and directed the church through written letters.

involves the pastor's swift move to another location (often without disclosing the reason for the transfer). The assumption is that the pastor will not repeat the illicit behaviors amid threat of repercussions or "because the shame of being found out once again would be too painful," yet this "geographic cure" rarely works.[3]

The biblical restoration outlined in section 4 requires a different approach—one that designates an overseer to ensure the integrity of the restoration process and ministerial licensure. This denominational leader or representative is responsible not only for the spiritual health and protection of the fallen minister but also for the minister's family, victim(s), affected congregation, and the congregation to which the minister is assigned if church reassignment is appropriate.

Quoting the seventeenth-century Benedictine mystic Dom Augustine Baker, Richard Foster rightly states that the overseer "is only God's usher, and must lead souls in God's way, and not his own."[4] The overseer must demonstrate genuine maturity, compassion, and commitment and be transparent and truthful. As Foster elsewhere asserts, "in our day, the desperate need is for the emergence of a massive spiritual army of trained spiritual directors who can lovingly come alongside precious people and help them discern how to walk by faith in the circumstances of their own lives."[5]

The overseer's responsibilities begin with a complete and impartial investigation of the charges, as discussed in chapter 7. If charges are validated, the overseer is responsible for determining whether restoration is allowed and, if so, to what extent. For example, the overseer may determine a violator is eligible only for a limited ministerial restoration in which the violator is allowed to fill administrative roles but prohibited from direct pastoral oversight. Having identified the allowances, the overseer is responsible for constructing the restoration team and plan. The overseer is also responsible for facilitating ministerial support for the violated. Specifically, this includes the victim(s), the violator's family members, and the affected congregation.

The overseer must maintain a nonattachment attitude during the investigation and restoration analysis. Though this overseer will have repeated contact with the violator, such meetings aim not to counsel but to obtain a comprehensive assessment to develop a proper restorative plan.

Because the restoration plan will require spiritual, emotional, and familial counsel, the violator must grant the overseer access beyond the offense's detailed and honest account. This access includes spiritual health

---

3. Laaser, *Healing the Wounds*, 50–51.
4. Foster, *Celebration of Discipline*, 185.
5. Foster, "Spiritual Formation Agenda," 31.

assessment and family relations, past emotional trauma and boundary violations suffered by the perpetrator, determination of emotional stability, and psychiatric analysis pertinent to the violation and related behaviors.[6] Obtaining this and other information requires informed consent in which the violator (1) grants full release by which the overseer or his designee is allowed to talk to anyone he deems necessary, (2) affirms that there will be no off-the-record communication, (3) acknowledges the evaluator's role as a mandatory reporter, and (4) acknowledges that failure to complete the restoration plan will result in the loss of ministerial standing.[7] Such consent allows overt rather than covert observation.

The overseer should interview the violator and the victim(s) and carefully review police reports and legal filings. The evaluator should interview key church members, colleagues, the minister's supervisor, and family to gain insight into the sexual misconduct and determine whether adverse behaviors were evident before the violation. Church minutes from previous years may also prove beneficial.

If restoration is deemed appropriate, the overseer is responsible for forming a threefold cord to pull the minister from the grip of destruction. This cord comprises a Christian mental health professional, capable mentors, and a spiritual congregation. Each will come alongside the violator and provide continuous counsel and accountability.

THE ROLE OF CHRISTIAN MENTAL HEALTH PROVIDERS

"Nothing is easier than to denounce the evil doer; nothing is more difficult than to understand him."

— Fyodor Dostoyevsky

---

6. The Health Insurance Portability and Accountability Act (HIPAA) Privacy Rule requires signed HIPAA release for any use or disclosure of protected health information (45 Code of Federal Regulations § 164.508). The authorization must include a description of the information that will be used/disclosed, the purpose for which the information will be disclosed, the name of the person or entity to whom the information will be disclosed, an expiration date or expiration event when consent is withdrawn, and the right of the individual to revoke authorization. Even with authorization, the overseer must adhere to the Minimum Necessary Rule, which stipulates that the disclosure of Protected Health Information (PHI) must be limited to the minimum necessary for the stated purpose.

7. This list draws from Mosgofian and Ohlschlager, *Sexual Misconduct in Counseling and Ministry*, 240.

Without question, godly character is of greater worth than a minister's passion or wise counsel.[8] Therefore, restoration must identify and rectify deformative factors contributing to illicit behaviors. Victims and violators also require "safe and intentional spaces" in which they can discuss their struggles, woundings, failures, and identities.[9] In addition, violators may struggle with mental health issues such as depression, anxiety, and attentional disorders. The violator may require outpatient or intensive inpatient treatment, and significant mood disorders may require psychiatric medication.

Such understanding requires counseling beyond the spiritual to address emotional and behavioral issues.[10] This counsel can include professional Christian psychotherapy (especially one using a cognitive-behavioral approach), group therapy, and marital and family therapies. Such matters demand the care and guidance of a trained professional who is distinctly Christian in life and practice. Through systemic processes such as guided discovery and collaborative empiricism, the mental health professional and the patient can work together to identify critical issues involved in the individual's struggles, examine the evidence that supports or refutes his beliefs, and establish common treatment goals.

Ministerial restoration programs often omit this therapeutic approach. For example, Tim LaHaye's popular eight-step restoration process includes genuine repentance, rebuilding the spiritual life and marriage, helping the minister find work, establishing a waiting period, a restoration service, considering ministry other than a pastorate, and ongoing voluntary accountability.[11] This list is strong but does not mention the emotional and social factors prevalent in many decision-making processes.

In addition, the inclusion of psychological counsel may challenge the preference of Christian leaders who prefer the exclusive use of biblical counsel for fear of "diluting the tradition's distinctiveness" or

---

8. Tim Sensing captures this truth when he evaluates Robert Reid's summary of the three canons of persuasion. Reid rightly asserts, "Congregants come to trust wise counsel (*logos*) from the preacher who seems to possess good character (*ethos*), who becomes appropriately passionate (*pathos*) about matters that the community views as central to their corporate shared identity" (Reid, *Four Voices of Preaching*, 17). Sensing further asserts that *ethos* is the primary of the three when one considers the preacher's credibility and authenticity (Sensing, *Qualitative Research*, 5).

9. Briggs, *Fail*, 17; Carnes, *Out of the Shadows*, 15; Clinton and Laaser, *Quick Reference Guide*, 130.

10. Treatment includes elements of ontology (how one views oneself), phenomenology (how one identifies the meaning of the lived experience), and epistemology (how one comes to know).

11. LaHaye, *If Ministers Fall, Can They Be Restored?*, 171–84.

introducing secularism into the solution.[12] What follows are three points for consideration.

The first challenge to limiting care to biblical counsel alone is that we do not reside entirely in the spiritual realm. Furthermore, our knowledge of that realm (let alone the others) is remarkably dim (1 Cor 13:9–12). God has perfect knowledge, yet "Scripture and history make it clear that *we* do not."[13] Second, the biblical directive to "not be conformed to this world, but be transformed by the renewing of your mind" (Rom 12:2) often requires that one understand and correct emotional brokenness not directly addressed in Scripture.[14] This understanding is critical for creatures of fragile constitutions relentlessly tossed about by selfish and cultural forces beyond our control. Third, one goal of psychology is to discover how one should be fully human and find lasting fulfillment. Is this not a primary call of Christian discipleship?

While secular psychology often neglects (and sometimes negates) spiritual aspects of this journey, it fully recognizes the brokenness of the human condition. Christianity should accept the subsequent diagnoses and prognoses and would do well to consider their benefits and the heritage of psychology itself.[15] Therefore, the inclusion of Christian psychology, informed by yet independent of the broader field and one that defines human meaning and action through solid theological understanding and spiritual formation, is of immeasurable worth.[16]

---

12. Johnson, *Psychology and Christianity*, 23.

13. Hathaway and Yarhouse, *Integration of Psychology & Christianity*, 24.

14. Willimon, *Pastor*, 116. As a result, many who try to overcome emotional wounding through spiritual effort alone are left discouraged and confused.

15. Many argue that the heritage of psychology is parallel to, if not drawn from Christian tradition (for example, Johnson, *Psychology and Christianity*, 10–14). Dennis Okholm argues that psychology is rooted in aesthetic and monastic theology of the fourth through seventh centuries, and notably that of Evagrius, Cassian, and Gregory (Okholm, *Dangerous Passions Deadly Sins*, 6–8). In addition, the terms "uncovery," "discovery," and "recovery" that Donald Hands and Wayne Fehr use to describe a patient's journey from darkness to light bears remarkable similarities to mystic descriptions of the "purgative," the "illuminative," and the "unitive" aspects of progress toward God (Hands and Fehr, *Spiritual Wholeness for Clergy*, xii).

16. Johnson, *Psychology and Christianity*, 36–37; McMinn, *Psychology, Theology, and Spirituality in Christian Counseling*, 24. Successful incorporation of Christian psychology requires sound theoretical integration that holds the theological and psychological in productive tension yet allows expanded understanding in and through both. William Hathaway's hermeneutical-process model of integration, which is centered on Gadamer's "fusion of horizons," provides a strong example. See Hathaway and Yarhouse, *Integration of Psychology & Christianity*, 89.

The holistic restoration model encourages the Christian mental health professional(s) to apply a transformational psychology view. Indeed, psychological care is "too heavily focused on repairing what is broken and fixing pathology rather than on promoting growth and health."[17] Conversely, transformational psychology is a teleological approach that discovers a person's psychology through observable realities understood by faith, truths from Scripture, and the experience of the Spirit. The "hope-focused couple approach" is a commendable option for marital counseling after a ministerial moral failure.[18] This pragmatic approach offers hope for change by engaging well-researched theories within a fluid structure that centers on Christian disciplines, thus allowing tailor-made strategies unique to the individuals and circumstances. Notably, the approach is strength-focused rather than problem-focused. The therapy identifies their strengths (as individuals and as a couple) and then uses those strengths to overcome weaknesses and help them mature as individuals and as a couple.

Such an approach carries the goal of spiritual and emotional transformative growth.[19] The inclusion of spiritual mentors further aids this effort.

THE ROLE OF SPIRITUAL MENTORS

"When it comes to mentors, we tend to look for one 'North Star,' one brilliant and trustworthy voice who can guide us through the dark nights. But sailors know that it takes more than one star; it takes a constellation."

— GLENN PACKIAM

The mentor is a non-negotiable aspect of restoration because "you cannot give yourself grace and you cannot restore yourself. That has to be a gift, first from God, and then from significant persons in your life."[20] The gift is multifaceted as it balances guidance with correction, encouragement with warning, opportunities with restrictions, and the listening ear with honest appraisal.

---

17. Hathaway and Yarhouse, *The Integration of Psychology & Christianity*, 13.
18. See Ripley and Worthington, *Couple Therapy*.
19. Coe and Hall, "Transformational Psychology View," 200–203. See also Benner, *Psychotherapy and the Spiritual Quest*; Hall and Coe, *Psychology in the Spirit*, 85–86; Johnson, *Psychology and Christianity*, 37–38; Tan, *Counseling and Psychotherapy*, 371–72.
20. London and Wiseman, *Pastors at Risk*, 81.

In its truest sense, the mentor is a conduit that leads from darkness to light. Such transit is easier said than done. The fallen minister would rather reside in darkness, not necessarily in dark deeds, but in the security of hiddenness. The errant minister was adept at hiding sexual dysfunction so that an ideal image could remain in view. Now fallen, he will typically reverse this approach and become hidden when the sin comes into view. The tomb of isolation and shame perpetually deepens because "sin demands to have a man by himself [and] withdraws him from the community. The more isolated a person is, the more destructive will be the power of sin over him, and the more deeply he becomes involved in it, the more disastrous is his isolation. Sin wants to remain unknown."[21]

God's sanctifying grace is the key to change, and the Spirit is the agent of change, but learning and accepting truths about self and God are the catalysts for change. That is why the mentor is a conduit—such learning is a relational journey, a perichoretic progression of the violator, mentor, and Spirit.

Trust is necessary to navigate the vast array of challenges that await. Building trust is not easy, and revealing shame is not easy where trust is absent. Therefore, having a spiritual mentor who is a close or respected associate is enormously beneficial.[22] While a church board or denominational authority may assign the mentor, "spiritual direction is first born out of natural, spontaneous human relationships. A hierarchical, or even organizational system, is not essential to its function and is often destructive to it."[23]

Though not a requirement, those with relatable experiences are of immeasurable worth. Indeed, the wounded should see the spiritual "as a fellow-patient in the same hospital who, having been admitted a little earlier, could give some advice."[24] Those who have overcome similar struggles have intimate knowledge of felt shame, the grace God extends, and the

---

21. Bonhoeffer, *Life Together*, 112.

22. This trust is akin to Carl Rogers' core conditions for therapeutic improvement: empathy, congruence (the counselor is genuine), and unconditional positive regard (the client is confident to speak without fear of criticism or judgment). Furthermore, the mentor should be male for male violators and female for female violators due to the nature of the offense and the counsel that will follow.

23. Foster, *Celebration of Discipline*, 186.

24. These words fittingly introduce restored adulterer Gordon MacDonald's very personal and poignant work (MacDonald, *Rebuilding Your Broken World*, loc. 145). MacDonald is quoting C. S. Lewis, "Letter to Sheldon Vanauken" (April 22, 1953). MacDonald dedicates the book to his wife and "the Angels, a remarkable team of godly men who once surrounded us and determined that here was one broken-world experience that was going to be rebuilt" (loc. 275). See also McMinn, *Psychology, Theology, and Spirituality in Christian Counseling*, 28, 216.

support the violator desperately needs (2 Cor 1:3–5). As Henri Nouwen rightly asserts, the "great illusion of leadership is to think that man can be led out of the desert by someone who has never been there."[25]

Self-inventory is a necessary first step despite any experience the mentor may bring. Paul directs those who are spiritual to restore such a one . . .

> ". . . in a spirit of gentleness; each one looking to yourself, so that you are not tempted as well. Bear one another's burdens, and thereby fulfill the law of Christ. For if anyone thinks that he is something when he is nothing, he deceives himself. But each one must examine his own work, and then he will have reason for boasting, but to himself alone, and not to another. For each one will bear his own load" (Gal 6:1–5; cf. 2 Tim 2:24–25).

What does the apostle mean by "looking to yourself"? Nine considerations anchor a proper self-evaluation:[26] First is an honest evaluation of the mentor's abilities and motives. Restoration results from neither pity nor obligation but committed compassion. Second, the prospective mentor must be a humble person of prayer with sufficient theological knowledge to avert doctrinal error. The mentor must also possess the spiritual maturity to discern and follow God's plan over an emotionally driven response. Third, the prospective mentor must be able to confront the violator with love and gentleness. A mentor candidate who is judgmental or punitive should step down from this opportunity. Fourth, there can be no emotional or professional need for the violator's approval, which may diminish the strength or objectivity needed to confront the individual. Fifth, the mentor's conscience must be clear in this area. If not, the mentor will likely project struggles into the violator's situation. Sixth, the mentor should have a working knowledge of psychology and be able to identify conditions that might require professional therapy. Seventh, the mentor must be able and willing to follow through to completion. Biblical mentorship is a process that takes years and requires a tireless, selfless commitment and resolve. Eighth, a mentor should be mindful of confirmation bias, which is the tendency to search for, favor, and interpret information in ways that confirm or support one's beliefs. Ninth, a mentor with predetermined expectations should not enter the program. While one may expect specific spiritual characteristics and results, God must be allowed to reform the violator as he sees fit. As Dietrich Bonhoeffer notes, "God does not will that I should fashion the other person

---

25. Nouwen, *Wounded Healer*, 72.

26. This list builds upon Laaser, *Healing the Wounds*, 140, and Gemignani, *Spiritual Formation for Pastors*, 93–96.

according to the image that seems good to me, that is, in my own image; rather in his very freedom from me God made this person in His image."[27]

A mentor must also see the individual not only as the violator but also as a victim of sin's deceit.[28] Jesus' Good Samaritan parable illustrates this well (Luke 10:30–37). The parabolic victim was vulnerable, shamed, and powerless to save himself. Unlike the priest and Levite, who likely prioritized purity and ministerial obligations, the Good Samaritan entered the victim's situation with compassion and intent. The Good Samaritan immediately treated the victim's wounds, provided a safe place for rest and recovery, and covered costs.[29]

However, the spiritual mentor differs from the Good Samaritan in notable ways. For example, the spiritual mentor must not leave the victim in another's care but instead commit to a ministry of presence. The spiritual mentor also provides biblical counsel that usually requires a difficult but necessary exploration.[30] The Good Samaritan did not question whether the traveler's poor choices subjected him to danger. He did not ask why the traveler was on that road alone or whether he took appropriate steps to avoid harm. These are questions the mentor must ask.[31]

The violator must be honest with God, himself, and the mentor, but honest dialogue is difficult. Some violators will minimize or even deny their culpability. Some will blame others. Some will try to manipulate the process. Even those who genuinely repent and desire restoration often struggle with an intimacy disorder, which renders the violator incapable of emotional vulnerability (which likely contributed to their decision to meet emotional needs elsewhere).[32] However, if properly understood, the violator's struggle with emotional vulnerability can be a powerful tool in the restoration process. The violator is typically unable or unlikely to speak about his failure(s) because he fears that loved ones would reject and abandon

---

27. Bonhoeffer, *Life Together*, 93.

28. Admittedly, this can be difficult, but "just as the complainant is entitled to loving, compassionate concern, so is the accused" (Grenz and Bell, *Betrayal of Trust*, 165).

29. The term "doctor" originates from the Greek *doceo*, which means "teacher"— those who taught the nature of illness and truth about the body (Willimon, *Pastor*, 122). This well describes the spiritual mentor's primary role. See also Mosgofian and Ohlschlager, *Sexual Misconduct in Counseling and Ministry*, 244.

30. The English word "spleen" comes from the Greek word for *splanchnon*, which is translated as "compassion" throughout the New Testament. Put another way, to be truthful is a compassionate act that takes guts (Willimon, *Pastor*, 121).

31. For an short example of mentor questions, see "Excursus 4: Restoration Resources."

32. Clinton and Laaser, *Quick Reference Guide*, 144; Laaser, *Healing the Wounds*, 55.

him if they truly knew him—and they are the people he most fears losing. However, the violator is less afraid of losing the mentor. Therefore, the swift establishment of safe communication spaces provides a working buffer that enables holistic counsel while protecting (from the violator's perspective) the already strained but cherished relationships.

Establishing boundaries is an excellent way to build trust. These boundaries establish acceptable behaviors within the counseling sessions and are to be agreed upon by the mentor and violator alike. The boundaries protect the violator and others and will hold the violator accountable for holistic growth within those parameters. A basic example of such boundaries follows.

> We are going to talk about [topic]. We have the liberty to explore the depths of this topic, but we will take this at a comfortable pace. This subject can easily lead us into any number of other discussions. Because this topic is essential to our restoration goals, I will nudge us back on track as needed. I mean no offense, and I am happy to discuss the other issues, but I will do so at an appropriate time.
>
> No masks are allowed in here. I am eager to hear and understand what's on your heart, but we must commit to honest dialogue. I am not interested in hearing from a fabricated, plastic preacher. Be real with me, and I will be real with you. You're safe here. What is said here will stay here unless you express a desire or intent to inflict harm on self or others.
>
> We may laugh together, and I hope we do. We may cry together, and I suspect we will. Both are acceptable. We have permission to be human.
>
> I know that some things we discuss will be painful. I will help you bear that cross. Some things you hear from me may be painful. My comments may make you uncomfortable or angry, but these are not personal attacks. I have no right or intent to judge you as a person, but I commit to share the truth about the decisions you have made and will make as we proceed.
>
> Therefore, I commit to be honest with God, you, and myself. I will speak that truth with love. I will do my best to respect your questions and perspectives. I will seek grace, receive grace, and extend grace. I will listen to understand, not simply to respond. And I will listen for what the Spirit is saying throughout.
>
> Will you commit to doing the same?

Such an agreement opens the door to attentive support. However, the violator can exit through the same door, so Paul prescribes gentleness for the fallen minister who enters in a fragile and broken condition (Gal 6:1). While the mentor does not condone the sin, neither does he condemn the sinner. Christlike correction is so tender that it does not break a bruised reed.[33]

The delicate ebb and flow that follows requires probing questions and critical yet compassionate listening. The mentor should encourage the violator to think out loud to externalize considerations. Carefully consider what the fallen minister says (and what he fails to say). The mentor must help the violator realize the flaw in his thinking and sometimes challenge the violator's attempts to evade or resist. Conversely, the mentor must offer an empathetic ear when the minister addresses painful issues and temper his possibly painful counsel with unconditional and accepting love.[34]

As safe and trusted dialogue ensues, it will soon be necessary to establish boundaries that address the violator's familial, professional, and personal activities. These relationships are essential to holistic (re)formation. An eighty-five-year study in which Harvard researchers looked to determine the key to happiness illustrates this well. The study began in 1938 and included 724 participants (and later expanded to include the men's thirteen hundred offspring). Researchers found their answers through biennial interviews and evaluations of health records and life events. The primary source of happiness was not career achievement, physical health, or personal wealth. Positive relationships result in flourishing and longer, fulfilling lives.[35]

As such, the familial, professional, and personal boundaries will be specific to the individual circumstances and adjust as the violator progresses or digresses. Of course, boundaries are only effective when followed. Therefore, the mentor must hold the violator accountable for holistic growth within those parameters.

A tenable accountability plan includes a clear purpose, periodic evaluation, revision of expectations, and closure. Such commitment stifles the unhealthy tendencies inherent to isolation and autonomy by requiring the violator to be open and forthright in all communication, decisions, and

---

33. Isa 42:3; Matt 12:20; cf. Prov 12:18.

34. Willimon, *Pastor*, 116, 217. See also Bonhoeffer. *Life Together*, 97, 99; Hetzendorfer, *Pastoral Counseling Handbook*, 12–15; McMinn, *Psychology, Theology, and Spirituality in Christian Counseling*, 200; Nichols, *Lost Art of Listening*, 62; Seamands, *Ministry in the Image of God*, 150–53. Laura McKnight Barringer poignantly defines empathy as "the ability to feel what someone else feels, to exit our own feelings and enter the experience of others . . . the ability to see the world through others' pain" (McKnight and Barringer, *Church Called Tov*, 100). Cf. Prov 17:17.

35. Mineo, "Harvard Study."

processes. This openness will include disclosure of thoughts and events that led to the illicit behavior, discussion of relational patterns before and after, and honest appraisal of the violator's reconciliation with his family.[36] Such honesty is critical because infidelity resides not only in sex but also in secrecy. Indeed, "it isn't whom you lie with. It's whom you lie to."[37]

While the mentor/violator relationship is most effective when compatibility, regularity, and trust exist, the mentor is not alone in this effort. The outworking of grace and growth takes place within the Christian community.

THE ROLE OF THE CONGREGATION

> "[Spiritual] formation is *the* task of the church. Period. It represents neither an interesting, optional pursuit by the church nor an insignificant category in the job description of the body of Christ. Spiritual formation is at the heart of its whole purpose for existence."
>
> — JAMES WILHOIT

The holistic restoration program answers Cain's pointed question, "Am I my brother's keeper?" with resounding affirmation (Gen 4:9). Yes, I am! Indeed, (re)formation leading to restoration is emotional, spiritual, *and* communal.[38] Significant portions of biblical discipleship and holistic formation occur in and are impossible apart from the church construct.[39]

---

36. Clinton and Laaser, *Quick Reference Guide*, 139.

37. Thoburn and Whitman, "Clergy Affairs," 493.

38. Here, we see a pragmatic correlation to the Great Commandment—love of God, self, and others (Matt 22:26–40). Much like the military unit that stands in *formation*, or a football team that approaches its opponent in a defined *formation*, holistic formation is a unitive act in which the Christian demonstrates selfless discipline and esteems others in service to a greater goal.

39. Boa, *Conformed to His Image*, 35, 429–36. The author presents seven formative purposes unique to the church: corporate love and compassion (cf. Col 3:12–14); corporate identity and purpose (cf. Heb 10:22–25); corporate nurture and service (cf. Eph 4:12); corporate discernment (cf. 1 Cor 14); corporate forgiveness and reconciliation (cf. 1 Cor 2:6–11; Eph 4:32); corporate authority and submission (cf. Matt 8:5–10; Heb 13:17); corporate worship and prayer (cf. Eph 5:19–20, Col 3:15–16). Grace enables transformation, and these communal processes are primary conduits through which grace flows. Furthermore, spiritual disciplines that "are to be practiced in community, in relationship with others of kindred spirit and intent." Formation occurs in Christ through the teaching, affirmation, and protection exclusive to the Christian community, where we learn to "trust God and others with me" (Willard et al., *Kingdom Life*, loc. 4899). For this reason, biblical guidance regarding restoration often includes direction

Of course, one may ask, "why should my church get involved in such a mess?" The reasons are many.

First, relational interactions are crucial to emotional health and healing. Ignoring the quintessential dimensions of humanity deprives people "of ways to heal from trauma and restore their autonomy. Being a patient, rather than a participant in one's healing process, separates suffering people from their community and alienates them from an inner sense of self."[40] In addition, transformation by renewing one's mind (Rom 12:2) has neurobiological and ethical implications, and both are communal. Notably, human connections and experiences within the community shape and sustain cognitive structures and create meaning.[41] In addition, virtues "need a community where they are engendered, fostered and refined" to hone the habits of mind and heart that develop moral reasoning.[42]

Second, excluding a repentant violator denies the individual's inherent worth and violates the *imago Dei*.[43] Exclusion further damages the fallen minister as his sin and shame thrive in darkness and isolation.[44] Sin must be brought to the light (John 1:3, 3:21; Eph 5:11–14) so that the Spirit and communities of grace can (re)form the sinner.

Third, a refusal to restore is detrimental to the church. A church that cannot forgive and restore cannot be Christlike. Furthermore, refusing to extend mercy does not deny that mercy to others. One cannot divert God's mercy. Such refusal effectively removes the church from God's movement toward the one in need.[45] Therefore, the only mercy that is lost is your own.

Simply put, we are in this together. Christian ministry is multivocal—the minister's inner call must be tested and confirmed by the church's

---

from responsible individuals or groups who are responsible to the church. See also Johns and White, "Ethics of Being," 296.

40. van der Kolk, *Body Keeps the Score*, 38.

41. Markham, *Rewired*, 186; Siegel, *Developing Mind*, 16, 21.

42. Hauerwas, *Community of Characters*, 115.

43. Volf, *Exclusion & Embrace*, 67. See also Augustine, *Trinity*, 284–86; Hildebrand, "Trinity in the Ante-Nicene Fathers," 105, 115–16; and Murray, *Saving Truth*, 97. Each person in the triune God finds distinct identity in relationship with the others. As Stephen Seamands rightly notes, "Personhood is therefore freedom *for*, not freedom *from*, another" (Seamands, *Ministry in the Image of God*, 118).

44. Physiologically, isolation decreases the mind's flexibility and resilience, which hinders its ability to overcome emotional trauma and shame (Thompson, *Soul of Shame*, 68). Spiritually, rescinding Christianity from a social to a solitary religion "is indeed to destroy it" (Wesley, *Sermon on the Mount*, 123).

45. Without question, the sexual impurity of one individual can contaminate a body of believers (1 Cor 5:6–7, 13). Conversely, the humble mercy of that body can contribute to that individual's purification and restoration (2 Cor 7:11).

outer call.[46] In the event of transgression, restoration must occur within the church for the sake of the transgressor and the church's public testimony.[47] The church plays an indispensable and required role in ordination *and* restoration. Therefore, the overseer should select a spiritually mature congregation to host the violator and, if applicable, his family throughout the process.[48] This church is where love, guidance, and accountability are deliberately offered and sought. Such commitment requires priority, planning, and the expenditure of energy and time.[49]

Herein lies a problem. We earlier discussed "functional dysfunction" and noted that dysfunction arises primarily from one's family structure. As most Christians have learned, the church is a spiritual family with functional dysfunctions of its own.[50] Several factors, such as a lack of biblical literacy, undue influence of culture, or the domination of personal preference, can result in wrong views and responses. Some churches do not believe ministerial restoration to be necessary. Others do not think it is effective. Some churches do not see themselves as responsible for implementing ministerial restoration, and some believe such restoration is not in their best interest.[51]

Overcoming the variance within these Christian communities will prove challenging. Even the church that extends grace will face significant challenges when that grace faces personal, congregational, denominational, and cultural preferences.

Still, this "messy grace" we call the church is also a spiritual family whose corporate identity is rooted in Christ's love (Eph 3:17).[52] Its biblical structure enables believers to speak truth to one another (Eph 4:15, 25), confess sins to one another (Jas 5:16), set right the one who has gone astray (Matt 18:10–20; Jas 5:19–20), and equip for the work of ministry (Eph

---

46. Willimon, *Pastor*, 44; Niebuhr, *Purpose of the Church and Its Ministry*, 64. This dual role is evident from the early church forward. For example, Cyprian, *Epistle* 5.4, loc. 97075.

47. Keener, *Galatians*, 530. See also May, *Body for the Lord*, 62; Hawthorne et al., *Dictionary of Paul and His Letters*, 776. Cf. 1 Cor. 5:1, 5; 6:1, 6.

48. Reintroduction is not immediate or automatic and depends on numerous factors. For example, reintroducing a minister who struggles with pornography into a church setting could likely take place sooner than for a minister who had a consensual adulterous affair.

49. Trask, et al., *Pentecostal Pastor*, 21.

50. Chapter 5 addressed the adverse influence secular culture has on the individual. It is equally necessary to understand that churches create their own cultures and socialize acceptable behaviors—and many are unhealthy.

51. Conversely, biblical leadership demonstrates spiritual authority and credibility through its message and example (Matt 7:28–29).

52. As described by Boa, *Conformed to His Image*, 427.

4:12).[53] The biblical community is a haven where the battered vessel can experience, express, and rightly direct feelings uncovered in the counseling process and recover "the affective life he had to abandon to survive in childhood."[54]

Therefore, the biblical response equally rejects meaningless inclusion and merciless exclusion. Though often viewed as virtuous, exclusion for purity's sake contradicts Christ's purifying example.[55] Conversely, Jesus' merciful inclusion does not eliminate the need for repentance but instead enables the reception of grace. Sinful behavior is neither excluded nor accepted but forgiven and overcome.

Such inclusion demands shaping and recovering one's character, which "requires confrontation by the community."[56] As Miroslav Volf rightly notes, "an approach that rests fundamentally on the moral assignment of blame and innocence" will find no success. Therefore, "the work of reconciliation should proceed under the assumption that, though the behavior of a person may be judged as deplorable, even demonic, no one should ever be excluded from the will to embrace, because, at the deepest level, the relationship to others does not rest on their moral performance and therefore cannot be undone by the lack of it. . . . [The violators] need not be perceived as innocent in order to be loved, but ought to be embraced even when they are perceived as wrongdoers."[57]

Humility is the hallmark of the restorative church. Those who are spiritual do not judge from the moral high ground.[58] Neither haughtiness nor condescension should stand between the spiritual and the broken. Only God's word stands between (and judges) both.[59] As Dietrich Bonhoeffer rightly asks, "How can I possibly serve another person in unfeigned humility if I seriously regard his sinfulness as worse than my own? Would

---

53. Loving and selfless participation is of immeasurable worth as the spiritual community provides a fuller presence of Christ and the Holy Spirit and shares unique gifts, ministries, experiences, and wisdom. A church may be spiritually gifted, theologically astute, full of miracle-working faith, generous to a fault, and even willing to die for Christ—but if it lacks love, it lacks everything (drawn from the analysis of 1 Cor 13 in Kinnaman and Ells, *Leaders That Last*, 110–11).

54. Hands and Fehr, *Spiritual Wholeness for Clergy*, loc. 603.

55. Herzog, *Jesus, Justice, and the Reign of God*, 176–77. Cf. Matt 9:9–13; Mark 2:15–17; Luke 15:1–7; John 4:7–30; 8:1–11.

56. Stassen and Gushee, *Kingdom Ethics*, 56.

57. Volf, *Exclusion & Embrace*, 84–85. Though Volf addresses ethnic reconciliation, the biblical truth he presents has application in all manners of reconciliation.

58. It is not condemnation but God's goodness that brings repentance (Rom 2:4). Why would any church take a different approach?

59. Bonhoeffer, *Life Together*, 107.

I not be putting myself above him; could I have any hope for him?"[60] The German pastor/theologian echoes Thomas à Kempis's charge to "not think that you have made any progress until you look upon yourself as inferior to all others."[61] Both echo the wisdom of Paul, the "chief of sinners" who admonishes believers to humbly "consider one another as more important than yourselves" (Phil 2:3–8; 1 Tim 1:15).

Rather than "combat and conquer them and never yield an inch," the meek ought to be treated with meekness "to encourage them to a better hope."[62] In such understanding, the church would do well to consider how quickly (and easily) Paul shifts from his condemnation of shameless immorality to condemnation of judgmental self-righteousness (Rom 1:18—3:8). Sadly, the old cliché remains true: the Christian army as the only army that shoots its wounded.[63]

Once again, we are missing the mark. It is time we lay down our arms. The communal responsibility is not idealistic moral perfection but the resemblance of God "by including enemies in our mercy, compassion, loving action, as God does."[64] Such resemblance includes prayerful support, Spirit-led direction, and sanctified attitudes that will prevent legalism, judgment, and haughtiness from encroaching and are possible only through the power of Christ's cross, which is communal. The cross stands as a sacrificial satisfaction in which Christ paid another's debt and took the sins of others to see that sin destroyed. The cross enables the body of Christ to do the same, to "bear one another's burdens, and so fulfill the law of Christ" (Gal 6:2). The Christian "must bear the burden of a brother. He must suffer and endure the brother. It is only when he is a burden that another person is really a brother and not merely an object to be manipulated. . . . It is the Fellowship of the Cross to experience the burden of the other. If one does not experience it, the Fellowship he belongs to is not Christian."[65]

Acceptance and application of this biblical construct are anything but easy. As C. S. Lewis rightly notes, "Everyone says forgiveness is a lovely idea

---

60. Bonhoeffer, *Life Together*, 96–97.
61. à Kempis, *Imitation of Christ*, II.II.4.
62. Gregory Nazianzen, *Oration* 11.28–33.
63. As attributed to psychiatrist Dwight L. Carlson in Hetzendorfer, *Pastoral Counseling Handbook*, 11.
64. Stassen and Gushee, *Kingdom Ethics*, 342. Cf. Luke 6:32–36.
65. Bonhoeffer, *Life Together*, 100–101. While Bonhoeffer is providing a general statement in regard to support for a Christian brother, this application of costly grace would certainly include a fallen minister who entered a Christian community with a desire for spiritual (re)formation.

until he has something to forgive."[66] Violations of the innocent or weak and of the sacred trust are not easy to forgive, yet (re)formation is impossible apart from forgiveness. Therefore, the healing community to which a fallen minister is assigned should demonstrate maturity, divine forgiveness, and godly unity developed through communal formation and centered on biblical relationships.

In summary, the congregation rightly expects Christlikeness from its minister. God expects the same of his church. Whether in the context of formation or (re)formation, one's life in Christ supports yet is simultaneously fed by corporate life in Christ. Therefore, the "church must assist rather than punish and deny this essential work to know the creation of a pure heart and an empowered church."[67] The spiritual Christian and congregation are the conduits through which the Spirit heals and reforms. The holistic restoration each provides enables deliverance *from* sin and *into* the community.[68] This deliverance is the hallmark of mutual love. The Spirit unites with those who are spiritual to bring such godly love to bear in the holistic restoration of broken ministers and ministries. This process transforms the individual through the community and the community through the individual.

THE ROLE OF THE VIOLATOR

"Cheap grace is the preaching of forgiveness without requiring repentance, baptism without church discipline, communion without confession, absolution without personal confession. Cheap grace is grace without discipleship, grace without the cross, grace without Jesus Christ, living and incarnate."

— Dietrich Bonhoeffer

That the violator has responsibilities goes without saying. That list begins with confession and repentance These terms are not synonymous.

To confess requires admission and acceptance of responsibility for one's actions.[69] Concern, godly sorrow, and regret are indicators of such

---

66. Lewis, *Mere Christianity*, 115.

67. Mosgofian and Ohlschlager, *Sexual Misconduct in Counseling and Ministry*, 287.

68. McMinn, *Psychology, Theology, and Spirituality in Christian Counseling*, 241; Stassen and Gushee, *Kingdom Ethics*, 337.

69. Anderson, *Steps to Freedom in Christ*, 31; Lazare, *On Apology*, 8–9; Newman, *Concise Greek-English Dictionary*, s.v. "ὁμολογέω," 125. See also Pss 25:11; 32:3–5; Prov

confession. However, emotion alone does not meet the biblical requirement for repentance.[70] Dallas Willard warns that it is common "to hear Christians talk of their 'brokenness.' But when you listen closely, you may discover that they are talking about their wounds, the things they have suffered, not about the evil that is in them."[71]

Two words of warning are necessary regarding confessions. First is the danger of a confession that comes out of compulsion. Achan provides a good example (Josh 7). God gave repeated opportunities for voluntary confession, but Achan offered a lackluster admission only after God revealed him as the culprit. "Some people think they have done a wonderful thing if they own up when at last the matter is found out. But if there was a chance that it would never be discovered, they were content to go on in silence. Therefore, their confession of sin, when at last it was made, was no real confession at all and did not bring to them the forgiveness of God."[72]

Second, those with oversight must be cautious of quick confessions. The violator may wish to put the issue behind him to (seemingly) protect his ministry and reputation. Though truthful about his actions, the violator may not yet accept the truth of himself.[73] The violator typically believes he is in control and able to quit at will. He has likely devolved into a delusion that his behavior is neither wrong nor harmful. A violator unwilling to confess or who substitutes confession with excuses is unlikely to understand his hurtful and destructive nature.

Still, confession is not enough. Biblical repentance demands a decided turn from sin and movement toward God—a reversal of direction that leads the individual into God's divine life and fellowship.[74] Holistic restoration cannot proceed if the violator remains rooted in denial and is resistant.

28:13; Jas 5:16; 1 John 1:9, etc.

70. The command to repent is addressed fifty-three times in the New Testament. Notable examples include Matt 4:17; Luke 13:3, 5; 15:7; Acts 2:38; 3:19; 17:30; 20:21; 2 Pet 3:9; Rev 2:5.

71. Willard, *Renovation of the Heart*, 60. Cf. Isa 6:5.

72. Hession, *Forgotten Factors of Sexual Sin*, locs. 945–53. Indeed, Paul describes a "godly grief produces a repentance that leads to salvation without regret, whereas worldly grief produces death" (2 Cor 7:10).

73. Such failure is inherent to the people Christians are to avoid (2 Tim 3:1–8). That group, like those who fall short of the biblical repentance described here, turn away others from the truth (3:6), always learning but never come to know the truth (3:7), because their corrupted minds resist the truth resulting in a worthless faith (3:8).

74. Erickson, *Christian Theology*, 865–68. Erickson demonstrates the reversal of direction inherent to repentance through analysis of the Hebrew *shuv* and the Greek *metanoeo*. See 2 Chr 7:14; Luke 13:3; Acts 3:19; 8:22; Heb 10:26; 1 John 3:8–10; Rev 2:5.

God does not reform an autonomous being in his image.[75] As Hollis Gause rightly asserts, "The will of the sinner is essential to repentance. Sin is a willful act; therefore, repentance must also be a willful act."[76] The violator's repentance (or lack thereof) enables the restoration team to differentiate between those with hard hearts and those with scarred hearts.

Repentance is a lordship issue in which the individual abdicates the throne of his life so that God can take his rightful place. A reversal of attitude and behavior marks the decision to serve the Spirit leading to life rather than sin leading to death. The church is to disassociate the violator who refuses to turn from sinful behavior (Matt 18:15–18; 1 Cor 5:1–5). While "intensely painful for everyone . . . it is the most caring thing to do, and the most honest."[77]

Conversely, the acts of repentance, reception of forgiveness, and restoration to fellowship "do not automatically carry with them the privilege of pastoring or leading a congregation."[78] The qualifying traits of a blameless reputation, marital faithfulness, and wholesome family life must be current and enduring character traits (1 Tim 3:1–13; Titus 1:6–9). Rebuilding such character and trust is neither easy nor quick. The sacramental aspects of ministerial leadership demand repentance and submission to biblical authority. Restoration to functional leadership requires a comprehensive and continuing review of the violator's personality and inclinations.

Because biblical repentance enables one's right standing with God and others, there is no allowance for the "cheap grace" described above.[79] Repentance demands contrition and is evident in godly sorrow and humble submission to the Spirit's conviction and leading. As such, biblical repentance begins an unmasking—removing the deceptive façade constructed

---

75. This restriction is especially true for those who justify sexual immorality by appeal to a divine endorsement such as "God told me to be with this person" or "God knows my heart and loves me anyway." Such people fail to realize that sexual immorality makes it difficult for them to hear God clearly or at all (Keener, *Spirit Hermeneutics*, 106). Therefore, rebuke and remove the false prophets who support indulgence or claim that the Spirit condones sexual immorality (Jer 23:14–18; 2 Tim 4:3; 2 Pet 2:1–3; Rev 2:14).

76. Gause, *Living in the Spirit*, 22.

77. Laaser, *Healing the Wounds*, 145. Some congregants will have great affection or appreciation for the pastor and demand forgiveness without responsibility. These members will likely challenge such dismissal as unchristian. However, Jesus did not say "make him" like a heathen but said "let him be" as a heathen (Matt 18:17). The individual's choices determine his path. Church leadership simply accommodates the choices made. In addition, notice that it was not the sin that led Paul to cast the immoral believer from the congregation but his refusal to repent.

78. Blomberg, *1 Corinthians*, 111.

79. Bonhoeffer, *Cost of Discipleship*, 44.

to protect image and ego and keep all else hidden. Chapter 10 more fully addresses this process. However, the restoration team can expect difficulties from the onset because most ministers (fallen or not) believe that pretending is safer than honesty and vulnerability.[80] Restoration demands both and thus forces the violator to face truths that result in significant embarrassment, shame, and lack of acceptance. Many ministers are ill-equipped to handle these factors, a shortfall that likely contributed to the illicit behaviors.

The apostle Paul speaks to desire before listing ministerial qualifications (1 Tim 3:1–7). Paul uses the word *oregomai*, which implies stretching forward and reaching with longing, craving, and yearning.[81] Moral failure indicates that desire is amiss. Violators must first acknowledge "that all of their strivings to satisfy their thirsts are abysmal failures. They must discover and embrace what they are truly thirsty for."[82]

Returning one's desire to God "sets us on the difficult path of self-emptying and self-denial, of losing our lives so that we may lay hold of Christ's life."[83] This effort is in vain if the violator desires restoration of ministry or reputation more than restoration unto God. Jesus made himself of no reputation and obediently submitted to death on the cross (Phil 2:5–8). The minister's reputation must not keep him from taking up his cross.

The restoration process, therefore, demands a radical reorientation of thought and life. This reorientation begins with rejecting one's autonomy and control, a necessity inherent to Jesus' direction that his followers lose their lives to gain his (John 12:25). There, the Greek word *apollumi* does not speak of misplacing or modifying but destroying that old life.[84]

The fallen minister can only hope to regain ministerial competency through holistic (re)formation. Such competency speaks not to one's technical skill but to the quality of moral integrity that God forms through sanctification and spiritual disciplines, which is evident in action and attitude. Such integrity qualifies for ordained office (1 Tim 1:18–19). It is a non-negotiable aspect, as the ministry is not a career but a calling "that encompasses all that a person is and does" and cannot tolerate a "dichotomy between private lifestyle and public conduct."[85]

---

80. Scazzero, *Emotionally Healthy Spirituality*, 12. Such was the author's confession.
81. Newman, *Concise Greek-English Dictionary*, s.v. "ὀρέγομαι," 127.
82. Laaser, *Healing the Wounds*, 124.
83. Boa, *Conformed to His Image*, 168. Cf. Matt 10:38–39.
84. Newman, *Concise Greek-English Dictionary*, s.v. "ἀπόλλυμι," 22.
85. Grenz and Bell, *Betrayal of Trust*, 62.

Confession and repentance begin the sanctifying process that will undo behaviors, often decades in the making, and begin to rectify consequences that resulted, but this is neither easy nor swift. Furthermore, confession and repentance are not exclusive to the initial phase. The violator will need to confess and repent when he falls short in subsequent struggle and as the restorative process reveals sinful actions and attitudes of which he was ignorant or had buried, forgotten, or even excused. Indeed, repentance is not a one-time event that covers all future sins; forgiveness is granted to future sins only when confessed and forsaken.[86]

While removing masks is difficult, vulnerability and humility endure added strain in times of public confession and repentance. Both are public acts, as "there is no sin in thought, word, or deed, no matter how personal or secret, that does not inflict injury upon the whole fellowship."[87] Indeed, what one does in darkness must be brought to the light (Luke 12:2–3). That does not mean the fallen minister must stand before the entire congregation and identify every detail of his moral failure. But Scripture does require the minister to confess to everyone he has violated—God, victim(s), family members, and the church leaders and members. Again, caution is warranted.

First, the quick or complacent confession does not adequately address those whom he has hurt. There is no allowance for generalized confessions with vague admission to various wrongs. Because the violator committed each sin individually, he must confess and repent of each sin individually. Furthermore, an apology for "whatever I may have done" fails to acknowledge the offense, while the statement, "if you were hurt, I am sorry," is a conditional acknowledgment that suggests the victims' sensitivity may be the problem.[88]

Second, the fallen minister may argue that confession is to God alone. However, God commanded that we confess our sins to one another, and with good reason.[89] One overcomes sin, which thrives in darkness and

---

86. 1 John 1:9; 2:1–2; Prov 28:13; Ps 66:18.

87. Bonhoeffer, *Life Together*, 89. The Lutheran pastor declares that "sin has lost all his power" in the humble confession that overcomes proud autonomy. Bonhoeffer does not require confession to the whole church, but to those directly offended (pp. 113–14).

88. Lazare, *On Apology*, 8–9.

89. Jas 5:16; cf. John 3:21; Eph 5:11–14. While narcissistic and unrepentant violators are quick to make such claim, the repentant minister who is broken and ashamed is sometimes hesitant to stand before those he has hurt. However, this is an essential act for the reasons noted above. And as Dietrich Bonhoeffer rightly opines, it should be easier to confess to a Christian than to God since the former is sinful as we are while the latter is a holy and just judge of evil and all disobedience (Bonhoeffer, *Life Together*, 115). The ease or struggle with which we confess to either is telling.

isolation, by bringing it to the light. In addition, biblical confession and apology are like keys that unlock the prison of hurt and shame. There are steps the victim must take to walk in freedom, but this is a significant act toward setting a captive free. Sometimes, the one who caused the hurt can bring help and healing.

In summary, only the truly repentant and properly prepared violator can take the corrective steps to remediate the past to fulfill his ministry. The good news is that God does not require one to rebuild what is broken alone. To do so is an exercise in futility. As Karl Barth rightly notes, a man who will not seek God's help must help himself, only to hope God will help him to help himself.[90] King David, who is well acquainted with repentance and restoration, offers a better option. "The Lord is near to the brokenhearted and saves those who are crushed in spirit" (Ps 34:18). And the Lord brings others alongside to hold the minister accountable and help him bear this burden. Success will require total commitment and submission to the work ordained by the Spirit and administered by the violator's overseer, mentor(s), and church community. Therefore, the following chapter provides guidance for constructing a tailor-made restoration plan that allows the minister to rebuild the walls, restore the temple, and resume ministry to God and others.

---

90. Barth, *Church Dogmatics*, 462.

9

Building the Restoration Plan

"It is abundantly manifest by the Scripture that God's manner of dealing with men is to 'lead them into a wilderness, before he speaks comfortably to them,' and so to order it, that they shall be brought into distress, and made to see their own helplessness and absolute dependence on his power and grace, before he appears to work any great deliverance for them."

— Jonathan Edwards

Our discussion has shifted from the battered ship to rebuilding a temple destroyed by a perfect storm. Here, we shift the metaphor once more. Sometimes, the most precious item lost to the storm is not the structure but a cherished item within.

Take vessels, for instance. They are often fragile and don't often endure catastrophe. That is especially painful for vessels of remarkable value. Sometimes, we fail to recognize the inherent worth. Such was the case for a fifteenth-century Ming dynasty box that sat unnoticed for decades in an attic but sold for $358,000 in 2023. A nice find, to be sure, but that is chump change in the world of collectible vessels. A small Ming dynasty bowl sold for a record $36.3 million in 2014. The previous record was $32.3 million paid in 2010 for a vase from Emperor Qianlong's imperial court. That same year, survivors preparing an estate sale included a decorative vase precariously perched atop a bookshelf for decades. Unknown to the family until the auction appraisal, that vase also originated under the rule of Qianlong, the Qing dynasty's fifth emperor. Insured for $1,300, the vase sold for $69 million.

Remarkable, to say the least. Before you ransack the attic, I would venture to guess that you have something of far greater worth in your possession. Perhaps it is a clay flowerpot crafted alongside a cherished childhood friend, the cast iron skillet your mom used to teach her favorite recipes, or a birdhouse built with a dearly departed grandfather. Indeed, these may prove more precious than the aforementioned items.

Why bring this up? Because we are all vessels shaped by God, precious in his sight, and filled with blessings of immeasurable worth. Unlike the safety deposit boxes, fireproof safes, and hidden vaults in which people store their valuables, God places his glorious treasure in fragile and seemingly ordinary vessels that are easily broken and often discarded (2 Cor 4:7).

Consider your home's cups, bowls, vases, pitchers, and pots. Some hold food items or craft supplies. Some hold investment value. Some contain the memories of generations that passed them down the line. Some vessels serve as decoration. Some emerge only when the company comes for dinner on special holidays. Vessels serve many purposes. God has one purpose for all vessels he creates. God desires to fill the vessels he forms.[1]

But what happens when a vessel becomes broken? In our society, a vessel that cannot be used is a useless vessel. God views broken vessels in a different light.

The Japanese art of *kintsugi* (golden joinery) provides a beautiful analogy. *Kintsugi* uses lacquer mixed with gold to repair and restore broken pottery. The visible seam does not devalue the vessel but increases its worth by filling its brokenness with gold. Better still, the restored flaw urges telling the vessel's story and reminds onlookers that one can transform imperfections into beauty. How much more can the God of all creation restore a broken vessel? Even in the wake of apparent destruction, God can exchange beauty for ashes (Isa 61:3). Even when the clay is resistant, God does not throw it away but reforms the clay into another vessel, shaping it as it seems best to him (Jer 18:2–4).

The following chapter considers ways God restores some broken vessels. Each restoration is as unique as the cracking patterns that emerge, and effective plans recognize and rectify the personalities, liabilities, and contributing factors that led to the brokenness. Still, some commonalities exist within every restoration plan.

Notably, sexual moral failure severs the right relationship with God, authentic self, and others.[2] Therefore, every restoration plan must follow the biblical order: to God, family, the people of God, and, in certain situations,

---

1. Cf. Acts 9:17; Eph 3:19, 5:18; Col 1:9.
2. This threefold alienation is first evident in humankind's fall (Gen 3:8–16).

the pastoral calling of God.[3] A violator deemed ineligible for restoration to the fourth category will find this holistic restoration program provides considerable guidance for recognizing and overcoming the factors that have adversely affected the other three categories.

The overseer establishes responsibilities for the mentors and congregation to which he assigns the violator for the restorative period. Because the violator is responsible for his actions and recovery, the program must remain fluid to accommodate struggle, address unforeseen conflicts, and include meaningful and measurable goals that balance formative growth with accountability.

This approach aligns with John Wesley's assertion that true theology first describes what Christianity looks like, then promises "this character shall be mine (provided I will not rest till I attain)," and ultimately explains how one may attain it.[4] The following subsections provide the *kintsugi*, as it were, for restoring broken vessels—the steps by which one picks up the pieces, restores function, and beautifies the cracks. Topics include emotional (re)formation to overcome brokenness, misshapen identity, and the illicit behaviors that become coping mechanisms; spiritual (re)formation through an analysis of passages as they are understood and applied through historical and theological development; and consideration of obstacles that can thwart the restoration plan.

CONSIDERATIONS FOR EMOTIONAL (RE)FORMATION

> "I appreciate God's forgiveness, but I want something more: I want deliverance. I need forgiveness for what I have done, but I need also deliverance from what I am."
>
> — WATCHMAN NEE

As noted in chapter 4, mental and emotional malformation often contributes to feelings of inferiority, identity struggles, and misshapes individual patterns of relating to others. How individuals view and relate to others rarely originates in adulthood but is often imprinted through childhood experiences. As a result, much Christian leadership "is exercised by people who do not know how to develop healthy, intimate relationships and have

---

3. The biblical order identifies relationship with God as ultimate (Mark 12:30, cf. Matt 10:37), with family relations as second and a qualifier for ministry, which comes third (1 Tim 3:4–5, 5:8).

4. Wesley, *Plain Account of Genuine Christianity*, locs. 104–21.

opted for power and control instead. Many Christian empire-builders have been people unable to give and receive love."[5]

Immoral behaviors are thus understood not only as sinful and destructive but as misguided attempts to escape shame, find loving approval, and earn significance. As a result, many illicit behaviors such as sexual malfeasance start as coping mechanisms for dysfunctional relationships, abandonment, physical and emotional trauma, and the like (cf. Eccl 7:29). Therefore, this section opens with counseling techniques to identify deformative and traumatic life events to help the violator heal longstanding wounds and overcome undeveloped and wounded emotions.

The bulk of emotional (re)formation falls to the Christian mental health professional. Because that professional's findings will inform the subsequent restoration plan, all participants should have a working knowledge of the factors in play. Team members should also look for signs and tendencies that emerge when the violator is more relaxed in non-counseling or "natural" settings.

The restoration team can expect despair to accompany the revelation of moral failure.[6] The human tendency is to fight or flight—retaliate through denial, entitlement or arrogance, or withdraw physically or emotionally "to not deal with the conflict and discomfort and to avoid future opportunities to be hurt."[7] Indeed, violators work to protect their secret world and will grieve its loss. Anger is the predominant emotion that marks this undetermined period.[8] The revelation through Christian counseling of personal responsibility abates the anger but often finds a violator unable or unwilling to address the brokenness and behaviors that led to malfeasance. Instead, the violator attempts to bargain with God and others to manage the chaos, alleviate the pain, and bring life back into order.[9] Many violators enter a stage of depression when the negotiations fail. The restoration team should not attempt to push the violator through this stage. While not a destination, depression is an ordinary and necessary stage of grief. Relational trust is critical, enabling the vulnerability needed for honest and informed self-appraisal.[10] Such appraisal centers mainly on the deformative factors and traumatic events that have a misshapen identity and subsequent behaviors.

5. Nouwen, *In the Name of Jesus*, 60.
6. The process that follows is drawn from Briggs, *Fail*, 123–31.
7. Briggs, *Fail*, 38.
8. Anger is not necessarily an expression of sin but a natural reaction to one's condition that may solidify into hostility toward God and others.
9. While this is a step in the right direction, the violator is far from victorious as these negotiations indicate a failure to release full control to God and the process.
10. A lack of trust may find the violator rescind into anger or isolation, or attempt

Descriptions of crucial aspects of this process follow. The violator who accepts his diagnosis can proceed with the proper prognosis toward healing and restoring hope. This progression is anything but easy. Holistic healing first requires examining past wounds and critically analyzing one's morals, then demands conscious changes in behavior, thinking, and spiritual life.[11]

As noted above, most sexual offenses result from causal factors unique to the individual and circumstances. These factors can be biological, social, cultural, emotional, or related to core neuropsychological systems. Both nature (particularly brain development) and nurture (social learning and circumstances) contribute to individual vulnerabilities.[12] As Terrence Real rightly asserts, "Too often, the wounded boy grows up to become a wounding man, inflicting upon those closest to him the very distress he refuses to acknowledge within himself."[13] Others seek inordinate happiness and self-worth through approval and achievement to their detriment.

Emotional (re)formation begins with a careful exploration of brokenness. This investigation requires patient yet probing discussions of the violator's upbringing, ministry history, and circumstances leading to the failure. Team members should look for traumatic life events such as an abandoning omission (e.g., a deformative lack of affirmation) or an invasive commission (e.g., a destructive violation of innocence). The perpetuation of illicit behaviors to relive traumatic events, what Sigmund Freud called "the repetition compulsion," results in the negative transference of dysfunction in subsequent relationships. For example, attachment profoundly influences how one relates to God. Therefore, the projection of blame upon God serves as a tell-tale sign that attachment is unhealthy or lacking.[14]

---

to control themselves, others, and any perceived threat.

11. Hetzendorfer, *Pastoral Counseling Handbook*, 7.

12. For example, some paraphilias are associated with differences in neuroanatomical brain structure and functioning, while others appear to result from earlier exposure and modeling, sexual abuse, and relational deficits (Yarhouse and Tan, *Sexuality and Sex Therapy*, 251–52).

13. Real, *I Don't Want to Talk About It*, 24.

14. Martin Luther provides a strong example. Numerous familial, religious, physical, professional, and cultural factors shaped the reformer's theology. Notably, Luther was subjected to a harsh and strict upbringing by his father, Hans Luder, and never felt he lived up to his father's expectations or gained his father's approval. That Luther ultimately displaced that perspective onto God is without question, as "Luther's relationship with God is a remarkably volatile one. He cowers before God's wrath against sin; he takes sharply to heart God's unrelenting demand for righteousness; he knows God's love is both fierce and tender; and he makes bold to call God to account" (Strohl, "Luther's Spiritual Journey," 152). Luther's theological development reveals his struggle with worth and salvation amid conflict within himself and nearly everyone he encountered. Yet intertwined within is marked development as a Christian and theologian as

Conversely, enmeshment and dissociation are common indicators of boundary violations. The latter is arguably the more serious of the two and may involve emotional stasis or suppression of memories.[15] Humiliation leading to shame is common in boundary violations involving sexual abuse by someone loved and trusted. "Because the relationship was based on manipulation, deception, and secrecy, this becomes the basis of other relationships."[16] Other signs include a lack of trust and care for others, emotional isolation, and difficulty with physical affection or relational communication.

Careful analysis will reveal the malformations that serve as building blocks for inaccurate self-assessments (e.g., worthlessness) as well as wrongful sexual arousal and behavior. Still, team members should expect such analysis to be arduous for four reasons. First, the failures often reside within the family structure. As noted above, individuals are reluctant to acknowledge familial dysfunction and harm.[17] Second, those wounded learn and live the "three unholy rules" of dysfunctional families (don't think, don't feel, don't talk) well into adulthood.[18] Third, those for whom illicit sexual behavior has become a coping mechanism know their behavior is dangerous, yet "inside them is a child who knows giving up that behavior will cause great pain" before it brings emotional healing.[19] Fourth, the struggling individual who harshly judges himself often expects a similar response from others should they come to know the history of his brokenness. This scenario is identical to the "fear-of-intimacy cycle" that first drove

---

Luther submits to God's transformative work. This is most evident in matured reflections on his theology that Luther provides in later years. The origin of Luther's struggle with self-doubt and self-loathing was not exclusive to external forces, as he likely suffered from cyclothymia, a rare mood disorder known for emotional ups and downs, though not as extreme as those seen in bipolar disorder (Ebeling, *Luther*, loc. 254). Some even argue that Luther's legacy was "the projection of one man's neurosis on the whole of human history" (Strohl, "Luther's Spiritual Journey," 149).

15. These symptoms especially demand professional care as "we cannot heal what we cannot feel" (Bradshaw, *Healing the Shame That Binds You*, 54).

16. Hetzendorfer, *Pastoral Counseling Handbook*, 96.

17. The Beaver System Model, which classifies families within five levels of health, is helpful in this regard. See Scazzero, *Emotionally Healthy Spirituality*, 90–91.

18. Mosgofian and Ohlschlager, *Sexual Misconduct in Counseling and Ministry*, 121. Bradshaw's "dysfunctional family rules" adds control of all interactions, feelings and personal behavior; perfectionism to hide the flawed, vulnerable self; blame to cover shame, and distrust of everyone to avoid disappointment (Bradshaw, *Healing the Shame That Binds You*, 62–63). Sandra Wilson identifies five rules intended to conceal family imperfections: be blind, be quiet, be numb, be careful, be good (Wilson, *Released from Shame*, 41). See also Laaser, *Healing the Wounds*, 78–86.

19. Laaser, *Healing the Wounds*, 158.

the individual from intimacy sources (his wife, for example) to persons or things that provide a temporary sense of intimacy (such as pornography, prostitutes, or extramarital affairs).[20] Yet, his attempt to meet a legitimate need illegitimately left him "feeling empty, lonely, ashamed, and guilty."[21] The violator, already ashamed of what was done *by* him, is fearful that others will learn what was done *to* him, thus plunging him further into despair.

Diane Chandler advances this understanding by addressing the significance of a critical incident—a "catalyzing starting place" such as a thought condition, intention, event, or action that prompts a significant decision or response that results in a leader's unethical behavior.[22] This "trigger event" might result from a substantial loss of anything ranging from a loved one to one's job or might be the product of anything from an increasingly inflated ego to the gradual decrease of self-worth. Behavioral responses developed amid deformative or traumatic life events can tip the scales before, during, and after critical incidents in sometimes identifiable directions.

That said, dysfunction and traumatic deformation are not evident in every individual who sexually misbehaves. Many confounding variables might contribute to sexual moral failure. Confounding variables refer to any number of circumstances and conditions that, taken together, contribute to pastors' sexual immorality. Examples of confounding variables include (1) length of time in the pastoral ministry, (2) burnout disposition, (3) tendency to self-isolate, (4) unresolved conflicts, (5) undealt-with anger, (6) unresolved family of origin issues, (7) lack of an adequate support system, (8) personal temperament and personality, (9) lack of intimacy in marriage, and (10) previous sexual trauma.

For example, previous sexual trauma often contributes to illicit sexual behaviors in adulthood. However, not everyone who suffers from sexual trauma will demonstrate such behaviors, and not everyone who demonstrates such behaviors has experienced sexual trauma. Violators with no history of sexual trauma may still be disposed to narcissistic tendencies, impulse control deficits, or abnormalities within the dominant behavioral system. However, conditioned responses to deformative life events, such as sexual trauma, are often apparent and must be considered when addressing holistic restoration. Unreasonable behaviors are a tell-tale sign in such cases. Emotions drive conditioned responses because they develop in the

---

20. Thoburn and Balswick, "Prevention Approach to Infidelity," 47. The counselor is encouraged to occasionally include the violator's spouse in this therapeutic process to address intimacy and heal the resulting wounds (Mosgofian and Ohlschlager, *Sexual Misconduct in Counseling and Ministry*, 247).

21. Thoburn and Balswick, "Prevention Approach to Infidelity," 47.

22. Chandler, "Perfect Storm of Leaders' Unethical Behavior," 71, 84.

early years before the complete formation of cognitive function or from traumatic events in which sensations override reason.

Without Spirit-led and Spirit-enabled correction, deformation will develop neural pathways that increasingly look externally rather than internally to cope with stress and low self-worth. Sometimes, decisions that aim to provide personal relief by easing emotional distress see appetite drive intellect. Through holistic formation, decisions that align with Scripture enable personal growth through reasonable responses forged by surrendering the intellect, emotions, and will to the Holy Spirit.

Despite the offending minister's previous victimization, he is also a violator. Though he may have intended to heal the brokenness that was not of his making, illicit sexual activity remains a selfish, deceptive, and destructive act.[23] Accepting this truth will result in further brokenness, and necessarily so, as "only something that is broken can be made new."[24] The violator must accept his brokenness and take responsibility for his caused brokenness; he must agree to amend harmful effects and commit to change.

CONSIDERATIONS FOR SPIRITUAL (RE)FORMATION

> "As long as I remain imperfect and refractory [divided], neither obeying God by practicing the commandments nor becoming perfect in spiritual knowledge, Christ from my point of view also appears imperfect and refractory because of me. I diminish and cripple Him by not growing in Spirit with Him."
>
> — MAXIMUS THE CONFESSOR

God must work *in* the minister before fully working *through* the minister. Indeed, "no one who is deliberately rejecting the known will of God in one area of life can expect to receive His enabling to live supernaturally in other areas."[25] But this is not for lack of trying.

---

23. Clinton and Laaser, *Quick Reference Guide*, 137; Grenz and Bell, *Betrayal of Trust*, 75.

24. Goldingay, *Psalms Vol. 2*, 133, cf. Ps 51:1–10. Still, this revelation leaves the violator vulnerable—and this at an unpredictable time when he may be facing criminal or civil proceedings in addition to the potential loss of licensure. The painful alienation of family adds to his intense shame. Since the violator could become suicidal, the restoration team must be ready to provide crisis intervention and other methods to bring stability.

25. McQuilkin, "Keswick Perspective," 152.

BUILDING THE RESTORATION PLAN

Many who struggle with and often succumb to temptation employ one of two strategies. The first strategy sees renewed commitment to spiritual disciplines in a usually frustrating effort to strengthen righteousness and withstand the devil's onslaughts. Such exercise is a necessary endeavor. However, the endeavor can quickly descend into ineffective legalism if not united with sanctification. More on that in a moment.

The second approach shifts the blame on others. Rather than take responsibility, we blame society, our parents, the pastor, and the government for our actions. This approach is not new. Having tasted the forbidden fruit, Adam blamed Eve and, indirectly, blamed God (it was the woman *you* gave me!). Eve blamed the serpent, which remains a favorite excuse: the devil made me do it! No, he didn't. We blame Satan for destroying our lives when, in reality, the spiritual forces do little more than entice. Sin enters when the individual acts upon those sinful desires. Individuals may be co-conspirators with their passions, but none are victims of their passions. The individual is responsible for his choices, and a way of escape is available (1 Cor 10:13). Jerusalem's first pastor explained this cycle and solution well.

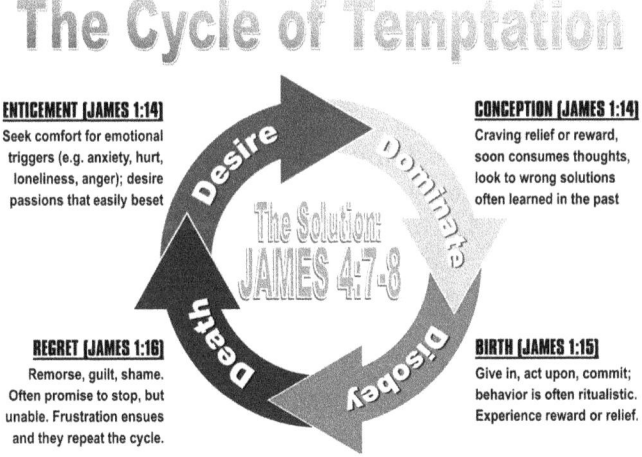

Temptation is not a sin. After all, Jesus was tempted in all things yet was without sin.[26] Like salvation and sanctification, sin is participatory.[27] Such participation begins in the diagram's second element. "Conception" is

---

26. Heb 2:18, 4:15; cf. Matt 4:1–11; Mark 1:12–13; Luke 4:1–13.

27. Note how James later presents faith as participatory through works (Jas 2:14–26).

a reversal of repentance, a turning away from God to fixate on fulfillment. It is an agreement with, even if not acted upon. The believer here fails to take that thought captive to the obedience of Christ (2 Cor 10:5). This is dangerous ground. Being addicted to ourselves, justifying our actions comes rather easily.

To sever temptation is to silence the tempter. Therefore, the restoration plan must equip the minister to sever temptation before sin conceives and brings death. James provides the solution, though in quoting the solution, many Christians strangely omit the essential half. "*Submit therefore to God.* But resist the devil, and he will flee from you" (Jas 4:7, emphasis added). Submission to God is an open invitation to sanctification, which delivers immediately from the penalty of sin, progressively from the plague of sin, and eschatologically from the presence of sin.[28] The battle resides in the second aspect, our progressive sanctification. Victory requires a proactive rather than reactive approach to temptation.

Indeed, sanctification is more than a purge of causative factors. While one may disdain the desires and decisions that prove rotten to the core, sanctification targets the root of that bad fruit. Why do you have these desires? How can you easily justify these behaviors? Why do you fail to recognize the evil nature that dominates? Why do you deny responsibility for the sin that results?

Continuous sanctification reverses this tendency by making believers holy through five stages: separation, purification, imitation, assimilation, and perfection/maturation.[29] This activity is of utmost importance, for without sanctification, no one will see God (Heb 12:14).

Let's begin by considering the need for separation. The Hebrew word most translated as "holiness" is קָדַשׁ (*qadash*). It means "to set apart" or "to consecrate" and speaks specifically to removing persons or things from the realm of the common or profane.[30] The priests and holy vessels of the tabernacle and temple provide a familiar picture. Their holiness was a matter of condition as well as position. As Stanley Horton rightly notes, "It was not their separation from ordinary use that made them holy. They were not holy until taken into the tabernacle and used in the service of God. So we are saints, not merely because we are separated from sin and evil, but because we are separated to God, sanctified and anointed for the Master's use."[31]

---

28. As presented by Randy Maddox when defining Wesley's three dimensions of human salvation (Maddox, *Responsible Grace*, 143).

29. Cf. Lev 16:30; 22:21; Deut 7:6; Ps 24:3–4.

30. Vine et al., *Vine's Complete Expository Dictionary*, s.v. "qadash," 6942.

31. Horton, "Pentecostal Perspective," 132. This is one reason "good works" are never good enough. One must progress from the good to the godly.

Later writings (particularly the Psalms and Prophets) extended the concept to all of God's people and presented holiness in ethical terms—a call to righteous behavior centered on the preeminence of love, compassion, and mercy (Ps 15:1–2) and the need to act justly and walk in humility (Mic 6:8). Thus, sanctification is a verb and an adjective; it is positional regarding the believer's right standing with God and propositional in its invitation to the continual development of Christlike character.[32] The Greek rendering of *hagios* (holy) strengthens the ethical emphasis of holiness by requiring the sanctified believer to demonstrate God's righteous character in external actions *and* internal attitudes.[33]

Hebrews 10:14 provides the exegetical cornerstone in its declaration that "by one offering He has perfected for all time those who are sanctified." The Greek *teleioo* (perfected) is in the perfect tense, which notes a completed action.[34] The following word, *dienekes*, means "forever, continuously, and for all time" and solidifies this completion.[35] Indeed, Jesus' sacrifice was "once for all" (Heb 9:28), making the believer's positional sanctification immediate and complete. However, the Greek *hagiazo* (sanctified) is in a continuous form of the verb, which notes the need for continued cleansing and purifying by the blood of Jesus, the Spirit of God, and the Word of God.[36] Therefore, sanctification relates to the beginning, continuation, and goal of the Christian life.[37]

It is here that separation must progress to purification—complete surrender of autonomous spirituality and repentance of all that is ungodly. Sadly, many examples of ministerial restoration do not progress beyond this point. Many Christians are eager to change the world but are unwilling or unable to change themselves. Some are afraid of repercussions if they come

---

32. This approach to positional and conditional sanctification is anchored in the theologies of John Calvin (where it is commonly referred to as definitive and progressive) yet has acceptance and development well beyond the Reformed tradition. The new covenant finds its priesthood of believers positionally sanctified (set apart) upon conversion; they are "in Christ" and, therefore, seated in heavenly places (1 Cor 1:30; Eph 2:4–6; Col 2:11–12; Heb 2:10–11; 13:12). However, the fallen condition demands continued sanctification and growth in Christlikeness (1 Cor 3:1; Eph 4:22–24; Col 3:5–10; 1 Thess 4:3–5; Heb 10:14; 2 Pet 1:4–8; 3:18; 1 John 1:7).

33. Vine et al., *Vine's Complete Expository Dictionary*, s.v. "*hagios*," 40. Cf. Matt 5–6; 1 Pet 1:15–16.

34. Vine et al., *Vine's Complete Expository Dictionary*, s.v. "*teleioo*," 5048.

35. Vine et al., *Vine's Complete Expository Dictionary*, s.v. "continual," 1467; "ever, forever, evermore," 3842.

36. Vine et al., *Vine's Complete Expository Dictionary*, s.v. "*hagiazo*," 37. Cf. John 17:17; Rom 15:16; 1 Cor 6:11; 2 Thess 2:13; 1 Pet 1:2, 22.

37. Williams, *Renewal Theology . . . Vol. 2*, 86.

forward. Others opt for semi-Pelagian solutions that prove ineffective and exhaust the individual in therapeutic "good works" and ministerial duties that neither eliminate ungodly character nor cultivate Christian character. Ministers with spiritual experiences apart from a personal sanctifying work may mistakenly believe they are doing fine and fail to realize their relational lives are fractured and their emotions disordered.[38] This misconception leaves them frustrated, angry, and often questioning the possibility of spiritual growth. Exacerbating the problem is an anhedonic acceptance by which society—including the church—has grown accustomed to the normality of dysfunction. Ministers who fail to purge the dysfunction can expect a return to past actions and attitudes when relief from ministerial pressures is needed. If armed only with deficient spiritual formation, they are helpless to survive the spiritual warfare that ensues.

This shortfall was evident to Dietrich Bonhoeffer, who squared off against a church whose compromised character led to the assimilation of liberal theologies and Adolf Hitler's Third Reich. The German pastor/theologian centered Christian formation within the need to recognize God's sovereignty, receive God's sanctifying grace, and become an active member of God's body.[39] This re-creation requires a complete renunciation of the old life and a firm commitment to spiritual disciplines. In Bonhoeffer's view, Matthew and Peter might have enjoyed religious experiences had they remained at the tax table and Galilean shore, but "the road to faith passes through obedience to the call of Jesus. . . . Only he who believes is obedient, and only he who is obedient believes."[40] Thus, Bonhoeffer stresses the symbiotic unity between faith and obedience, a submissive partnership that recognizes external ministry is naught if not preceded by internal transformation. Conversely, disobedience is the tell-tale sign an individual is trying to keep something under his control.

When individual responsibility evokes a sanctified response, Augustine's disordered loves are reordered and put "in their place with reference to what is good under God . . . progressively replacing our destructive images and ideas with the images and ideas that filled the mind of Jesus Himself."[41]

---

38. Scazzero, *Emotionally Healthy Spirituality*, 16.

39. Such commitment is equally evident in Donald Whitney's approach. He identifies three primary catalysts God uses to sanctify and reform believers in his image: People (Prov 27:17), circumstances (Rom 8:28), and spiritual disciplines (Whitney, *Spiritual Disciplines for the Christian Life*, 10–11).

40. Bonhoeffer, *Cost of Discipleship*, 62–63.

41. Willard et al., *Kingdom Life*, locs. 740 and 771. Indeed, the need for sanctification is not limited to sinful sexual behaviors but extends to causal factors that manifest as temptation. These include mental and emotional malformation, struggles with

Such sanctified reordering moves beyond cognitive judgment and behavior modification to (re)form one's nature, character, and identity. This reordering is a critical distinction: one who is sound in theological judgment yet deficient in spiritual formation can still (and likely will) be consumed by vile affections and heretical actions.[42] Knowledge and willpower are insufficient to produce godly thoughts that lead to godly character.[43] Mere avoidance of sin does not correct one's attitude toward sin. Trying to perfect the sinful nature, which is dead, is futile. Any "success" in this effort only renders the individual a "whitewashed tomb" who has traded sexual for self-righteous behavior.

Conversely, holistic (re)formation seeks to meet Christ's ethical standard and form Christlike character. This endeavor requires a sanctifying psychopathology, a participative commitment to reconstruct self-oriented patterns of thought and malformed behaviors. Veli-Matti Kärkkäinen explains that this interplay of grace and assent may see the Spirit draw, "but people must consent. The Spirit helps us, but we are also coworkers with God."[44]

For this reason, holistic sanctification requires committed and continual participation. Because uncreated grace resides in relational presence, it is resistible and "does not continue to act upon a soul unless the soul reacts upon God."[45] Like all personal relationships, sanctification "deepens (or widens) over time because God respects and awaits our progressive response."[46] As Gregory Clapper rightly asserts, "The final shape or form of our heart is to a great extent the result of own evaluations, judgments and decisions about how we choose to cooperate with God's grace."[47]

Cooperation with the Spirit purifies passions and heals systemic hurts. As noted above, some cases of sexual immorality result when isolated and ill-equipped ministers seek to meet legitimate needs in illegitimate ways. Indeed, the man who knocks on the door of a brothel does so seeking God.[48] Ministers who lack holistic formation may revert to self-oriented solutions

---

inferiority and identity, dysfunctional relationships and abandonment, and the effects of trauma.

42. Jer 17:9; Matt 15:18–19; 23:13–33; Jas 2:19.

43. For the deficiency of knowledge alone, see Rom 2:17–24. For the deficiency of willpower, see Matt 26:41; Mark 14:38; Rom 7:14–23.

44. Kärkkäinen, *One with God*, 85. Cf. 2 Cor 6:1; Phil 1:19.

45. Wesley, "Sermon: 'The Great Privilege,'" 339.

46. Maddox, *Responsible Grace*, 87.

47. Clapper, *Renewal of the Heart*, loc. 423.

48. This quote is often attributed to G. K. Chesterton but comes from Bruce Marshall's 1945 novel *The World, the Flesh and Father*.

drawn from past dysfunction to cope with woundedness, loneliness, and lack of self-worth. Hence the need for holistic sanctification. Justification does not remove the "infection of nature" (sinful passions and tempers); justification removes sin's guilt and controlling power, but not its inclination.[49] Indeed, there remains a heart that is "more deceitful than all else and is desperately sick" (Jer 17:9).

This condition is why the Holy Spirit's purification of the heart comes through replacement rather than refurbishment. David affirms this truth in his petition that God "create in [him] a clean heart" (Ps 51:10). The word בָּרָא (bara') expresses creation out of nothing; creation of something that did not previously exist.[50] This new heart is understood to be טָהוֹר (tahor), a clean that lacks impurity, filthiness, defilement, or imperfection.[51]

The uncreated grace inherent to holistic sanctification progressively heals the plague of sin and enables further participation in divine presence and power, a "sharing" in the life of God.[52] This holistic work enjoins "divine affectivity (Spirit as bond of love) and human affectivity."[53] Sanctification releases the heart from rebellion and frees the soul to love God and others actively. This multi-faceted (re)formation enables recovery of moral righteousness and "the image of God, a renewal of soul after His likeness."[54] The focus is not on inner spirituality but on inward cleansing leading to outward love.[55] The result is a new and undivided heart—what Clapper describes as *orthokardia*, or "right heart."[56] The new heart allows the fulfillment of the Great Commandment, which is "the goal of our calling to which we must ever look if we would answer God when he calls."[57]

Thus, participation with God in sanctification develops relational anthropology that views proper relationships as central to authentic human

---

49. Wesley, "Sermon: 'On Sin in Believers,'" 341. See also Maddox, *Responsible Grace*, 82.

50. Vine et al., *Vine's Complete Expository Dictionary*, s.v. "bara," 1254. The need for a new heart is similarly echoed by God in Jer 24:7; 31:33; 32:39 and Ezek 11:19; 18:31; 36:26.

51. Vine et al., *Vine's Complete Expository Dictionary*, s.v. "tahor," 2889.

52. Alston, "Indwelling of the Holy Spirit," 223–52.

53. Coulter, "Introduction," 7.

54. Wesley, "Sermon: 'The Witness of Our Own Spirit,'" 267.

55. Dieter, "Wesleyan Perspective," 27. This marks a key difference between the original Wesleyan doctrine of entire sanctification and the position of the nineteenth-century Holiness Movement that would follow.

56. Clapper, "Orthokardia," 259.

57. Calvin, *Institutes of the Christian Religion*, 3.6.2.

existence.[58] Repentance restores the right relationship with God, enabling the purification and healing of root issues that cause many illicit behaviors. Then, by knowing, loving, obeying, and enjoying God through participative relationships, the individual experiences proper relationships with others through loving service.

These healthy relationships enable a proper relationship with oneself and a realization of true identity in and through Christ, which leads to self-acceptance and counters self-condemnation.[59] The individual progresses from "*barely* human, to the *truly* human, to the *fully* human."[60]

In summary, holistic sanctification is "a gradual therapeutic process that grows out of our responsive participation in God's forgiving and empowering grace."[61] This process enables forsaking illicit desires and entrusting oneself with God's loving presence. Robert Louis Wilken captures this critical need in his powerful and poignant observation that "desire feeds on absence; love lives off presence."[62] Desire yearns to possess something that is (or perceived to be) lacking; illicit appropriation results in the privation of good. True fulfillment is found only in the originating source—divine love.

Participation in God's presence reforms the *imago Dei* and enables the believer to love God, others, and self rightly—and find fulfillment in each. Right relationships lead to *orthokardia* (right heart), which works in conjunction with *orthodoxy* (right beliefs), *orthopathy* (right affections), and *orthopraxy* (right action or behavior) to form "the fullest definition of what it means to be a Christian."[63] Yet there are many challenges the fallen minister must overcome.

---

58. Maddox, *Responsible Grace*, 68.

59. The twelfth-century abbot and mystic Bernard of Clairvaux presents this progressive fulfillment in four stages: (1) "love of self for one's own sake," which seeks gratification and fulfillment through illicit desires; (2) "love of God for one's own sake," which sees a response to God's grace, but in hope of consolations; (3) "love of God for God's sake," in which the individual no longer desires consolations, but the God who gives the consolations; and (4) the "love of self for God's sake" (Bernard of Clairvaux, *On the Love of God*, chs. 8–10).

60. Maddox, *Responsible Grace*, 146 (author's italics).

61. Maddox, *Responsible Grace*, 192. Here, the word "therapeutic" is not meant in the secular definition that seeks self-oriented spiritual (typically non-Christian) treatment, but the Wesleyan sense that heals the spiritual, emotional, and physical disease of sin.

62. Wilken, "Blessed Passion of Love," 36.

63. Clapper, "Orthokardia," 259.

SECTION THREE: WHEN DISASTER STRIKES

STRONGHOLDS AND THE PROBLEM OF PORNOGRAPHY

"Save us from weak resignation to the evils we deplore."

— Harry Emerson Fosdick

Baasha was the king of the ten northern tribes called Israel (1 Kgs 15:16–22). He established a fortress at Ramah to control the people and to diminish the authority and power of Asa, the king of the two tribes called Judah. Baasha's actions are significant because God required the people to worship him in Jerusalem. However, this stronghold kept the people from the place of prayer, worship, and sacrifice. More to the point, this stronghold kept the people from God's presence.

Satan acts similarly. He does not need a legion of devils to keep you from God. All he needs is one stronghold that will cause you to come up short in your worship and sacrifice, prayer and praise. Just one stronghold will prevent you from standing in God's presence.

These massive fortresses don't pop up overnight. The enemy first lays a foundation, then fortifies his castle brick by brick, layer upon layer. His quarry is rife with various stronghold stones, such as pride, loneliness, depression, and fear of rejection or abandonment. Unhealed emotional wounds and unresolved trauma are popular options. Decisions or actions that reject biblical revelation provide the fortifying mortar. And chiseled upon many stronghold stones are phrases such as "look out for number one," "do what's right for you," and "find your own truth."

Regarding sexual immorality, pornography has become a preferred building block. While pornography use is significantly lower among Christians than non-Christians, the Barna Institute quantifies usage as a crisis within Christianity. A 2016 survey of nearly three thousand U.S. teens, adults, and Protestant youth and senior pastors asked about their perceptions of pornography, their use of pornography, and how they feel about their use of pornography. More than half of Christians between 18 and 24 seek porn at least occasionally. One in five youth pastors and one in seven senior pastors—more than fifty-thousand US church leaders—admit they currently use porn. Two out of three youth pastors and more than half of senior pastors say porn is a current or past struggle.[64] Unfortunately, many ministers spend more time on Pornhub than Bible Hub (not that any time on the former is acceptable).

---

64. Barna Group, *Porn Phenomenon*, 77–78.

BUILDING THE RESTORATION PLAN

Is pornography sexual immorality? Is viewing porn commensurate to adultery or fornication? The citadel's strength is evident in the responses that often follow. Defenders contend that porn is not a problem but instead provides an acceptable alternative to actual sex. Because it involves consenting adults, it does not harm. Allow me to dismantle this stronghold one brick at a time.

What is the problem? Pornography is a sin that violates the divine image and intent. Viewing porn (as well as sex without commitment) is dehumanizing. The viewer sees the other party as a sexual consumable rather than a person created in God's image with inherent dignity and worth. This individual is objectified, considered only as an instrument to satisfy selfish desires, and valued for imagined sexual proficiency.[65] Pornography use also violates sexuality's divine intent. Though sexuality is commercialized, and deviance has progressed (digressed?) from toleration to celebration, sexuality remains sacred.[66] As Carl Trueman rightly asserts, pornography divorces sexual activity from any moral content, desecrates the holy, and "repudiates any notion that sex has significance beyond the act itself."[67]

But isn't pornography an acceptable alternative to actual sex? No. Pornography will put asunder that which God has joined together, even if both spouses are willing participants. The two become one through intimate trust and vulnerability. Such intimacy is deeply relational—a progressive giving of the authentic self in response to the patience, humility, emotional listening, and selfless support the other offers. In the divine design, the sexual act is a teleological apex of physical, spiritual, and emotional unity. Pornography circumvents that path to provide sexual reward without all the work. Of course, the individual loses the greater reward of unity and intimacy, and this deficiency drives him to repeat the cycle in a vain search for fulfillment.

---

65. Clinton and Laaser, *Quick Reference Guide*, 158, Hettlinger, *Sex Isn't That Simple*, 80, Struthers, *Wired for Intimacy*, 45. See also the subsection "Old Testament: Sexual Immorality Violates the *Imago Dei*" in chapter 2. The sex act cannot be separated from the personhood of the human beings who engage in it, especially for the Christian whose body is the temple of the Holy Spirit and is commanded to "honor God with your body" (1 Cor 6:19–20). Thus, every sex act becomes a powerful theological statement (Grenz and Bell, *Betrayal of Trust*, 75).

66. If sexual activity outside of marriage is not a violation of conscience, why must one be "seduced"? Why do state and federal laws differentiate between physical and sexual assault? Because the former are beaten, but the latter are violated (Murray, *Saving Truth*, 135; see also Hession, *Forgotten Factors*, loc. 270).

67. Trueman, *Rise and Triumph of the Modern Self*, 99.

Pornography also causes separation from God, as willful sin is a purity issue.[68] Purifying the heart was a primary purpose of Christ's passion (Matt 5:8; Titus 2:14). A lack of purity prevents conformity to Christ, who is the perfect image of God. A lack of conformity prevents unity with God and others, which is the essence of love and the greatest commandment (Matt 22:36–40). There can be no unity if one is sinful and the other holy.

But we are consenting adults, so what is the harm? Much. First, consider the physical, spiritual, emotional, and financial enslavement experienced by countless souls in the industry. Christians set captives free; we do not contribute to their captivity. Further harm may come when pornography, which may start as a substitute, leads to unrealistic sexual expectations, more significant deviation from the divine intent, and participation in the act. A need to satisfy deep emotional and spiritual longings creates sexual fantasy as the individual perceives sex to be the solution for love, touch, nurture, and affirmation. Pornography escalates the intensity of that fantasy to higher and higher levels of lust. Here, the viewer learns that pornography is neither an emotionally nor physiologically neutral experience. Addictive tendencies soon form; changes in the brain's neural patterns indicate pornography becomes as addictive as cocaine and heroin. Like those drugs, tolerance builds and demands more dangerous or exciting forms. It is no wonder that porn—which is often violent, degrading, and extreme—contributes to violence against women, child pornography and abuse, and sex trafficking.

More than forty years of peer-reviewed research have demonstrated that porn adversely shapes how we think about gender, sexuality, relationships, intimacy, sexual violence, and gender equality. The issue is so bad that many on Capitol Hill now argue this is a public health crisis rather than a private matter.[69] The damaging findings include:

- Eighty-three percent of US college men studied reported seeing mainstream pornography, and those who did were more likely to say they would commit rape or sexual assault if they wouldn't be caught than men who hadn't seen porn in the past twelve months. The same study found that porn consumers were less likely to intervene if they observed a sexual assault taking place.

---

68. Contrary to some fringe theologies, it is sinful to view pornography. Jesus flatly said that to lust is to commit adultery (Matt 5:28). Cf. Prov 15:29; Isa 59:2; Rom 8:7–8; 1 Cor 6:9–10; Eph 2:1–3.

69. Dines, "Is Porn Immoral?" Also worth considering is the sociologist's book *Pornland: How Porn Has Hijacked Our Sexuality*.

- In a study of young teens throughout the southeastern United States, 66 percent of boys reported porn consumption in the past year; this early porn exposure was correlated with perpetration of sexual harassment two years later.
- A recent meta-analysis of twenty-two studies between 1978 and 2014 from seven countries concluded that pornography consumption is associated with an increased likelihood of committing acts of verbal or physical sexual aggression, regardless of age.

In summary, porn is a problem, it is not an acceptable alternative to traditional sex, and it results in much harm. If you don't believe any of these apply to you, get comfortable in the enemy's stronghold. You may be there for a while and find its dungeons delve deeper than you imagined.

Instead, I invite you to take residence in a different stronghold. David called God "my fortress."[70] The Hebrew word used is *metzudah*, from which we get the word "Masada." That word remains revered in Israel. Masada is a historic location atop a high desert plateau overlooking the Dead Sea. It took a Roman force of roughly fifteen thousand men and enslaved people almost two years to subdue the fortress, which a force of fewer than one thousand men, women, and children defended. The remarkable Jewish zealots preferred death to enslavement. The would-be conquerors found that the defenders, led by Eleazar ben Jair, had taken their own lives. The Jews destroyed everything in Masada except the food and storehouses to show the Romans that they chose death over slavery.

God is your "Masada" as well. That does not mean the enemy will not attack. Protection comes by ascending to an elevated place with God. This climb requires you to recognize what is above you and what is beneath you. You must be willing to make your stand and put the flesh to death rather than be enslaved by sin. You must be willing to pay the price for your freedom in Christ.

To enter this Masada, one must abandon sexual immorality, including pornography. If married, spouses must make this journey together. Identify sexual desires or actions that are unbiblical or make you uncomfortable. Repent of your actions and renounce the enemy's lies. With the help of a qualified counselor or mental health professional, use cognitive restructuring to change your illicit thoughts (more on that in chapter 11).

The true meaning of sexual intercourse discloses itself within a proper context (marriage) and with a proper intent (to express unconditional, covenantal love). This "beautiful symbol of mutual commitment and mutual

---

70. Ps 71:1–3. See also 1 Sam 22:4–5; 23:14; 24:22; Pss 18:1–3; 91:1–2; 144:2; Prov 18:10.

submission" is the biblical counter-narrative to sexual activity outside of the marriage bed, "which all too readily becomes an expression of self-gratification, infidelity or exploitation."[71]

---

71. Grenz and Bell, *Betrayal of Trust*, 75.

Section Three Summary

> "We ought to be interested in that darkest and most real part of a man in which dwell not the vices that he does not display, but the virtues that he cannot."
>
> — G. K. Chesterton

THIS SECTION OUTLINED STEPS for determining a fallen minister's eligibility for restoration and building a restoration team and unique restoration plan when appropriate. Five assertions are central to this restoration paradigm:[1]

1. Holistic restoration demands biblical confession and repentance that originates from godly rather than worldly sorrow (2 Cor 7:10). Furthermore, the fallen minister is to repent for violating the victim, the office, and the image of God.

2. Holistic restoration requires honest self-appraisal and painful appraisal from God and others. The fallen minister must reverse course and submit to a restorative plan that looks beyond the behaviors and addresses the root causes of unethical or immoral behavior.

3. The goal is restoration to God and calling rather than ministry vocation. Such restoration is impossible apart from restoration to family and others, necessitating a holistic approach that must look upward, inward, and outward.

4. Ecclesiastical counsel and care are critical to success. The selection and participative support of leaders and the church body is essential. Those who are spiritual must restore in truth and gentleness, careful not to violate grace in the name of toleration or purification.

---

1. Matt 7:1–5; 18:15–18; Luke 17:1–4; Gal 6:1–2; Jas 5:19–20. Cf. Prov 3:27.

5. Long-term holistic and ministerial restoration requires perpetual commitment. Therefore, the guidelines in section 4 include an open-ended timeline with systematic analysis and continual accountability.

Biblical restoration is a team effort. The individuals or agencies necessary to the restorative process include (1) the overseer, (2) the Christian mental health professional, (3) the spiritual mentor, (4) the church, and (5) the violator. This Spirit-led and competent team can complete its transformative work with such skill that it makes the great Michelangelo's work look like a preschool art project. In fairness to the artist, his four "prisoners" who struggle to break free from stone bondage are impressive and analogous to the task.

Rather than fashion the stone into an ideal minister, each team member serves as a unique tool the Holy Spirit uses to chip away the excess stone that keeps the beautiful and true character entombed. The beauty of it is this: Michelangelo sometimes quit a sculpture in frustration, saying the stone refused to release the prisoner. Not so with the Holy Spirit. He that began a good work in you shall complete it (Phil 1:6).

The overseer leads this symbiotic effort and is responsible for the spiritual health and protection of the fallen minister, the minister's family, victim(s), the affected congregation, and the congregation to which the minister is assigned, if and when a church reassignment is appropriate. The Christian mental health professional helps establish a formal diagnosis and provides counsel toward healing emotional brokenness and halting the illicit coping behaviors learned in response. The spiritual mentor establishes boundaries that will protect the violator and others. He holds the violator accountable for holistic growth within those parameters through compassionate correction, encouragement, and honest appraisal. A designated congregation provides a fuller presence of Christ and the Holy Spirit. God's grace is extended and effectual through church members' loving and selfless participation. The violator is responsible for confessing and repenting, counting costs, committing to correction, and recouping competency.

There are four anticipated obstacles to successful ministerial restoration: (1) the human condition; (2) the lack of self-appraisal; (3) the lack of specific biblical guidance; (4) the preference for and influence of secular reasoning resulting in a lack of congregational participation and support.

The first and significant obstacle to an effective holistic formation and ministerial restoration is and will likely remain the failure to understand and acknowledge the reality of the human condition. Without question, to "be like God" remains the timeless temptation.[2] Individualism promises

---

2. If only Adam and Eve had looked at the serpent and asked, "if the freedom to

SECTION THREE SUMMARY

freedom yet results in bondage.[3] Individuals pursue those things that will (seemingly) provide stability, purpose, and worth in life. These pursuits become commitments, and commitments become servitude. When expectations are unmet, individuals typically endure or escape through learned behaviors and coping mechanisms. This tendency often becomes addictive amid increasing struggles. The flesh justifies these destructive behaviors with familiar statements such as "it is no one's business," "you are not hurting anyone," "you deserve this," and "it will be much worse if you don't have an outlet."

Honest self-appraisal is the second obstacle. A typical example begins with the tendency to measure ministerial success by secular principles such as attendance and income. This "successful" minister soon relegates relational and righteous requirements to secondary or tertiary status. There is no reason for spiritual inventory when adoration equates to anointing. As such, he is increasingly ignorant or dismissive of moral weaknesses that emerge when squeezed by ministerial pressures. While that minister may be able to resolve external conflicts, only learned (and often illicit) behaviors can appease the internal conflicts that inevitably develop.

Honesty also applies to the restoring community. As noted above, many congregations forced to deal with ministerial moral failure choose to suppress information in a vain attempt to maintain resources and protect reputations. Such actions violate the biblical mandate that links truth-telling and community (Eph 4:15-16).[4]

The lack of specific biblical guidance is the third obstacle to ministerial restoration. This results in various approaches, such as the destroy/defer/disregard descriptors explained in chapter 7.

In fairness, there is a lack of detailed instruction regarding ministerial restoration. Scripture offers neither a casuistic law that would mandate explicit behavior nor apodictic commands that regulate all restorations. Still, such a lack can be beneficial since each moral failure is an individual endeavor predicated on a confluence of spiritual, psychological, physiological, and contextual factors that are both personal and social in scope. The restoration process cannot be reduced to one prescription when each event is as unique as the causal circumstances in which the participant partook.

---

define good and evil elevates one to godlike status, why haven't you sunk your teeth into that fruit?" It is a good question to ask your serpent, as well.

3. Prov 16:18; 23:19-21; Eccl 8:10-13; Oba 3; 1 Pet 5:5-6.

4. See Eph 4:15-16. Indeed, mentors and congregations must avoid "CEO disease" which is the information vacuum created "when people withhold important (and usually unpleasant) information," thus restricting the reliable analysis essential to personal improvement (Goleman, *Primal Leadership*, 93-95).

With that said, it is possible to construct a biblical restoration paradigm from the identifiable commonalities shared by individuals and circumstances. The bulk of this book stands as proof—it supports the paradigm by presenting a systematic review of appropriate biblical principles, historical and theological analysis of doctrines and practices, and careful exegetical appraisal of terms and concepts. While the findings necessitate interactive processes between the individual, congregation, and God, those within the Christian community whose theology has deeper roots in secular rather than scriptural considerations stand as the fourth obstacle.

Numerous studies have found that the laity often affirms or rejects restoration for personal reasons or provides allowances only within specific parameters that reflect secular reasoning over and above biblical truth.[5] For example, some churches will take a very liberal approach and demand restoration with little, if any, corrective measures. On the other hand, more legalistic churches will place rigid requirements if restoration is allowed. Both approaches are in error. The first lacks the biblical call for a righteous standard centered on repentance, while the latter negates the grace and forgiveness inherent to the Gospel.

Such variations result from divided concepts of truth that have become characteristic of Western culture and have inundated the Western church. Described by Nancy Pearcey as the "secular/sacred split," this dichotomy has seen society increasingly view secular and scientific reasoning as factual and public while forcing religious activity to reside in the realm of personal values. This worldview has effectively held Christianity in cultural captivity that results in "double minds and fragmented lives," as religious adherents often (and often unknowingly) ascribe to secular ethics and ideals but "Christianize" such concepts with the inclusion of proof texts and Scripture taken out of context.[6]

Pearcey's understanding is critical in formulating a holistic (re)formation. It is necessary not only that the *message* is biblical but that the *method* is biblical—it is not sufficient to determine *that* Scripture affords a violator's restoration; one must equally determine *how* Scripture dictates that restoration is to transpire. Avoiding secular tendencies and preferences requires a comprehensive understanding and acknowledgment of how culture and one's worldview influence ethics and action. Failure to recognize or reject such tendencies is tantamount to tasting the fruit of the first Adam's rather than the second Adam's tree.

---

5. Barna Group, *Porn Phenomenon*, 118; Sutton et al., "Does Gender Matter?," 647; Sutton and Jordan, "Evaluating Attitudes Toward Clergy Restoration," 865; Sutton and Thomas, "Can Derailed Pastors be Restored?," 596.

6. Pearcey, *Total Truth*, 25.

SECTION THREE SUMMARY

Restoration demands biblical response and accountability from the Christian community. Although some congregants and pastoral leaders may feel unqualified for the task or oblivious to their biblical responsibilities, restoration is a communal act. Those spiritual within the church, not just its leaders, must restore the victims and violators in gentleness. Above all, complete submission to and participation in the Holy Spirit's sanctifying work is central.

In closing, holistic (re)formation and ministerial restoration demand recognition, repentance, and responsibility. Recognition goes beyond the sinful activity to identify the causal factors and affirm the consequences born by others, namely the minister's victim(s), family, and church. Repentance goes beyond confession to require a turning away from established behaviors. Responsibility goes beyond the fallen minister to encompass the duty of others to aid in this endeavor. Like Nehemiah's work crew, all parties are to show up with a sword in one hand and a tool in the other.

Now, let's get busy restoring this temple.

SECTION FOUR
Restore, Rebuild, and Reinforce

> "Jesus rises from his knees and calls his disciples. 'Rise, let us be going,' he says, and goes before them—to the Cross. There is the pattern of leadership for the church."
>
> — Lesslie Newbigin

The restoration team is assembled but looks upon a seemingly impossible task. The once-magnificent temple lay decimated in the wake of a perfect storm. The remnants serve only as reminders of the former glory. How can one clean up this mess, let alone rebuild something in its place?

This question also plagued Zerubbabel. Judah's tribal leader rebuilt the Jerusalem Temple seven decades before Nehemiah arrived to rebuild the city's wall. His was a mountainous endeavor—quite literally, as we shall see. Yet the project's enormity was not the most significant problem. Opposition and complacency pushed this five-year restoration project into a twenty-three-year ordeal.

Temple restoration can be tough.

Zerubbabel's commissioning to restore the temple came upon his release from Babylonian captivity. Things started well. He led a group of exiles, including Joshua, the high priest, who brought with them the sacred gold and silver vessels Nebuchadnezzar had stolen.[1] Under Zerubbabel's leadership, God's people rebuilt the altar, restored ordained worship, and relaid the temple's foundation (Ezra 3:2–13, 4:2–3).

Laying that foundation was a monumental achievement. Solomon's Temple was epic. Solomon obtained colossal stone blocks from subterranean

---

1. Ezra 1:7–11; 2:1–60, 5:2; Neh 7:7, 12:1.

quarries for the foundation and walls. The Temple Mount lacked sufficient level space, so Solomon constructed a massive masonry wall—more than two hundred feet high in some places—across the southern and eastern sides. The king created vast cisterns in the rocky hill to supply sufficient water. One cistern, the "great sea," could hold two million gallons of water.

Its bronze altar of sacrifice, where priests offered flesh to God, measured twenty-two and a half feet square, stood fifteen feet high, and was accessed by a twenty-foot ramp from the east.[2] Gold-plated cedar paneling from the forests of Lebanon covered the interior walls and boasted majestic carvings of flowers and cherubim. No stonework was visible.

But Nebudchanezzar and the Babylonian army razed Solomon's Temple. Only a massive pile of rock and rubbish remained. How would Zerubbabel remove this mountainous mess, let alone shape and position the gigantic stones that would take its place? Solomon had a massive workforce of nearly two hundred thousand (1 Kgs 5:13–18). What could this remnant do?

Here, God gave Zerubbabel a word that all restoration teams would do well to remember: "'Not by might nor by power, but by My Spirit,' says the Lord of armies. 'What are you, you great mountain? Before Zerubbabel you will become a plain; and he will bring out the top stone with shouts of "Grace, grace to it!"'" (Zech 4:6–7).

Soon, the mountainous debris was removed, except for one stone. That singular stone became the foundation for the new temple.[3] Its installation ignited shouts of "grace!" that echoed across the platform and into the heavens.

It was a glorious and victorious day, indeed. Unfortunately, darker days were ahead. Zerubbabel's task was not only mountainous but opposed (Ezra 4). This turn of events gives every restoration team reason for caution.

The Samaritans, who were not in right standing with God, wanted to help rebuild the temple and share in its use. Zerubbabel and his restoration team were committed to doing it God's way. There was no need for social influence or syncretism. The Samaritans lashed out in response. Their verbal attacks discouraged and frightened God's people. The Samaritans inundated Persian officials with lies and bribes, and the Persian king soon withdrew his support. The restoration program was at a standstill. In fairness, Zerubbabel

---

2. In comparison, the first altar of sacrifice was built three months after the Israelites departed Egypt and accompanied their forty-year journey through the wilderness (Ex 19:1; 27). Made of acacia wood and covered in bronze, the altar measured seven and a half feet square and stood four and a half feet high.

3. Boda, *Haggai, Zechariah*, 276.

SECTION THREE SUMMARY

and his team are not without fault. They were busy building costly homes for themselves, contributing to the sixteen-year delay (Hag 1:1–11).

After a stern rebuke from God, Zerubbabel and the people resumed their task and dedicated the temple five years later, on March 12, 515. It was a joyous and phenomenal celebration that coincided with Passover (Ezra 6:16–19). Even so, the festivities found some with heads hung low (Hag 2:1–4; cf. Ezra 3:12). It is not hard to understand why. Zerubbabel's Temple was as large (possibly larger) as Solomon's but lacked the former's magnificence and splendor. More importantly, this temple lacked the ark of the covenant and, therefore, the *shekinah* glory of God's divine presence and his Ten Commandments. The Babylonian Talmud (Yoma 21b) asserts that Zerubbabel's Temple also lacked the sacred fire with which God ignited the altar of sacrifice, the spirit of prophecy, and the Urim and Thummim worn by the high priest.

The lack was a sad reminder of what once was. Zerubbabel's restoration was not so glorious. Or was it? God encouraged the restoration team to take courage, for God would fill this house with glory; the latter glory would be greater than the former, and the temple would be where God gives peace (Hag 2:4–9). God's people renovated Zerubbabel's Temple many times in the years that followed, with the most significant expansion completed by King Herod. In that temple, the infant Jesus was dedicated (Luke 2:22), the boy Jesus astounded the teachers (Luke 2:46–49), and the great minister taught (Mark 12:35; Luke 19:47; John 7:28, etc.).

Indeed, Zerubbabel's Temple held a far greater glory—and so does yours (cf. 1 Cor 3:16; 6:19–20). But like Solomon's Temple, our temples sometimes become a mountainous mess. Like Zerubbabel's Temple, ours can become defiled.[4] The following subsections provide the architectural plans, as it were, for temple restoration. Specifically, steps to restore the foundation, rebuild the walls, and reinforce the structure.

Chapter 10 restores the foundation. Like Zerubbabel's restoration efforts, one stone amid the rubbish is the cornerstone.[5] Through Christ, the violator can be reconciled to God and find forgiveness and identity in Christ.

Because moral and spiritual formation are inseparable, this effort must extend beyond a "head, hearts, and hands" approach to discuss the crucial

---

4. Chapter 2, subsection 3 addresses Antiochus's desecration of this temple. Note also that Jesus cleansed this temple at the beginning and conclusion of his earthly ministry. For first cleansing, see John 2:13–22. For second, see Matt 21:12–13; Mark 11:15–17; Luke 19:45–46.

5. Ps 118:22; Isa 28:16; Matt 21:42; Mark 12:10; Luke 20:17; Acts 4:11; Eph 2:20; 1 Pet 2:6–7.

areas of thinking, being, relating, and doing.[6] Therefore, chapter 11 looks to remove the rubbish, reform the mind, and reinforce spiritual disciplines.

A minister's moral failure is often the culmination of poor decisions years in the making. Rectifying and reversing those tendencies requires a similar commitment of time and effort. Therefore, chapter 12 addresses the periodic appraisals and protective measures designed to help the restored minister maintain his personal and professional purity. Steps include the establishment of personal boundaries, restrictions on ministerial function, and continued accountability and mentorship. Handling ministerial stress, avoiding burnout, and overcoming societal influence also receive specific attention.

---

6. Kretzschmar, "The Education of Prospective Ministers," 3.

10

Restore the Foundation

"The way is long if one follows precepts but short and helpful, if one follows patterns."

— Seneca

As noted in chapter 5, foundations are everything. One must ensure sufficient depth and strength to support the structure and bear subsequent load. While Christ is the cornerstone, obedience to Christ provides the foundation that withstands any storm (cf. Matt 7:24–27).

Obedience to the divine word and work will restore one's relationship with God, authentic self, and others. It is necessary to keep those in proper order. While the violator may understandably prioritize restoring his family, ministry, and reputation, the corrective steps must first bring reconciliation with God. If one does not rightly love God, he cannot rightly know and love his authentic self. If he does not rightly know and love his authentic self, he cannot rightly see and love others (Matt 22:37–40). Furthermore, God is not simply a means to an end. Restoration of one's communion with God is paramount, even if God does not restore the broken family, ministry, or reputation.

As noted above, repentance is the catalyst to reconciliation, which opens the door to restoration. More than a confession, repentance requires a turning from sin and movement toward God. Humility is the first step in that movement.[1] Consider the example provided by the parable of the prodigal son (Luke 15:11–32). Poor choices find the prodigal in a pig pen. It

---

1. Do you recount from the section 4 introduction how Zerubbabel's team laid the capstone with shouts of "grace!"? Restoring your temple also requires grace, which God gives to the humble (Jas 4:6–7; 1 Pet 5:5–6).

is a symbolic location that is pertinent to our topic. Jews who touched pigs were four times as unclean as those who visited a prostitute. The prodigal hit rock bottom, and no one offers to help. He is starving, stooping so low as to eat the slop meant for pigs, yet nothing satisfies. It is not until the prodigal "comes to himself" that the solution reveals itself. The prodigal needs to go home.

Though preservation rather than restoration drives his confession, he is on the right path. The prodigal prepares a speech that he hopes will win over the father's heart, which tells us that he didn't know the father's heart. The prodigal never gets to share what was sure to be a well-rehearsed speech (more on that in a moment).

Suffice it to say the first step in solving a problem is admitting there is a problem. Granted, many things are wrong in this world, and you have likely endured many wrongs. We tend to fixate on those wrongs and overlook our own. Instead, admit there is something wrong with you. Admit that your actions were wrong. Take responsibility for that wrong and seek the solution outside of yourself.

And head home.

RECONCILIATION IS THE CORNERSTONE

"People may spend their whole lives climbing the ladder of success only to find, once they reach the top, that the ladder is leaning against the wrong wall."

— Thomas Merton

Applying reverse engineering to the greatest commandment, we see that one must rightly love self to rightly love others. But to rightly love oneself, one must rightly love God. To rightly love God requires a relationship. Such a relationship requires reconciliation.

How can one reconcile after committing such an egregious betrayal? How can the fallen minister gain God's trust and convince the Father to return? He can't; any effort to do so is a legalistic works doctrine.[2] But if a prodigal repents and returns, he will be met by the Father's compassionate embrace long before he arrives home. Indeed, the parabolic father had been watching and saw the prodigal while he was still a long way off.

---

2. Don't be surprised if the fallen minister tries to do so. The "performance leading to acceptance" is likely an inherent approach and may be what lead him into trouble in the first place.

And what did the father see? He saw that his son had abandoned the pig pen. More to the point, his son abandoned his wrongful choices and desires. The prodigal once sacrificed everything for one thing. Reconciliation came when he sacrificed that one thing for everything. Similarly, reconciliation comes when you sacrifice that "one thing" to obtain everything.

It is time you present yourself as a living sacrifice.

Levitical sacrifices offer a strong typology. The priest first presented the sin and guilt offerings to address the sin that severs relationship with God, then the burnt offerings and grain offerings that express consecration to God, and finally the peace or fellowship offerings that symbolize communion with God (cf. Lev 9:8–21).

Christ has provided the atoning sacrifice that addresses the first issue. What, then, must one surrender for consecration and the hope of communion with God? To achieve the greatest purpose, one must sacrifice the thing that holds his greatest love.[3]

What is the one thing you wrongly love or desire above all else? What follows is a simple test that may provide insight. Do not try to determine a "right" or "appropriate" answer. Instead, capture the first word or phrase that comes to mind. Ready? Fill in the blank:

I would be happier if I had more _____.

A heartfelt response reveals who or what has lordship in our lives. Contemplate your answer and discuss it with mentors and mental health professionals. How the desire to obtain this "one thing" drives you and defines all others will soon become evident. Though it may be difficult, please leave it in the pig pen.

By giving up his one thing, the prodigal receives everything. The prodigal's choice to do so evoked a response by the father so radical that it offended his other and seemingly faithful son. The father immediately covered the prodigal's filth with a robe (a restoration of righteousness), placed a signet ring on his finger (a restoration of authority), put shoes on his feet (a restoration of journey), and called for a feast of epic proportion (a restoration of fellowship).[4] Here is where most restoration plans will miss the mark. These items are not merely gifts but guidance. In our context, the restored son must remain clothed in Christ, rightly wield his authority, walk with God, and live in communal fellowship. How does one do so? Chapter

---

3. After all, that's what God did. He gave his only begotten son; he offered his spotless lamb for the higher good of redemption.

4. Here, we see that Rabbi Abraham Heschel is correct to challenge Aristotle's definition of God as "the unmoved mover" and more accurately identify God as "the most moved mover" (Heschel, *Between God and Man*, 25).

11 elaborates. However, it is critical to recognize that repentance and return are the starting line rather than the finish line of restoration.

Such grace may not seem fair, especially to the overseer, mentors, and congregation. Rest assured, it is not. Be careful not to follow the older brother's example. Yes, the prodigal disgraced the family and squandered his fortunes, yet the older brother is more lost than the younger—and cannot see his lostness. The older brother lives with the father but is far from the father. He is afraid of being excluded. He is self-righteous. He grew judgmental and angry. One brother was a prodigal, and the other was in proximity, yet neither truly knew the father until that fateful day.

Such grace may not make sense. Rest assured, it eventually will if the prodigal walks this out (hence, the shoes). As Augustine and Anselm rightly taught, faith seeks understanding. Put another way, we need not understand to follow; instead, we follow to understand. This dynamic is why Jesus bids his would-be followers to "come and see" (John 1:39). Or consider Jesus' first command: "Follow me, and I will make you become fishers of men" (Mark 1:17). The all-too-common approach reverses Christ's guidance and first seeks one's purpose or calling (fishers of men), then works to be or do what God wants (I will make you) in the hopes of being worthy of a closer walk with God (follow me). The biblical approach requires we first follow Christ so that he may develop our biblical character (I will make you) and empower our biblical calling (fishers of men). In this approach, we respond *to* God, begin to live *from* God, and then rightly live *for* God.

Allow a quick consideration before we proceed. What do you suppose the prodigal did in the days and weeks following his return? No doubt, he marveled at his father's love and grace. Perhaps he tried to reconcile with his brother. And most likely, he wrestled with anger and self-loathing. For this reason, holistic restoration requires forgiveness. The fallen minister must forgive God and those who may have caused emotional harm leading to deformation.[5] He must also forgive himself.

As Ambrose of Milan rightly asserts, "the wicked man is a punishment to himself, but the upright man is a grace to himself—and to either, whether good or bad, the reward of his deeds is paid in his own person."[6] Therefore, forgiveness of self is necessary to progress from wicked to upright and thus "halt the juggernaut retribution."[7]

---

5. Matt 5:23-24. God has done no wrong and, therefore, has no need for forgiveness. However, the wounded soul often projects blame or disappointment upon God, and these wrong attitudes must be released.

6. Ambrose, *De Officiis*, 1.12.

7. Yancey, *Scandal of Forgiveness*, 89.

Charizomai is an oft-used New Testament word for forgiveness. It means to deal graciously with or bestow favor unconditionally.[8] To forgive is to release our resentment, declare that only God can change another person, and entrust justice to God. Such forgiveness is so unappealing and difficult that many consider it to be "the real 'F word.'"[9]

Forgiveness requires mercy.[10] Yet many ministers who can provide a robust theological description of God's love and forgiveness cannot offer an experiential testimony of the same. Especially those who find identity and worth in the malformed roles learned through dysfunction and trauma.[11]

For the fallen minister reading this book, how do you view yourself? Helpless? Unlovable? Unworthy? A failure? Let's get this straight: you failed. Own it. It is difficult to learn from your mistakes while denying them. Own up to your mistakes, but know that failing does not make you a failure. And know that God is not in the habit of rejecting ministers who fall short. Just ask Jeremiah, who frustratingly rejected his call, or Jonah, who ran from his. Ask Timothy, who wrestled with anxiety and ulcers and had to stir up the spiritual gifts to keep moving forward. Ask Aaron, a people-pleaser who created a golden calf, called it "Yahweh," and quickly blamed others for his error. Or Moses, whose attempt to do God's will left a man dead. Moses met the call to resume his ministry with a five-point argument detailing why he was unfit for service. Peter also believed himself unqualified after he denied Christ and quickly returned to his old way of life. And let us not forget David. So significant and pertinent are his failure and restoration that chapter 3 details both.

Though your past damaged you, it does not define you. Forgive yourself, pick yourself up, and walk with God.[12] Leave the negative labels in the pig pen. Look at it this way: if someone told a series of lies but humbly repented and committed to truth-telling, would it be fair to view him as a

---

8. Vine et al., *Vine's Complete Expository Dictionary*, s.v. "forgive, forgave, forgiveness." Notable is how this word is used in 2 Cor 2:6–8.

9. Grenz and Bell, *Betrayal of Trust*, 129.

10. Mercy carries the "privilege of burying and forgiving" (Bonhoeffer, *Life Together*, 103). There is need for mercy *in* ministry, but also mercy *for* ministry. Perhaps this realization explains Paul's addition of "mercy" to his typical greeting of "grace and peace" in his three pastoral epistles to Timothy and Titus.

11. See chapter 4. The overseer, Christian psychologist, and spiritual mentors who guide the violator as he extends and accepts forgiveness must anticipate and work through three significant obstacles: (1) the need for vulnerability and the fear this evokes, (2) the depletion of self-worth when the individual removes the deceptive façade constructed to protect image and ego, and (3) the need to face and renounce the shame that misshapes identity and fuels ungodly behaviors.

12. Cf. Ps 37:23–24; Prov 24:16; Mic 6:8, 7:8; 2 Cor. 4:8; Phil 1:6; 3:13–14.

liar forevermore? Perhaps you committed adultery. Should you be labeled "adulterer" for the rest of your life (by self or others)? Is that a fair and accurate reflection of your culminated character? No, it is not. Such terms identify behaviors but fail to recognize the complexity of the human condition and divine renewal. They also betray the divine directive to forgive and embrace the renewed and (re)formed identity in Christ, which is our next topic.

REALIZE WHO(SE) YOU ARE

"Almost all problems in the spiritual life stem from a lack of self-knowledge."

— Teresa of Avila

The people of Babel were in a restoration program of sorts. Noah's flood had wiped everything away. The people decided to build a tower that reached into heaven (Gen 11:1–4). It would seem a commendable endeavor, but there were many problems. They used the wrong materials and did not follow God's direction. Of specific concern is their desire to work their way into heaven and make a name for themselves. When a person seeks to make a name for himself, he either does not know who he is or feels that others do not (but should) know who he is.

A favorite cartoon strip finds a young, enthusiastic boy named Calvin staring into the seemingly endless abyss of the night sky. He soon bellows, "I'M SIGNIFICANT!" After a few moments, the downcast youth adds, "screamed the dust speck."

Calvin certainly is not alone in his estimation. I have felt that way, and chances are, you also have. We want to know that we are significant and that we matter. As has been repeated throughout this book, we often seek that self-worth in achievements and what (we think) people think about us. Many will (mis)shape their identities this way and devolve into self-deceit and self-centeredness—what the Bible describes as confusion, futility, and darkness (Rom 1:21–2; Eph 4:17).

Moses knew a thing or two about confusion, futility, and darkness. Moses knew he was called to deliver God's people but didn't know himself well. Let's face it: Moses struck out big time when he first stepped up to the plate (Ex 2:11–14; Acts 7:22–25). One man was dead, a lot of people were offended, and Moses ran into hiding in the backside of the desert. He struggled for forty years with his identity and purpose.

It is likely that thought of what might have been, what should have been, consumed Moses. Things changed the day he saw a bush on fire but not consumed (Ex 3:7–10). God's calling to Moses from the bush would appear to be the most significant moment of Moses' life. It marked his second chance, his shot at redemption! The Lord was ready to deliver his people out of bondage and to the land of promise, and God called Moses to lead this great work. Moses would go forth in the anointing and power of God. The time had come. The prayers would be answered. The call would be fulfilled. The bondage would be broken. The promise would be realized. And how does Moses respond? Is he eager? Excited? Elated?

Not even close.

Moses did not exclaim, "Here am I! Send me!" Moses did not submit to God's will at all. Instead, he pointed to his poor performance and the opinions of others. From this, Moses offered five excuses for not being able to do this great work. "I'm a nobody" (Ex 3:11–12). "I don't know God as I should" (Ex 3:13). "No one is going to listen to me, and why should they?" (Ex 4:1). "I'm not a good speaker" (Ex 4:10). "Somebody else can do it better" (Ex 4:13).[13]

Moses had too eagerly defended a Hebrew slave earlier in his life. Why the change of heart and loss of confidence in his calling? Moses intervened in a fight between two Hebrews the day after he killed the Egyptian. One of the Hebrews asked, "Who made you king and judge over us?" The question haunts him forty years later. At the burning bush, one of Moses' pressing questions is, "When I am asked 'who sent you,' what is my answer?" Moses' hesitation to obey God is rooted in a previous conflict with his fellow Hebrews. Their challenge contributed to his alienation from God's people and call. It left a lasting wound and internal struggle for self-image and self-worth. It was so devastating that even God's audible commission could not (initially) break its power over Moses.

Perhaps you have followed that path. Wilderness isolation has a way of assimilating identity with injury. Soon, it is difficult to know who you are apart from the brokenness you have endured. You define yourself by how much you produce, how much you are liked, or how much you accomplish. And it is never enough.

The apostle Paul provides a better approach. Paul offered a pointed response when church members challenged his qualifications and authority. "It is a very small thing that I should be judged by you or by any human court. I do not even judge myself," Paul said. "I am not aware of anything

---

13. How many times has God called a restored servant and only heard excuses in response? Don't let that be your testimony. You never need say "I am not" once God has declared "I Am!"

against myself, but I am not thereby acquitted. It is the Lord who judges me" (1 Cor 4:3–4).

That was Paul's polite way of saying, "I have a very low opinion of your opinion of me, and I have an even lower opinion of *my* opinion of me." Paul did not value what others said about him and did not listen to self-condemnation. Don't misunderstand; Paul knew he had issues—he considered himself the chief of sinners (1 Tim 1:15; cf. Phil 3:12–14). Yet, neither their judgments nor his own mattered. Why? Because the Lord had judged Paul, and the Lord's was the only opinion that mattered.

What do you think the Father sees when he looks at you? A failure? A poor excuse for a minister? A poor excuse for a spouse? A poor excuse for a parent? No, like the prodigal's father, our Father sees his beloved child when he looks at you. You are more sinful and flawed than you dared believe, yet you are more accepted and loved than you ever dared hope.[14]

Granted, you are not everything God wants you to be. You have not done everything God has called you to do. You do not have the victory in all your battles. You have not made all the wrongs right. You have not solved all the problems or fixed all the issues. But God is not done with you yet! He began the good work, so trust him to finish it (Phil 1:6). Lay aside everything that holds you back, look to Jesus, and follow his example when opposition arises (Heb 12:1–3). Forget those things behind, reach forward to those ahead, and press for the prize (Phil 3:13–14).

This approach enabled Paul to boldly declare that "by the grace of God I am what I am, and His grace toward me did not prove vain" (1 Cor 15:10a). Get that in your spirit: I am who *I Am* says I am. God's opinion is the only one that matters, and what he says will not be in vain.

Indeed, the restored minister can neither know nor fulfill God's heart for others until he knows God's heart for himself. Therefore, self-knowledge is a critical step toward freedom in Christ as it enables one to recover the affective life possibly abandoned to survive in childhood.[15] However, self-knowledge may lie buried beneath self-defense and self-deception. Exposing the true self requires a vulnerability that starkly contrasts the protective (though illicit) behaviors learned in response to the individual's malformation.[16]

Many would prefer to reside in Egypt's perceived safety than risk the wilderness path leading to God's promise. Yet this promise awaits, and the

---

14. Keller, *Meaning of Marriage*, 44.
15. Hands and Fehr, *Spiritual Wholeness for Clergy*, loc. 526.
16. See "Excursus 4: Restoration Resources" for examples of self-reflection questions and exercises.

passage requires one to reveal the most broken and hidden parts so that God may heal that brokenness. Equally valid is that such vulnerability appears dangerous, even terrifying, to the wounded soul. Honest openness places one's long-hidden hurts at the mercy of spiritual mentors who may inflict further harm through ignorance or intent. Even amid compassionate care, to fully avail oneself is to reveal painful histories and characters that the individual has long hidden. These revelations can evoke fear of isolation and abandonment—an assumption that others, including God, will not (cannot) accept the individual once the truth about the individual is known.[17]

Having revealed the origin of negative thoughts and behaviors, the fallen minister must "own" what he is . . . and what he is not. Success requires the restoration team's compassionate yet uncompromising guidance. As psychotherapist Carl Jung rightly asserts, the "acceptance of oneself is the essence of the whole moral problem and the epitome of a whole outlook on life."[18] The fallen minister may willingly extend patience, forgiveness, and love to "enemies" who have brought harm yet fail to see that his greatest enemy resides within. Once revealed, the human condition more easily condemns and rages against the broken self rather than extends grace. What God declares "beloved," the self declares "unloved." For this reason, the individual ignores, represses, or hides the wounded self behind masks of self-sufficiency and success.

The tendency is not unlike Scrooge's encounters with two horrid children, Ignorance and Want, hidden beneath the robe of the Ghost of Christmas Present.[19] Rather than comfort the repulsed and frightened miser, the ghost warns Scrooge to beware of both children and especially Ignorance, upon whose brow is written the word "doom." We would do well to heed that warning.

Like the ravenous children lurking beneath the spirit's robe, the uncomfortable truths revealed amid self-evaluation can be startling. Ignorance is oblivious to the moral standard that self-interest suffocates and the moral injury that results. Want embodies the relentless hunger born from deprivation and trauma. And Scrooge did not want to look upon either.

Earlier that day, the wicked old screw was shrouded in the fog of indifference as he traversed London's crowded streets. Not much had changed

---

17. Notable is Ted Haggard's statement that "the reason I kept my personal struggle a secret is because I feared that my friends would reject me, and abandon me, and kick me out, and that the church would exile me and excommunicate me. And that happened and more" (Alexander, "Telling the Truth About Sex," 122).

18. Jung, *Modern Man in Search of a Soul*, 235.

19. Dickens, *Christmas Carol*, 56.

at this point. Scrooge wished to hide Ignorance and Want under the cloak—out of sight and out of mind. Similarly, there is a desire to hide one's flaws and failings. We don't want to see them and certainly don't want others to see them, so we try to lock them away deep down inside.

This approach is pointless. Our inner dungeons have a key, which is usually in the possession of others. They need only say or do something to open the door and let those undesirable characters run amuck. This approach is also perilous, stifling genuine repentance, negating accountability, and fostering environments where unhealthy character can persist.

Why do we make such an effort? Because many wrongly equate holiness with the ability to hide one's undesirable character and project the desirable (yet fabricated) image.[20] Lock away the undesirables so they can never violate your conscience or Christian standing! In truth, those characters are just as much a part of you as anything else. The key is not to hide them but to deliver them.

The haunting warning of the Ghost of Christmas Present exemplifies the need to uncover these painful truths. In the ministerial context, this means actively addressing and working through Ignorance and Want. Don't be like Scrooge and allow the chain of indifference to grow link by link and yard by yard. Engage in truth-telling, repentance, (re)formation, and sometimes, tough love and discipline. Confront Ignorance and Want to prevent doom.

Ignorance and Want were not to blame for their condition. Powerful forces beyond their control hurt them, and the indifference of Scrooge and others condemned them to remain in that pitiful state. But grace and love were able to overcome and heal the harm done. Scrooge's transformative journey concludes with a man who became "as good a friend, as good a master, and as good a man as the good old city knew."[21] By committing his resources and, more importantly, his attention through compassion for and benevolence toward the poor, he brought the children out of the hiding he once demanded and helped them live healthy and happy lives.

God desires to do the same for you, but you must sacrifice the fabricated "good image" and face the Ignorance and Want you long kept hidden. Only when fully known can one be fully loved and fully love God, self, and others.[22] Unmasking centers on removing the "persona," a façade often

---

20. Notable is Paul's renunciation of outward forms people use to control sin: "do not handle, do not taste, do not touch" (Col. 2:20–23).

21. Dickens, *Christmas Carol*, 78.

22. Bonhoeffer, *Ethics*, 21; Grenz and Bell, *Betrayal of Trust*, 133; McMinn, *Psychology, Theology, and Spirituality in Christian Counseling*, 239; Scazzero, *Emotionally Healthy Spirituality*, 48; Thompson, *Soul of Shame*, 126.

constructed of authentic spiritual experiences and disciplines but designed to cover real feelings and failures that seemingly inhibit relationships with others.[23]

For example, can you "read a room" and act accordingly to gain acceptance or please the group? That is a mask. Can you muster enthusiasm to hide your anger, frustration, or depression? That is a mask. Through feigned affirmation and a charming smile, are you able to encourage people to accept and commit to your ideas? That is a mask. Are there people for whom you care little but think of themselves as your friends or cherished church members? That's because you wear a mask.

Removing the masks exposes truths the individual has worked long and hard to keep hidden. Therefore, unmasking surrender does not come easy. Even more challenging is that some masks are so convincing that even the person behind the persona begins to believe the mask is his true identity. The part of me that does those bad things and has those bad thoughts is the imposter. "That's not who I really am!" they exclaim. In truth, that is exactly who you are. One's thoughts and actions provide a far more accurate depiction of one's true self than the fabricated yet convincing personas we portray. Out of the heart comes "evil thoughts . . . acts of adultery, other immoral sexual acts" and the like (Matt 15:19; cf. Prov 23:7).[24]

The individual who loves the created persona has little, if any, love for the authentic self.[25] Yet that authentic self yearns to be free, known, and healed. Release yourself from versions of you that you created to survive.

Again, this is easier said than done. Fallen ministers often desire and even demand to quit at the point of unmasking. Such attitudes should not be mistaken for defiance. Identifying and acknowledging one's condition adds a seemingly unbearable weight of guilt and shame upon self-worth shattered by sexual moral failure. Resignation from ministry often seems a quick and easy solution. However, this will perpetuate rather than ease his pain. The restoration team must emphasize that God offers invitation rather than condemnation (Rom 8). The endeavor is humbling but not meant to be humiliating, as it replaces depravity with dignity and divinity.

It is a significant understatement to say the subsequent removal of one's mask will be an emotional experience. Realigning long-distorted or

---

23. Willimon, *Pastor*, 400. Cf. Heb 12:1–2.

24. "I'm only human" is another common assertion. However, this statement is "an abuse of the word human [and] a degradation of the ministerial vocation" (Willimon, *Pastor*, 377). Sin is inherent to our fallen condition, not the original human condition. Jesus is the true human; thus the goal of Christian formation is to become truly human.

25. Bradshaw, *Healing the Shame That Binds You*, 34; DeGroat, *When Narcissism Comes to Church*, loc. 449.

denied emotions often results in the expressive and painful release of pent-up feelings. The restoration team should not stifle these natural expressions. Because (de)formation frequently causes the violator to view his feelings as wrong, bad, or even destructive, (re)formation of the *imago Dei* must view emotions as healthy and unique attributes that define one's humanity. Indeed, in "neglecting our intense emotions, we are false to ourselves and lose a wonderful opportunity to know God. We forget that change comes through brutal honesty and vulnerability before God."[26] Similarly, the restoration team should not judge the feelings expressed as right or wrong but instead, allow a safe space for expression and guidance so that the broken soul may know God's restorative truth.[27] Cognitive restructuring enables individuals to identify false beliefs, adopt logical and biblical truths, and progressively reinforce positive changes.

Ultimately, the individual fully unmasks when he faces and renounces shame. This victory enables biblical forgiveness of self and those who inflicted emotional harm. This forgiveness neither accepts hurtful behavior nor asserts that painful feelings no longer exist. Instead, forgiveness is not allowing the hurt and pain to control or dominate one's life. Biblical forgiveness agrees "to live with the consequences of another person's sin."[28]

Beyond surrendering one's right to retribution, forgiveness rediscovers the humanity of those who caused hurt and appropriately revises one's thoughts and feelings.[29] Such forgiveness marks a turning point in holistic healing and (re)formation, but it doesn't turn on a dime. Indeed, it often takes six to nine months "before feelings of forgiveness catch up to the decision."[30]

Removing the false self enables forgiveness and honesty, which are necessary to restore a right relationship with God, others, and self. Relational connectivity is critical as only the faithful Christian community can form (and re-form) faithful Christians.[31] This hallmark may prove an excit-

26. Allender and Longman, *Cry of the Soul*, 24–25.

27. For example, misdirected pain or anger is often met with the statement "you should not feel that way." Well-meaning mentors and counselors have no right to tell a victim how he should feel. Instead, reveal how God feels and lead the individual to explore whether his feelings rightly align. In addition, mentors and counselors should not say "I know how you feel." The individual's emotions and experiences are unique and should be honored as such. While experiential connection is of great worth, this is better achieved by modifying the statement to "I know how I felt when I experienced a similar situation."

28. Anderson, *Steps to Freedom in Christ*, 22.

29. Ripley and Worthington, *Couple Therapy*, 287; Smedes, *Art of Forgiveness*, 5–6.

30. Hetzendorfer, *Pastoral Counseling Handbook*, 52.

31. Johns and White, "Ethics of Being, 295–96. It is also worth noting that Jesus

ing and rewarding time for the violator as he basks in the light of godly and communal love after years of struggling in darkness and emotional isolation. He may demonstrate significant progress and be eager to return to ministerial function. The restoration team must resist this premature return and allow patience to have its perfect result (Jas 1:4).

Removing the false self will reveal the *authentic* self but not the *true* self. Put another way, removing the façade reveals who the violator is but not who he is called to be. Therefore, the violator who rightly rejects the false self and accepts his authentic self must now discover his true self in Christ (Eph 4:22–24). This true self "will not come as long as you are looking for it. It will come when you are looking for Him."[32]

Where do we find him? How far is he? The distance from your knee to the floor. While chapter 11 addresses the disciplines inherent to this search, kneeling is the first step. Such understanding is reminiscent of Carl Jung's reflection on the lack of relational engagement with God. Why do we not experience God? Why do we not hear from God? The founder of analytic psychology recounted a rabbi's profound wisdom: "Nowadays, there is no longer anybody who can bow low enough."[33] Therefore, humble yourself under God's mighty hand so he may exalt you at the proper time (1 Pet 5:6). Only from a place of humility can one develop and demonstrate power through weakness.

RESTORE POWER THROUGH WEAKNESS

> "The real man is at liberty to be his Creator's creature. To be conformed with the Incarnate is to have the right to be the man one really is. Now there is no more pretense, no more hypocrisy or self-violence, no more compulsion to be something other, better and more ideal than what one is. God loves the real man. God became a real man."
>
> — DIETRICH BONHOEFFER

Those living on the coast know that a powerful storm will rob you of power. Power loss leaves its victims with few options. You can go without power, but that will be an uncomfortable decision that will likely cause further

---

derived his identity from his relationship with the Father (see Matt 11:19; Mark 2:16, 6:3; Luke 11:53–54; John 1:46; 7:4–5; 8:41; 8:48).

32. Lewis, *Mere Christianity*, 226.
33. Jung, *Man and His Symbols*, 91.

problems as damage to the structure goes unaddressed. You can depart for another location with power, but that is a temporary fix. A portable generator is a third option. You need a good fuel source as the generator needs constant refilling. Even at capacity, major appliances are not an option. That means you will lack the comfort of air-conditioning and cannot cook, wash clothes, and the like. There is power, but just enough to get by.

A final option is to invest in a home generator system that kicks on the moment you lose electricity and provides all the power needed to function at normal capacity. You cannot install this generator the day after the storm ravages your home. These generators require the expenditure of time, finances, and effort. You must pull permits, run natural gas lines, build foundations to support the generator, and connect the machine to your electrical system. If done right, the home generator provides a means of empowerment to help you endure the storm and function until the regular power sources are repaired and restored.

Where do we tap into such power when the spiritual storms rage? Not where one might expect.

To illustrate, let's consider a first-century church in south-central Greece. Indeed, the church in Corinth bears remarkable similarities to the contemporary church. Its people were sinking into an abyss of individualism and self-glorification. The surge in religious interest was superficial and naïve.[34] People wanted contact with the supernatural; amulets, curse tablets, astrology, and miracles filled the atmosphere of enchantment as the people became engulfed in superstition. Salvation centered on matters of health, wealth, protection, and sustenance. Religious consumerism centered on events—banquets, parades, festivals, dances, and dramas. Corinth also embraced preachers whose speeches centered on powerful deliveries geared to public tastes and to win applause, as "truth and knowledge were sacrificed on the altar of popular acclaim."[35]

The church in Corinth also struggled with false apostles and sexual immorality from the onset.[36] The believers would repent but soon rescind

---

34. Savage, *Power Through Weakness*, 25–27.

35. Savage, *Power Through Weakness*, 30.

36. Paul founded the church on his first visit in AD 50–52 (Acts 18:1–17). The letter that now serves as 1 Corinthians was written in late 56 or early 57. Timothy came to Corinth soon after (Acts 19:21–22; 1 Cor 4:17–19; 16:10–11) and found the situation had deteriorated from bad to worse. Timothy went to Ephesus to report the situation to Paul, who voyaged immediately by sea on what has become known as the "painful visit," one marked by humiliation (2 Cor 2:1; 11:1–21). Paul later addressed the Corinthian errors by way of a "severe letter" delivered by Titus. This led the Corinthians to repent, and Titus brought the good report when he returned to Paul at Macedonia (2 Cor 7:2–16). This is the catalyst of Paul's "letter of thanksgiving," which now stands

into sinful behavior. The problems piled up. Paul noted eight consequences of division caused by the false apostles: quarreling, jealousy, anger, selfishness, slander, gossip, conceit, and disorder (2 Cor 12:20). Paul then turned his attention to sexual immorality. He had eviscerated the Gnosticism that plagued the Corinthian church, but that heresy's openness to sexual immorality remained. Such is evident as Paul lists a triad of sins for which the people are guilty and unrepentant: ἀκαθαρία, or sexual impurity (cf. Rom 1:24; 6:19); πορνεία, or fornication (cf. 1 Cor 5:1; 6:13, 18; 7:2; and ἀσέλγεια, or licentiousness, (cf. Rom 13:13).[37]

Notably, the false leaders publicly challenged the messenger rather than his message (2 Cor 11:4, 12–15; 12:3, 20). Though for different reasons, the restored minister is likely to hear similar objections. What right do you have? What authority could you possibly carry? You failed big time.

In such cases, the restored minister would do well to follow Paul's example. The apostle was considered weak and lacking power. Paul acknowledged the charge with enthusiasm.

The Corinthians said Paul's previous visit lacked spiritual boldness and power. The apostle had threatened to address wrongdoers "with a whip" (1 Cor 4:21) but was perceived as timid and ineffective when he faced the Corinthians (2 Cor 10:1–10). The would-be leaders quickly assailed Paul and boasted of their worth (2 Cor 10:7b–12, 11, 12:21b–23). Questions regarding Paul's credentials and conduct soon became demands for proof that Christ spoke through Paul. They demanded a display of power—no doubt something on the magnitude of what happened to Elymas, who was struck blind for trying to thwart Paul (Acts 13:11), or the salvation of the Macedonian jailer after empowered praise opened the prison doors (Acts 16:25–40).

To demand godly power as proof of ministerial authority is a blatant error. Any effort to evaluate, assess the claims, or test the credentials of Christ and his designated ministers in this way is to reduce Christ to a powerful genie who performs spectacular tricks on command. "As long as people are assessing him, they are in the superior position, the position of judge. As long as they are checking out his credentials, they are forgetting that God is the one who will weigh them."[38]

Furthermore, the demand for proof reveals the self-serving nature of the Corinthians' faith, a woeful lack of spiritual discernment, and utter

---

as 2 Cor 1–9.

37. Corinth was not alone in succumbing to this struggle. The same trio of sins is addressed in Gal 5:19; the first two are named in Eph 5:3 and Col 3:5; the last-named is addressed in Eph 4:19 and 1 Pet 4:3.

38. Savage, *Power through Weakness*, 20.

confusion about apostolic sufficiency and authority. As such, they would receive proof that Christ's power was working through Paul, but this would not come in the way they expected.

Paul's response included a little boasting, which may seem out of character. To boast in one's anointing or ministry is tantamount to a theological error in Paul's perspective, as a minister ought to boast only in the Lord and what the Lord had done. Yet the apostle knew that Corinthian culture considered boasting a prized, even honorable activity. Indeed, his opponents had boasted to glorify themselves and assert supremacy over others (2 Cor 11:18). Therefore, the apostle joined the boasting battle but boasted of his weakness, a topic that would have elicited extreme contempt among his proud readers (2 Cor 11:30).

Paul noted that he could match their proclaimed powers, experiences, and labors, but they could not match his record of suffering and persecution on behalf of Christ. Though he pointed to signs, wonders, and miracles as "signs of an apostle" wrought among the Corinthians (2 Cor 12:12), Paul placed greater worth on times of perceived weakness—times in which he was imprisoned, flogged, lashed, stoned, shipwrecked, imperiled, hungry, thirsty, and stripped naked (2 Cor 11:23–29).

Paul's famous "theology of suffering" is the hallmark of 2 Cor 10–13. The pericope centers on power through weakness. Just as holiness is the proof of justification, weakness is the proof of godly power and the mark of genuine ministry (2 Cor 13:3). Paul identifies himself as a testimony to this. If he had achieved anything, it was only because of God's power working through a weak but consecrated vessel (cf. 2 Tim 2:20–21). Therefore, Paul did not deny, justify, or excuse his weakness but instead embraced it as the conduit through which the power of God worked. In three pericopes where Paul reflected on power, he addressed the hardships that beset his ministry.[39] Such hardship and weakness enabled the revealing of Christ's power through miracles, Paul's preaching, and the conversion of sinners who were washed, sanctified, and justified.[40]

That is not to say that Paul lacked boldness or confidence in his calling. The apostle later responded in force to the wayward believers who demanded proof of his power and calling. Patience and love had restrained a harsh response. However, such patience cannot come at the expense of obedience to Christ. Thus, Paul warned that his pending third visit would not

---

39. 2 Cor 4:7–5:10; 6:3–10; 11:16–12:10.

40. Gräbe, *Power of God in Paul's Letters*, 154. For revelation through miracles, see 2 Cor 12:12; Rom 15:19; Gal 3:5. For revelation through Paul's preaching, see 1 Cor 2:4. For revelation through the conversion of sinners, see 1 Cor 6:11.

spare any of those causing division or committing sexual immorality.⁴¹ Paul also included "any of the others" (literally, "all the rest"), which refers to any he might find guilty of sin upon arrival. This "hit list" includes those who had shown leniency toward or ignored these sinful behaviors. "To Paul's mind there are no 'innocent bystanders' in what has happened at Corinth."⁴²

Paul's purpose was not to demonstrate godly power but rather the source of that power. The true power of ministry comes by following Christ's example. Continuing participation in Jesus' death results in continuing participation in Jesus' power. Such understanding is of great significance because many in the contemporary church, like the Corinthians, desire the power of God to overcome weaknesses. Paul let the power of God work through his weakness. He did this by dying to the world's system and being crucified with Christ.

The understanding that power is made perfect in weakness "constitutes the Magna Carta of the Christian experience."⁴³ That is not to say that God's power is revealed *as* weakness, but rather *amid* weakness and through the broken existence of our earthen vessels (2 Cor 4:7–12). The more a believer surrenders his ego and facades, the more room is available for God's power to manifest.

Paul acknowledged that the Corinthians sought δοκιμή (proof). The apostle has "conceded to the church the right to examine his work. In fact, he welcomed this opportunity. But the nub of the debate is that the criteria chosen by the Corinthians to evaluate his work are wrong."⁴⁴ The word δοκιμή carries the idea of passing the test. Paul's use of the word reveals that he was not the one tested. They were. The proof was not in miracles but in ministry. If Christ was among them through Paul's ministry, then Paul carried Christ's authority and power—and they must repent.

---

41. 2 Cor 13:2. Paul's warning was extended to προαμαρτάνειν, or all who have persisted in their sin (2 Cor 13:2). Paul mourned over these individuals (2 Cor 12:21). However, he also noted the nature of their sin by using a perfect active participle of προαμαρτάνειν, which indicated persistence in sin, and the aorist participle from μετανοεῖν with ἔπραξαν, which indicated that some continued to sin despite an earlier visit or letter by Paul. They had the opportunity to change (the aorist), but did not take advantage of it (the perfect) (Martin, *WBC: 2 Corinthians*, 467). In light of such unwillingness, Paul was unwilling to spare anyone. Martin asserts that φείδεσθαι is a military term that speaks to sparing an enemy in battle though the opportunity to take the life is present (Martin, *WBC: 2 Corinthians*, 472). Such would not be the case in Corinth. Though Paul would not spare those who deserve punishment, the perfect προημαρτηκόσιν suggests persistence in sin, which indicates Paul would not punish those who repent.

42. Garland, *New American Commentary*, 542.

43. Gräbe, *Power of God*, 262.

44. Martin, *WBC: 2 Corinthians*, 473. Cf. 2 Cor 10:12; 11:12, 17; 12:11–18.

So, power and weakness, which seem contradictory, are symbiotic. The Corinthians wanted signs, wonders, and miracles (2 Cor 12:12), but Paul pointed to submission and servanthood. It is meaningful ministry rather than a demonstrable form that validates; "it is not a performance to amaze people, but a word to address them, and so (Paul is sure) to have an effect in their lives."[45] While most try to overcome their weaknesses, God is satisfied using weakness for his purposes. "God's means of working, rightly understood, is not making people stronger, but weaker and weaker, until the divine power alone is seen in them."[46] As such, weakness is not the mark of an inferior or false apostle but rather the essence of a true believer—and the transformed lives that result are the proper validation of ministerial authority.

Paul committed to follow the example of the Lord, who set aside his rights and prerogatives as God, was not willing to punish those who opposed him, and humbled himself to the point of death on the cross (Phil 2:1–11). For Paul, this is power at its purest. By sharing in Christ's weakness, one enters the paradox of Jesus Christ: comfort from suffering, strength from weakness, wisdom from foolishness, and life from death.

The Corinthians demanded proof of Paul's calling and authority, but the question was not whether Christ was speaking in Paul but whether Christ was living in them. The answer required self-examination, conviction of the Holy Spirit, repentance, and prayerful support.

The minister who has done likewise and developed power through weakness will have the strength to rebuild the temple walls.

---

45. Bultmann, *Theology of the New Testament*, 244.
46. Hawthorne et al., *Dictionary of Paul*, 967.

11

Rebuild the Walls

"You must learn, you must let God teach you, that the only way to get rid of your past is to make a future out of it. God will waste nothing."

— Phillips Brooks

As noted in chapter 7, Nehemiah inspected Jerusalem's walls to assess specific damage and determine needed repairs (Neh 1:1–4:11). He assembled a capable team that worked "with all their hearts" to achieve measurable goals amid many challenges. Ultimately, the team built a strong, new wall atop the existing foundation while repelling repeated and familiar attacks (Neh 4:15–23).

Unlike Zerubbabel's foundation, the rebuilt city walls included reclaimed stones and materials. Ministerial restoration programs, by necessity, also make use of repurposed material. Some of that material is beneficial. Some of it is not. Some may be functional only if they serve a new purpose. Therefore, a thorough inspection is essential to ensure that the chosen materials make the grade.

When it comes to home restoration, reclaimed and recycled materials are not synonymous. Reclaimed materials do not require significant reprocessing. The wood maintains its original form even when used for a different purpose. This approach provides historical authenticity that new material may replicate but cannot duplicate. However, the salvaged material can bear damage and unseen weakness and has the potential for contaminants.

Recycled wood is broken down, processed, and reconstructed into a usable product. The recycling process requires energy and expense but is a cost-saver compared to new material. Functionality and durability can vary; some recycled materials have sufficient strength, while others lack original integrity. Recycled material is not recommended for load-bearing beams and walls, as it cannot bear the weight.

When it comes to temple restorations, we can learn much from King Solomon. His temple was breathtaking to behold. Two twenty-seven-foot brass pillars flanked the entrance. The previous chapter addressed the importance of a solid foundation. These pillars were important, as well. They opened the way to God's presence; they were stable, supportive, and uplifting. These pillars did not waver. They were strong enough to bear the burden because they had integrity.[1]

Solomon named his pillars Jachin, which means "God has established," and Boaz, which means "strength within." These same pillars are invaluable in your temple restoration. Moral failure erodes what "God has established," while shame and a fabricated identity drain the "strength within." If the enemy can muster a storm strong enough to topple one or both of these support structures, he will significantly diminish your ability to access and share God.

The subsections on reforming the mind and reinforcing spiritual disciplines will help construct those strong pillars. Before putting them into place, it is necessary to clear the debris and determine the suitability of reclaimed and recycled components that will complete the structure. Put more directly, some of the minister's character is worth keeping, and some is rubbish that should be removed.

REMOVE THE RUBBISH

"No man is free who cannot control himself."

— Pythagoras

Nehemiah's team rebuilt Jerusalem's walls with difficulty. Enemy attacks were relentless, and the area was so littered with rubbish that the workers could hardly make progress (Neh 4:10). Rubbish terminates restoration. Allow the rubbish to remain, and workers will soon grow tired and discouraged—and discouraged people are defeated people.[2]

Ministerial restoration must remove rubbish, as well. Specifically, restoration must dump the debris deposited by the flesh, world, and devil.

---

1. Much like James, Peter, and John, whom the apostle Paul called the "pillars" of the early church (Gal 2:9).

2. After all, it was a handful of doubters who discouraged the people of God, which kept the Israelites from entering the promised land (Num 13:25–14:4, 32:7–13).

Removing this residual refuse requires partnership with the Holy Spirit and the restoration team. This progressive sanctification provides a cleansing from and empowered avoidance of whatever displeases God, whether internal or external to the believer.

Despite his moral collapse, the minister retains some good material that could aid in his temple restoration. Restoration also uses the opportunity to strengthen areas that proved weak and unable to withstand. However, any impure materials that weaken the structure must be identified and removed. Such understanding nods to the sinful nature expressed in Augustinian thought and the loss of God's likeness due to humankind's fall, as described in Eastern thought.

Though Augustine's insight into sin's origin and function is invaluable, the resulting doctrine of original sin proves deficient for holistic restoration. Augustine's influence generally affects Western traditions by viewing human creation as complete and perfect. The fall brings inherent guilt, depravity, and powerlessness apart from God's grace. Conversely, Eastern theology views humanity as innocent and dynamic yet incomplete at creation. Participation in divine life and grace (deification) enables a progressive realization of *imago Dei*. However, the fall brings death, corruption, and loss of the Spirit's immediate presence. Deprivation of this essential relationship debilitates the individual and leads to moral depravity.[3]

Reformed and Wesleyan ontologies reflect these differences well. The Augustinian Reformed view centers on two inner and contending natures, the "old nature" and the "new nature." The Spirit's sanctifying work deals with the pollution of sin and acts as a counterbalance against sinful nature. Renewal is a change of direction rather than a change in substance.

The Wesleyan view, presupposed here, draws from Eastern theology to argue that Jesus' human nature replaces the sinful nature that dies with Christ in salvation.[4] Contention within the affections remains because humans are "bound by their own delight to created realities."[5] The Spirit's sanctifying work reorders one's desires—the tendencies and behaviors

---

3. Maddox, *Responsible Grace*, 65–66, 74, 81.

4. The argument that Christ had two natures, and believers are to be Christlike, is acknowledged. However, the Spirit's activity in Jesus' incarnation ensured he had a human nature (natural will) but not a sinful nature (gnomic will). That Christ had two wills, human and divine, was established by Maximus the Confessor and Pope Martin I at the Rome Synod of 649. See also John 3:3–5; Rom 6–8; 2 Cor 5:16–17; Gal 2:20, 6:14–15; 1 Pet 2:24; 2 Pet 1:4.

5. Coulter, "Introduction," 7. This is the heart of the existentialist philosopher's contention that the human's normal state centers on the desire to build its identity around something other than God (Kierkegaard, *Sickness Unto Death*).

learned while a sinful nature leads the individual. Therefore, sin is always a personal choice that resides in the passions and is never an act of nature.

Christian thought understands the detriment of and responsibility for the passions from its onset. Clement of Alexandria defines passion as an excessive impulse (movement of the mind) contrary to nature and disobedient to reason. While impulses arise from fundamental appetites and can become virtuous or vitious, Gregory of Nyssa presents the passions as unfavorable.[6] Like much of antiquity, Gregory's view understood passions as deriving from the fundamental human impulses of desire (yearning to possess what we do not have) and fear (aversion to what we do not want).[7]

Aquinas would categorize passions as "intellect influenced by appetite."[8] The irrational soul's repeated indulgence and disregard of reason prove deformative to the will, resulting in a dysfunctional character. Conversely, affections are "appetites influenced by intellect." The Spirit's uncreated grace elevates human will.[9] The individual's virtuous and voluntary response to prevenience is a reasonable action of the rational soul.[10] Rightly directed desire provides the basis for participation in divine love, which sanctifies the soul.[11]

Holistic sanctification is not an infusion of virtue, contrary to Augustine, but results from deepening participation in divine life and power that transforms the sinful nature and enables the "recovery of the holiness of life that God intended for us."[12] As Anthony Hoekema explains, "In sanctifying us, God does not equip us with powers or capacities that are totally different from those we had before; rather, He enables us to use the gifts He gave us in the right way instead of in sinful ways. Sanctification empowers us to think, will, and love in a way that glorifies God, namely, to think God's thoughts after Him and to do what is in harmony with His will."[13] Thus, sanctification

---

6. Coulter, "Introduction," 11. The author quotes from Gregory of Nyssa, *De anima et resurrectione* (PG 46.57B-68A).

7. Wilken, "Blessed Passion of Love," 35.

8. Aquinas, *Summa Theologiae*, I-II, 13, 5.

9. Western theology generally assumes grace is divinely created righteousness or obedience bestowed upon humanity in response to sin. Eastern and Wesleyan theology assumes grace is uncreated; it is not given to humanity but "is the accompanying effect of the Divine energies present in our life through the Holy Spirit" (Maddox, *Responsible Grace*, 86).

10. While embracing reason, Wesley does not fully align with Aquinas and rejects the intellectualist tradition that views reason as subordinating and controlling emotion in human actions (e.g., Wesley, "Sermon: The End of Christ's Coming," 376).

11. Clapper, *Renewal of the Heart*, loc. 712; Coulter, "Introduction," 19.

12. Maddox, *Responsible Grace*, 48–55.

13. Hoekema, "Reformed Perspective," 62.

within holistic (re)formation is a synergistic endeavor that sees the restored minister serve out of submission rather than strength.

What does this mean for the fallen minister sifting through the debris of a destroyed temple? Being mindful of preferences and presuppositions (not to mention the human tendency to justify sinful behaviors), the minister must trust the Holy Spirit and the Spirit-filled restoration team to discern carefully which materials to keep and which to discard.[14] Some stones are building blocks, and others are stumbling blocks. Three dominate the latter category and are easy to spot but difficult to remove. They are fantasy, masturbation, and pornography.[15]

Stopping fantasies is arguably the most difficult of the three, as fantasies "don't develop randomly or without reason" but have a purpose—and the behavior is near impossible to stop until that purpose is understood.[16] With the help of a mental health professional, the minister should explore rather than ignore fantasies to understand emotional needs better and disengage the triggers and rituals that lead to sexual activity.[17] Beyond identifying the negative actions and attitudes, it is essential to recognize how the individual has internalized the trauma. Such knowledge will help the team develop healthy choices to meet these needs. Still, keeping fantasies in check is a difficult task that requires a disciplined thought life.[18] The minister also must monitor social interactions and media intake to limit the visual and verbal stimulation common to a sex-saturated society.[19]

Limitations of sexual activity are also in order. In this regard, treating sexual misconduct is more akin to food addiction than alcohol or drug addiction. Christopher West's exploration of three "diets" to fulfill universal longing provides worthy insight.[20] The first diet is starvation, in which the

---

14. *Skandalon* is the Greek word for "stumbling block." It appears fifteen times, and the corresponding verb appears thirty times. Watch out for stumbling stones, and do not become one (see Matt 18:6–9; Luke 17:1–2; Rom 14:13).

15. Cf. Heb 12:1.

16. Laaser, *Healing the Wounds*, 156–57. The author further explains that fantasies distract from painful emotions, meet otherwise unmet desires and needs, and recast experiences of past abuse. Regarding the latter, fantasies can recast past abuse by providing a different outcome or allowing the individual to be the initiator rather than the victim.

17. For example, HALT is an acronym used to identify four common triggers. Addictive behaviors often emerge when one is hungry, angry, lonely, or tired. Notably, Satan's primary temptations of Jesus happened in the wilderness when Jesus was hungry, lonely, and tired.

18. Phil 2:1–8, 4:8; 2 Cor 10:3–5.

19. Cf. Job 31:1; Ps 101:3; Matt 5:29.

20. West, *Fill These Hearts*.

individual exalts the soul to deny the body.[21] The second is fast food, in which the individual exalts the body and denies the soul.[22] The banquet represents the third and proper diet. It takes more time to prepare but provides a balanced meal well worth the wait.

Still, a temporary fast of sexual activity is necessary. Deliverance begins with a ninety-day (minimum) abstinence from all sexual activity, including masturbation and sex with a spouse.[23] Sex is an easy escape for those unable or unwilling to deal with shame, hurt, and loneliness. Orgasm releases dopamine, which effectively shuts down one's emotional center, the amygdala. For many, sexual activity seemingly replaces pain with pleasure. To overcome this self-destructive strategy, the violator, aided by a Christian mental health professional and spiritual mentors, must face and overcome the debilitating dependence. This detoxification reduces neurochemical tolerance levels, loosens dopamine dependence, and positions the individual to train his brain to find neurological relief through healthy means, as discussed in the following subsection.

And yet, much rubbish remains. Littering the broken-down temple are piles of lies and excuses, virtue signaling and victim mentalities, preoccupation with plaudits and popularity, and the demand to maintain one's rights and reputation. The fallen minister may have enough masks to form a mountain.

Removal will prove difficult, as rubbish can settle into the structure. Raze a pile of rubbish, and you may cause the collapse of a wall that had come to lean on that rubbish for support. Like Jesus' warning that indiscriminate removal of tares will uproot good wheat (Matt 13:24–30), the workers must carefully separate the two and deal accordingly. The trouble is that fallen ministers, like most Christians, prefer to keep their poisonous parts buried. Ministers encourage vulnerability in others but don't care to be vulnerable themselves. Worse, ministers "struggle with denial more than

---

21. For examples, see "Excursus 1: Review of Sexual Morality in Church History." Dietrich Bonhoeffer captures the danger of this approach in his criticism of monasticism, as its asceticism and individual achievement "transformed the humble work of discipleship into the meritorious activity of the saints. . . . The monk's attempt to flee from the world turned out to be a subtle form of love for the world" (Bonhoeffer, *Cost of Discipleship*, 47).

22. For examples, see "Contemporary Examples of Sexual Moral Failure" in chapter 1 and "Excursus 2: A Case Study of Pentecostal Pioneers." This approach provides instant gratification but lacks spiritual value just as fast food lacks nutritional value (and is a major contributor to many of the leading causes of death in the United States).

23. The latter requires mutual consent (1 Cor 7:5). The time normally devoted to sexual activity can be used to deepen emotional and spiritual life together through open conversation and participation in the spiritual disciplines.

anyone in the general population."²⁴ Yet, it is right and necessary to "remove our external props and force us to confront sinful and selfish attitudes and behaviors [which can] make us uncomfortably vulnerable before God."²⁵

It is here that the minister replaces his wishbone with a backbone. The task is not easy, and there is a genuine chance of failure. Conversely, the minister who develops the courage to be vulnerable can see and accept responsibility for his imperfections and mistakes.²⁶ If a thorough cleansing follows, a massive temple repair and renewal can result. Just ask King Josiah.

Josiah became king of Judah at the young age of eight. The eighth year of his reign saw a dedicated search for God. Within four years, Josiah had the idolatrous high places removed (2 Chr 34:3). A massive temple purification and restoration began six years later. Hilkiah, the high priest, discovered the Book of the Law during this time (2 Chr 34:8, 14). That's right, they had lost God's Word in God's Temple.

Upon hearing the sacred text, the repentant king realized that the nation's unfaithfulness would incur great wrath.²⁷ Josiah gathered the elders and headed to the temple, where he read the Law aloud and renewed the covenant before the Lord. God honored Josiah's response and withheld judgment (2 Kgs 22:14–22; 2 Chr 32:22–28). Religious renewal ensued. Josiah obliterated the pagan shrines and priests, reestablished the biblical feasts, and led the people in recommitment to God's covenant.

Like Josiah, the minister who corrects past decisions will better understand present problems and be able to formulate future solutions.²⁸ Therefore, integrate the past into the present and set your mind on what God has in store. Put another way, having removed the rubbish, it is time to (re)form your mind.

---

24. Kinnaman and Ells, *Leaders That Last*, 93, 96.

25. Boa, *Conformed to His Image*, 87.

26. Intrusive examination is non-negotiable. E.g., Lam 3:40; 1 Cor 11:28; 2 Cor 13:5; Gal 6:3–5, etc.

27. This outcome was foretold in Solomon's prayer at the temple dedication three hundred years prior (1 Kgs 8:46–53; cf. Deut 30:1–10).

28. The paradigm is powerfully evident in Moses' song after the Red Sea crossing. The first half celebrates the victory (Exod 15:1–12), while the second half anticipates future victories—specifically, the conquest of Canaan and worship at God's holy mountain (Exod 15:13–18). The apparent destruction brought a miraculous deliverance, and reflection on God's faithfulness despite their fear enabled a prophetic *telos* and progression toward the promise. For a more contemporary example, see the remarkable story encapsulated in Viktor Frankl's charge to live for meaning rather than happiness, and how the truth of such insight gave him and others the hope and will to survive the Nazi death camps (Frankl, *Man's Search for Meaning*).

SECTION FOUR: RESTORE, REBUILD, AND REINFORCE

(RE)FORM YOUR MIND

"A belief is not merely an idea the mind possesses.
It is an idea that possesses the mind."

— Robert Oxton Bolton

Have you lost your mind? If not, it's time you did.

How one thinks affects how one relates to God.[29] Thoughts influence actions, forming habits that build character. This subsection focuses on physiological techniques that "retrain the brain," thus replacing destructive perceptions and responses with healthy and godly thought patterns.

The violator took the first steps toward freedom by repenting, identifying the root cause(s) of sexual transgression, and removing the rubbish. However, wounded individuals do not easily "unlearn" illicit behaviors formed to compensate for brokenness (getting what I did not deserve) and lack (not getting what I did deserve).

God created "thinking people" who feel, but when feelings dominate, we become "feeling people" who think. Emotions rather than logic and preference rather than truth guide such individuals. Suppose emotions overpower the anterior cingulate cortex (where we choose right from wrong). In that case, good judgment becomes a passing thought (at best) as impulsive decision-making seeks to satisfy perceived needs.[30]

That is why a pastor's fall may appear sudden but is nearly always "a consequence of years of deeply rooted unhealthy and unrecognized patterns of behavior."[31] These habits form when the brain converts sequential action into a routine called "chunking." This process creates neural pathways that deepen over time and increasingly constrict the will. The habits that govern such behaviors are difficult to break and transform.[32] Simply put, the more one succumbs to temptation, the more likely one is to do so.[33]

---

29. Prov 23:7; Matt 15:18–19; Mark 7:20–23; Luke 6:45; Rom 8:5–7; Phil 3:19.

30. Jennings, *God-Shaped Brain*, 40. Habits also have neurophysiological aspects. For example, addiction to sex and pornography (as well as many substances) causes hypofrontality, a reduced functioning of the frontal cortex that is symptomatic of several neurological conditions such as attention deficit hyperactivity disorder (ADHD), bipolar disorder, and major depressive disorder.

31. Kinnaman and Ells, *Leaders That Last*, 96. See also Trull and Carter, *Ministerial Ethics*, 174.

32. These patterns and behaviors were formed by a fallen nature and informed by secular worldviews. Cf. Rom 12:2; Eph 4:17–24; Phil 2:3–8; Col 3:2.

33. As Aristotle rightly asserts, "Virtues are formed in man by his doing the actions." Will Durant's interpretation, often attributed to Aristotle, is more direct: "We

Like the "old programs" featured in *The Matrix* trilogy, your old behaviors do not easily vacate. Ingrained thought patterns are a living part of you (which is why it hurts when we are wrong or make a mistake). Therefore, deletion is not an option. Instead, you must learn to build new structures that render the old obsolete. Sledding provides a good example.

In my youth, a race to a favorite hill followed every significant snowfall. The first sledder had a difficult task, as fresh powder does not make for an exhilarating trek, but the multitude soon carved a distinct groove down the slope. Each run assured the next sledder a faster and farther ride.

However, challenges could darken the day (and put a dent in your medical record). Meager snowfall meant the sled path would soon diminish. The hard ground lurking beneath would repel the merriment by grabbing, bumping, or redirecting sleds without warning. The hill's popularity resulted in increasing wait times, and the presence of bundled tots (not to mention their vocal photo-happy moms) urged caution that we had thrown to the wind. Frigid seasons would see the adjacent cove teem with ice skaters gliding across the frozen waters. The lack of skaters served as a stark warning. Successful rides would require the sledder to employ the Fred Flintstone foot brake or turn into a hill that launched riders like a rodeo clown, lest they take an unintended polar bear plunge.

Neural paths formed by illicit behaviors work much the same way. The journey is exciting, even exhilarating, but there comes a point when the path becomes dangerous or takes you further than you want to go. That does not mean you should hang up the sled and never return. But perhaps it is best to forge a new path in some fresh snow. Granted, it isn't easy to push through the first runs, and everyone on the other path seems to be having a good time, but keep packing the powder into a viable path. You will be glad you did.

Holistic (re)formation does not try to improve the problematic paths. It does not persist in the dysfunctional tendency to bury or manage feelings and memories. Instead, holistic (re)formation cuts new paths using neuroplasticity, which uses the brain's adaptive ability to form and reorganize synaptic connections.

Some refer to this process as "rewiring" the brain. Although Paul was not a neuroscientist, the apostle called this a "renewing of the mind" (Rom 12:1–2). Though Scripture correctly translates the Greek word *metamorphoō* as "transformed" in that familiar passage, the prefix *meta-* in Greek composite verbs also carries the meaning of reversal, much like the

---

are what we repeatedly do." Similarly, Friedrich Nietzsche held that every "great man" was merely a play actor of his own ideal. There was much Nietzsche had wrong, but he got that right.

prefix *re-* in English.³⁴ It is an important distinction. Transforming alters or changes into something entirely new that had not existed (for example, progressing from egg to caterpillar to pupa to butterfly). To reform returns to a previous state. Such understanding raises the question, Does God seek to transform you into something you have never been or reform you in the image of God—the image in which God created humankind but the fall shattered?

Whether transformed or reformed, God changes the believer by renewing the mind. The individual learns to forego ingrained thought patterns and responses so that he may imitate and ultimately assimilate godly character.

Renewing the mind toward biblical thinking begins by dying to self— our fleshly desires, erroneous preferences, and preconceived notions. Despite the pain, illicit thoughts must die to establish the truth and allow the divine life to enter (John 12:24–26; 1 Pet 2:24).

Next, the individual must replace dysfunctional thoughts. The violator must "renounce then announce"—renounce the evil idea system(s) that led him away from God and declare allegiance through thought and action to the idea system embodied by Christ.³⁵ Failure to change your way of thinking will cause harmful experiences to be recycled time and again. Conversely, the (re)formed believer interrupts these destructive thoughts to focus on God's truth. This effort forms new neural pathways that develop new habits that create a new character.

Rightly aligning one's passions (unruly emotions) and affections (right and rational actions) purges the passions that drive illicit sexual desires and heal the brokenness on which those passions feed. Reordered attitudes enable reordered actions. Therefore, the restoration plan must elicit virtuous choices and behaviors. Because habits form character, and righteous habits facilitate the Spirit's formation of righteous character, the minister must imitate Christ and emulate his seasoned saints.³⁶ Indeed, a proven way to acquire virtue is to behave as if you already have it.³⁷ That does not mean

---

34. Adapted from Bacon, *Scariest Word in the Bible*, 29, which references Ladner, *Idea of Reform*, 42.

35. Willard, *Renovation of the Heart*, 98. Cf. Phil 2:1–8; 4:8; 2 Cor 10:3–5.

36. 1 Cor 11:1; Heb 6:12; 13:7; 3 John 1:11. One does not achieve imitation through rudimentary applications of "WWJD" in daily life. Rather, intentional acts that demonstrate Christlikeness are required. While some Christians contend godly behaviors exclusively result from sanctification, godly behaviors also lead to sanctification (Rom 6:19; 1 Thes 4:1–8).

37. This approach has been embraced by thinkers ranging from Aristotle to C. S. Lewis. Its success is why Thomas à Kempis's *Imitation of Christ* remains one of the

"fake it until you make it." It means we should imitate God's character until we assimilate God's character.

Virtues and vices are moral qualities one acquires, habits that lead to character development and eventually seem natural to the individual. These can be cultivated or eliminated over time. As Richard Foster notes, the scholastic maxim *actio sequitur esse* (action follows essence) "reminds us that our action is always in accord with the inward reality of our heart. This approach, of course, does not reduce good works to insignificance, but it does make them matters of secondary significance, effects rather than causes."[38]

Repeated thoughts and behaviors deepen the new paths inherent to the renewed mind. Such formation moves beyond religious formalism to see God's truth embodied and habituated "into attitudes, patterns of response, and reflexive action."[39] This adaptation and regeneration of brain cells enables the brain to adjust behaviors in response to new learning, experiences, or damage. In the early twenty-first century, researchers learned that activating specific neural networks through intentional thought results in more easily activated and permanent networks. Essentially, "neurons that fire together wire together," and the individual becomes that about which he thinks.[40]

That is why making good choices makes good choices easier to make. Have you noticed that you can reason well when your conscience is clear but cannot think straight when guilt-ridden? It's a balancing act. Reason, decision-making, and other executive control functions occur in the dorsolateral prefrontal cortex (DLPFC). The regulation of conscience and emotion resides in the orbital frontal cortex (OFC) and the ventral medial prefrontal cortex (VMPFC). Sound judgment results when these regions work together, but imbalance has detrimental effects.

---

great Christian works. Such an approach has also had its share of opponents, to include church father Augustine and the great reformers Martin Luther and John Calvin. For them, any assertion that external imitation of Christ would result in Christian life was superficial at best and Pelagian at worst.

38. Foster, "Spiritual Formation Agenda," 30; see also Roozeboom, *Neuroplasticity, Performativity, and Clergy Wellness*, 11; Sullender, *Ancient Sins*, 68.

39. Ortberg, "Can Neuroscience Help Us Disciple Anyone?," 22. Research suggests these new behavioral paths also influence the coding of new proteins within the DNA and could have an epigenetic consequence. That means the new patterns not only transform your genes, but might transform your subsequent generations.

40. Thompson, *Soul of Shame*, 47; cf. Rom 8:5–7. Similarly, neurotheology (the study of the brain as believers think and pray about God) has demonstrated the brain-altering power of practices such as prayer and praying in tongues. See Newberg and Waldman, *Why We Believe What We Believe*.

As Timothy Jennings explains, "when we respond to God's love and practice his methods, our higher brain regions grow stronger. But when we choose selfishness, our limbic systems grow stronger, guilt increases and prefrontal-cortex function is impaired."[41]

For example, depression kicks the OFC and VMPFC into overdrive. Intense feelings of inadequacy and shame result and render any reasonable argument ineffective. The brain's emotional center (amygdala) evokes a sense of fear and apprehension, while the pleasure center (nucleus accumbens) becomes unresponsive. Diminished interest, social withdrawal, and emotional paralysis are common. The individual often turns to learned behaviors for adequate stimulation and adopts that identity as more and more thoughts slide down that same sled path.

The paralytic at the pool of Bethesda provides an example (John 5:1–9). Jesus asked, "Do you want to get well?" His failure to respond to the possibility of freedom indicates he had adopted the identity of a paralytic. Worse, his physical paralysis had become an emotional paralysis, evident by the fact that the man projected blame onto others. "I have no one to put me into the pool when the water is stirred up, but while I am coming, another steps down before me." In other words, no one will help me, and someone will always steal my blessing.

Like the paralytic at the pool, healing requires movement. While medication may provide a necessary regulation of hormones and chemicals, Christian psychotherapy and counseling can change rational and emotional cognition to form new neural pathways. Simply put, they can create new ways of thinking.[42]

While the reprogramming of neural pathways requires significant effort by the individual and restoration team, this renewing of the mind is a gracious work of God's Spirit and strengthened through spiritual disciplines. The result is a blending of common grace and common sense—new ways of thinking for those trapped in destructive perceptions, behaviors, and addictions. This approach necessitates a holistic reorientation of mind, soul, and body in which the individual destroys all mental stronghold and arguments, all arrogance and proud obstacles raised against the knowledge of God, and takes every thought captive to the obedience of Christ (2 Cor 10:3–5). This reorientation is critical to one's (re)formation into the *imago Dei*, enabling the believer to imitate and ultimately assimilate Christ's character rightly.

---

41. Jennings, *God-Shaped Brain*, 84; see also 37–39.

42. For examples of exercises and approaches that can be used to promote neuroplasticity, see "Excursus 4: Restoration Resources."

To be (re)formed by renewing your mind is not a matter of control through behavior modification but sanctification through the Spirit. Allow the Spirit to redirect, then partner with him to form new neural sled paths. While fresh snow proves difficult, exercising spiritual disciplines will deepen those new paths.

REINFORCE THE SPIRITUAL DISCIPLINES

> "All of humanity's problems stem from man's inability
> to sit quietly in a room alone."
>
> — Blaise Pascal

A group of God's anointed once labored to advance God's kingdom (2 Kgs 6:1–7). While cutting down trees to build a new facility, a worker saw his axe head fly into the river. He lost his cutting edge. If an axe head starts to work loose, a good woodsman needs only to tap the little wedge at the end of the axe handle to keep the head tight. It would seem the young prophet took his axe head for granted. Perhaps he assumed the wedge was securely fixed and the axe would serve his purpose whenever needed. He neglected to check his axe head, and he lost his edge.

The scenario is familiar to every temple restoration. You've lost your edge when people are obstacles rather than opportunities. You've lost your edge when it takes considerable effort to forgive. You've lost your edge when you need a pep talk to evoke your praise. You've lost your edge when you serve out of obligation instead of dedication.

To regain your edge, you must admit you've lost it—something many refuse to do.[43] Instead, these ministers take the time to polish their handles to a pretty sheen but swing away in vain, leaving little more than bruised trees and frustrated souls.

Admit that you've lost your edge, then identify where. Notice that the young prophet points to the exact spot where he lost the axe head. At what point did you grow weary in your well-doing? Did it happen when you were constantly running and stretched yourself thin? Did it happen when the response to your willingness was expectation rather than appreciation? Was it because you were always there to help anyone in need but felt no one was there for you? Did you grow weary of holding your tongue while

---

43. A sad fact, as one must know truth to experience freedom (John 8:32).

people continued to say hurtful things? Did constant criticism bury your best efforts?[44]

Having identified where you lost your edge, it's time to cut a branch from a tree and cast it into the water. Why does Elisha go to such an effort? Everyone was cutting down trees, so wood littered the ground. True, but when you've lost your edge, you can't expect help from a dead stick. Regaining a lost edge requires a living branch (cf. Isa 11:1–5). Not only do we cast our cares on Jesus, but we also cast Jesus upon our cares. Then, when you see your blessing surface, follow Elisha's guidance and pick it up for yourself.

Indeed, rebuilding the temple is an arduous task that will bring you to your breaking point. There is no need to fly off the handle. Do not follow the young prophet's example and neglect what is most important. Instead, tap that little wedge regularly, and you will maintain your cutting edge. How does one do this? I'm glad you asked.

Spiritual disciplines play a vital role in restoration. The *lectio divina*, or sacred reading, is especially effective. This approach, introduced to the West by the Eastern desert father John Cassian early in the fifth century, consists of four elements: *lectio* (reading), in which one absorbs a selected short text by repeated reading; *meditatio* (meditation), in which the individual reflects on the words and phrases; *oratio* (prayer), in which the internalized passage is offered back to God in personalized form; and *contemplatio* (contemplation), in which the believer yields in silence in God's presence. Martin Luther's *tentatio* (struggle) is added to this list and presented as a critical component in Christian character formation.

Other disciplines include fasting, simplicity, solitude, submission, confession, engagement with nature, journaling, and worship. In totem, this endeavor is interactive and ongoing, individual and communal; the process "concerns how the Spirit works in us, among us, and through us to achieve Christlikeness."[45] The goal is spiritual formation, so Jesus' actions and attitudes become a natural outflow of reformed character.

There are three significant challenges to applying spiritual disciplines in a holistic restoration program. First, many fallen ministers may practice these and other spiritual disciplines. However, their motives and methods may prove ineffective. For example, a minister who reads his Bible and prays daily may do so only to meet ministerial requirements or to appease God and thus avoid judgment. Second, the fallen minister may be unfamiliar

---

44. This approach is another illustration of the need to move past the bad fruit (flying off the handle) to identify the bad root (the cause of our behaviors) and offer right response.

45. Chandler, *Christian Spiritual Formation*, 71. Cf. Rom 8:29; Eph 4:15; 2 Cor 3:18.

with the intentional steps inherent to spiritual disciplines and find its revelations quite painful. Therefore, these disciplines must be modeled and guided by a spiritual mentor who serves as a reading partner for accountability and shared insight. Lastly, each approach to spiritual disciplines has inherent weaknesses. For example, the *lectio divina* has been a hallmark of spiritual formation for centuries. While the approach is contemplative, it lends itself to solo reading rather than reading that encourages reflection with others. The holistic restoration program could draw from *lectio divina*'s inherent strengths but also prioritize a tailor-made devotional reading plan that meets the individual's unique needs and facilitates relational growth with God through the guidance of the spiritual mentor.

This symbiotic approach to the spiritual disciplines sees them not as duties but as doorways through which one can access God's presence. The spiritual disciplines do not produce the change but bring the individual to a place where change can occur through nurture and development as the Holy Spirit works, reveals himself, comforts, guides, and instructs.[46] The result is an awakening, a move from self-orientation to self-realization that allows the fallen minister to apprehend God through personal encounters. Because the approach is experientially holistic, the fallen minister can obtain healing and wholeness and thus come to know his true self (fulfilling Augustine's passionate prayer *"novem te, novem me"*—may I know you that may I know myself!).

Spiritual disciplines ride the paths of a renewed mind to drive behaviors from the sexual to the spiritual, from the "immediate other" to the "eternal other." Returning to the divine relationship's forgotten "first love" restructures the fallen minister's devotional life (cf. Rev 2:2–5). Formative practices are catered to the violator's unique struggle and situation and should remain flexible to accommodate progression or digression. The mentor guides reflective participation in each step. Weekly meetings enable strong accountability as they facilitate discussion of designated passages, enable deeper connectivity in prayer, strengthen fellowship, and provide an opportunity to share struggles and celebrate victories.[47]

What follows is a brief discussion on *lectio divina*'s core elements.

---

46. Foster, *Celebration of Discipline*, 8.

47. For fuller connection with and submission to the Spirit's work, it is recommended that each gathering open with prayers that focus on formative passages such as Pss 19:14; 119:9–16, 25–27; 139:23–24; Rom 12:2; 13:12–14; Phil 4:8–9; Heb 6:12.

Benefits of *Lectio* (Reading)

A renewed approach to Scripture and prayer are non-negotiable, as these remain the primary conduits through which God engages his people. Yet it is here that the mentor is likely to encounter resistance, if not outright opposition, as many fallen ministers consider themselves adept and anointed in such matters. Some even qualify as Bible scholars. The issue is not knowledge but application, specifically, whether spiritual competencies have extended beyond professional duties into personal development.[48] Indeed, those who know the truth are set free (John 8:82), and there is freedom in the Spirit's presence (2 Cor 3:17). Conversely, bondage to sexual sin violates Scripture and upends the minister's conscience. This upheaval creates an internal dilemma of shame and hypocrisy that likely distances him from God's Word and, thus, the power to overcome. Guided renewal in devotional life invites the breath of God to enliven the text and minister to the soul.

Humility as a learner rather than instruction as the teacher predicates formative engagement with Scripture. *Lectio* centers on the daily and repetitive reading of short Bible passages related to the individual's situation. This endeavor is intimate and sometimes invasive but results in a self-discovery that enables the broken minister to encounter God's love and grace in new and much-needed ways. Much like the path from the pigpen to the father's house, this approach facilitates a return to the simplicity of being God's beloved son.

Mentors should be aware of significant challenges that may arise. These include the prevalence of selective literalism (adhering to Scriptures one is willing or able to accept while discarding the rest) and moral relativism (measuring specific scriptures against self-defined truth claims). The mentor can be attentive to the violator's biases and cultural influences, as these can twist Scripture to fit within his tainted worldview. Scripture reading with a mentor helps the reader recalibrate his relationship with God. The individual can next determine the pertinence of such truth in his life and ministry through meditation.

---

48. Notably, a 2022 national poll found that more than two-thirds of pastors who have considered quitting and more than half who have not considered quitting said personal spiritual formation takes a back seat to pastoral responsibilities (Barna Group, "For Pastors Who Want to Quit," figure 2).

Benefits of *Meditatio* (Meditation)

Rather than empty one's consciousness—techniques common to Buddhism, Hinduism, and the New Age movement—biblical meditation seeks to fill one's consciousness and feed a broken soul with the truth of God's revealed Word.[49] Rumination provides a more contemporary analogy. The individual slowly and carefully "chews on" the passage to extract every possible nutrient. Diligent attention and reflection on every nuance help one clarify and apply biblical truths.

Deep consideration of God and self will sharpen the contrast between God's righteous standard and the violator's flaws and reveal causal factors leading to moral failure. These can include weak personal and familial structures or emotional and spiritual malformation. Mentors should anticipate significant struggle, as this may evoke the sorrowful realization of one's selfish preoccupation and alienation from God and the depth of personal suffering the fallen minister has caused. However, the goal is neither judgment nor self-condemnation but diagnosis leading to prognosis—an ability to acknowledge, confess, and renounce such behaviors and be healed by Christ (Matt 9:12; Mark 2:17; Luke 5:31). As Socrates rightly opined, "the unexamined life is not worth living."

Research shows that fifteen minutes of daily meditation results in "measurable development" of the prefrontal cortex, especially in the anterior cingulate cortex (where we experience love, compassion, and empathy). "The healthier the ACC, the calmer the amygdala (alarm center), and the less fear and anxiety we experience. Truly, love casts out all fear!"[50]

The meditative minister next determines how to apply revealed biblical truths in his life through prayer and contemplation.

Benefits of *Oratio* (Prayer) and *Contemplatio* (Contemplation)

Having internalized the Scripture and identified the profoundly personal struggle within, the individual now offers the revealed truths to God through personalized prayer. *Oratio* is a loving communion with God. Marked by attentive dialogue, such prayer seeks to listen more than speak.

As Elijah demonstrates in his time of despair, God's voice often comes not in displays of thunderous power but in a gentle whisper (1 Kgs 19:11–13). Such whispers amplify in places void of internal and external distractions, where one commits to patient silence and stillness before

---

49. Cf. Deut 6:4–4; Ps 1; 119:43–48; Rom 8:5; Phil 4:8; Col 3:1–2; 2 Tim 2:15–16.
50. Jennings, *God-Shaped Brain*, 132.

God.[51] There, God's Word acts upon the unconscious; truth silences the false self and thus creates an opportunity for the authentic self to emerge and be made whole.[52]

Appropriately taken, the steps above lead to *Contemplatio* (Lat. roots *com* and *templum*, "with" and "temple"), an overwhelming awareness of God's loving presence. Here, the individual stands on holy ground. The proximity that affords direct beholding is a matter of discovery rather than achievement. As John of the Cross rightly asserts, "Seek in reading and you will find in meditation; knock in prayer and it will be opened to you in contemplation."[53]

Ministers often neglect their spiritual reading and prayer life, substituting a task-oriented life. The soul sleeps while the mind is in motion. But the direct beholding of God's grace and goodness initiates a radical reorientation resulting in the proper intention of the heart (*intentio cordis*), purity of heart (*puritas cordis*), and humility of heart (*humilitas cordis*). Such (re)formation is critical as every believer steadily conforms to what he most loves and comes to resemble what he reveres.[54]

Kenneth Boa summarizes this approach well in defining spiritual life as "the life of Christ reproduced in the believer by the power of the Holy Spirit in obedient response to the Word of God."[55] From this perspective, he contrasts spiritual life with what it is not. Specifically, spiritual life (1) is not based on knowledge but obedience, (2) is not external but internal, (3) is not automatic but cultivated, (4) is not the product of effort but of divine enablement, (5) is not a dream but a discipline, and (6) is not a list of rules but a life relationship.

Benefits of *Tentatio* (Struggle)

The fallen minister and mentors alike should expect spiritual assaults to intensify at this point as ever-opportune demonic forces tempt through appeasement and question God's love and purpose. One should not avoid this

---

51. Cf. Pss 4:4; 46:10; 62:5; 119:33–37; Hab 2:20. Such practices were indispensable in Christ's life and ministry (Matt 4:1–11; 14:23; 26:36–46; Mark 1:35; Luke 5:16, 6:12–13; John 6:15).

52. Boyce and Erkert, "Spiritual and Relational Formation," 28. Notably, the authors assert that avoidance of silence is particularly acute in those plagued by inner torment.

53. John of the Cross, *Sayings of Light and Love* 158, 97.

54. Boa, *Conformed to His Image*, 154; Beale, *We Become What We Worship*, 22. Cf. Hos 9:10; 2 Cor 3:18.

55. Boa, *Conformed to His Image*, 102.

agonizing internal struggle, which Martin Luther would call *"Tentatio,"* as it is a primary means by which God's Word and Spirit destroy yet bring life. As C. S. Lewis rightly asserts, "God whispers to us in our pleasures, speaks in our conscience, but shouts in our pain."[56]

Here, the spiritual mentor provides invaluable support as an encourager, as many contemporary Christians (ministers included) would prefer "safe spaces" to suffering. Social presumptions add to the problem by wrongly defining happiness as autonomous individualism that minimizes or rejects suffering.[57] Contemporary society is ill-equipped to deal with suffering and far more traumatized by its presence. As a result, the materialist seeks personal happiness, and the naturalist only looks to survive. Both try to manage suffering by controlling their environment and others. If they cannot, they try to control their responses and behaviors.

Holistic restoration does not eliminate suffering but rather sees pain as purposeful for maturation.[58] "Christianity teaches that, contra fatalism, suffering is overwhelming; contra Buddhism, suffering is real; contra karma, suffering is often unfair; but contra secularism, suffering is meaningful. There is a purpose to it, and if faced rightly, it can drive us like a nail deep into the love of God and into more stability and spiritual power than you can imagine."[59]

Though difficult, the struggle with one's brokenness and the subsequent violations of God and others is necessary and formative. This struggle exposes and refines the heart (Deut 8:2–5; Zech 13:9), restores hope through the development of perseverance and resilient character (Prov 3:11–12; Rom 5:4), and affords the wayward minister the redemptive opportunity

---

56. Lewis, *Problem of Pain*, 91.

57. For example, atheism views creation as bearing "pitiless indifference" (Dawkins, *River Out of Eden*, 96, 132–3) and the attempt to find meaning in the face of suffering as "infantile" (Dawkins, *God Delusion*, 360). Timothy Keller also provides an insightful summary of four ways society responds to suffering and evil (Keller, *Walking with God through Pain and Suffering*, 17–18). These include the moralistic view (pain and suffering are a "wake-up call" that the victim needs to change his or her ways and live rightly), the self-transcendent view (evident in Buddhism, which teaches that individualism is an illusion and suffering results from unfulfilled desires), the high view of fate and destiny (circumstances are set by the stars or by supernatural forces and the highest virtue is to stand one's ground honorably in the face of hopeless odds), and the "dualistic" view (the world is a battleground between the forces of darkness and light).

58. Job 23:8–10; Ps 119:67–72; 2 Cor 12:7–10, etc.

59. Keller, *Walking with God through Pain and Suffering*, 30. The author goes on to analyze Gregory's *Moralia* to reveal how different kinds of suffering serve "a number of purposes in the divine economy" (p. 47). For example, some suffering corrects past wrongs (Jonah) and some prevents future wrongs (Joseph sold into slavery).

to affirm his faithfulness to God through proper response.[60] Furthermore, struggle enables the fallen minister to recognize and accept his vulnerabilities and limitations and often evokes a greater sense of compassion for the suffering of others.[61] Struggle also develops "indirect preparedness" for success in overcoming future trials.[62]

For example, Paul instructs deacons to be proven (1 Tim 3:10). That Greek word (*dokimazō*) and its related forms speak to being tried in the fire, refined and tempered to reveal impurities and cracks in character.[63] Similar is the scriptural process by which fire refines silver. Indeed, God refines, purifies, and strengthens his people in the fires of adversity.[64] Refining or purifying silver positions the precious metal over scorching flames. The heat separates impurities that would otherwise reduce the silver's value and strength. The silversmith carefully monitors the process; remaining in the fire a moment too long destroys the silver. How does the craftsman know when to pull his precious possessions from the furnace? Purified silver will reflect his image.[65] The same is true for you. When the fiery trial has burned away your impurities, God will see his image looking back at him. Is it any wonder the psalmist would declare, "I will see Your face in righteousness; I shall be satisfied when I awake in Your likeness" (Ps 17:15)?

In summary, susceptibility to moral failure increases as the spiritual condition decreases. Because ministerial training generally lacks substantive emotional and spiritual formation, some who struggle under the inexplicable burdens of ministry see a return to learned illicit behavior(s) as the only recourse to numb their pain, meet relational needs, or satisfy a lack of self-worth. While confession and repentance rightly identify and take responsibility for the "bad fruit" that emerged, that bad fruit is merely the product of a bad root (Matt 7:17–18; 12:33; Luke 6:43).

Removing bad fruit proves beneficial only for a season. Holistic (re)formation looks past the fruit to uproot the causal factors and facilitate growth in holiness. This endeavor is, first and foremost, an internal matter in which the individual partners with God to remove the ungodly and reform the divine image. As such, God's initial response to the believer's

---

60. Indeed, suffering precedes glory, the culmination of transformative identification with Christ (Luke 24:26; Rom 8:17–18; 2 Cor 4:17–18; Phil 3:10, 21; 1 Pet 1:11; 4:13).

61. Hall, "Suffering as Formation, 73–74.

62. Willard, *Spirit of the Disciplines*, 153.

63. As in Prov 27:21; 1 Cor 3:12–15; 1 Pet 1:7; Jas 1:2–4.

64. Ps 12:6; Mal 3:2–3; 1 Pet 4:12–13.

65. Cf. Prov 27:21; 1 Pet 4:12–13.

surrender of lordship does not focus on the upward or outward but on that which is inward.

Cooperation with divine sanctification anchors one's (re)formation. The goal is to break illicit tendencies and reintroduce the fallen to the true source of freedom and happiness. Such victory requires the minister to renew his mind and rebuild neural thought patterns. Habitual and virtuous behaviors and commitment to the spiritual disciplines allow one to "move slowly from an absurd to an obedient life, from a life filled with noisy worries to a life in which there is some free inner space where we can listen to our God and follow his guidance."[66]

As Paul explained, the minister must put away the old self, be renewed in the spirit of his mind, and then clothe himself with the new self (Eph 4:22–4). The "new you" is now ready for intentional yet incremental growth. Such maturation is rooted in self-control and contentment, progressing in partnership with the Spirit and spiritual community.

---

66. Nouwen, *Making All Things New*, 27.

12

Reinforcing the Structure

"By a Carpenter mankind was made, and only by that Carpenter can mankind be remade."

— Desiderius Erasmus

The intensive ministerial restorative plan described above will likely take up to two years, though individual needs and circumstances determine duration. However, effective holistic formation and (re)formation are incremental and lifelong endeavors. Even when Christ restores character and calling, the subsequent ministry takes place in the world. Successful restoration requires long-term applications to handle ministerial stress, avoid burnout, and overcome societal influence. Therefore, the program implements protective measures with periodic appraisals to help the restored minister maintain his personal and professional purity.

Make no mistake, there will be struggles. The restored minister is much like a mariner, happy to leave an unsuitable harbor and head for new horizons. With excitement, the minister hoists the sails. But favorable winds inevitably turn contrary and force him to contend with the flesh, the world, and the devil, the elements of our "perfect storm." Each of the three urges a return to the "safety" found in previous harbors, where the minister can anchor once again in the comfort of his illicit tendencies, if only for a brief visit.

As the adage goes, any port in a storm.

The minister who resists the urge to return to port must navigate the treacherous forces that rage beneath the surface. Here, he will face two significant challenges. First, as is seen in the journeys of Jonah and Paul, is the fearful reaction of inexperienced sailors who often discard precious cargo (in this case, spiritual disciplines and healthy relationships) in a vain effort to keep their vessel afloat (cf. Jonah 1:5; Acts 27:13–20). Second, persistent storms can cause even experienced sailors to lose hope and possibly abandon ship. The minister who grows weary fighting adverse winds and waves can easily, even willfully, sink into a spiritual apathy called "sloth." Thomas Aquinas rightly describes this condition as "an oppressive sorrow."[1] Ministerial sloth desires security and success but without the sacrifice and struggle necessary to achieve either. Grief over the loss or lack of spirituality leads to a diminished willingness to attain the same. The once-thriving pastor who recedes into this ministerial melancholy will eventually demonstrate a weary aversion to spiritual growth and life and increasingly lacks self-confidence or self-regard.[2]

Even in the best examples, the restored minister will have times when he cannot bear the considerable burden of past actions or recurring temptations, let alone weather new storms. Such struggle demands continuous accountability by seasoned spiritual mentors to ensure the restored minister reaches a suitable harbor (cf. Ps 107:28–30). Such mentors are familiar with the minister's tendencies and struggles and can identify when the minister falls short.

Unfortunately, national research shows that nearly 80 percent of pastors "do not have a network of close, mentoring friendships."[3] That is a tragic truth when studies show that "three or more incidents of intense stress within a year (say serious financial trouble, being fired, or a divorce) triple the death rate in socially isolated middle-aged men, [but] have no impact whatsoever on the death rate of men who cultivate many close relationships."[4]

The experienced mentor uses periodic appraisals to identify spiritual maelstroms and dangers threatening the vessel's integrity. Sailors call these scouting missions a "horizon scan," a concept that is at the heart of Jesus' command to "watch and pray so that you will not fall into temptation" (Matt 26:41). Rapid course corrections are sometimes required. The mentor is also

---

1. Aquinas, *Summa Theologiae*, IIaIIae Q. 35, Art. 1.

2. The digression from "intent" to "intend" is a tell-tale indicator that spiritual sloth has set in. The individual who intends has yet to act and may never do so. Conversely, intentionality speaks of purposeful action. The well-meaning "intend" is a deceptive justification of inaction. One may want to help, plan to help, be eager to help, agree to help . . . but none of these things help. Similarly, it is not enough that the restored minister intends to grow. The intentional minister will commit to action, primarily through the spiritual disciplines.

3. Kinnaman and Ells, *Leaders That Last*, 93, 96.

4. Goleman, *Primal Leadership*, 6–7.

responsible for setting new waypoints—meaningful and measurable goals unique to the individual and circumstance. And in times of relative calm, the mentor takes the opportunity to sharpen the minister's proficiency in spiritual and personal disciplines.

General orders for all watch standers require accountability in three key areas: personal behavior, professional conduct, and ministerial resiliency. These protective measures can help the minister avoid the tempest called temptation. The following subsections give attention to each category.

PERSONAL ACCOUNTABILITY

> "Holy sexuality consists of two paths: chastity in singleness and faithfulness in marriage. Chastity is more than simply abstention from extramarital sex; it conveys purity and holiness. Faithfulness is more than merely maintaining chastity and avoiding illicit sex; it conveys covenantal commitment."
>
> — Christopher Yuan

Accountability in personal behavior is arguably the most challenging of the three. Violators who have been misshapen by deformative life events will often view feelings as too painful and to be avoided. Accountability seems right and good—until external pressures and internal strife inevitably return. The violator who instinctively returns to illicit activities views accountability, which he formerly accepted and perhaps embraced, as inhibiting the "freedom" to find some measure of relief. The mentor must help the minister weather seasons of grief, self-loathing, and hopelessness. His guidance will enable the violator to find peace and strength through godly means, and accountability ensures the minister maintains course.[5]

Personal accountability cannot be a solo endeavor for this and other reasons. It was not good for man to be alone (Gen 2:18). It is not good for those with holistic wounding and malformation to be alone, as many will rectify loneliness through illicit behaviors that are considerably worse than "not good." Similarly, it is "not good" when one fights the battle for sexual and relational purity alone.[6]

---

5. As noted above, some sexual violators and addicts are master manipulators. Others find open dialogue to be embarrassing or painful. Therefore, a list of questions to initiate discussion for accountability purposes is provided in "Excursus 4: Restoration Resources."

6. Notably, solitary confinement is considered the worst kind of incarceration. Leaving a person alone for an extended periods is considered punishing, even

The violator must rebuild his relationship with God and family before he rebuilds his ministry.[7] While the restoration program is unique to the individual, the healing of brokenness that enables godly intimacy and the development of godly character bears common and evolving requirements. Restoring relational intimacy with God requires attention to many topics addressed above. These include fidelity in the spiritual disciplines; a teachable, humble, and obedient spirit that considers circumstances from a biblical worldview; understanding of personal worth and calling; and continued development of healthy relationships and habits. Commitment to each does not meet legalistic demand but centers on the biblical requirement for justice, mercy, compassion, and relationship.[8]

Restoring relational intimacy with family members can be more complex and calls for professional counsel. It is necessary to "vent," to talk through issues, and to be heard. It is also essential to have an unbiased analysis of each person's beliefs and behaviors. While tempting to turn to friends and family when communication with the spouse is especially strained, their insight is not unbiased and likely lacks the depth of understanding needed for proper diagnosis and prognosis. For example, human memory is highly selective and protects the ego by default. As a result, struggling couples "often disagree about the facts of their shared history, with both partners overestimating their positive intentions and behaviors in the events."[9]

The tendency to overestimate one's contribution while underestimating another's proves especially problematic when loved ones enter the discussion. Their validation may seem beneficial but is not constructive when rebuilding a marriage. Supporters may urge divorce in a well-meaning but wayward attempt to protect their beloved from further harm. Despite their love for you, they don't understand your love for the other. They do not know the intricacies of your relationship and may not see the plan or power of God at play. Therefore, relying on friends and family for counsel is to be avoided by husband and wife alike.

Instead, the violator is responsible for rebuilding a trusting and loving relationship with his betrayed spouse while the mentor and mental health

---

torturous. Isolation decreases cognitive and emotional resilience. The same is true in emotional prisons. Sin thrives in darkness and isolation. The answer to bring it to the light. A struggle unaddressed remains unresolved.

7. As noted above, the biblical order identifies relationship with God as ultimate (Mark 12:30; cf. Matt 10:37), with family relations as second and a qualifier for ministry, which comes third (1 Tim 3:4–5; 5:8).

8. Ps 89:14; Mic 6:8; Matt 9:13; 12:7; 23:23; Gal 6:1–2.

9. Ripley and Worthington, *Couple Therapy*, 287.

professional hold him accountable. Start by reading the subsection "Hearing and Healing the Victim(s)" in chapter 7. Then, with the assistance of the restoration team, establish measurable goals to ensure the betrayed spouse's fears and hurts are heard and acted upon.[10] The violator must be fully present and listen to hear rather than respond. He should be available to answer questions and prepared to accept angry or painful outbursts. A tsunami of negative thoughts can arise anytime, so always be ready to get her to higher ground.

Several steps can help initiate progression in the right direction. The violator should dedicate time to spend with his wife. Don't fit her into the schedule, but demonstrate that she is the priority. Rekindle your relationship with date nights that focus on the things she enjoys. Don't simply tell her that you love her; tell her what you love about her. Daily displays of affection are beneficial. Don't smother her, but think of small ways to say to her that she is in your heart and thoughts.[11] Little gestures go a long way.

While responsibility for marital reconciliation falls mainly on the violator, the betrayed spouse contributes to success in several ways. For example, expressing belief in him will profoundly affect him, as he probably doesn't believe in himself. A man who believes himself to be a failure will prove himself right. That same man will move heaven and earth to prove right a wife who believes him able.

Beyond acknowledging her feelings, the fallen minister should assure his wife that she is cherished. Most men are not naturally affectionate, and most who partake in sexual malfeasance find vulnerability especially difficult. A dysfunctional upbringing in which physical and verbal affection was nonexistent or abusive compounds the struggle. Therefore, significant effort and patience are needed to establish healthy communication.[12]

A word of warning is in order. Many violators feel genuine hurt that they have hurt a loved one. Because most are ill-equipped to discuss feelings or handle criticism, the violator may desire (or demand) the issue be forgiven and forgotten, never to be addressed again. After all, how can we move forward if we keep digging up the past?

10. Relational listening is invaluable for mentors when meeting with the restored minister, and the restored minister when conversing with his wife. Tips for relational listening are provided in the subsection "Tips for Relational Communication" in "Excursus 4: Restoration Resources."

11. *The Love Dare* is a great starting point, as the bestseller provides specific ways to demonstrate unconditional love over forty days (Kendrick and Kendrick, *Love Dare*).

12. For example, individuals give and receive love in very different ways. *The 5 Love Languages* is recommended as one way to ensure both individuals know how to say "I love you" in ways their partner will understand (Chapman, *5 Love Languages*). The "love language" quizzes and other helpful items are available at www.5lovelanguages.com.

REINFORCING THE STRUCTURE

Grab a shovel, friend.

Here, we see a practical application of "power through weakness," as discussed in chapter 10. The same shovel used to bury your feelings now digs up anything she desires to discuss. Hopefully, your mentor and mental health professional will also have shovels in hand and questions at the ready. Like Mary and Martha, whom we discussed in chapter 8, you may prefer to keep dead things buried. Don't be deterred by your dirt. After all, Adam was just a pile of dirt when God drew close and breathed life within (Gen 2:7).[13]

The priest/prophet Ezekiel provides a good analogy when he comes upon a valley of dry bones (Ezek 37:1–14). God asks, "Can these bones live?" Consider the difficulty (impossibility?) of this task. There are 206 bones in the human body. Assembly would be difficult if this were just one skeleton puzzle, but this is a nation. To live, one must locate, separate, and assemble 206 unique bones for seemingly innumerable people.

Can these bones live? The prophet rightly responds, "God, only you know the answer." In fact, God is the answer. He commands Ezekiel to prophesy to the bones—to speak the living word over a dead situation. Ezekiel hears a rattling as broken, separated, and strewn pieces are united. Ezekiel sees muscles emerge, restoring strength, and then flesh emerges as God covers them once more.

Don't bury your bones. Prophesy to the bones and watch God restore, strengthen, and cover what was dead. Still, those bones are not alive. Similarly, a marriage or a ministry can have the attributes, form, and features of Christ's body, but it's all for naught if we lack Christ's life.

God tells Ezekiel, "Prophesy to the breath, prophesy, son of man, and say to the breath, 'Thus says the Lord God, "Come from the four winds, O breath, and breathe on these slain, that they come to life."'" In the Hebrew, the word is *ruach*, and in the Greek, it is *pneuma*. Both mean wind, breath, and Spirit. When we restore form and function, the Spirit of God restores life.

God's Spirit enlivened Adam. God's Spirit revived Ezekiel's dry bones. God's Spirit rebuilt Zerubbabel's Temple. God's Spirit empowered the early church at Pentecost. God's Spirit will revitalize, revive, rebuild, and empower your marriage and ministry.

So, how do we assemble the broken pieces? Here are some helpful tips:

---

13. Paul identifies himself as a testimony to this. If he had achieved anything, it was only because of God's power working through a weak but consecrated vessel (cf. 2 Tim 2:20–21.) Therefore, Paul did not deny, justify, or excuse his own weakness but rather embraced it as the conduit through which the power of God worked. See 2 Cor 4:7–5:10; 6:3–10; 11:16–12:10–12. Cf. Rom 15:19; 1 Cor 2:4; 6:11; Gal 3:5.

- For the violator, be honest with yourself, responsible for your actions, and open to others' perspectives. For the betrayed, remember that your spouse is flawed. That is not to excuse, but it may help explain his decisions.

- Express negative feelings but avoid accusatory or threatening language. Look to construct rather than condemn. Express your feelings with I-centered sentences.

- Avoid conversations when extremely angered or overwhelmed by emotion. Set a designated time to address the issues, preferably in the presence of a neutral third party.

- Commit to forbearance and avoid coding, triangling, triangulation, and virtue signaling.[14] Speak directly and honestly with your spouse to help them understand your experience and what they can do to help you overcome.

- Commit to honest communication with your children. Expressing vulnerability builds confidence in relationships; it teaches children that they are not alone in their weaknesses or their solutions and that they are right to share feelings and uncertainties in healthy ways.

- Pray for and with each other. Couples who do demonstrate increased trust in as few as four weeks.[15]

The restored minister is accountable not only to God and family but also to himself. As such, he is responsible for the ABCs of accountability: avoidance, boundary setting, and cost covering.[16]

The list necessarily begins with avoidance. James and Peter instruct believers to resist Satan (Jas 4:7; 1 Pet 5:8), and Paul instructs believers to "flee immorality" (1 Cor 6:18). The contrast reveals the power of sexual temptation. Joseph's story illustrates this power and proper response. The young man flees sexual temptation with such force that Potiphar's wife, who refuses to let go, is left holding his abandoned garment (Gen 39:11–15).

Similarly, the restored minister must flee every time temptation lays hold. Yet the minister's story differs from Joseph's in one significant area: temptation often presents itself through gateway sexual behaviors such as fantasy, masturbation, and the use of pornography long before a potential

---

14. The explanation of each is in the Definition of Terms.
15. Ripley and Worthington, *Couple Therapy*, 51.
16. Though the restored minister is responsible for these activities, he is likely to falter if not held accountable by others. Therefore, a list of accountability questions is provided in "Excursus 4: Restoration Resources."

partner stands in proximity. Therefore, the minister must intentionally avoid mental and physical spaces where temptation is likely.

Fantasy emerges from the need to satisfy deep emotional and spiritual longings. The individual perceives sex as the solution to the need for love, touch, nurture, and affirmation. Pornography escalates the intensity of that fantasy to higher and higher levels of lust. When an activity becomes routine, addictive tendencies commonly progress to more dangerous or exciting forms. There is ample evidence that viewing pornography is not an emotionally or physiologically neutral experience; instead, behavioral patterns show an identifiable lack of control over time.[17] Therefore, abstinence from such behaviors is required.

The spiritual mentor works to ensure the restored minister remains mindful of his vulnerabilities, is heeding the warning signs, avoids inappropriate behaviors, and rightly addresses unresolved issues. Strategies for maintaining accountability in this area include computer software that blocks illicit content and alerts a third party of access. Prescribing medication to regulate hormones and chemicals may be necessary because pornography changes the brain's neural patterns and proves as addictive as drugs such as cocaine and heroin. Building new neuropathways and establishing new, positive rituals may require additional counseling.

Next comes boundary setting, which helps foster and maintain the right relationships. Boundaries are not designed to limit one's freedom (though it may seem this way to the violator). Instead, boundaries enable true freedom in Christ as they defend against negative influences and form a safe space where the fallen can focus on reconciliation with and restoration through God. This safe space requires recognizing and removing bad company that speaks doubt and discouragement into your life or leads you astray.[18] Simply put, the restored minister cannot nurture what God said to neuter. Release anything or anyone not of God, and ask, "Does this support the life I'm trying to create?" If not, let it go.

Boundaries not only keep the unwanted out but keep that which is precious within. As such, continuous family counseling is a critical and arguably non-negotiable need. The spiritual mentor should monitor the minister's progress and encourage him to maintain commitment in such matters.

Counting and accepting the cost is the third aspect of personal accountability. Jesus warns that discipleship comes at great cost (Luke

---

17. Struthers, *Wired for Intimacy*, 68–69.

18. Cf. Rom 16:17; 1 Cor 15:33; 2 Cor 6:14; 2 Tim 3:2–5. Notable is Paul's query in Gal 3:1, in which he asks the "foolish" Galatians "who [not what] has bewitched you?"

14:28–29). You have undoubtedly learned that accepting the call to ministry came at great expense. Restoration to the ministry carries additional expense. There will always be doubters and naysayers. There will always be suspicions. Worse yet, the restored minister must contend with the agonizing struggle resulting from the damage and hurt he has caused. Restoration does not negate repercussions—just ask King David.[19]

The most significant cost will not be monetary and may prove a price the violator is unwilling to pay if not properly prepared. The fallen minister must carefully consider the adverse impact of a lengthy restoration process on his ego, family, and professional and social standing. As Richard Foster posits, people "may genuinely want to be good, but seldom are they prepared to do what it takes to produce the inward life of goodness that can form the soul. Personal formation into the likeness of Christ is arduous and lifelong."[20] The significant burden may soon overtake the violator who fails to count this cost and prepare accordingly. Some will cut the emotional costs by returning to hidden behaviors or leaving the ministerial calling.

In short, restoration to God, self, family, and ministry is a costly endeavor. The one who chooses to fight may lose. However, the one who chooses not to fight has already lost. Therefore, the weight of this burden urges continued reliance on the restoration team. Remember that even Jesus needed help carrying his cross.[21]

And as a minister, the cross you bear is not only personal but professional.

PROFESSIONAL ACCOUNTABILITY

> "He who is required by the necessity of his position to speak the highest things is compelled by the same necessity to exemplify the highest things."
>
> — Pope Gregory I

Professional accountability initially prohibits the restored minister from ministerial or counseling oversight of others. Progress rather than duration

---

19. As a result of David's actions against God in the rape of Bathsheba and murder of Uriah, God declares the sword would never depart David's house, his wives would be taken by another, and the firstborn of David and Bathsheba would die (2 Sam 12:10–14). Indeed, David's secret sexual murderous sins were practiced openly by his sons, Amnon and Absalom. In addition to rape and murder, the latter rebels against David and two civil wars tore the kingdom apart. See also Num 14:20–24; 1 Cor 10:11; Rom 15:4.

20. Foster, "Spiritual Formation Agenda," 31.

21. Matt 27:32; Mark 15:21; Luke 23:26.

governs the decision to resume ministerial duties. Overseers should err on the side of caution when allowing any ministerial duties that would involve one-on-one counsel, as the "pastor-congregant relationship is most susceptible to abuse when it arises in a counseling situation."[22] The therapeutic relationship often finds two people meeting alone to discuss secret and intimate details of life. Unless distance is maintained, "therapeutic privacy can evolve into illicit secrecy," and even well-meaning compassion may lead to corruption.[23]

Overseers may enact a limited restoration of pastoral counseling that does not allow the restored ministers to counsel the opposite sex, and similar restrictions may be self-imposed. Restoration of full privileges should see the counseling of females occur only during office hours and in spaces that allow others to view the activity easily through a window or open door. Physical contact should be kept to a minimum if not avoided outright. The restored minister should be especially mindful that the intimacy of spiritual counsel avails itself to emotional transference.[24] Specifically, female congregants needing emotional and spiritual support will sometimes develop feelings for the pastoral caregiver, who may be the first person to listen and appreciate her in quite some time. Sometimes, a counselee who seeks affirmation, stability, or strength begins to see such qualities in the pastoral figure and believes the idealized minister to be her solution.

Conversely, the pastoral counselor should expect intense feelings to emerge occasionally. The proper response includes moral integrity and a readiness to respond accordingly. The minister should reveal and address matters such as transference and feelings of arousal in accountability sessions. The minister should cancel future counseling sessions if these feelings do not abate. Emotional connections lead to emotional bonding, which creates an emotional affair, leading to a physical affair.

Professional accountability also seeks to negate the devastating effects of burnout.[25] As noted in chapter 6, most ministers operate dangerously

---

22. Grenz and Bell, *Betrayal of Trust*, 45.

23. Mosgofian and Ohlschlager, *Sexual Misconduct in Counseling and Ministry*, 19. The authors further state that a conservative estimate finds that more than one million women have been sexually exploited by a helping professional, approximately 90 percent of all sexual misconduct is perpetrated by men, adult women comprise about 85 percent of the victims, and about 70 percent of therapists report having a counselee who was exploited by another therapist (p. 52).

24. Patton, *Pastoral Counseling*, 56, 144, 171; Trull and Carter, *Ministerial Ethics*, 80; Willimon, *Pastor*, 218–19.

25. Notably, 38 percent of full-time pastors and 46 percent under the age of 45 who were surveyed at the end of 2021 said they considered quitting ministry within the past year. This total was up from 29 percent at the beginning of the year. Burnout

close to crush depth. While crippling an untold number of ministers in various ways, burnout is especially dangerous to the restored pastor who works tirelessly to right his past wrongs. Diminished capacity leads to diminished returns. The demoralization and discouragement that results likely drove the minister to engage in illicit behaviors in the first place.

The minister is neither able nor required to earn favor through works.[26] Such understanding may take considerable effort, experience, and encouragement, but it is necessary if the minister is to be guided by God's Spirit rather than misguided expectations. The mentor will play a key role by holding the minister accountable for rightly prioritizing his calendar during this process.

Establishing work limits is an excellent strategy to keep ministers operating at safe depths. This approach creates a buffer zone that can prevent implosion. Richard Swenson calls this space "personal margin," defined as the area between capacity and commitment.[27] To illustrate, imagine a circle inside a larger circle. The inner circle represents everything you are currently doing, and the outer circle represents everything you have the time, energy, and resources to do. Margin is the area between completion and capacity. The closer the lines of completion and capacity become, the closer you are to a physical, spiritual, or emotional breakdown.

For this reason, Swenson sounds the alarm. "We must have some room to breathe. We need freedom to think and permission to heal. Our relationships are being starved to death by velocity. No one has the time to listen, let alone love."[28]

A pervasive accountability program reveals the tendencies that eradicate the minister's margin, thus allowing the team to establish the boundaries that will optimize proficiency. Holistic formation should include the scheduling of sufficient daily, weekly, and annual time off, as well as commitment to physical activity and healthy eating, both of which reduce stress. In short, self-care is not selfish. Self-care is a non-negotiable component of spiritual, emotional, and ministerial health and vitality.[29]

---

is a primary factor, as roughly one-third of pastors scored "excellent" or "good" in six well-being categories (Barna Group, "38% of U.S. Pastors").

26. 1 Sam 16:7; Prov 29:25; John 2:24; Eph 2:8–10; Gal 1:10.

27. Swenson, *Margin*, 22. The author notes that while the drive for achievement has brought progress in the physical, material, and cognitive environments, the effect has been catastrophic in the social, emotional, and spiritual domains.

28. Swenson, *Margin*, 22.

29. Holistic formation will also include commitment to physical activity and healthy eating, both of which reduce stress. For more on this, see Rediger, *Fit to Be a Pastor*.

There is great wisdom in Vance Havner's assertion that "some of us would do more for the Lord if we did less."[30] And if we let patience have its perfect work (Jas 1:2–4). Rehabilitating means restoring one's ability, but one must never rush proper rehabilitation.

PATIENCE AND PERSISTENCE

> "Remember that every flower that ever bloomed had to go through a whole lot of dirt to get there."
>
> — Barbara Johnson

Lifelong Christian formation looks back to heal past wounds and forward to develop godly character. There "are few shortcuts in the journey from being a sin-dominated person to becoming a spiritually empowered, Christlike person."[31] The progressive development of a godly character is neither immediate nor straightforward. Virtuous character emerges gradually, eventually growing into a complex reality.

Indeed, mature Christians consider it a joyous matter when we "encounter various trials, knowing that the testing of your faith produces endurance. And let endurance have its perfect result, so that you may be perfect and complete, lacking in nothing" (Jas 1:2–4). No doubt most readers can quote that passage, but can you live it? Indeed, it is easier said than done.

Patience wouldn't be so bad if it didn't take so long. Such duration, though frustrating, is of great benefit as biblical patience builds resilient perfection, which is in woeful lack.[32] Beyond the perfect storm of the flesh, world, and devil, the restored minister must contend with the doubters and naysayers addressed above. Chances are good that their accusations and condemnations will pale compared to the charges you level at yourself. God will change your perception (and hopefully theirs) through patient resilience.

To illustrate, we return to our discussion in the subsection "Realize Who(se) You Are" in chapter 10. The apostle Paul's low opinion of others' opinions, and even lower opinion of his own opinion, is worth further exploration. Instead, let's reflect on Moses' predicament. The shepherd lacked

---

30. Arterburn, *100 Days of Peace*, Day 48.
31. Chandler, *Christian Spiritual Formation*, 25.
32. Jack Hayford's "discipline of time" provides a powerful conveyance of the need for patient restoration (Hayford, *Restoring Fallen Leaders* 25–26).

confidence in himself, giving five reasons why he was no longer qualified. Moses also lacked confidence that God's people would accept the resumption of his divine purpose (Exod 4:1–9). God told Moses to throw down his staff. It became a serpent, then God instructed Moses to handle the venomous threat (picking it up in a dangerous fashion, no less, as the head was free to strike). Next, God told Moses to put his hand inside his robe. His skin became leprous; a return to the robe brought restoration. Here, God said something remarkable: "If they will not believe you nor pay attention to the evidence of the first sign, they may believe the evidence of the last sign" (Exod 4:9). Why would they believe the second if not the first? After all, doesn't every minister have (or feign) the authority to manhandle serpents and all the power of the enemy? Perhaps. But Moses' first response was to run from the snake. He could not run from his fleshly affliction. He could muster the courage to kill the snake but could not conquer his fleshly condition. There was no grasping that—only God holds that solution.

There is an even more profound analogy between leprosy and moral failure. Leprosy is a devastating disease that starts as a slight affliction but soon progresses into painful visible sores. The victim eventually loses parts of himself to the disease. The disease eats inward from the flesh to the bones; what begins as an external infection soon becomes an internal affliction. Leprosy reduces its victims to social outcasts condemned to die a little bit at a time. As this disease slowly consumes his flesh, so also does it consume his hopes and dreams, his future, and his family.

Because this program centers on temple restoration, we would do well to relate such understanding to the purification and restoration of a leprous house (Lev 14:33–53). The owner's first obligation when the disease appeared was to tell the priest (confession). The house was closed to allow cleansing and purification. If the disease remained upon reinspection, the owner discarded the infected stones outside the city. The house was abraded and rebuilt using new stones and plaster. If there was no sign of the disease upon reinspection, the priest declared the house clean and suitable for habitation. If, however, the disease remained, it was deemed a persistent, leprous disease. The priest ordered the unclean house torn down and had its stones, timber, and plaster discarded in an unclean place outside the city.

It is a complicated and laborious procedure—and with good reason. "The complex, phased process that returned a person to normality . . . [implied] the enormity of the fall from purity that had occurred."[33] Similarly, by allowing the complicated and laborious process inherent to ministerial restoration, God demonstrates the magnitude of the change he accomplished.

---

33. Gane, *Leviticus, Numbers*, 249–50.

Like the leprous house, restoring the temple that is the fallen minister centers on purification and sanctification. The latter is both definitive and progressive; it occurs at a certain point in time yet is a lifelong process. While instantaneous sanctification is wonderful (and instant), holistic (re)formation typically and necessarily reflects an ongoing process as God reveals and restores illicit thoughts and behavioral responses decades in the making. The result is progressive intellectual, affective, volitional, relational, and moral transformation.[34]

To reiterate, ministerial restoration is not an administrative allowance but a Spirit-led affirmation by designated leaders that holistic (re)formation has taken place and promises to continue. While ministerial restoration may culminate at a specified date, holistic (re)formation (emotional, spiritual, communal, and professional) is a lifelong journey through uncharted territories with uncertain outcomes.[35]

The hope is that, over time, the fallen minister is (re)formed by a renewal of thought resulting in changed behavior. Simply put, active reflection leads to reflective actions.[36] The fallen minister must reject ingrained thought patterns and responses to imitate and ultimately assimilate godly character fully.[37] This approach rejects the contemporary therapeutic approach to behavior modification and embraces a divine transformation of heart and affections. In much the same way holistic (re)formation centers on a synergistic partnership with God, this virtue ethic gradually sees one's being influence his doing, and his doing shapes his being. Character informs conduct. Therefore, the question that drives holistic (re)formation is not "What should I do?" but "what should I be?" Only a long-term commitment to character development will result in moral and ministerial integrity.[38]

Incremental character formation further develops self-control, a critical attribute that protects against future failures. Self-control is simply placing oneself under God's control, but such surrender is neither quick nor

---

34. Bekker, "Scriptural Formation," 101–102. Bekker draws this from Louise Kretzschmar, "Authentic Christian Leadership," 41–60. Similarly, Kretzschmar builds this paradigm upon Francis of Assisi's work.

35. This truth is conveyed in the Greek verb *katartidzo*, which conveys restoration as sustained, ongoing, and continual.

36. Johns and White, "Ethics of Being," 302.

37. 1 Cor 11:1; Phil 2:5–11; 1 Pet 2:22–24.

38. Notably, the root of "integrity" is "integer," meaning "one." The minister who walks in such integrity will be one person no matter the circumstance. There is no more need for personas. Furthermore, moral and ministerial integrity indicates that the individual is one with God.

easy. Peter sees self-control as emerging from moral excellence mediated by the Scriptures, thus enabling perseverance, godliness, brotherly kindness, and godly love (2 Pet 1:4–7). Indeed, the discipline of self-control is a hallmark of holistic formation (1 Cor 9:25; 1 Tim 4:7), a fruit of the Spirit (Gal 5:23), and a requirement for ministers (1 Tim 3:2; Titus 1:8). Conversely, the lack of self-control is an opportunity for Satan (1 Cor 7:5) and a hallmark of worldly character (2 Tim 3:3).

Ultimately, patient participation with the Spirit delivers one from fleshly desire into divine love. God's gracious presence enables the recovery of prelapsarian holiness of life, through which the right relationship with God, others, and self can actualize.[39] Through instruction and encouragement, the mentor builds a resiliency that can keep the minister from giving up or giving in when seas grow contrary.[40]

---

39. 2 Cor 4:16; 1 Thess 4:3–7; Jas 1:12, etc.

40. As Paul directs, believers should "aim for restoration [and] comfort one another" (2 Cor 13:11; cf. Acts 27:36; 1 Thess 5:11; 2 Tim 1:6–7).

Section Four Summary

"Those who dive into the sea of affliction bring up rare pearls."

— Charles Spurgeon

Holistic restoration requires personal and professional accountability that builds resiliency. Success requires continuous appraisal and accountability of the restored minister to ensure the re-formative efforts result in further growth and fruit-bearing. Even in successful restoration, no minister is completely delivered (Prov 16:18; 1 Cor 10:12). Peril awaits the solo sailor who believes himself capable of navigating the turbulent times and temptations that lie ahead. Periodic appraisals allow experienced and level-headed mariners to come aboard, discern God's direction, and find safe harbor (Ps 107:28–30). Careful inspection and introspection will enable the minister to evaluate his vessel properly, mend the broken pieces, and better prepare for future headwinds.

A strong accountability program sees the minister acknowledge his struggles and provides a godly perspective that may be lacking. For example, continuous struggles batter the isolated minister, leaving him weak and incapable. In truth, honest acknowledgment of such weakness and subsequent dependence on God are keys to effective ministry. God perfects and exhibits his power through weakness (2 Cor 12:9), which catalyzes servanthood and demonstrates the priority of love over knowledge and gift (1 Cor 8–10).[1] The weaknesses that threaten to destroy can become the minister's greatest strength. Periodic appraisal and continuous accountability enhance the restored minister's ability to establish good boundaries and behaviors that bring relational health to self, family, and ministry.

We rebuild temples devastated by perfect storms while anticipating the unseen storms that loom beyond the horizon. For this reason, patient perfection and resiliency are essential. As noted in the section 2 summary,

---

1. Hawthorne et al., *Dictionary of Paul and His Letters*, 966.

the two Galilee storms demonstrate how Christian maturation sees one progress from certain destruction to peaceful presence to a miraculous walk with Christ. Indeed, the perfect storms are formidable, but Jesus has given you authority over every storm. The threatening waves are beneath you. Rather than topple you, they will carry you to your desired harbor so long as you keep your eyes on Christ and stay in step.

In closing, I offer a prayer and a proclamation.

First, read Psalm 25, David's desperate plea for protection, guidance, and pardon. Make his prayer your own. Engage the passage through the elements of *lectio divina*, addressed in chapter 11, every day for the foreseeable future. Emulate the psalter's honesty, vulnerability, and trust.

Second is a proclamation made by the existentialist philosopher Søren Kierkegaard: "Now, with God's help, I shall become myself."[2]

Become. And blessings on your journey.

---

2. Kierkegaard, *Papers and Journals*, entry 19 April 48 VIII I A 641.

Conclusion

"Coming together is a beginning. Keeping together is progress. Working together is success."

— Henry Ford

We have likened the cataclysmic effects of sexual moral failure to the "perfect storm," a convergence of three powerful forces that oppose the spiritual walk: the flesh, the world, and the devil.[1] Each storm draws strength from the wounds and trauma, especially those that occurred in formative years. These identifiable and measurable events result in brokenness and emptiness, adversely shaping one's views of self and the world.

Our analogous journey set sail with the tragic tale of *Andrea Gail*, lost in 1991 in the North Atlantic's "perfect storm." The story became a bestseller and blockbuster movie. It is neither the first nor the last to do so. People seem enamored with shipwrecks and the stories of ill-fated passengers and crew. Songs, books, poems, paintings, and major motion pictures capture tales of heroism and heartache.[2] Numerous programs explore these sites and even "drain the oceans" for a better look. Countless divers spend millions annually to find and explore wreckage. Some do it for the sake of history. Some, in the hopes of finding lost treasure.

Shipwrecks lose their sense of wonder if you or a loved one were on board. Indeed, shipwrecks entomb countless men, women, and children who never made it to safe harbor. Each shipwreck represents the catastrophic loss of life, finances, and provision for the future. Countless hopes, dreams, reputations, plans, and promises rest within the watery graves.

---

1. Eph 2:2–3; cf. Jas 3:15; 1 John 2:16.

2. Though the movie's main characters were fictional, the tale of *Titanic* brought in more than $2 billion. Personally, I am moved by Horatio Spafford's tragic classic, "It is Well with My Soul," and recommend you research its origin.

SECTION FOUR: RESTORE, REBUILD, AND REINFORCE

Ministry vessels overcome by the perfect storm tell a similar tale. This book provided only a tiny portion of the losses, as most go unreported. There are an estimated three million undiscovered shipwrecks around the world. How many ministries have quietly slipped into the depths?

Holistic restoration provides a process by which some ministry vessels can be saved or salvaged. The process also provides healing, restoration, and protection for the victims adversely impacted by the minister's illicit behavior—specifically the abused, the violator's family, and churches left wounded in the wake of sexual impropriety.

The systematic and exegetical analysis of Scripture, theological doctrine, and Christian tradition affirms ministerial restoration after sexual moral failure is possible but is the exception rather than the rule. The contemporary church has demonstrated a woeful inadequacy in responding to these violations. Secular standards rather than scriptural guidance have driven countless decisions for and against ministerial restoration. Restoration programs have proven inadequate. Even worse, many churches and leaders who govern these programs are ill-equipped to address the numerous issues involved.

Conversely, the holistic restoration program acknowledges, assesses, and overcomes the flesh, world, and devil—three powerful forces that oppose the spiritual walk.[3] This sanctifying psychopathology reconciles, revives, and rebuilds the fallen minister. Specifically, this Spirit-led endeavor deals with the violator's shame, heals emotional wounds caused by trauma and dysfunctional relationships, reforms neural pathways, and replaces the negative self-image with one's identity in Christ. Holistic restoration overcomes the world by deconstructing narcissistic power structures, rightly identifying and rejecting negative cultural influence, and enabling the development of a biblical worldview. Lastly, the program addresses demonic oppression through the Spirit's sanctifying work by uprooting the causal factors and facilitating growth in holiness and the development of Christlike character. In partnership with the Spirit, the fallen minister rebuilds godly affections and commits to spiritual disciplines and continued accountability. Such (re)formation is a lifelong endeavor that enables a healthy and holy relationship with God, self, and others (Matt 22:34–40).

This endeavor begins with a crisis event that destabilizes the flawed structures that have long upheld the minister's façade. When the dust of the subsequent collapse finally settles, the pile of broken rubble that was his life and ministry, in many ways, resembles the mountainous ruins of Solomon's Temple that once lay before Zerubbabel (as discussed in chapter 11). How

---

3. Eph 2:2–3; cf. Jas 3:15; 1 John 2:16.

CONCLUSION

can one remove such debris, let alone rebuild a suitable temple and restore ministry to the Lord? Only by partnering with the Spirit.[4]

Ministerial restoration also necessitates the unified function of church leaders, mentors, mental health professionals, and a dedicated congregation. The restoration team should learn the fallen minister's history and tendencies and understand his weaknesses and behaviors better. This approach strengthens a personalized spiritual formation plan while indicating any potential areas of struggle or unbiblical tendencies and responses. Other preventative measures in this initial year include psychological assessments for ministerial candidates to identify narcissistic and illicit tendencies and assess sexual typology and recidivism.[5] Further screening should consist of background checks, social media checks, reference checks, and formal interviews that include direct questions relating to sexual morality. A minimum two-year ministerial internship training period would follow. Holistic formation would remain a priority throughout, while intense engagement with ministerial practice will allow ministerial trainers to learn the candidate's propensities and how the candidate handles the inherent stresses.

Acceptance into this holistic restoration program does not guarantee completion, and completion does not guarantee reinstatement. The overseers, mentors, and Christian mental health professionals who partner in this endeavor determine whether the minister has met and maintained the biblical standards for repentance and restoration. Furthermore, this process may reveal unrealized or unacknowledged spiritual and emotional inadequacies, thus disqualifying the minister from future service. Also, program leaders may recommend alternative ministerial duties, such as an administrative position, rather than approve a minister's return to a shepherding role.

God's grace invites the violator to participate in this purifying and redemptive work. Repentance and continued submission are the appropriate responses.[6] As noted, to repent is to change one's mind. Therefore, the violator must renounce all pride, self-righteousness, and self-orientation. Such change is neither easy nor enough. Because truth acknowledged is ineffectual until applied, right thinking helps produce right actions that form right

---

4. Ezra 3:8; 5:2; Hag 1:1–14; Zech 4:6–10.

5. As noted above, examples include the Minnesota Multiphasic Personality Inventory (MMPI), the California Psychological Inventory (CPI), the Rorschach, the Enneagram, the Sexual Addiction Screening Test, and the Sexual Addiction Inventory. Notably, researchers have found that most ministerial candidates score in Cluster B DSM-V spectrum of personality disorders, which feature narcissistic traits most prominently (DeGroat, *When Narcissism Comes to Church*, loc. 298).

6. Rom 1:5; 16:26; cf. Ps 119:30; Heb 10:22–23.

habits, which develops right character. Therefore, restoration begins in the cognitive but fully develops in the affective. The sanctification of thoughts progresses to the sanctification of actions that develop sanctified character. Still, the need for sanctification is not restricted to sinful sexual behaviors. It extends to the causal factors exacerbated by the stresses of ministry, the inability to manage such stress, and the general thwarting of being spiritually formed into Christlikeness.

This Spirit-led participatory process, in many ways, uses disintegration to enable reintegration. This destructive reconstruction centers on the emotional and spiritual (re)formation that acknowledges the harm he has suffered and has shared. It then requires the minister to take responsibility for its consequences and end its negative influence. The fallen minister cannot restore the brokenness around him until he restores the brokenness within him.

While restoration requires brokenness, God does not leave the violator in a broken state. The Spirit removes the debris by probing emotional trauma and encouraging the fallen minister to acknowledge the harm others inflicted upon him—violations long buried beneath denial and shame. This work includes the piece-by-piece removal of the persona created to disguise the minister's self-orientation, lack of self-worth, and hypocrisy. Though remarkably painful, such exposure is necessary to receive healing, extend forgiveness, and better understand how emotional brokenness has misshaped his view of self and others. Through this sanctifying psychopathology, God removes the impurities that would otherwise weaken the new structure.

These processes will see the violator who hid his flaws become hidden in Christ (Gen 3:8; Col 3:3). Rather than pretend to be someone else, the violator accepts his identity in Christ (Gen 27:5–29; 1 Cor 15:9–10). Rather than clothe himself in works of righteousness, the violator clothes himself in Christ's righteousness.[7]

Beyond purification is the necessary radical reorientation of thought and life.[8] Such (re)formation is a work of the heart, "the arena of the individual person where Christian truth is either exhibited or found wanting."[9] Amid this cleanup and construction, the minister will likely realize the indescribable harm he has caused others. Extending and receiving forgiveness takes considerable time for all parties involved, as does rebuilding trust.

---

7. Isa 64:5–6; Rom 13:14; Phil 3:1–8.

8. Such understanding is in keeping with John Wesley's "main doctrines" of repentance, faith, and holiness, presented in "Principles of a Methodist Farther Explained."

9. Clapper, *Renewal of the Heart*, loc. 417.

CONCLUSION

Like Ezra, Nehemiah, and Zerubbabel, the restored minister will likely meet opposition throughout this endeavor. He may contend with the relentless temptation and condemnation of spiritual forces and the distrust and disregard of fellow ministers and Christians. But restoration done well allows the restored minister, like the ministers of old, to experience God's glory in greater measure than before.

Holistic restoration is thus an outcome of God's active goodness. The willingness to acknowledge woundedness and rebellion and to accept responsibility for his behaviors and the harm he has caused enables the fallen minister to experience the right relationship with God, leading to the right relationship with himself and others. Personal commitment and submission to God's ongoing work bring healing, deliverance, and development in Christlikeness. There are no shortcuts, only the exhortation that one continues to strive to reach this goal (Phil 3:12–14). Maturation of godly character leads to godly behavior and enables the restored minister to participate in God's kingdom work.

While the holistic restoration program addresses individuals and affected churches, the *telos* embodies a holiness standard reflecting a holy God. For the corporate body of Christ, this demands intentional movement from the prescriptive to the preventative.[10] A proactive rather than reactive approach to sexual moral failure requires the church to remove the plank from its eye first. The first step is full-scale transparency. Silence is a statement and sometimes reflects complacency and complicity. For Christendom to elevate righteousness over reputation, denominations must articulate and apply a coherent restoration theology for violators and victims. Rebuilding trust will be painful, but being viewed as untrustworthy is more so.

Transparency also requires churches to report confirmed instances of ministerial sexual moral failure. This effort should include constructing a multi-denominational database of offenders, as this would remove the autonomy and secrecy that has thwarted the healing and health of violated individuals and church communities. Such disclosure will also help ensure that violators cannot covertly resume ministerial function in other locations or denominations unaware of past behaviors.

Obtaining such data will prove difficult, at best. This difficulty is ironic, considering that most Christian churches rightly devote time and resources to fighting sex trafficking, defending women's rights, and funding shelters for battered women. Still, many church organizations and denominations remain reluctant to release such data for many reasons, such as legal

---

10. 1 Thess 4:3–8; cf. 1 Cor 6:12–20; 2 Cor 4:1–2.

considerations, protection of victims, and the desire to maintain a good reputation and standing.

The increasing tendency of churches and Christians to be guided by personal preference and secular standards rather than biblical principles is also problematic. Social acceptance or rejection of various behaviors may contribute to a sliding response scale. In addition, identifying and applying biblical principles among biblically illiterate people may prove challenging.

Still, churches that commit to the holistic approach, whose restoration programs are rooted in Scripture and guided by the Spirit, will experience indescribable moments of grace as violators and victims progress from care to cure and from coping to conquering. Indeed, the path to ministerial restoration is straight and narrow. Yet, those who find and follow this path will experience God's remarkable grace and presence.[11] Some will be poised to grace others in similar measure and, perhaps, even prevent similar failures in future leaders (2 Cor 1:3–5).

Through it all, God will be glorified.

---

11. 2 Cor 7:1; Eph 4:24; 1 Thess 3:13; Titus 2:14; Heb 12:10, 14.

Excursus 1

Review of Sexual Morality in Church History

> "The past is never dead. It's not even past."
> — William Faulkner

CHRISTIANITY'S RESPONSE TO SEXUAL moral failure and its restoration of victims and violators has been inconsistent, but the early church started well. For two centuries, the early church held close to the Pauline theology of sexuality, detailed in chapter 2. Christians were a counterculture to the sexual revolution of their day, which paradoxically considered male sexual relationships with slaves, prostitutes, and young boys to be proper, legitimate, and "even necessary to keep lust and other passions in check."[1]

Christians differentiated in three ways, and by this, "Aphrodite was slain by the Christians."[2] The first was sexual exclusivity in marriage, a commitment that saw everyone from Aristides and Justin to Clement and Lactantius blast adultery and fornication as contrary to godly life and happiness.[3] For this reason, adultery often headed the list of vices in early Christian writings such as the Didache, the church's oldest discipline manual. Christianity's second differentiation saw opposition to divorce and remarriage, which arguably began with Athenagoras's pointed argument

---

1. Harper, *From Shame to Sin*, 49.
2. Harper, *From Shame to Sin*, 135.
3. Hunter, *Marriage and Sexuality in Early Christianity*, 14; Yamauchi and Wilson, *Dictionary of Daily Life*, 24.

that second marriage was merely "respectable-looking adultery."[4] One's responsibility for maintaining purity marked the third point of differentiation and initiated Christendom's progressive and profound changes regarding sexuality and marriage in ministry.

The early church generally understood sex within monogamous marriage as good. Christians believed the sanctity of marriage to be God's creative intent. Some, such as Basil the Great and Gregory of Nyssa, viewed sex as a glorious part of God's creation and sexual immorality as a consequence of sin.[5] Adherents endorsed sexuality within marriage, and the ecumenical church generally supported marriage for ministers.

Restoration to ministerial function was generally available for those who violated the biblical ethic even as standards became increasingly strict. David Hunter provides a robust breakdown of these accommodations from Basil's writings. Basil presented restoration in stages rather than entirely excluding those with moral failure. For example, Basil gave total allowance for the marriage of ministers but viewed remarriage as "restrained fornication." The Cappadocian father urged a one-year exclusion for digamists (second marriage) and five years for trigamists.[6] Violators were worthy of being hearers after two to three years, later permitted to stand with the congregation but excluded from communion, and ultimately restored to Eucharist when the fruit of repentance was evident. Fornicators were to endure a similar four-year restoration, though the first year required they "be expelled from the prayers and weep at the doors of the church."[7] Basil later extended this to seven years.[8] In addition, restorative exclusion of adulterers runs fifteen years: four years of weeping, five as a hearer, four kneeling, then

---

4. DeVille, *Married Priests in the Catholic Church*, 8.

5. For example, Gregory contrasts that "in the cases where it is possible at once to be true to the diviner love, and to embrace wedlock, there is no reason for setting aside this dispensation of nature and misrepresenting as abominable that which is honourable" (Gregory of Nyssa, *On Virginity*, 24).

6. Hunter, *Marriage and Sexuality in Early Christianity*, 227–38. The author cites Basil of Caesarea, *Letter 188 to Amphilochius*, 4.

7. Hunter, *Marriage and Sexuality in Early Christianity*, 240. The author draws from Basil of Caesarea, *Letter 199 to Amphilochius*, 22.2. Despite this seemingly harsh sentence, Basil's views on fornication were equally liberal, as is evident in *Letter 217 to Amphilochius*, 26, in which he urged that those united in fornication be separated, but "if they are completely happy living together, let them submit to the penalty for fornication but without separation, so that nothing worse may happen."

8. Hunter, *Marriage and Sexuality in Early Christianity*, 243. The author quotes Basil of Caesarea, *Letter 217 to Amphilochius*, 59.

two standing with the congregation but without communion until fruits of repentance are evident.⁹

The priest who unknowingly entered an illegitimate marriage could retain his seat but should entreat the Lord with tears and refrain from all other activities as "pardon is enough."¹⁰ Basil further asserted that it "would not make sense for someone who ought to be treating his own wounds to be blessing another. For to bless is to impart holiness." Lectors who had intercourse with their betrothed before marriage were allowed to read after a suspension of one year and to remain without promotion. Ministers and lectors with "secret relations without betrothal" were removed from the ministry.¹¹

The emerging Roman Catholic Church took a similar approach, but two debates signaled inevitable change. First was the increasing resistance to the remarriage of ministers following adultery by or death of the spouse. Second was the contention that celibacy (rather than chastity) best reflects the moral standard.¹² Challenges to the purpose and purity of sex, even in monogamous marriage, gained quick momentum.

The digression of sexuality from celebrated to tolerated to eviscerated did not happen overnight. When Christians (especially ministers) could not control their carnal desires, leaders soon blamed sex. The subsequent emphasis on celibacy defined purity in a ministerial rather than marital context and viewed sex as less than ideal and even ungodly. Their pursuit of purity centered on an arguably misconstrued emphasis on asceticism, the disciplined avoidance of indulgence. In many ways, their methods resembled Plato's philosophy more closely than Holy Scripture.

The Christian standard eventually shifted from chastity to celibacy and ultimately to virginity.¹³ This contentious journey significantly altered

---

9. Hunter, *Marriage and Sexuality in Early Christianity*, 243. The author quotes Basil of Caesarea, *Letter 217 to Amphilochius*, 58.

10. Hunter, *Marriage and Sexuality in Early Christianity*, 241. The author quotes Basil of Caesarea, *Letter 217 to Amphilochius*, 27.

11. Hunter, *Marriage and Sexuality in Early Christianity*, 243. The author quotes Basil of Caesarea, *Letter 217 to Amphilochius*, 69.

12. The early church defined chastity as abstention from unlawful sexual activity, and celibacy as the abstention from all sexual activity.

13. For example, the Shepherd clearly refers to chastity as fidelity and not celibacy (Osiek and Koester, *Shepherd of Hermas*, 110). Contrary to his consistent urging that even those married remain celibate, Methodius of Olympus also defines and affirms chastity as control of sexual desire that enables the chaste to fly above the concerns of mortals and see the immortal realm (Methodius, *St. Methodius*, 106). See also Cullum, "'Give Me Chastity,'" 624; Hunter, *Marriage and Sexuality in Early Christianity*, 22.

Christian views toward sexuality and continues to challenge ministerial sexual ethics.

PROGRESSION FROM CELEBRATION TO CELIBACY

The mid-second century saw a significant shift in the church's approach to sex and marriage. Rather than celebrate chaste sexuality as inherently good and given by God, an increasing urgency for celibacy emerged even within biblical marriage. Adherents believed celibacy expresses a higher spirituality and commitment to God. The first significant push came when Tatian formed an ascetic Christian sect called the Encratites (Chaste Ones). Followers asserted that restoration to prelapsarian life in God requires the rejection of all intercourse. In refutation, Irenaeus of Lyons, Tertullian, and Clement of Alexandria defended biblical marriage and urged sexual purity. But these refutations soon revealed cracks in their foundation.

Clement presented the married state as preferable because it allows the believer to practice self-control.[14] Not only in avoiding sexual impropriety but also in practicing self-control that prevents one from feeling lust even for one's spouse. One must love that spouse, but self-control ensures procreation remains "a reverent, disciplined act of will."[15] Clement also affirmed the benefits of celibacy, which some heard as him elevating celibacy as superior.[16] Whether celibate or married, one's self-control must combine chastity and rationality to remain unyielding to the inferior "lower standard" and thereby acquire greater merit in God's eyes.[17] In this, sex that is to be beautiful and unitive becomes an exercise of the will, and those who master this will have favor with God.

Remarriage, especially by ministers, also came under direct attack. The Shepherd of Hermas provided early guidance that allowed remarriage after a spouse's death but inferred "greater honour and glory with the Lord" if the person remained single.[18] The mandate warned against lust and fornication, which brings about one's death, yet required a husband to take back a repentant, unfaithful wife—but only once.[19] Then Tertullian added some

---

14. Clement of Alexandria, *Stromateis*, 293.

15. Clement of Alexandria, *Stromateis*, 292.

16. Hunter, *Marriage and Sexuality in Early Christianity*, 22. Conversely, see Hägg, "Continence and Marriage, 137.

17. Clement of Alexandria, *Stromateis*, 304.

18. Hermas, *Shepherd*, Commandments 4.4, loc. 22083.

19. Hermas, *Shepherd*, Commandments 4.1, loc. 22049. This direction closely parallels the Shepherd's much contested assertion that believers are allowed post-baptismal

nitrous oxide to this gradual shift. The Latin father composed three treatises on the subject: "To His Wife" advised his spouse against remarriage after his death, though he admitted remarriage is not a sin. In "An Exhortation to Chastity," his attitude hardened, and he declared remarriage opposes God's positive will. Tertullian's third treatise, "On Monogamy," ultimately rejected and equated remarriage to adultery.

Similarly, Origen equated remarriage to fornication, making one "unfit for ecclesiastical honors."[20] In his view, remarriage and fornication are blemished and "not of the Church" but relegated one to a "second rank" of those saved but not crowned by Jesus.

Key leaders increasingly opposed remarriage by ministers and gave the laity sparing allowance. The increasing view that sex (including biblical sex) is a necessary allowance for procreation and never for pleasure fueled this change.[21] Similarly, the Shepherd permitted marriage and procreation "as a lesser evil than adultery; it remains a less virtuous alternative to celibacy."[22] But the proverbial straw that broke Tertullian's back came when Pope Callistus issued "Decree of 217," which offered forgiveness for seven sins, including adultery and fornication, that previously prohibited Christians from the Eucharist.[23] This decree outraged Tertullian and significantly contributed to his departure from the Catholic Church.[24] His angst was evident in his pointed response, "On Modesty." Notably, he declared the "frenzies of passions" and all other sexual vices to be "beyond the laws of nature, we banish not only from the threshold, but from all shelter of the Church, because they are not sins, but monstrosities."[25]

Tertullian's treatise "To His Wife" also foreshadowed a notable turn in Christian sexual ethics as he asserted that marriage is good, but abstinence is better.[26] Sex remained exclusive to marriage, but even then, it was suspect. Marriage is a necessity, but a necessity by nature depreciates what it allows.[27]

---

repentance only once (Commandments 4.3, loc. 22076).

20. Origen, *Homilies on Luke*, 75.

21. Such assertions were not new. For example, see Justin, *1 Apology*, 29, and Athenagoras, *Plea for Christians*, 33.

22. Meawad, "Sexuality, Angelification, and Divine Indwelling, 589.

23. The other sins included murder, idolatry, fraud, apostasy, and blasphemy. Callixtus also allowed clergy to marry before and after ordination. These and other changes led to schism and the election of Hippolytus, the first anti-pope.

24. Tertullian saw sin as external and soundly rejected anything worldly, including the circus and theater, while he advocated strict adherence to the moral law.

25. Tertullian, "On Modesty," 4.5, loc. 67144.

26. Tertullian, "To His Wife," 1.3.2, loc. 65960.

27. Tertullian, "To His Wife," 1.3.2, loc. 65963.

At this point, intercourse, even from a biblical perspective, had become an obstacle to chastity. Pope Siricius, in 385, solidified this thought by issuing the first papal decretal enforcing continence on married Catholic clerics.[28]

FROM SANCTITY IN MARRIAGE TO SANCTITY IN MINISTRY

The fourth century saw more emphasis on acquiring virtue and asceticism as the increasing solution. Gregory of Nyssa's three-stage "perpetual ascent" (*epektasis*) was a dominant approach that called for purification or detachment from fleshly passions, strengthening the soul, and union with God.[29] However, monogamous marital sex was increasingly suspect and seen as "lesser goods" by leaders such as Ambrose, Jerome, and John Chrysostom. For example, Chrysostom suggested marriage is good as it "creates a safe place to deal with the sexual appetite."[30] But Chrysostom's ascetic duality was evident when he inferred that sexual passion (not the sexual act) is morally and spiritually dangerous. Thus, marriage is God's provision for the management, not the unleashing or enjoying of sexual passion. For Chrysostom, marital sex does not lead to impurity or shame, merely "to a waste of time."[31]

While clerical celibacy gained a foothold in Chrysostom's writings, Augustine of Hippo kicked the door down. Arguably the greatest of the Latin fathers, Augustine saw marriage as good but continence as better.[32] Sexual procreation was part of God's original intent, not a concession to sin. However, Augustine argued that sexual relations between Adam and Eve before humankind's fall would have been entirely rational and void of "concupiscence of the flesh" or the irrational impulses and disordered desires that characterize fallen humanity.[33] In this view, sexual passion is not a part of God's good creation but a consequence of humanity's fallen condition.

Augustine understood he was flawed in this regard and admittedly gave no theological allowance to the flesh. His reasonings are evident in his

---

28. Canon 33 of the Council of Elvira (ca. 306) may provide an earlier rule requiring celibacy of ministers, married or otherwise. However, questions persist regarding the council's dates and contents and whether the list is a compilation of various synods.

29. Meawad, "Sexuality, Angelification, and Divine Indwelling," 583.

30. Wehr, "Virginity, Singleness and Celibacy," 92.

31. Wehr, "Virginity, Singleness and Celibacy," 92. The author cites Chrysostom, *On Virginity*, 30.2. See also Chrysostom, *Homily 20 on Ephesians*, 5.4, 7.4.

32. See Augustine, *Good of Marriage*, VIII.8.

33. Hunter, *Marriage and Sexuality in Early Christianity*, 30–1.

Confessions, which reveal that Augustine had an unhappy childhood in a dysfunctional family, was prone to theft and dishonesty, and was addicted to sex and food. Augustine took a lover in his teen years, lived with her for a decade and a half, and they had a child out of wedlock. This unnamed woman was likely enslaved or from a lower social class.[34] Augustine later affirmed he used this woman for her body and viewed her as a sexual object that he could cast aside.[35]

The bishop of Hippo admitted that "foul was the evil, and [he] loved it."[36] He acknowledged hedonistic sexual desire and aversion to self-restraint kept him bound to worldliness apart from God.[37] He eventually realized how desire grows and, if given satisfaction, forges habit. When habit passes unresisted, a compulsive urge solidifies.[38] Augustine ultimately personified these "empty nothings" as a habitual tyrant who endlessly attempted to persuade Augustine that he could never live without such pleasures. Still, in his misery, the young Augustine famously prayed, "Grant me chastity and continence, but not yet." The pause resulted from the fear that God would hear and soon deliver from "the disease of concupiscence, which I desired to have satisfied rather than extinguished."[39]

Augustine found hope in Christianity.[40] He soon determined that inauthentic intimacy makes an end of a means and thus idolizes the illegitimate.[41] One is to enjoy God only; using everything else is toward that end. One must strictly control affections to ensure God and all else are loved appropriately and proportionally.[42] One must recognize that which is corrupt as it seeks to lure the soul "into the depths of nothingness and further and further from Being."[43]

---

34. Litfin, *Getting to Know the Church Fathers*, 220.

35. Augustine, *Confessions*, 4.2.2; Augustine, *Good of Marriage*, 5.5.

36. Augustine, *Confessions*, 2:4:9.

37. Augustine, *Confessions*, 8.11.26. See also his address of the "monstrous thing" in 9.21, 10.22.

38. Augustine, *Confessions*, 8.5.10.

39. Augustine, *Confessions*, 8.7.17.

40. This happened in the summer of 386, when a childlike voice urged "*Tolle, lege*" (Latin, "Take, read"). Augustine received this as a divine command and randomly selected Rom 13:13–14 which holds the command to "put on the Lord Jesus Christ, and make no provision for the flesh, to gratify its desires." A thirty-three-year-old Augustine was later baptized by Ambrose of Milan and ordained in 391.

41. Augustine, *Confessions*, 3.6.10.

42. Augustine, *On Christian Doctrine*, 27.28.

43. Smith, "Redeeming the Affections," 45–46.

In such understanding, Augustine renounced everything he deemed worldly and remained celibate from his adult conversion.[44] Augustine conversed with women only from a distance, primarily through written correspondence regarding theological and ministerial matters.[45] While such devotion is commendable, Augustine's asceticism and theology reveal an underlying truth. The bishop never shook his Hellenistic upbringing and maintained a negative view of the material world. A modified dualism was inherent to his asceticism. Augustine assumed undisciplined passions cause sin, thus rendering the "active" life inferior to the "contemplative" life of prayer and meditation. Augustine's approach elevated the spiritual discipline of celibacy above the physical allowance for marriage and sexuality.

Augustine's relentless renunciation of passions and its almost synonymous relationship between biblical purity and ascetic celibacy did not go unchallenged. Theologians such as Ambrosiaster opposed this ascetic, declaring marriage and biblical sexuality inherently good aspects of God's creative intent.[46] They reached back to second-century writers such as Clement of Alexandria, who rejected ascetic claims of spiritual authority, and Ignatius of Antioch, who argued celibacy disrupts the Christian community.[47] However, the momentum of fourth-century asceticism effectively silenced these arguments.[48] Jovian's treatment provides a good example. He declared celibate and married Christians are equal in God's sight and equated asceticism with Paul's warning of "false teachers" (1 Tim 4:1–5).[49] In Jovian's view, one who compels acts of renunciation denies the value of creation and allies

---

44. Ellens, *Sex in the Bible*, 8. The author calls this "an overreaction to the first half of [Augustine's] life," which is debatable.

45. Smither, "Pastoral Lessons from Augustine's Theological Correspondence with Women," 1–2. Augustine has correspondence with fifteen women, constituting nineteen of his 252 known letters. The letters address various questions about Christian life, thought, and practice, including sexual morality. Notably, "Letter 150" congratulates a young woman who decided to become a consecrated virgin, a topic addressed below. In "Letter 208," Augustine encourages a consecrated virgin not to be surprised by moral failure among church leaders, as Paul warns these things would happen, but instead to put her hope in God.

46. See Ambrosiaster, *Commentary on the First Letter of Paul to the Corinthians*, 7:6, 7:9.

47. Hunter, *Marriage, Celibacy, and Heresy in Ancient Christianity*, 91–92.

48. In fact, Augustine's Christianized Platonism remained essentially intact until Thomas Aquinas engaged the works of Aristotle in the thirteenth century.

49. Jovian was condemned by synods in Rome and at Milan, led respectively by Siricius and Ambrose.

oneself "with demons and other errant spirits."[50] In response, the church condemned Jovian as a heretic.

Indeed, the early church was replete with examples of Christians going to extreme lengths to destroy sexual passions and ascend in personal spirituality. Origen of Alexandria, ironically known for interpreting Scripture as allegory, took Jesus' analogy of eunuchs (Matt 19:12) literally and castrated himself to become a "eunuch for the kingdom of heaven."[51] Chrysostom did not go to such extreme, but to overcome sexual temptation, he committed four years of ascetic rigor in the mountainous region near Antioch, followed by two years of isolation in a cave. Chrysostom believed that weakening his flesh would weaken his fleshly desires.[52]

While some subjected their bodies, others subjected radical asceticism to the church and further diminished the view of inherent goodness in marriage and biblical sexuality, sometimes in alarming ways. The *Acts of Thomas* provide a telling example. The opening act finds Jesus urging newlyweds in their bridal chamber to "refrain from this filthy intercourse" and thus become holy temples, free of trials and difficulties, and not drown in the cares of life and children that lead only to ruin.[53] The following morning, the bride gleefully tells her father that she had no intercourse with "a temporary husband," as this ends only in lust and bitterness of soul.[54]

Jerome provided another contentious example. His scathing attack "Against Jovian" went beyond a defense of celibacy and displayed overt hostility toward marriage. Jerome consistently presented marriage as "a lesser evil than fornication, not something truly good in itself."[55] Augustine countered with "The Good of Marriage" "to demonstrate that it was possible to maintain the superiority of celibacy (against Jovinian) and yet to uphold the genuine goodness of marriage (against Jerome)."[56] Despite this defense of marriage, Augustine's well-established preference for celibacy in ministry soon saw church leaders define sexual purity within the sanctity of ministry

---

50. Hunter, *Marriage, Celibacy, and Heresy in Ancient Christianity*, 95.

51. Litfin, *Getting to Know the Church Fathers*, 156. Origen later regretted the act and wrote that others should not follow suit.

52. Litfin, *Getting to Know the Church Fathers*, 193.

53. Anonymous, *Gospel of Thomas*, 37. The author quotes *Acts of Thomas*, Act 1.12.

54. Anonymous, *Gospel of Thomas*, 38. The author quotes *Acts of Thomas*, Act 1.14.

55. Hunter, *Marriage and Sexuality in Early Christianity*, 28.

56. Hunter, *Marriage and Sexuality in Early Christianity*, 28. This writing established Augustine's three "goods" of marriage (offspring, fidelity, and the sacramental bond) and identified procreation as the "one honorable fruit" of intercourse. For Augustine, sex to satisfy sexual desire within biblical marriage was regrettable but permissible under Paul's "concession" in 1 Cor 7:5–6.

rather than marriage. This development quickly progressed from a demand for celibacy to a demand for virginity, which became the epitome of virtue and evidence of spiritual martyrdom.[57]

FROM CELIBACY TO VIRGINITY AS THE IDEAL

The church's exaltation of virginity, especially among ministers, did not form overnight. Cyprian's "The Dress of Virgins," written in 249, is the earliest treatise dedicated to Christian virgins (defined as those who commit themselves to perpetual celibacy). A moderate encratism—the requirement of Tatian's ascetic sect to reject all intercourse—weaves through this work as it compares virgins to the angels who neither marry nor are given in marriage.[58]

The bishop of Carthage also advanced, albeit questionably, the traditional sexual ethics noted above. For example, Clement demanded self-control of the celibate and married alike to acquire greater merit in God's eyes.[59] While the Shepherd of Hermas suggested "greater honour and glory with the Lord" for the person who remained single, Cyprian elevated virgins further and declared they would receive better dwelling places, greater grace, and greater sanctity.[60]

Jerome's "Against Jovian" went even further by comparing the martyrdom of the married Peter to the preservation of the (supposedly celibate) John. Jerome declared this as evidence that "virginity does not die and not even the blood of martyrdom washes away the defilement of marriage."[61] The swift challenge of many theologians met Jerome's egregious assertion but could not impede the elevation of virginity.

As noted above, Methodius described the chaste—those who control sexual desire—as flying above the concerns of mortals to see the immortal

---

57. The virgin life is long understood to demand strict and continual discipline and exists in expectation of spiritual conflict. Athanasius's "The Life of Antony" demonstrates this well. When spiritual disciplines enable Anthony of the Desert, the "Father of Monasticism," to repel the devil's various assaults, the deceiver ultimately resorts to take "the shape of a woman and imitated all her acts simply to beguile." Anthony's Christlike nobility enables him to thwart this final and most dangerous attack (Athanasius, *Life of Antony*, 5).

58. Hunter, *Marriage and Sexuality in Early Christianity*, 121; Luke 20:34–36.

59. Clement, *Stromateis*, Book 3 7.58, 12.79.4.

60. Hunter, *Marriage and Sexuality in Early Christianity*, 122.

61. Hunter, *Marriage and Sexuality in Early Christianity*, 28. The author is citing "Against Jovinian" 1.26. In 26.3, Jerome further asserted that "only the virgin recognized the virgin" when Jesus stood on the shore and John had to tell Peter "It is the Lord" (John 21:7).

realm. On the other hand, virginity is a divine gift that finds one's head in the heavens while still walking on earth.[62] This higher spirituality was evident in other works that evoked virginity's pure ideal, such as Chrysostom's "On Virginity," Gregory of Nyssa's "On Virginity," Ambrose of Milan's "Concerning Virginity" and the anonymous Acts of Thomas.

As Western Christianity entered the fifth century, it vehemently contended that "virginity was ideal, marriage acceptable, sex beyond marriage sinful, [and] same-sex eros categorically forbidden."[63] Christians could marry, but this relegated them to a second-class citizenry incapable of curbing fleshly passions. As such, marriage for ministers was suspect and met with strong opposition. An ontological link soon emerged between celibacy and priesthood, asserting marriage divides a priest's love between parish and home.[64] Church leaders, leaning heavily on Augustine's theology of the "lesser good," saw the participant of biblical sex as impure and unable to administer the Eucharistic sacrifice. Celibacy was a must among ministers—and became obligatory for priests at the Lateran Council of 1123.

Such restrictions did not emerge in Eastern Orthodox theology. The Council in Trullo, convened in 692 by the Byzantine emperor Justinian II, furthered Basil's guidelines for ministerial marriages.[65] The canons do not permit clerics in Holy Orders to marry after ordination. Though prior marriage is acceptable, all priests must maintain continence rather than chastity. Married priests, deacons, and subdeacons are not to live with their wives on days they approach the holy mysteries. Ministers convicted of sexual immorality are subject to the same penalties as the laity.[66] However, those involved in prostitution are deposed.[67]

SUMMARY

The *imago Dei* in which God created man and woman reflects a plurality in unity. The image of God is "very good" (Gen 1:31), a description that "is less about aesthetics and more about purpose."[68] Such understanding is inherent to biblical sexuality yet lost within Augustine's Christianized Platonism and the ascetic push for purity over passions.

62. Methodius, *Symposium*, 42, 106.
63. Harper, *From Shame to Sin*, 135.
64. DeVille, *Married Priests in the Catholic Church*, xiii–xiv.
65. For example, Canons IV, XXVI.
66. For example, Canon XLIV.
67. Canon LXXXVI.
68. von Rad, *Genesis*, 52.

As noted in chapter 2, the biblical teachings of Jesus and Paul present marriage and human sexuality as blessed aspects of God's good creation. While both categories see humankind in a perpetual struggle with sin and its consequences, these categories are "subsidiary rather than essential to being human."[69] Indeed, Augustine was right to identify "disordered loves" as a consequence of humanity's fall and the pursuit of the "lesser good" as a sinful act. However, the inherent goodness of marriage and sexuality should not be similarly categorized—even when sin dominates either's expression. Sexual immorality is a matter of misappropriation, the illegitimate pursuit of a legitimate need. The sinful nature that births such desire and allows the desire to habituate is a "pervasive pollution of our essential identity" that does not define *who* we are but *how* we are.[70]

Each person is subject to an unchosen condition but responsible for personal choices. Such understanding is essential to a holistic formation that seeks to overcome sexual immorality by sanctifying the spirit, soul, and body—failure to recognize sexuality as a spoiled good leads to legalistic moralism. Failure to recognize one's responsibility leads to liberality and abuse of grace. To deny the ontological truths inherent in the *imago Dei* regarding human gender and sexuality allows personal experience to "supersede essence—what I feel is who I am."[71] In this, psychology usurps biology.

Similarly, the Augustinian denial of created reality in Christian sexual ethics sees philosophy usurp theology. These errors amplify the need for holistic formation. However, acknowledging the biblical role of holistic formation does not necessarily convey holistic acceptance—a painful truth the contemporary church knows all too well.

---

69. Kapic, "Anthropology," 184.
70. Yuan, *Holy Sexuality and the Gospel*, 30.
71. Yuan, *Holy Sexuality and the Gospel*, 22.

Excursus 2

A Case Study of Pentecostal Pioneers

> "Everyone wants to be clothed with power
> but no one wants to be stripped of self."
> — Leonard Ravenhill

THIS EXCURSUS ADDRESSES THE emergence of the Pentecostal Movement, which served as a critical conduit through which holistic sanctification progressed from the Evangelical Awakening through the nineteenth-century Holiness Movement and into contemporary Christianity. By way of example, the subsection highlights two key Pentecostal patriarchs—Benjamin Hardin Irwin (1854–1926), founder of the Fire-Baptized Holiness Church, and Charles Fox Parham (1873–1929), a father of the modern Pentecostal Movement. Both fell prey to sexual immorality and failed to respond with their holistic theologies. The excursus concludes with an analysis of the inadequate response within the Pentecostal Movement to their moral failures.

Notably, both men revealed little to no personal accountability as authority figures but instead reflected increasing neglect of spiritual disciplines as each struggled to meet unrelenting ministerial requirements. Church leaders failed to require biblical correction and restoration, thus compounding the far-reaching consequences.

Both men continued to minister, albeit with diminished authority, for the rest of their days. Irwin's restoration included confession and repentance, though he soon returned to the same sinful condition. Parham neither confessed nor repented. Some within various Pentecostal denominations shamed and shunned Parham, but failure to bring biblical correction or expulsion allowed Parham to preach increasingly unbiblical doctrine in alternate settings.

THE MORAL FAILURE OF BENJAMIN HARDIN IRWIN

Irwin preached holiness so vigorously that even radical elements within the denomination were taken aback.[72] Irwin added neckties to established restrictions on extravagant dress. He denounced dances, theater, county fairs, coffee, card playing, and recreation "not in conformity with spiritual worship and the Lord's work."[73] Everyone was to keep Old Testament dietary laws. Irwin also demanded believers keep a pseudo-sabbatical law. Christians were not allowed to ride in cars, read the newspaper, or indulge in any worldly pleasures on Sundays—even ministers were not to conduct visitation on the holy day.[74] In Irwin's view, "no man can be on friendly terms with this wicked world, no matter what his ostensible purpose or object may be, without being an enemy of God. . . . As Christians we must be completely separated from evil and from evil associates and entirely devoted to God."[75]

However, Irwin began taking extended breaks, and no one, not even his wife, knew his whereabouts. As it turns out, Irwin was returning to the drinking, smoking, and womanizing common in his youth. On April 20, 1900, Irwin penned "A Desert Place Apart," his last correspondence to the Fire-Baptized Holiness Church's official magazine, *Live Coals of Fire*. The article, published two months before Irwin's double life was exposed, explained how he had been "almost incessantly engaged in active evangelistic work" for nearly nine years.[76] It is an important observation. As noted above, illicit behaviors are often conditioned responses learned to cope with spiritual and emotional malformation.

Things came to a head when Irwin was recognized after emerging drunk from a bar and smoking a cigar in June 1900. The preacher attempted to bribe the witnesses but ultimately confessed. The subsequent inquiry also

---

72. Synan, *Holiness-Pentecostal Tradition*, 57–59.
73. Phillips, *Quest to Restore God's House*, loc. 2669.
74. Phillips, *Quest to Restore God's House*, loc. 2665.
75. Irwin, "The Friendship of the World," 2–3.
76. Synan and Woods, *Fire Baptized*, 225. Vinson Synan thus asserts the gross neglect of private devotions due to exhaustion from constant travels and preaching is a likely cause of Irwin's "repeated failures" (p. 97).

found financial indiscretions. In one instance, Irwin took $900 that was given to build a church and spent it on liquor and prostitutes.[77]

J. H. King, the general overseer of the Fire-Baptized Holiness Church, offered a telling response that described the revelation as "a tremendous shock, and yet I was not altogether surprised."[78] Others described discernment that something was amiss, yet no record of anyone addressing these concerns with Irwin or other church leaders exists.

The revelations shattered the Fire-Baptized Holiness Church.[79] Irwin moved to Oregon without his wife, Anna. He temporarily returned to the practice of law and soon added "bigamist" to his list of misdeeds when he married Mary Lee Jordan, a Texan from a socially prominent family.

Irwin attended a Pentecostal service in Salem, Oregon, in October 1906. He later claimed that he confessed to backsliding, repented in sackcloth and ashes, and made restitution at the meeting.[80] Irwin soon resumed his ministry, and Mary proved a strong partner, often at the expense of their children. Irwin continued to womanize throughout their marriage. He abandoned the family in early 1910 and ran off with a younger woman. In response, Mary described Irwin as "definitely immoral and a slave to his passions."[81] Irwin eventually returned to his Primitive Baptist roots, preached an extremely radical Calvinism, and posited that all life's actions are predestined.

Unfortunately, Irwin's is not the only example of moral failure among Pentecostal pioneers.

THE MORAL FAILURE OF CHARLES FOX PARHAM

Charles Parham was another influential Pentecostal pioneer who experienced moral failure. Parham's belief that *glossolalia* is the outward evidence of Spirit baptism was anything but common when he opened a Bible school in Topeka, Kansas.[82] Opinions began to change when Agnes Ozman

---

77. Synan and Woods, *Fire Baptized*, 225.

78. Synan and Woods, *Fire Baptized*, 79.

79. Most followers in Tennessee and Western North Carolina join the newly formed Church of God. Churches in Florida, Virginia, and all others west of the Mississippi River are closed. When the dust settles, only two conventions remain: North Carolina and Georgia.

80. After speaking in tongues, Irwin publicly rejected his former fire, dynamite, lyddite, and oxidite "baptisms." He officially transitioned from Holiness, which he preached for twenty years, to Pentecostalism, which he preached for the next four years.

81. Synan and Woods, *Fire Baptized*, 84–87.

82. Faupel, *Everlasting Gospel*, 174.

spoke in tongues on New Year's Eve of 1900. William Seymour, an African American student forced to sit outside the classroom, soon took Parham's doctrine to Los Angeles and launched the Azusa Street Revival.[83]

Many lauded Parham as a father of the Pentecostal Movement. However, unspecified rumors of immoral behavior emerged as early as January 1907.[84] That spring, leaders of the Apostolic Faith movement, which Parham founded, decided to "disfellowship" Parham and rescind his ministerial credentials. Parham vigorously protested their claims and actions, but on July 19, 1907, thirty-four-year-old Parham and twenty-two-year-old J. J. Jourdan were arrested in San Antonio and charged with "an unnatural offense"—sodomy, to be precise. Parham was released on a $1,000 bond. He never was brought to trial, but his ministry never fully recovered.

Civilian news accounts varied. The *Houston Chronicle* reported a supposed confession in which Parham asserted, "I will swear, however, that I never committed this crime intentionally. What I might have done in my sleep I cannot say, but it was never intended on my part."[85] The paper later reported that Parham rescinded the confession, citing coercion, and claimed the arrest was part of a plot to destroy his ministry. Jourdan refused to comment throughout the ordeal.

Parham's susceptible followers soon pointed an accusatory finger at Wilbur Glenn Voliva, successor to John Alexander Dowie's multi-million ministry and Zion City, located sixty miles outside Chicago. They viewed the charges as a smear campaign in response to Parham's previous attempt to take control of the fledgling group when a stroke forced Dowie's resignation.[86] While Voliva used the scandal to further his ministerial ambitions, Leslie Dawn Callahan effectively argues that "it strains credulity to think him able to orchestrate Parham's arrest from hundreds of miles away, complete with an eyewitness, affidavits, and the participation of the constable. . . . The most reasonable conclusion about the arrest is that while Parham's enemies might have profited from the scandal, the specific charge had some basis in fact."[87]

---

83. Hollenweger, *Pentecostalism Origins and Developments Worldwide*, 19.

84. Callahan, "Fleshly Manifestations," 141–42.

85. Callahan, "Fleshly Manifestations," 141–42.

86. Parham's narcissistic need for control and affirmation saw similar behaviors in his vocal opposition to William Durham's "Finished Work" theology. Beyond theological considerations, Parham used the issue to regain his position as projector of the movement. Parham saw Durham's untimely death in 1912 as vindication and reignited his claims for control, but to no avail.

87. Callahan, "Fleshly Manifestations," 157.

Still, unsubstantiated claims soon emerged in the *Zion Herald*, the official publication of Vovila's church. A scathing story published on July 26, 1907, was said to be a quote from the San Antonio Light newspaper. Still, it included references to eyewitnesses and a written confession that was not part of the local coverage.[88] The *Waukegan Daily Sun* ran essentially the same story the following day, and this version appeared nearly two months later in the Holiness circular the *Burning Bush* (Waukesha, Wisconsin).

Parham stuck to his conspiracy claims and neither confessed nor repented, though he did come close in a 1913 article published in *Apostolic Faith*. Parham stated, "I realize, and need not be reminded that my past life and conduct has fallen short of that of the Master; inaccuracies and weaknesses of the flesh and mind have cropped out time and again." But any hint of confession was quelled when he turned attention to the "scandalous lies and slanderous reports."[89]

Still, tendencies common to ministerial moral failure were evident in Parham's life. Rumors of immoral behaviors were prevalent before the San Antonio allegations. In addition, toxic leadership was apparent in his attempts to strong-arm to overtake Zion City, and the Assemblies of God, and narcissistic tendencies emerged in Parham's defiance against anyone who charged him with wrongdoing. As is demonstrated below, ecumenical charges in response to sexual moral failure were few and far between.

THE (NON)RESPONSE OF EARLY PENTECOSTALISM

As addressed above, sexually immoral ministers often surround themselves with sycophants and acolytes who fail to bring accountability and even intentionally or unintentionally facilitate illicit behaviors. Such adverse influence grows into toxic church cultures that enable sexual sins to flourish and often see church leaders protecting their reputations at the expense of truth. This tendency was evident in the emerging Pentecostal movement as talk of moral failure and restoration grew silent in the years following Irwin's and Parham's failures.[90]

88. Goff, "Fields White Unto Harvest," 239–41.

89. Parham, "Greeting," 8.

90. Irwin and Parham are not the only early Pentecostal leaders to face matters of sexual immorality with little public recourse. Revivalist, faith healer, and megachurch pastor Aimee Semple McPherson was widowed after two years of marriage. Her second marriage ended in divorce and was soon followed by the famous "kidnapping incident" in 1926. McPherson disappeared for five weeks and claimed to have been kidnapped, though critics contend she went to a love nest with Kenneth Ormiston, an announcer from her Los Angeles radio station. McPherson officially organized the International

Two articles addressed restoration to membership after Parham's fall. A 1910 article in the *Church of God Evangel* requires that "a name continue to remain on the roll if the person has gone back into sin and refuses to repent, straigten [sic] up his life and live for God. If one who is a member should be overcome and get back into sin, proper steps should be taken by the church to restore him, but if after having complied with the Scriptural directions he is still not restored, then it is the duty of the church to disfellowship him and blot his name from the church roll."[91]

At roughly the same time, *The Latter Rain Evangel* published a March 1910 message preached in Chicago. Charles F. Hettiaratchy asserted that a "spirit of forbearance" was needed because love covers a multitude of sins.[92] The sermon urged hearers not to shun the fallen but to restore in the spirit of meekness. Divine love is the mark of true Christianity, as the devil cannot imitate divine love, but the lack of forbearance keeps many from God.

Some leaders outside the Pentecostal Movement offered a pointed response to Irwin and Parham. However, their comments did not center on the sacred trust of ministry, holiness, or repentance. Instead, some who denied sanctification as a second work of grace pointed to the illicit actions to substantiate their claims. Radical evangelicals in the Holiness Movement took aim at Parham with particularly scathing and long-lasting criticisms, going so far as connecting his "devilish 'tongues' craze" with the "sin of sodomy."[93] Although Ruben A. Torrey endorsed Spirit baptism and believed it accompanies manifestations of *charismata*, he (like many in Evangelical revivalist circles) rejected speaking in tongues as initial evidence. Torrey said

---

Church of the Foursquare Gospel the following year. Though early Pentecostalism uniformly rejected remarriage, McPherson in 1931 married her third husband, David Hutton, a vaudeville and cabaret performer who had a questionable past with alcohol and womanizing. The couple separated in 1933 and divorced in 1934. Also of note is M. S. Lemon, a prominent leader during the Church of God's (Cleveland) formative years who was one of three to lead the ouster of the denomination's first general overseer, A. J. Tomlinson, for questionable financial practices. However, very little is known of Lemon's apparent moral failure, as the files were seemingly sealed at the family's request (in addition to significant personal influence, his wife Mattie was a beloved matriarch in the early church).

91. Church of God Evangel, "Keeping of Records," 1–2.

92. Hettiaratchy, "But the Greatest of These Is Love," 12.

93. Callahan, "Fleshly Manifestations," 159. The charges appear in the radical Holiness magazine *The Burning Bush* on Sept. 19, 1907, exactly two months after Parham's arrest.

such belief was "utterly unscriptural and anti-scriptural."[94] He later declared the doctrine was "emphatically not of God, and founded by a Sodomite."[95]

Pentecostal leaders did little to counter the attacks or prevent further failure in the following years.[96] Irwin's actions were never directly addressed. Parham's name appeared in the second edition of *The Apostolic Faith* (October 1906) in a general history of the young movement but was not mentioned again in any major Pentecostal publication until October 1908, when G. B. Cashwell mocked Parham's reported effort to locate the ark of the covenant.[97]

The Apostolic Faith Movement's *Gospel of the Kingdom* in April 1910 became the first to address Parham's moral failure directly but did so in his defense. The edition included an unrelated article by Parham and commentary by editor J. G. Campbell. The latter provides an example of a "susceptible follower," one of three essential elements in Padilla's "toxic triangle" described above. Campbell argued that allegations against Parham were organized by those who seek control and warned readers not to be "equally guilty of false accusation."[98] In numerous publications, Campbell noted the pointed rejection of Spirit baptism and speaking in tongues and concluded Satan was "at the bottom" of the attacks on Parham's character and doctrine.[99]

Some leaders, such as E. N. Bell, eventually challenged Parham's behavior. In 1912, Bell warned readers to ignore Parham's leadership claims because Parham was repudiated, refused to "hear the church," and was a "heathen and a publican" until he repented and confessed.[100]

94. Anderson, *Spreading Fires*, 23–24.

95. Synan, *Holiness-Pentecostal Tradition*, 146.

96. This observation comes from an electronic review through the Consortium of Pentecostal Archives (pentecostalarchives.org), a collaborative effort initiated by repositories of Pentecostal archival materials to make their materials accessible online. The library includes twenty-nine publications provided by eight denominations and universities. These publications provided detailed reports of leaders' actions, and most denominational leaders use the publications as primary conduits to convey doctrine and polity.

97. Cashwell, "Letter From Bro. Cashwell," 4. The same publication later prints a report from China missionary Thomas Junk, who suggests that rather than finding the ark of the covenant, Parham should "look up his covenant with God [and] study his Bible prayerfully" (Junk, "Letter From Thomas Junk," 1).

98. Campbell, "Pentecostal Papers," 2.

99. Campbell, "Pentecostal Papers," 2.

100. Bell, "Notice About Parham," 3. This is the official publication of the Church of God in Christ (White). Bell's comments could serve an ulterior motive as Parham was attempting to seize control of the Assemblies of God following Durham's death. Bell later becomes the denomination's first general overseer.

Still, most Pentecostal leaders and publications failed to address Parham's actions.[101] Even when one removes Irwin and Parham from the equation, discussion of moral failure is noticeably absent from the first four decades of Pentecostal periodicals. Such activity was denounced but typically in testimony or passing. For example, an electronic search of periodicals found that "moral failure" appears only nine times, typically in the general context of forbidden practice. None of the related articles identify specific actions or appropriate responses.

In comparison, the term "adultery" appears 591 times, the overwhelming majority of which address divorce and remarriage. The term "immorality" appears 305 times but covers everything from inappropriate behavior to conducting a revival without approval from a district minister. The words "restore" and "restoration" appear hundreds of times in the decade after Irwin's fall, but nearly all speak of the restoration of faith, the *charismata*, personal health, Israel, or the biblical church. None address restoration to ministry. Irwin had moral failures and was a bigamist, yet he was allowed to preach after his 1906 repentance. This allowance evidences some sense of restoration, yet the early periodicals did not address the processes involved (let alone why or when) in making such determinations.

The first defined call for personal sexual purity in the context of moral failure appeared in May 1932, when W. E. Moody presented the issue as "one of if not the most vital question that has confronted the church."[102] He said, "Impurity in its most insidious and shameless forms, is stalking through the land, and is making tremendous inroads into the Church. . . . missionaries, pastors, evangelists, and other prominent workers are being overcome." Moody argued that such behavior would lead to increased divorce rates and secret self-abuse and that God would hold the church responsible for the "criminal silence" of pulpit and platform.[103]

Pentecostal denominations did not directly address the consequences of moral failure in ministry again until the 1940s; even then, it was in passing. The reprint of a 1942 Christmas letter sent to Assemblies of God ministers is noteworthy. General Superintendent Ernest S. Williams closed by addressing the issue of moral failure. He acknowledged that "every year there are a few, a very small percent, thank the Lord, whose names must be published as dropped from the fellowship because of a moral failure. Most of these failures could have been prevented if the minister had been

---

101. It is equally telling that none report Parham's death.
102. Moody, "Personal Purity," 6.
103. Moody, "Personal Purity," 6.

alert in his walk with God."[104] These things do not usually happen suddenly, Williams warned. The devil endeavors to find any weak spot in a minister's character. An unguarded trigger event places the minister at risk of "ruining his whole future, to say nothing of the ruination of his own soul."[105]

The reasons early Pentecostal periodicals withhold reports of moral failure and detailed guidance for correction and restoration are unknown. It stands to reason leaders may have been motivated by a desire to keep negative publicity to a minimum, given the fragile nature and challenges faced by the young movement. Regardless, Pentecostals arguably did more harm than good in their failure to fully address the issue of moral failure and the omission of deliberate accountability proved disastrous.[106]

SUMMARY

It cannot be known whether or to what extent conditioned responses to deficient emotional or spiritual formation played in the moral failures of Irwin and Parham. Both endured the death of an infant. One cannot determine, but neither should one overlook, the effect of such tragedy. In addition, both exhibited narcissistic tendencies that suggest malformation. More evident was their failure to maintain the spiritual disciplines amid unrelenting ministry schedules. Such stress, combined with the ego-boosting status they carried as Pentecostal pioneers, provided fertile soil for an attitude of entitlement that justifies unacceptable behavior.[107] This perfect storm, strengthened by a lack of accountability to ministerial authorities, saw both succumb to their respective trigger events.

A holistic restoration program could have seen Irwin and Parham restored to God and, if appropriate, to ministry. Of course, both continued to minister, but illicit behaviors and diminishing effects are evident throughout their remaining days. There are similar results in dozens of illicit sexual behaviors among contemporary ministry leaders. The sexual moral failure of ministers continues to see subsequent failures by church leaders to apply biblical restriction or restoration as appropriate.

---

104. Williams, "Assemblies of God Minister's Letter."
105. Williams, "Assemblies of God Minister's Letter."
106. Trask et al., *Pentecostal Pastor*, 21.
107. Chandler, "Perfect Storm of Leaders' Unethical Behavior," 77.

Excursus 3

The Role of Free Will

> "If you're willing to repair your life, God is willing to help.
> If you're not willing to repair your life, God is willing to wait."
>
> — Marie T. Freeman

While debates regarding free will are evident throughout Christian history, the differing views on providence and participation captured in the sharp dialogue between Martin Luther, Desiderius Erasmus, and John Wesley remain foundational when discussing what role (if any) free will has in holistic formation.[108] While Luther engaged free will in developing outward relationships with others, he omitted its role in one's inward relationship with God. Conversely, Erasmus presented free will as participative with the divine rather than a means to achieve divine favor. Wesley presented free will in the context of a progressive transformation that balances divine sovereignty and human responsibility.

This excursus briefly explains why Erasmus's and Wesley's views are favored over Luther's and concludes with more recent scholarship on free will.[109]

---

108. For more on the ways in which these doctrines can and should be rectified, see Bacon, "Pentecostal Paradigm That Reconciles," 85–102.

109. Luther defined this surrender of free will as faith—and proper faith is not a matter of simply offering right words or religious activity to achieve surrender. Proper faith is not the mental assent to certain understanding or even the right application of sacraments. It comes by grace alone.

MARTIN LUTHER'S POSITION ON FREE WILL

For Luther, right standing with God comes by surrender rather than the operation of free will. The moral law's requirements are endless, and humankind is incapable of any work that could overcome the sinful condition. Furthermore, it is possible to obey such requirements "while remaining a quite wicked person."[110] Therefore, efforts to fulfill the moral law are fruitless and lead only to bondage. In this view, "The gospel, the Christian faith, and even God himself are denied if the freedom of the will is asserted as the power of man to choose his salvation for himself."[111]

Luther's view of free will becomes problematic when his "two kingdoms" paradigm alters Augustine's doctrine of "two cities" and asserts a symbiotic relationship shared by the kingdoms of God and the world. As such, believers must "function within both kingdoms, practicing one ethic in our life before God and a different ethics in our life before the world."[112] This approach finds the Christian "perfectly free Lord of all, subject to none" yet "a perfectly dutiful servant of all, subject to all."[113] This approach was necessary because Luther viewed believers as "*Simul Justus et Peccator*" (sinners and justified simultaneously).

The deficiency in Luther's ontological assessment was that it offered a role for free will in developing outward relationships with others but not in one's inward relationship with God. Luther affirmed humankind is "abundantly and sufficiently justified by faith inwardly," and the believer must (in subjugation to the Spirit) discipline the attitudes and actions so that the outer man will conform to the inner man.[114] Though Christians are free from all work, Luther spoke of the need to empty themselves, take the form of servants, and serve their neighbors. "This he should do *freely*, having regard for nothing but divine approval."[115] The obligation and initiative reside with the individual to act without compulsion for reward but approval

---

110. Wogaman, *Christian Ethics*, 118.

111. Ebeling, *Luther*, loc. 2274.

112. Wogaman and Strong, *Readings in Christian Ethics*, 122.

113. Wogaman and Strong, *Readings in Christian Ethics*, 123.

114. Wogaman and Strong, *Readings in Christian Ethics*, 125.

115. Wogaman and Strong, *Readings in Christian Ethics*, 126, italics mine. The editors are quoting Luther's treatise "Concerning Christian Liberty." The reformer also addressed the distinction between works and grace in "On the Bondage of the Will" (an essentially Augustinian account of bondage either to sin or grace), and "The Heidelberg Disputation" (1518). Regarding the latter, the first section (theses 1–12) states the demands of God's law and human powerlessness to fulfill it. The second section (theses 13–18) addresses the limits of free will.

from God alone. Luther went so far as to declare "wicked" those who would choose to rest in the sufficiency of faith and do no works.[116]

This approach denied a participative role in developing a relationship with God yet demanded participation with the Spirit in developing relationships with others. Willful actions are essential to satisfy divine requirements for the outer man but unnecessary (even contrary) for the inner man. Such an approach begs the question: since the Great Commandment (Matt 22:34–40) addresses our relation to God and others, why would God be pleased with willful obedience applied to others but not to himself?

DESIDERIUS ERASMUS'S POSITION ON FREE WILL

Pressured by many to respond, Desiderius Erasmus presented free will as something that participates with the divine rather than a means to achieve divine favor. In his view, "Grace does not work *through*, so much as *in*, free choice."[117] Erasmus viewed the human will as a source of freedom rather than bondage when cooperating with God's grace, which is the primary of the two.[118] Rather than seeing humankind as incapable of doing anything good, the Catholic humanist asserted, "There is nothing that man cannot do with the help of the grace of God and that therefore all the works of man can be good."[119]

Erasmus arguably struggled to equal Luther's exegetical prowess, but an abundance of patristic sources support his views.[120] He charged Luther and company with "immeasurably" exaggerating original sin to say that "even though justified by faith, a man cannot of himself do anything but sin. . . . and yet the same people assert that even when he has received grace, a man does nothing but sin."[121] Erasmus countered that God's grace is not a divine response to utter human depravity but "divine assistance to a humanity that has not been totally corrupted by the fall."[122]

Erasmus certainly did not attribute to human beings the ability to redeem themselves. Everything for him was grace; free will was an act of grace that enabled the individual to turn toward other graces. Not allowing

---

116. Wogaman and Strong, *Readings in Christian Ethics*, 126.
117. Wogaman and Strong, *Readings in Christian Ethics*, 136.
118. Wogaman and Strong, *Readings in Christian Ethics*, 121.
119. Wogaman and Strong, *Readings in Christian Ethics*, 134. Here, the editors are quoting from Erasmus's work, *On the Freedom of the Will*.
120. Miller, *Erasmus and Luther*, 42, 148, 191.
121. Miller, *Erasmus and Luther*, 137.
122. Wogaman, *Christian Ethics*, 135.

this eliminated any human responsibility and ethical demand.[123] To do so necessitated the attribution of human evil to God. In Erasmus's view, "It would be the highest level of sin if one were to insult God by accusing him and holding him accountable as the originator of sin."[124]

The differences espoused by Luther and Erasmus have not abated, and the topic remains relevant to holistic formation. Erasmus rightly questioned whether Luther's "freedom" could become an excuse for complacency and inaction. Furthermore, how is there reward without merit or judgment without a weighing of merits? Why does God demand unceasing prayer and labor for what he has already decreed? If God works all good and evil, then a person who cannot author good works cannot author evil works. How, then, can the person be judged in either capacity?[125] How one answers these questions determines how one lives out his Christian existence with God and others.

Though significant, the five centuries since Luther and Erasmus have seen no reconciliation between providence and participation. One reason is the difficulty reconciling Luther's theology, in which freedom and bondage, as well as concealment and revelation, are neither mutually exclusive nor alternatives but coexist. While Luther holds the two kingdoms of humankind and God in symbiotic tension, the holistic approach asserts that Jesus didn't come to influence or transform the world into a better place. He came to redeem people out of the world. Scripture identifies the kingdoms of the world to be under satanic control and in opposition to the kingdom of God.[126]

This tension is evident when Luther observed that believers still see and succumb to sin, though that sin was taken and defeated by Christ. He answered that God ignores your sin because he put it on Christ.[127] Sin now belongs to Christ, and no one can rob Christ of what rightfully belongs to him. Though somewhat beautiful, the analogy fails to meet the scriptural and practical standards espoused by Luther's theology of the cross. Does such an understanding find continuation in sin acceptable? Luther would vehemently deny such an idea and assert that the individual who has accessed God through faith must serve God and man in love. This solution seemingly embraces the work of free will, which Luther eviscerates in his theology of glory.

123. Bayer, *Martin Luther's Theology*, 188.
124. Bayer, *Martin Luther's Theology*, 195.
125. Wogaman, and Strong, *Readings in Christian Ethics*, 121, 134–36.
126. Matt 4:8; 12:26; Luke 4:5; 11:18; 2 Cor 4:4.
127. Paulson, *Lutheran Theology*, locs. 1926–30.

Conversely, Erasmus's questions on reward and punishment have yet to be satisfied. Some theologians even try to force the theology of free will into a providence that wants none of it. Such struggle is evident in the views of Reformed theologian Wayne Grudem, who states, "God causes all things to happen, [but] he does so in such a way that he somehow upholds our ability to make *willing, responsible choices*, choices that have *real and eternal results*, and for which we are *held accountable*."[128] Grudem's theologies are consistent with Luther's view that salvation is a work of grace while subsequent actions and obedience are required yet ordained. He goes so far as to say that humans are not free to make decisions apart from God's will but are free to make willing choices with real consequences.[129] How is this possible? Grudem's explanation is simple: Scripture does not explain this to us.[130]

In the view of Luther, Grudem, and others, the believer is free to choose, but God has already ordained that choice. The believer (not God) is responsible for that ordained choice. Even though God ordained the evil choice, he is neither the author of that evil nor accountable for its results.

Erasmus would likely charge these with neglecting the willful obedience required by Scripture.[131] That is not to say the believer is responsible for any success in fulfilling God's desired plan—God makes the way, reveals the way, and gives the believer everything necessary to remain in the way.[132] Erasmus would also take issue (as he did with Luther) with the view of evil in the context of providence. Grudem notes that God does indeed cause evil events and deeds but argues that God does no evil.[133] Scripture does not bear this out. The omniscient and omnipotent God uses the willful actions of evil persons to influence others and help bring about his ultimate purpose but does not originate these for his purposes.[134]

Erasmus rightly views free will as central to the sinful condition and its solution. Illicit behaviors result from the immeasurable influence that deformative life events have on the fallen nature and are exacerbated by spiritual attacks. Conversely, willful participation in sanctification purifies, overcomes, and ultimately reforms through further grace and discipline.

128. Grudem, *Systematic Theology*, 321.
129. Grudem, *Systematic Theology*, 331.
130. Grudem, *Systematic Theology*, 322.
131. Deut 28:14; 1 Sam 12:20; Prov 4:27; Matt 7:13–14; John 1:7; 3:20–21, 36; Acts 5:32; Rom 1:5; 2:4–11; 16:26; Eph 2:10; 4:2–24; 2 Thess 1:8–10; Heb 5:8–10; Jas 4:17; 1 Pet 4:16–18; 1 John 1:6; 2:3–6; 2 John 4–6, 9. These and other passages present obedience as a critical element of salvation.
132. Jer 10:23; 1 Cor 4:7, 15:10; Jas 1:17.
133. Grudem, *Systematic Theology*, 328.
134. Gen 50:20; Rom 8:28; Jas 1:17; 1 John 1:5.

The restoration of a fallen minister begins with willful repentance, leading to atonement. Christ's atoning death was a willful act. Similarly, accepting the natural (prelapsarian) human will Christ offers is an individual and willful act. Only the new creation in Christ can form Christlike character, which is necessary to fulfill God's purpose of forming us rather than forcing us, enabling the believer to *be* something rather than to *do* something. John Wesley provides a more developed and mediating approach to this holistic formation.

JOHN WESLEY'S POSITION ON FREE WILL

Wesley's doctrine of Christian Perfection, or entire sanctification, presented this progressive transformation in a delicate balance between divine sovereignty and human responsibility. In his holistic approach, Wesley argued that deliverance from willful resistance of God is possible because the indwelling Spirit cleanses the believer's heart. This purification of dedications and desires heals the crippling wounds caused by original sin. Yet cooperation with this Spirit-led transformation is necessary as the believer recovers the *imago Dei*—a lifelong endeavor Wesley would call the "glorious privilege of every Christian."[135] Such growth in holiness renders one free from evil thoughts and tempers, which allows a wholehearted love of God that guides subsequent actions and attitudes. Such a believer is "purified from pride, for Christ was lowly of heart. He is pure from self-will or desire, for Christ desired only to do the will of his Father and to finish his work. And he is pure from anger, and the common sense of the word, for Christ was meek and gentle, patient and long-suffering."[136]

Essentially, right actions and attitudes toward God and others become a natural outflow of character.[137] Such growth requires a willful commitment to spiritual disciplines. The godliness it achieves requires divine enablement in partnership with self-control;[138] the minister must place himself under God's control for continuous development and refinement.

---

135. Wesley, "Plain Account of Christian Perfection," 1035.

136. Wesley, "Sermon: Christian Perfection," 411.

137. This was Paul's cry as he likened spiritual formation to the pain of childbirth until Christ is formed in the believer (Gal 4:19).

138. Cf. John 15:4–5; Gal 5:16–25; 1 Tim 4:7.

MORE RECENT SCHOLARSHIP ON FREE WILL

More recent scholarship presents holistic perspectives that are pertinent to this topic. For example, C. S. Lewis affirms psychoanalysis is necessary for the removal of "abnormal" and "quite unnatural feelings" that result from "things that have gone wrong in [one's] subconscious."[139] He defines "bad psychological material" not as sin but as a disease that "does not need to be repented of, but to be cured."[140] Analytical measures that identify and then correct illicit tendencies provide the individual "better raw material for his acts of choice."

Yet Lewis eviscerates Sigmund Freud's assertion that removing these ingrained tendencies results in morality. In Lewis's view, overcoming one's emotional deformation does not solve the moral problem but allows the individual to address that problem rightly. "However much you improve the man's raw material, you have still got something else: the real, free choice of the man, on the material presented to him, either to put his own advantage first or to put it last. And this free choice is the only thing that morality is concerned with."[141]

The issue is how one chooses to live in relation to God, self, and others. As Lewis rightly asserts, every decision finds the individual slowly transforming into a heavenly creature that is in harmony with God, with other creatures, and with itself, or into a hellish creature that is in a state of war and hatred with God, and with its fellow-creatures, and with itself.[142] As noted throughout this book, three primary factors drive choices leading to the latter: the flesh, the world, and the devil. To overcome necessitates a break from inherent tendencies and reliance upon and submission to the Spirit's leading.

Contemporary theology further developed such understanding. The insight of Frank Macchia is notable. He views Luther's imputed righteousness as a "questionably biblical notion," a passive justice that removes all human transformation and cooperation.[143] While Luther drove the doctrine of justification from anthropology into Christology, Macchia posits the journey is incomplete until it arrives at pneumatology to facilitate synergistic participation of transformation with the Spirit. "If an emphasis on the Spirit over faith means putting Luther at some distance, so be it. We are obligated

---

139. Lewis, *Mere Christianity*, 89.
140. Lewis, *Mere Christianity*, 91.
141. Lewis, *Mere Christianity*, 90.
142. Lewis, *Mere Christianity*, 92.
143. Macchia, *Justified in the Spirit*, 47.

first to the biblical witness and not to Luther."[144] Our cooperation, which Macchia defines as "graced synergy," brings the life of the Spirit (Rom 5:18; 1 Cor 15:45) and participation in the Triune life.[145]

Contrary to Wesley's Christian Perfection, Macchia (who more closely aligns with the Finished Work theology) does not see God giving the believer power or assistance to help him mature. Instead, God gives himself. This divine self-giving was initiated at Pentecost and gave humanity its very being as God's living presence dethroned the reigning powers of sin and death to reign in their place.[146] The divine indwelling provides conveyed graces such as charismatic and spiritual fruit. These graces enable further sanctification and deification and deepen the love-based restorative relationship.

Diane Chandler expands Christian spiritual formation by defining this as "an interactive process" by which the Father fashions believers into the Son's image through the Spirit's empowerment. This process fosters development in seven primary life dimensions: Spirit, emotions, relationships, intellect, vocation, physical health and wellness, and resource stewardship. Such a definition is pertinent to ministers searching for restoration as the reformed dimensions "coalesce into an ethical lifestyle that witnesses to the unbelieving world of God's redeeming love."[147] This perpetual and grace-based formation enables the "Christian legacy," which is the restoration of *imago Dei* to form the *imago Christi* and all for *gloria Dei*.[148]

Dallas Willard also provides a strong example of holistic restoration and sustainment. His paradigm requires self-denial to replace self-adulation, which allows the effective organization of six basic dimensions of the human self around God: (1) thought, which includes images, concepts, and judgments; (2) feeling, which includes sensation and emotion; (3) choice, which includes will, decision, and character; (4) body, which includes action and interaction with the physical world; (5) social context, which includes personal and structural relations to others; and (6) soul, which is the factor that integrates the others to form one's life.[149] Willard centers this

---

144. Macchia, *Justified in the Spirit*, 54.

145. Macchia, *Justified in the Spirit*, 172.

146. Macchia, *Justified in the Spirit*, 32, 161. Cf. 1 Cor 15:44–46; 2 Cor 5:4. Macchia thus aligns with Martin Hegel in the understanding that the New Testament defines atonement not as a human abatement of God's wrath but God's "reconciliation to himself unfaithful creatures who had become his enemies."

147. Chandler, *Christian Spiritual Formation*, 19.

148. Chandler, *Christian Spiritual Formation*, 64.

149. Willard, *Renovation of the Heart*, 31–33; cf. Ps 16:7–9.

robust transformation on the acronym VIM: Vision (new birth), Intention (purposeful action), and Means (spiritual disciplines).[150]

Vision is a partaking of the divine nature resulting from new birth that makes our participation with God possible.[151] Failure to correctly grasp the vision will result in malformed or nonexistent intention, and the means implemented will be chaotic and ineffectual. Intention relates to the individual's trust in and submission to God and enables the vision's realization. This approach starkly contrasts the individualism and self-centered theologies that have allowed the emotion-driven therapeutic and results-driven managerial models of leadership to consume contemporary sanctuaries.[152] Only through such intention can one rightly identify and apply the means, the adopted practices through which God transforms character. Some means are under the individual's control, while others are God's actions toward and in the individual.[153]

The spiritual disciplines that serve as Willard's means are echoed and elaborated by numerous theologians with varying emphases. For example, Richard Foster's plan centers on a threefold typology of inward disciplines (meditation, prayer, fasting, and study), outward disciplines (simplicity, solitude, submission, and service), and corporate disciplines (confession, worship, guidance, and celebration).[154] Willard similarly divides the disciplines into two classes: those of abstinence (solitude, silence, fasting, frugality, chastity, secrecy, and sacrifice) and those of engagement (study, worship, celebration, service, prayer, fellowship, confession, and submission).[155]

Studying and meditating on Christ and Scripture are dominant disciplines. As Kenneth Boa rightly argues, spiritual life is "the life of Christ reproduced in the believer by the power of the Holy Spirit in obedient response to the Word of God."[156] Typically, receiving secondary status is the honest and consistent prayer that God will direct one's work and transform one's being. Biblical study, meditation, and prayer each demand the discipline of solitude, which Henri Nouwen describes as "the furnace of transformation."[157] Other disciplines common to formation plans include strong mentorship

---

150. Willard, *Renovation of the Heart*, 83–87. The acronym is a derivative of the Latin term *vis*, which means direction, strength, force, vigor, power, energy or virtue and sometimes means sense, import, nature or essence.

151. John 3; 2 Pet 1:4; 1 John 3:1–2.

152. Scharen, *Faith as a Way of Life*, 7.

153. Willard, *Renovation of the Heart*, 90.

154. Foster, *Celebration of Discipline*.

155. Willard et al., *Kingdom Life*, locs. 1588–771.

156. Boa, *Conformed to His Image*, 102.

157. Nouwen, *Way of the Heart*, 25–27.

and accountability, fasting, simplicity, confession, and worship. The study of saints whose lives displayed the nature of Christ receives lesser emphasis. Boa is an exception as he gives appropriate attention to the four elements of *lectio divina* or sacred reading: *Lectio* (reading), *Meditatio* (meditation), *Oratio* (prayer), and *Contemplatio* (contemplation).[158]

In summary, holistic restoration begins with the willful acceptance of the natural (prelapsarian) human will that Christ's atonement provides. This formation is lifelong and continually developed through participative submission to the Spirit's continuous sanctifying and transformative work. This ongoing process enables the minister to overcome temptations that lead to illicit behavior. Because thoughts form habits and habits form character, the righteous thoughts and habits that result from obedient submission will facilitate the Spirit's formation of righteous character. However, the minister cannot achieve (re)formation and potential restoration in isolation. An individual driven by malformed emotional wounding(s) and influenced by secular reasoning will inevitably choose a "good" that falls short of the ultimate good, which is God. Therefore, the minister must submit to and partner with God and the godly—specifically, the leaders above him and the laity around him.

---

158. Boa, *Conformed to His Image*, 96, 166. Discussion of this historic list in chapter 11 adds Martin Luther's *Tentatio* (trial and struggle).

Excursus 4

Restoration Resources

> "It takes considerable knowledge just realize the extent of your own ignorance."
> — Thomas Sowell

WHAT FOLLOWS ARE PRACTICAL tools to assess ministerial health, maximize meetings, build relational communication skills, maintain accountability, establish boundaries, and develop neuroplasticity. These items are not definitive but serve as general starting points to foster relational communication.

HOW CLOSE ARE YOU TO CRUSH DEPTH?

Numerous personal and ministerial factors contribute to any assessment of clergy health. However, the Social Readjustment Rating Scale provides a strong baseline for measuring life stress and stress-induced problems.[159] Forty-three life event questions have a Life Change Unit—numeric scores ranging from 11 to 100, determined by the trauma each event caused in a large sample of participants. By adding the LCUs an individual has experienced over the past year, the individual can identify significant stressors and better predict the degree to which stress-induced problems are likely.

---

159. Holmes and Rahe, "Social Readjustment Rating Scale."

The Holmes-Rahe Life Stress Inventory
The Social Readjustment Rating Scale

INSTRUCTIONS: Mark down the point value of each of these life events that has happened to you during the previous year. Total these associated points.

Life Event	Mean Value
1. Death of spouse	100
2. Divorce	73
3. Marital Separation from mate	65
4. Detention in jail or other institution	63
5. Death of a close family member	63
6. Major personal injury or illness	53
7. Marriage	50
8. Being fired at work	47
9. Marital reconciliation with mate	45
10. Retirement from work	45
11. Major change in the health or behavior of a family member	44
12. Pregnancy	40
13. Sexual Difficulties	39
14. Gaining a new family member (i.e.. birth, adoption, older adult moving in, etc)	39
15. Major business readjustment	39
16. Major change in financial state (i.e.. a lot worse or better off than usual)	38
17. Death of a close friend	37
18. Changing to a different line of work	36
19. Major change in the number of arguments w/spouse (i.e.. either a lot more or a lot less than usual regarding child rearing, personal habits, etc.)	35
20. Taking on a mortgage (for home, business, etc..)	31
21. Foreclosure on a mortgage or loan	30
22. Major change in responsibilities at work (i.e. promotion, demotion, etc.)	29
23. Son or daughter leaving home (marriage, attending college, joined mil.)	29
24. In-law troubles	29
25. Outstanding personal achievement	28
26. Spouse beginning or ceasing work outside the home	26
27. Beginning or ceasing formal schooling	26
28. Major change in living condition (new home, remodeling, deterioration of neighborhood or home etc.)	25
29. Revision of personal habits (dress manners, associations, quitting smoking)	24
30. Troubles with the boss	23
31. Major changes in working hours or conditions	20
32. Changes in residence	20
33. Changing to a new school	20
34. Major change in usual type and/or amount of recreation	19
35. Major change in church activity (i.e.. a lot more or less than usual)	19
36. Major change in social activities (clubs, movies,visiting, etc.)	18
37. Taking on a loan (car, tv,freezer,etc)	17
38. Major change in sleeping habits (a lot more or a lot less than usual)	16
39. Major change in number of family get-togethers ("")	15
40. Major change in eating habits (a lot more or less food intake, or very different meal hours or surroundings)	15
41. Vacation	13
42. Major holidays	12
43. Minor violations of the law (traffic tickets, jaywalking, disturbing the peace, etc)	11

Now, add up all the points you have to find your score.

150pts or less means a relatively low amount of life change and a low susceptibility to stress-induced health breakdown.

150 to 300 pts implies about a 50% chance of a major health breakdown in the next 2 years.

300pts or more raises the odds to about 80%, according to the Holmes-Rahe statistical prediction model.

Sources: Adapted from Thomas Holmes and Richard Rahe: Holmes-Rahe Social Readjustment Rating Scale, Journal of Psychosomatic Research, Vol II, 1967

MAXIMIZE YOUR MEETINGS

From mentorship to marriage reconciliation, success begins with the end in view. Indeed, goal setting will significantly enhance every facet of the restoration process. It provides structure, direction, and purpose. Focusing on tangible outcomes increases motivation and thus overcomes those overwhelming moments when success seems impossible.

Goals must be meaningful but also measurable.[160] One cannot improve what one does not manage, cannot manage what one does not measure, and cannot measure what one does not define. Therefore, treatment "should be directed toward clearly specified and mutually understood outcome goals, rather than determined by relationships or time limits."[161]

Allow the fallen minister to participate in goal setting. Doing so provides a sense of ownership that will likely increase engagement and commitment. Encourage the fallen minister to rely on support systems such as family, friends, and the church community to stay motivated and on track. Regularly review progress and adjust course as necessary.

Progress toward goals results in neurological joy; therefore, the greatest joy comes from aspiring to the greatest goal, which is God. Such understanding anchors Solomon's warning that "where there is no vision, the people perish" (Prov 29:18). The word "perish" literally means "go unrestrained" or "go their own way." It is an unfulfilling and unpleasant journey. These individuals feel like they are just spinning their wheels, making no progress. Because they have no idea where they are going, they don't know how to get there or whether they have arrived.

Habakkuk provides a better approach. The prophet experienced an oppressive burden crushing God's people (Hab 1:1–3). Soon, there came a knowing deep within. Habakkuk heard God's solution (Hab 2:1–3). In this moment, the burden became a vision or a divine goal. God instructed the prophet to write the vision. You would do well to follow his lead. Write the vision so you can stand on God's Word when the devil tries to talk you out of it. Write the vision so you can stand on God's promise when you wonder whether it will come to pass. Write the vision to know and follow God's will when the world offers an easier path. Write the vision so that one who reads it may run, which brings us to the next point.

---

160. A common approach uses the acronym SMART: Goals should be Specific, Measurable, Achievable, Relevant, and Time-bound.

161. Mosgofian and Ohlschlager, *Sexual Misconduct in Counseling and Ministry*, 243.

Keep a good record of the journey while headed toward the goal. The record of each meeting should include key markers that identify progress made and ways points for the road ahead, such as

- The date.
- The participants.
- Summary of a personal check-in (how are things personally and at home?).
- Review of goals and discussion of progress made.
- Points of encouragement and affirmation.
- Two or three things to address.
- What this person needs from me moving forward.
- What action steps are needed (identify the person responsible and due date)?
- How should I pray for this person until our next meeting?

While setting goals and maintaining records is a good start, successful mentorship centers on relational conversations, which is the next topic of discussion.

TIPS FOR RELATIONAL COMMUNICATION

The good seed of God's Word can bear much fruit, but spreading that seed is for naught if it lands on fallow ground. Therefore, the restoration team must sometimes break up hard hearts (and hard heads) so the seed can take root, resulting in spiritual growth.

Relational communication is an essential tool. Relational communication requires the mentor to see the fallen minister as a person rather than a project.[162] And not just a person but a priority. Give the individual your undivided attention to demonstrate such status. Converse with interest and enthusiasm. Remove distractions; don't doodle, tap your pen, and do not read or send text messages.

Empathetic engagement loosens hard hearts. The breaking up enables one to break through, but you must cultivate the soil further. Jesus' parable of the sower warns of stones and thorns—hard situations that halt and worldly desires that choke growth (Matt 13:1–23). A good farmer removes both to ensure an abundant harvest. Asking the right questions and listening

---

162. Pippert, *Out of the Saltshaker*, 10.

to understand rather than responding are proven ways to eliminate stones and thorns.

Ask the Right Questions

There are many benefits to asking the right questions. Requiring the fallen minister to clarify his position can help the mentor and the violator understand the individual. Specifically, his beliefs and experiences, the nature of his actions, awareness of sinfulness, and intentions regarding future behavior. What follows are probing questions that will help bring insight:

Self View

1. What is your purpose or goal in life? How has God uniquely gifted you?
2. When have you felt successful?
3. Have your spouse and children recognized your changes for the better? If so, what was their response? Have others recognized your struggles and achievements?
4. Describe your most difficult season or greatest disappointment.
5. How would you want to be remembered?

Situational Analysis

1. Can you describe the actions that led you here today?
2. What led you to make these choices?
3. How did you feel immediately after taking these actions? Did you experience any peace, anxiety, or guilt at that time?
4. Did you believe your actions might be against God's Word and will? Why or why not?
5. Looking back now, how do you feel about your actions?
6. Have your feelings about what happened changed over time?
7. What are you mad about? Glad about? Sad about?
8. What are you worried about?

9. Do you see yourself potentially repeating these actions? Why or why not?
10. What steps are you considering to align your future actions with your faith?

Spiritual Vitality

1. Tell me about your spiritual journey, starting with how you came to Christ.
2. Describe your view of and relationship with God.
3. Can you share a time when you felt close to God? When did you feel God's pleasure?
4. In what ways could your relationship with God grow?
5. In what ways does your life align with biblical truths? In what ways does it not? How can you improve on this?
6. How does your faith influence the way you are handling your current challenges?
7. What aspects of your life do you wish to see transformed through your faith?
8. What biblical stories or passages inspire you when facing difficulties?
9. Who in your life provides you with spiritual support?
10. What are your hopes for the future, and how does your faith influence these hopes?

General Exploration Questions

1. Could you help me understand/tell me more?
2. How did you draw that conclusion?
3. What do you mean by that?
4. How does that make you feel?
5. Why do you think that is?

Ignatius of Loyola's Prayer of *Examen* is a proven method for exercising spiritual disciplines and analyzing spiritual vitality.[163] In this five-

---

163. Ignatius of Loyola, *Spiritual Exercises and Selected Works*.

step approach, the individual intentionally enters God's presence with thankfulness, seeks grace to understand ways God is acting in his life, reviews the past day to contemplate specific feelings and responses, reflects on ways he was drawing closer to or drifting further from God's presence, and looks toward tomorrow with consideration of how he can more effectively collaborate with God's plan.

Emotional Vitality

1. What was life like growing up?
2. Describe your relationship with your mother and father. Did your parents love you?
3. What were some good things your parents did for you? What are some things you wished they had done or not done?
4. What were your parents' expectations of you?
5. What did you have to do to be noticed or appreciated?
6. How did your family address problems and conflicts?
7. Can you share your best and worst childhood memories?
8. What has been the biggest transition in your life?
9. What were your family's core values?
10. How were women viewed and treated by the men in your family?

Listen to Hear Rather Than Respond

Empathetic listening is a vital (and often neglected) aspect of holistic restoration. The first step is to be quiet (Jas 1:19–20). You can't listen when you're talking, and you cannot correct the problem if you do not hear the problem. As the old saying goes, we have two ears and one mouth, so we should listen twice as much as we talk. That is sound advice.

In addition, attentive listening prioritizes the person and validates his feelings. Sometimes, people just need someone to listen. As Dietrich Bonhoeffer rightly observes, "Christians, especially ministers, so often think that they must always contribute something when they are in the company of others. . . . They forget that listening can be a greater service than speaking."[164]

---

164. Bonhoeffer, *Life Together*, 97.

Paraphrasing helps to clarify his comments and demonstrates that you are carefully listening. Indeed, "Being heard is so close to being loved that for the average person, they are almost indistinguishable."[165] It is better to empathize than criticize. Do not counsel out of emotion or assumption. Put yourself in the fallen minister's shoes to better understand his choices and feelings. You do not need to acknowledge his choices as appropriate or reasonable, but be careful to avoid judgement. There will be a time to bring biblical correction, but this is a time to build trust.

BRINGING BIBLICAL CORRECTION

Attentive and empathetic listening requires honest feedback. Biblical correction helps restore and mature repentant believers while strengthening and purifying the church. However, "correction" is not a popular word in Christianity. Many Christians will accept your authority and guidance if they agree with what you say or believe your words to be in their best interest. Many will reject that authority and guidance once you correct their wrongdoing. Still, we have an obligation to provide biblical correction.[166]

The apostle Paul provides a robust biblical model for biblical correction in his correspondence with the church in Colosse (Col 1:3–12). Paul does not rush to address the issue but first prays. We would do well to follow his example. Pray for them. Pray for you. Pray that God would give wisdom and revelation. Pray that the Spirit would open ears to hear and hearts to receive.

When the time comes to address the matter, Paul doesn't enter with guns blazing. A brother offended is harder to win than a strong city (Prov 18:19). He opens by emphasizing the positive. The apostle notes how God's Word had brought them grace and caused them to bear fruit. He commended them for their excellent start and reminded them of their influence on others.

Having covered the matter in prayer and love, Paul brings the word of correction. He does so with compassion and grace, and so must we.[167] Harsh correction will not be well received, while soft correction will not be respected. The way you bring correction can speak far louder than the words of correction themselves.

What is our response if correction is not received? We follow Jesus' first instruction to the church, which addresses how we confront sin (Matt

165. Augsburger, *Caring Enough to Hear and Be Heard*, 12.
166. Gal 6:1–2; Heb 12:6–8; 13:17; 2 Tim 3:16–17.
167. Gal 6:1; 2 Tim 2:23–26; Jude 1:22–23.

18:15–17). Paul followed this guidance on more than one occasion.[168] He understood that love covers a multitude of sins, but it does not tolerate sin.[169]

ACCOUNTABILITY TALKING POINTS

Some sexual violators and addicts are master manipulators. Others find open dialogue to be embarrassing or painful. This list of questions can help initiate discussion for accountability purposes.

1. How did you engage God's Word since our last meeting?
2. How often and for what have you prayed since our last meeting?
3. What is God speaking into your life in your private times of prayer and reading?
4. In what ways has your flesh dominated your actions and reactions?
5. Did you give into temptation since our last meeting?
6. What steps are you taking to avoid temptation?
7. Have you exposed your mind to sexually inappropriate things?
8. Have you met your obligations to the individuals under your charge?
9. Have you been above reproach with your finances and your personal commitments?
10. Have you lied in any of your previous answers?

CODE OF ETHICS

Those restored to any ministerial function during or after this cumulative process, especially those who supervise or counsel others, should be required to review and sign a code of ethics that strictly prohibits sexual contact, communications, or innuendos with anyone other than the minister's spouse. Protecting those who will receive pastoral counsel from a restored minister is prioritized. While a code of ethics can be far-reaching, these four points are of critical concern:

---

168. Notably, Paul cast an unrepentant sexual sinner from the church in Corinth (1 Cor 5:1–5) and put two unrepentant sinning leaders out of the Ephesian church (1 Tim 1:20).

169. 1 Pet 4:8; cf. Rom 16:17–18; 1 Cor 15:33–34.

1. **The priority of personal relationships.** The biblical order identifies relationship with God as ultimate (Mark 12:30; cf. Matt 10:37), with family relations as second and a qualifier for ministry, which comes third (1 Tim 3:4–5, 5:8). The qualifying traits of a blameless reputation, marital faithfulness, and wholesome family life must be current and enduring (1 Tim 3:1–13; Titus 1:6–9). Therefore, the code should include pragmatic pledges for honesty in all communication, fidelity, and dedicated time for building and fostering familial relationships. In addition, the Trinity offers four characteristics on which our personal relationships are based: (1) full equality, (2) glad submission, (3) joyful intimacy, and (4) mutual deference.[170] The pledges could include measurable goals for formation in each category.

2. **Counseling and contact with persons of the opposite gender.** As noted above, the "pastor-congregant relationship is most susceptible to abuse when it arises in a counseling situation."[171] The intimacy of spiritual counsel avails itself to emotional transference. Therefore, another person (preferably another female) should be in proximity during counsel and conversation. Physical contact is prohibited. Reject any flirtatious talk or behavior by the counselee and report these behaviors to your mentor. It is necessary to address and eliminate these temptations before lust conceives, births sin, and brings death (Jas 1:15).

3. **Treatment of church staff and members.** As noted above, unethical ministers often surround themselves with sycophants and acolytes who fail to bring accountability and even intentionally or unintentionally facilitate illicit behaviors. Such adverse influence grows into toxic church cultures that enable sins to flourish, and church leaders often protect their reputations at the expense of truth and correction. Therefore, the restored minister should dedicate himself to the affirmation, recognition, and training of new church staff and members. Open dialogue and sharing concerns and ideas should be encouraged and facilitated, as this fosters growth, trust, and biblical unity.[172]

4. **Integrity in personal and ministerial finances.** Though this may seem unrelated to a sexual moral failure, many who participate in illicit behaviors struggle with poly-addiction. The inherent tendency is to replace the behavior or substance that is overcome with another

---

170. Seamands, *Ministry in the Image of God*, 35.
171. Grenz and Bell, *Betrayal of Trust*, 45.
172. Cf. Ps 133; Acts 4:32–33.

behavior or substance to ease the pain and anxiety. Therefore, it is beneficial to establish financial accountability teams to count/verify monies, oversee disbursements, and the like. The code of ethics can establish guidelines to ensure the minister is not guilty of inappropriate stewardship (or the appearance thereof). These can include audits, rules to govern spending, and presenting an annual report to parishioners. Such mechanisms prevent wrongful actions and accusations, fostering transparency and trust.

WAYS TO AID NEUROPLASTICITY

Several exercises and approaches can promote neuroplasticity. These include:

1. Eye Movement and Desensitization and Reprocessing (EMDR) uses eye movements and sound to tap unprocessed and painful memories. Side-to-side eye movement and memory tasks deactivate the amygdala, reducing the emotional responses such as "fight or flight" that ignite when trauma-related memories are evoked. The procedure further enables improved communication between the amygdala and the hippocampus (the center for learning and memory), which allows the individual and mental health professional to reprocess painful memories, reduce related stress and anxiety, and recode the emotional content.

2. Reflective journaling can help participants to process their experiences, thoughts, and emotions. This practice can enhance self-awareness and emotional regulation, contributing to neural adaptations in brain areas involved in self-reflection and emotional intelligence.

3. Biblical meditation, as described in chapter 11, affects brain areas related to attention, self-regulation, and stress reduction.

4. Acquiring new skills such as a language, creative hobby, or professional ability forms and strengthens neural connections.

5. Simulation exercises can help enhance the participant's cognitive flexibility. Similarly, interpersonal group discussions allow one to reflect and redirect perceptions as appropriate. These interactions provide reasonable and empathetic perspectives and stimulate neural pathways involved in social cognition and emotional regulation.

RESTORATION RESOURCES

6. Engaging in spiritual practices can reinforce neural pathways associated with spiritual experiences and values, enhancing the integration of spirituality into personal identity and ministerial practice.

7. A healthy lifestyle enhances cognitive functions and mental health, supporting the ongoing process of neuroplasticity and the development of more resilient and adaptive brain networks. Physical exercise increases the heart rate, thus delivering more oxygen, aiding brain cell growth. Diets rich in antioxidants, good fats, vitamins, and minerals also provide the energy and building blocks necessary for brain health. Healthy sleep patterns give the brain time to recover and rebuild, improve problem-solving skills, and enhance memory.

Glossary

Accountability: Personal acceptance of responsibility for one's behavior, which is necessarily aided and validated by trusted believers and spiritual leaders who provide support, counsel, and motivation.

Addiction: The compulsion to use a substance or activity to cope with everyday life.

Adultery: Consensual sexual activity—be it physical, verbal, or virtual—outside of heterosexual marriage.

Attachment: The emotional bond that forms between infant and caregiver. The exchange of comfort and care is the means by which the infant has primary needs met and the infant brain learns to organize and regulate itself.

Attachment theory: The assertion that human behavior is attributable to the quality (positive or negative) of early human attachments with primary caregivers, especially parents. These attachments, if unaltered, will transfer to adult relationships.

Character: The unity and continuity of self; the sum of one's consistent habits and patterns of thinking and acting over time.

Christian formation: A Spirit-led process that conforms an individual's spiritual, emotional, and physical conditions into the *imago Dei* (Lat. image of God) that rightly defines and develops Christlike character.

Coding: Verbal manipulation through key words or conveyance of unspoken rules through nonverbal body language.

Cognition: The mental process of acquiring knowledge and understanding through thought, experience, and the senses. Emotional, social, and spiritual factors that influence individual perception, thought, and action form cognition.

Congruence: The state in which a person's ideal self and actual experience are consistent or very similar. This requires accurate self-assessment, acceptance of responsibility for decisions made, and commitment to ethical behavior.

Constructionism: The assertion that a culture or organization is the product of the individuals who comprise it and is in a constant state of revision.

Cultural mandate: The divine command that those created in God's image are to exercise dominion over the creation, subdue it, and develop its latent potential (Gen 1:28).

Cyber-sex: Sexual relationships between consenting adults on the Internet.

Denial: A defense mechanism that ignores the reality of a situation or blocks awareness of external events to avoid anxiety; a refusal to acknowledge or experience.

Displacement: A defense mechanism that redirects an emotional reaction from the rightful recipient onto another person or object, typically a less-threatening subject.

Dissociation: A defense mechanism in which a person disconnects from their thoughts, feelings, memories, behaviors, or sense of identity as protection from emotional pain.

Emotional abuse: A process that includes verbal or nonverbal actions that systematically diminish and destroy the inner self and health of another.

Emotional formation: The development of godly character in one's capacity to identify, understand, express, and reflect upon one's learned relational behaviors, formative experiences, inherited worldview, neural/cognitive development, and social/cultural context as these constitute individual feelings, desires, and passions that must be expressed in healthy and God-honoring ways.

GLOSSARY

Empathy: The ability to enter the experience of others and emotionally understand what that individual feels, and thus, see the world through their point of view and pain.

Enmeshment: The lack of self-other differentiation resulting from inappropriate intrusion on each other's thoughts, feelings and communications. This violation of personal boundaries may severely hamper development of full personhood.

Epistemology: The study of knowledge, and specifically, what distinguishes justified belief from opinion. Christian epistemology is through divine revelation, which is eschatological, with spirituality and ecclesiology providing the method.

Escapism: A defense mechanism where a person ignores, avoids, or evades the real world in an attempt to find desired security and tranquility in a fantasy world.

Exhibitionism: Sexual gratification through exposure of one's genitals to non-consenting and unsuspecting strangers or being observed by others during sexual activity.

Fetishism: Erotic arousal or attachment to inanimate objects or asexual parts of the human body.

Forbearance: The willful restraint of emotionally negative expressions of hurt or anger.

Forgiveness: A decision to not allow hurt and pain to control or dominate one's life. Forgiveness includes surrendering one's right to retribution and appropriately revising one's thoughts and feelings to honor the inherent worth of those who caused hurt.

Fornication: Consensual sexual activity—be it physical, verbal, or virtual—between unmarried individuals.

Guilt: A self-conscious negative evaluation of one's self as a result of something done that negatively affects another.

GLOSSARY

The pronoun "he": Refers to the violating minister, although this masculine usage neither asserts that males alone can be pastors, nor does it deny that some female clergy are guilty of sexual misconduct.

Holistic formation: A Spirit-led process that conforms an individual's spiritual, emotional, and physical conditions into the *imago Dei* (image of God) that rightly defines and develops Christlike character.

Homeostasis: The regulation of physiological processes by which the aggregate components bring strength and balance to the part of the system that is out of balance.

Koinonia: The Greek word for fellowship, which refers to an intensely close and meaningful relationship shared by fellow believers. This relationship demonstrates the divine love and unity by which it is enabled.

Lovesickness: An affliction that can produce negative feelings when deeply in love, during the absence of a loved one, or when love is unrequited.

Mandatory reporter: One having a legal responsibility to report suspected abuse, neglect, and exploitation.

Masochism: Sexual gratification gained from one's own pain or humiliation.

Moral failure: Unethical behavior involving sexual sins.

Neuroplasticity: The brain's ability to modify, change, and adapt the structure and function of neural networks.

Objectivism: The assertion that a culture or organization has a reality separate from the individuals who comprise it, and this exerts pressures and expectations on individuals who thus conform to the requirements.

Ontology: The study of existence, being, becoming, and reality. Christian ontology asserts that God has given the creation (the reality), and humans are given the gifts of creativity, agency, and relationality.

GLOSSARY

Orthodoxy: The right or authorized theology and doctrine used to establish (and sometimes informed by) orthopathy and orthopraxy within a church or denomination.

Orthopathy: The right beliefs and affections toward and resulting from orthodoxy and orthopraxy within a church or denomination.

Orthopraxy: The right action and correct conduct (ethical and liturgical) resulting from orthodoxy and orthopathy within a church or denomination.

Paraphilia: Sexual deviations including pedophilia, voyeurism, fetishism, exhibitionism, masochism, sadism, and transvestism.

Pedophilia: A sexual attraction to and sexual behavior toward prepubescent children.

Perichoresis: The Greek word refering to the eternal movement of reciprocal giving and receiving, the "divine dance" in which the three persons of the triune God move and participate in one fluid motion.

Physical abuse: Acts of aggression intended to cause pain or injury to another or acts of negligence that result in bodily injury.

Pornography: Printed or visual illicit material containing explicit descriptions or displays of sexual organs or activities intended to stimulate sexual excitement.

Post-truth: The tendency to accept as truth a position based on preference or presupposition. Objective facts are less influential than emotion in shaping such belief.

Projection: A defense mechanism in which one attributes undesirable traits they find unacceptable in themselves onto another person, group, or object.

(Re)formation: The reconstitution of something that once existed but has been defiled or destroyed.

GLOSSARY

Regression: A defense mechanism in which an individual retreats to an earlier developmental stage to cope with stressful or anxiety-provoking relationships or situations.

Repression: The unconscious blocking of disturbing, unpleasant, or threatening emotions, memories, and thoughts from becoming conscious.

Restoration: A return to holiness and integrity after moral failure and marked by genuine personal repentance, the reciprocation of communal love, and oneness with God, which hopefully culminates in the total return to ministerial position and function.

Sadism: Sexual gratification gained by harming or humiliating one's partner.

Salvation: A juridical pardon by grace through faith that allows the believer to enter a gradual therapeutic and participative process in God's presence and through God's power by which the disease of sin is healed and likeness of God is restored.

Sanctification: A restorative repositioning to holiness that demands a cleansing from and empowered avoidance of whatever displeases God, whether that is internal or external to the believer, and enables the lifelong healing of sin-distorted affections.

Sexual abuse: Verbal, visual, or physical sexual activity performed without consent. It is an exploitation of the victim to satisfy an abuser's needs.

Sexual sin: The imagined or actual participation in sexual behaviors prohibited by Scripture, including fornication (sexual activity between unmarried individuals), adultery (sexual activity that violates the marriage covenant), and homosexuality (sexual activity between same-sex individuals).

Shame: A self-critical perception of being uniquely and hopelessly less than other human beings. Whereas guilt declares "I have done something bad," shame declares "I am a bad person."

Spiritual abuse: The coercive and controlling mistreatment by a religious authority of a person who is in need of spiritual support, guidance, or empowerment. This abuse often uses domination and manipulation to keep the person subjected to a weaker status or to affirm the abuser's (seemingly) stronger status.

Spiritual formation: Maturation in holiness through the Spirit-led sanctification process based upon Scripture and prayer.

Theoretical integration: The construction, synthesization, or correlatation of Christian thought with psychological theory.

Transcendental idealism: Immanuel Kant's view that the individual never perceives the world as it truly is (the *noumenal reality*) but perceives the world as it appears (the *phenomenal world*) through sensory input informed by *a priori* rationalism and empiricism.

Triangling: The delivery of a message through a third person to avoid direct deliverance.

Triangulation: The manipulative act (often by person with strong narcissistic traits) of bringing a third person into a relationship in order to remain in control.

Voyeurism: Sexual gratification gained by observing an unsuspecting person who is disrobing, naked, or engaged in a sexual activity.

Worldview: The beliefs and practices that shape an individual's priorities, relationships (to God and others), assess the meaning of events, and justify our actions.

Zeitgeist: The spirit of a time and culture.

Bibliography

à Kempis, Thomas. *The Imitation of Christ: Translated from the Latin into Modern English*. Milwaukee: Brucefc, 1940.

Abasili, Alexander Izuchukwu. "Was It Rape? The David and Bathsheba Pericope Re-Examined." *Vetus Testamentum* 61.1 (2011) 1–15.

Alden, Robert L. *Job*. The New American Commentary. Nashville: Broadman & Holman, 1993.

Alexander, Jonathan. "Telling the Truth about Sex: Rhetorical Responsiveness in the Case of Ted Haggard." *Journal of Advanced Composition* 34.1/2 (2014) 105–31.

Allender, Dan, and Tremper Longman III. *The Cry of the Soul*. Dallas: Word, 1994.

Alston, William. "The Indwelling of the Holy Spirit." In *Divine Nature and Human Language*, 223–52. Ithaca, NY: Cornell University, 1989.

Ambrose. "Letter 35." In *Ancient Christian Commentary on Scripture: Old Testament IV—Joshua, Judges, Ruth, 1–2 Samuel*, edited by J. R. Franke, 156–58. Downers Grove, IL: InterVarsity, 2005.

———. *De Officiis*. Translated by Ivor J. Davidson. Oxford, England: Oxford University Press, 2002.

Anderson, Allan. *Spreading Fires: The Missionary Nature of Early Pentecostalism*. Maryknoll, NY: Orbis, 2007.

Anderson, Neil T. *The Steps to Freedom in Christ: A Biblical Guide to Help You Resolve Personal and Spiritual Conflicts and Become a Fruitful Disciple of Jesus*. Grand Rapids: Baker, 2017.

Anonymous. *The Gospel of Thomas, with The Acts of Thomas, and The Book of Thomas the Contender*. Durham, UK: Aziloth, 2013. Kindle edition.

Apostles, The Twelve. *The Didache*. Oxford, England: Acheron, 2012.

Aquinas, Thomas. *Summa Theologiae* (Complete & Unabridged). Claremont, CA: Coyote Canyon, 2010.

Aristotle. *Nicomachean Ethics*, Bk II.1. In *Basic Works of Aristotle*, edited by Richard McKeon. New York: Random House, 1941.

Arizona Christian University. "AWVI 2020 Results – Release #11: Churches and Worldview." Oct 6, 2020. https://www.arizonachristian.edu/wp-content/uploads/2020/10/CRC_AWVI2020_Release11_Digital_04_20201006.pdf.

Armstrong, John H. *Can Fallen Pastors Be Restored? The Church's Response to Sexual Misconduct*. Chicago: Moody, 1995.

Arnold, Bill T. *1 & 2 Samuel*. The NIV Application Commentary. Grand Rapids: Zondervan, 2003.

Arterburn, Stephen. *100 Days of Peace: Daily Devotional*. Carol Stream, IL: Tyndale House, 2019.

Athanasius. *On the Incarnation*. Translated by Penelope Lawson. Lake Forest, CA: Blue Letter Bible, 2012.

———. *The Life of Antony*. Edited by Philip Schaff. The Complete Ante-Nicene, Nicene, and Post-Nicene Church Fathers Collection. London: Catholic Way, 2014.

Augsburger, David W. *Caring Enough to Hear and Be Heard: How to Hear and How to Be Heard in Equal Communication*. Scottdale, PA: Herald, 1982.

Augustine. *Christian Instruction, 3.21.31*. In *Ancient Christian Commentary on Scripture: Old Testament V—1-2 Kings, 1-2 Chronicles, Ezra, Nehemiah, Esther*, edited by Marco Conti and Gianluca. Downers Grove, IL: InterVarsity, 2008.

———. *Confessions*. Edited by Philip Schaff. The Complete Works of St. Augustine. Omaha: Patristic, 2011.

———. "Epistle to the Galatians, Letter 56." In *Ancient Christian Commentary on Scripture: New Testament VIII—Galatians, Ephesians, Philippians*, edited by Mark J. Edwards, 93. Downers Grove, IL: InterVarsity, 1999.

———. *On Christian Doctrine*. Edited by Philip Schaff. The Complete Works of St. Augustine. Omaha: Patristic, 2011.

———. *The Confessions of St. Augustine*. Translated by Edward B. Pusey. New York: Collier, 1909.

———. *The Trinity*. New York: New City Press, 2015.

Bacon, Lance M. "A Pentecostal Paradigm That Reconciles: The Theology of the Cross and Christian Perfection." In *The Holy Spirit and the Reformation Legacy*, edited by Mark J. Cartledge and Mark A. Jumper, 85–102. Eugene, OR: Pickwick, 2020.

———. *The Scariest Word in the Bible: Might You Be Wrong about Being Right with God?* Eugene, OR: Wipf & Stock, 2018.

Bailey, R. C. *David in Love and War: The Pursuit of Power in 2 Samuel 10–12*. Sheffield, UK: JSOT, 1990.

Bailey, Sarah Pulliam. "Mark Driscoll Removed from the Acts 29 Church Planting Network He Helped Found." *Christian Century*, Aug 11, 2014. https://www.christiancentury.org/article/2014-08/mark-driscoll-removed-acts-29-church-planting-network-he-helped-found

Baker, Warren, and Eugene E. Carpenter. *The Complete Word Study Dictionary: Old Testament*. Chattanooga, TN: AMG, 2003.

Balswick, Jack, and John W. Thoburn. "How Ministers Deal with Sexual Temptation." *Pastoral Psychology* 280 (1991) 277–86.

Balz, Horst, and Gerhard Schneider, eds. *Exegetical Dictionary of the New Testament: Vol. 1-3*. Grand Rapids: Eerdmans, 1990.

Barkley, Scott. "Southern Baptist Leaders Respond to Second Leaked Letter from Former ERLC President." *Baptist Press*, Jun 7, 2021. https://www.baptistpress.com/resource-library/news/southern-baptist-leaders-respond-to-second-leaked-letter-from-former-erlc-president/.

Barna Group. "America's Most (and Least) Bible-Minded Cities." Jun 22, 2017. https://www.barna.com/research/2017-bible-minded-cities/.

———. "Barna Survey Examines Changes in Worldview Among Christians over the Past 13 Years." Mar 9, 2009. https://www.barna.com/research/barna-survey-examines-changes-in-worldview-among-christians-over-the-past-13-years/.

———. "Competing Worldviews Influence Today's Christians." May 9, 2017. https://www.barna.com/research/competing-worldviews-influence-todays-christians/

———. "For Pastors Who Want to Quit, Self-Care & Soul-Care Slip." Jun 15, 2022. https://www.barna.com/research/spiritual-formation-back-seat/.

———. *Porn Phenomenon: The Impact of Pornography in the Digital Age*. Carol Stream, IL: Tyndale House, 2016.

———. "38% of U.S. Pastors Have Thought about Quitting Full-Time Ministry in the Past Year." Nov 16, 2021. https://www.barna.com/research/pastors-well-being/.

Barna, George, and David Kinnamon, eds. *The State of Pastors*. Carol Stream, IL: Tyndale House, 2017.

Barrett, Matthew. *God's Word Alone: The Authority of Scripture*. Grand Rapids: Zondervan, 2016.

Barron, Lynsey M., and William P. Eiselstein. "Report of Independent Investigation into Sexual Misconduct of Ravi Zacharias." Feb 9, 2021. https://www.courthousenews.com/wp-content/uploads/2021/02/zacharias-report.pdf.

Barth, Karl. *Church Dogmatics*. Translated by Geoffrey W. Bromiley and Thomas F. Torrance. Edinburgh, UK: T&T Clark, 1956.

Barton, Bruce B., et al. "Galatians." In *Life Application Bible Commentary*, edited by Philip Comfort. Wheaton, IL: Tyndale House, 1994.

Bayer, Oswald. *Martin Luther's Theology: A Contemporary Interpretation*. Grand Rapids: Eerdmans, 2008.

Beale, G. K. *We Become What We Worship: A Biblical Theology of Idolatry*. Downers Grove, IL: IVP Academic, 2008.

Bekker, Cornelius J. "Scriptural Formation: The Power of the Biblical Story." In *The Holy Spirit and Christian Formation: Multidisciplinary Perspectives*, edited by Diane J. Chandler, 91–106. Cham, Switzerland: Palgrave MacMillan, 2016.

Bell, E. N. "Notice About Parham." *Word and Witness* 8.8 (Oct 20, 1912) 3.

Benner, David G. *Psychotherapy and the Spiritual Quest*. Grand Rapids: Baker Academic, 1988.

———. *Strategic Pastoral Counseling: A Short-Term Structured Model*. Grand Rapids: Baker Academic, 2003.

Bergen, Robert D. *1, 2 Samuel*. The New American Commentary. Nashville: Broadman & Holman, 1996.

Bernard of Clairvaux. *St. Bernard of Clairvaux: On the Love of God & Selected Writings*, translated by Marianne Caroline and Coventry Patmore. re:SOURCE Digital Publishing, 2017. Kindle Edition.

Bissell, David Lawrence. "Restoring Fallen Pastors: A Study on Restoring and Reinstating Clergy Who Have Been Involved in Sexual Misconduct." PhD diss., Andrews University, 2005.

Black, Robert E. and Ronald McClung. *1 & 2 Timothy, Titus, Philemon: A Commentary for Bible Students*. Wesleyan Bible Commentary Series. Indianapolis: Wesleyan Publishing House, 2004.

Blair, Leonardo. "Chris Conlee Resigns from Highpoint Church after Andy Savage Scandal; Sex Abuse Victim Rejoices." *Christian Post*, Jul 12, 2018. https://www.christianpost.com/news/chris-conlee-resigns-from-highpoint-church-after-andy-savage-scandal-sex-abuse-victim-rejoices.html.

———. "Megachurch Pastor Resigns over Allegations of Sex with 18-Year-Old Members of Youth Group 17 Years Ago." *Christian Post*, Nov 29, 2019. https://www.christianpost.com/news/megachurch-pastor-resigns-over-allegations-of-sex-with-18-year-old-members-youth-group.html.

———. "Pastor Andy Savage Launches New Church as Beth Moore Offers Comfort to His Sexual Assault Victim." *Christian Post*, Oct 28, 2019. https://www.christianpost.com/news/pastor-andy-savage-launches-new-church-as-beth-moore-offers-comfort-to-his-sexual-assault-victim.html.

———. "Televangelist Perry Stone Slams Secular Media after Report Alleges Sexual Misconduct." *Christian Post*, Dec 27, 2021. https://www.christianpost.com/news/perry-stone-slams-secular-media-after-hes-accused-of-misconduct.html.

———. "Tullian Tchividjian's Uncle, Brother, GRACE Board Call Sex Scandal 'Gross Misuse of Power.'" *Christian Post*, Dec 8, 2016. https://www.christianpost.com/news/tullian-tchividjians-uncle-brother-grace-board-call-sex-scandal-gross-misuse-of-power.html.

Blocher, Henri A. G. "God and the Scripture Writers: The Question of Double Authorship." In *The Enduring Authority of the Christian Scriptures*, edited by D.A. Carson, 497–541. Grand Rapids: Eerdmans, 2016.

Blomberg, Craig L. *1 Corinthians*. The NIV Application Commentary. Grand Rapids: Zondervan, 1994.

Boa, Kenneth. *Conformed to His Image: Biblical and Practical Approaches to Spiritual Formation*. Grand Rapids: Zondervan, 2001.

Boda, Mark J. *Haggai, Zechariah*. The NIV Application Commentary. Grand Rapids: Zondervan, 2004.

Bonhoeffer, Dietrich. *The Cost of Discipleship*. New York: Touchstone, 1959.

———. *Ethics*. New York: Touchstone, 1995.

———. *Life Together: The Classic Exploration of Christian Community*. San Francisco: Harper Collins, 1954.

Boorstein, Michelle. "Evangelist Ravi Zacharias Engaged in Sexual Misconduct, Report Says." *Washington Post*, Feb 11, 2021. https://www.washingtonpost.com/religion/2021/02/11/ravi-zacharias-report-rape-misconduct-thompson/.

———, et al. "Top U.S. Catholic Church Official Resigns After Cellphone Data Used to Track Him on Grindr and to Gay Bars." *Washington Post*, Jul 21, 2021. https://www.washingtonpost.com/religion/2021/07/20/bishop-misconduct-resign-burrill/.

Bowlby, John. *Attachment and Loss: Vol. 3—Loss: Sadness and Depression*. New York: Basic, 1980.

Boyce, Kelly Breen, and Nanci Fisher Erkert. "Spiritual and Relational Formation: How Contemplative Prayer and Psychodynamic Therapy Enhance Loving God and Others." In *The Holy Spirit and Christian Formation: Multidisciplinary Perspectives*, edited by Diane J. Chandler, 19–32. Cham, Switzerland: Palgrave MacMillan, 2016.

Bradshaw, John. *Healing the Shame That Binds You*. Deerfield Beach, FL: Health Communications, 1988.

Briggs, J. R. *Fail: Finding Hope and Grace in the Midst of Ministry Failure*. Downers Grove, IL: InterVarsity, 2014.

Briggs, Megan. "Sexting, Spiritual Abuse, Rape: Devastating Full Report on Ravi Zacharias Released." Christian Leaders, Feb 11, 2021. https://churchleaders.com/news/390043-sexting-spiritual-abuse-rape-devastating-full-report-on-ravi-zacharias-released.html.

Brown, Raymond. *The Message of Numbers: Journey to the Promised Land*. The Bible Speaks Today. Nottingham, UK: InterVarsity, 2002.

BIBLIOGRAPHY

Browning, Don S., et al. *From Culture Wars to Common Ground: Religion and the American Family Debate.* Louisville: Westminster John Knox, 2000.

Brownson, James V. *Bible, Gender, Sexuality: Reframing the Church's Debate on Same-Sex Relationships.* Grand Rapids: Eerdmans, 2013.

Brueggemann, Walter. *First and Second Samuel.* Interpretation: A Bible Commentary for Teaching and Preaching. Louisville: Westminster John Knox, 1990.

Bryce, Heather. "After the Affair: A Wife's Story." *Leadership* 9 (Winter 1988) 58–65.

Buckley, Madeline. "Harvest Bible Chapel Elders Issue 'Public Rebuke' of Fired Pastor James MacDonald in Post that Accuses Him of Bullying and Extravagant Spending." *Chicago Tribune*, Nov 8, 2019. https://www.chicagotribune.com/news/breaking/ct-harvest-bible-chapel-james-macdonald-update-20191108-uob3qjdwbjbvjdo266jy5s756m-story.html.

Bultmann, Rudolf. *Theology of the New Testament 1.* Translated by Kendrick Grobel. London: SCM, 1952.

Byrne, Brendan. "Sinning against One's Own Body: Paul's Understanding of the Sexual Relationship in 1 Corinthians 6:18." *Catholic Biblical Quarterly* 45.4 (Oct 1983) 608–16.

Callahan, Leslie Dawn. "Fleshly Manifestations: Charles Fox Parham's Quest for the Sanctified Body." PhD diss., Princeton University, 2002.

Calvin, John. *Institutes of the Christian Religion*, edited by John T. McNeill. Translated by Ford Lewis Battles. Philadelphia, PA: Westminster, 1960.

Campbell, J. G. "Pentecostal Papers," *Gospel of the Kingdom* 3.1 (April 1910) 2.

Carnes, Patrick. *Don't Call It Love: Recovery from Sexual Addiction.* New York: Bantam, 1992.

———. *Out of the Shadows: Understanding Sexual Addiction.* Center City, MN: Hazelden, 2001.

Cartledge, Mark J. *Practical Theology: Charismatic and Empirical Perspectives.* Eugene, OR: Wipf and Stock, 2003.

———. *The Mediation of the Spirit: Interventions in Practical Theology.* Grand Rapids: Eerdmans, 2015.

Cashwell, G. B. "Letter From Bro. Cashwell," *Bridegroom's Messenger* 2.23 (Oct 1, 1908) 4.

Cassian, John. *The Conferences of Desert Fathers.* Translated by Edgar C. S. Gibson. Aeterna, 2015.

Chandler, Diane J. *Christian Spiritual Formation: An Integrated Approach for Personal and Relational Wholeness.* Downers Grove, IL: InterVarsity Academic, 2014.

———. "The Perfect Storm of Leaders' Unethical Behavior: A Conceptual Framework." *International Journal of Leadership Studies* 5.1 (Jan 2009) 69–93.

Chapman, Gary. *The 5 Love Languages: The Secret to Love that Lasts.* Chicago: Northfield, 2015.

Chrysostom, John. "Homilies of St. John Chrysostom, Archbishop of Constantinople on the Gospel according to St. Matthew." In *Saint Chrysostom: Homilies on the Gospel of Saint Matthew (Vol. 10)*, edited by Philip Schaff, 16–923. Translated by George Prevost and M. B. Riddle. New York: Christian Literature Company, 1888.

Church of God Evangel (uncredited). "The Keeping of Records." *Church of God Evangel*, 1.7 (Jun 1, 1910) 1–2.

Ciampa, Roy E. and Brian S. Rosner. *The First Letter to the Corinthians.* Pillar New Testament Commentary. Grand Rapids: Eerdmans, 2010.

BIBLIOGRAPHY

Clapper, Gregory S. "Orthokardia: John Wesley's Grammar of the Holy Spirit." In *The Spirit, the Affections, and the Christian Tradition*, edited by Dale M. Coulter and Amos Yong, 259–78. Notre Dame, IN: University of Notre Dame Press, 2016.

———. *The Renewal of the Heart Is the Mission of the Church: Wesley's Heart Religion in the Twenty-First Century*. Eugene, OR: Cascade, 2009. Kindle edition.

Clement of Alexandria. *Stromateis, Book 3*. In *Stromateis, Books 1-3*, translated by John Ferguson. Washington, D.C.: Catholic University of America, 1992.

Clinton, Tim and Mark Laaser. *The Quick Reference Guide to Sexuality and Relationship Counseling*. Grand Rapids: Baker, 2010.

Coe, John H., and Todd W. Hall. "A Transformational Psychology View." In *Psychology and Christianity: Five Views*, edited by Eric L. Johnson, 199–226. Downers Grove, IL: IVP Academic, 2010.

Comfort, Philip, and Walter A. Elwell. *The Complete Book of Who's Who in the Bible*. Carol Stream, IL: Tyndale House, 2005.

Cooper-White, Pamela. "Soul Stealing: Power and Relations in Pastoral Sexual Abuse." *Christian Century* 108 (Feb 20, 1991) 196–99.

Coulter, Dale. "Introduction." In *The Spirit, the Affections, and the Christian Tradition*, edited by Dale M. Coulter and Amos Yong, 1–28. Notre Dame, IN: University of Notre Dame Press, 2016.

Coutts, Jon. *A Shared Mercy: Karl Barth on Forgiveness and the Church*. Downers Grove, IL: IVP Academic, 2016.

Crabb, Larry. *Connecting: Healing for Ourselves and Our Relationships—A Radical New Vision*. Nashville: Word, 1997.

Cullum, Pat. "'Give Me Chastity': Masculinity and Attitudes to Chastity and Celibacy in the Middle Ages." *Gender & History*, 25.3 (Nov 2013) 621–36.

Cyprian. *Epistle 5*. Edited by Philip Schaff. The Complete Ante-Nicene, Nicene, and Post-Nicene Church Fathers Collection. London: Catholic Way, 2014.

Dalberg-Acton, John Emerich Edward. "Letter to Mandell Creighton, April 5, 1887." In *Essays on Freedom and Power*, 358–67. Glencoe, IL: Free Press, 1949.

Dart, John. "Swaggart Steps Down after Public Confession: Evangelist Admits Moral 'Sin,' Leaves for Indefinite Period." *Los Angeles Times*, Feb 22, 1988. https://www.latimes.com/archives/la-xpm-1988-02-22-mn-29975-story.html.

Davidson, Richard M. "Did David Rape Bathsheba? A Case Study in Narrative Theology." *Journal of Adventist Theological Society* 17 (2006) 81–95.

Dawkins, Richard. *River Out of Eden: A Darwinian View of Life*. New York: Basic, 1996.

———. *The God Delusion*. New York: Houghton Mifflin, 2006.

DeGroat, Chuck. *When Narcissism Comes to Church: Healing Your Community from Emotional and Spiritual Abuse*. Downers Grove, IL: InterVarsity, 2020.

DeVille, Adam A. J. *Married Priests in the Catholic Church*. Notre Dame, IN: University of Notre Dame Press, 2021. Kindle edition.

DeYoung, Rebecca Konyndyk. *Glittering Vices: A New Look at the Seven Deadly Sins and Their Remedies*. Grand Rapids: Baker, 2009.

Dickens, Charles. *A Christmas Carol*. Ottawa: East India, 2002.

Dieter, Melvin E. "The Wesleyan Perspective." In *Five Views on Sanctification*, edited by Stanley N. Gundry, 151–83. Grand Rapids: Zondervan, 1987.

Dines, Gail. "Is Porn Immoral? That Doesn't Matter: It's a Public Health Crisis." *Washington Post*, Aug 8, 2016. https://www.washingtonpost.com/posteverything/wp/2016/04/08/is-porn-immoral-that-doesnt-matter-its-a-public-health-crisis/.

———. *Pornland: How Porn Has Hijacked Our Sexuality.* Boston: Beacon, 2010.
Dostoyevsky, Fyodor. *The Brothers Karamazov: Illustrated.* New York: Dover, 2019.
Duke Divinity School. "Clergy More Likely to Suffer From Depression, Anxiety." *Duke Today*, Aug 27, 2013. http://today.duke.edu/2013/08/clergydepressionnewsrelease.
Dunn, James D. G. *Jesus Remembered.* Grand Rapids: Eerdmans, 2003.
Ebeling, Gerhard. *Luther: An Introduction to His Thought.* Minneapolis: Fortress, 2007.
Edwards, Mark J., ed. *Galatians, Ephesians, Philippians.* Ancient Christian Commentary on Scripture. Downers Grove, IL: InterVarsity, 1999.
Ellens, J. Harold. *Sex in the Bible: A New Consideration.* Westport, CT: Praeger, 2006.
Elliott, John. *What Is Social-Scientific Criticism?* Minneapolis: Fortress, 1993.
Ellis, Albert. *The Case Against Religion: A Psychotherapist's View.* New York: Institute for Rational Living, 1971.
Erikson, Erik. *Identity and the Life Cycle.* New York: W. W. Norton and Company, 1980.
Erickson, Millard J. *Christian Theology.* Grand Rapids: Baker Academic, 2013.
Evagrius Ponticus. *The Praktikos and Chapters on Prayer.* Translated by J. E. Bamberger. Spencer, MA: Cistercian, 1970.
Faupel, D. William. *The Everlasting Gospel: The Significance of Eschatology in the Development of Pentecostal Thought.* Sheffield, UK: Sheffield Academic, 1996.
Fee, Gordon D. *Paul, the Spirit, and the People of God.* Grand Rapids: Baker, 1996.
Fieguth, Debra. "After All These Years." *Faith Today* (Mar/Apr 1994) 29.
Fisher, Marc. "Clinton's Pastor with a Past." *Washington Post*, Sep 28, 1998. https://www.washingtonpost.com/wp-srv/style/daily/clinpastor0928.htm.
Flynn, James T. "Firewall: Health Essentials for Ministers and Their Families." *Christian Education Journal* 6.2 (Fall 2009) 309–24.
Fortune, Marie M. *Is Nothing Sacred? When Sex Invades the Pastoral Relationship.* San Francisco: Harper & Row, 1992.
———. and James N. Poling. *Sexual Abuse by Clergy: A Crisis for the Church.* Eugene, OR: Wipf and Stock, 2004.
Foster, Richard J. *Celebration of Discipline: The Path to Spiritual Growth.* New York: HarperCollins, 1998.
———. "Spiritual Formation Agenda: Richard Foster Shares His Three Priorities for the Next 30 Years." *Christianity Today* (Jan 2009) 28–33.
Frankl, Victor. *Man's Search for Meaning.* Boston: Beacon, 2006.
French, Rose. "Report: Protestant Church Insurers Handle 260 Sex Abuse Cases a Year." *Insurance Journal*, Jun 18, 2007. https://www.insurancejournal.com/news/national/2007/06/18/80877.htm.
Freston, Paul. "Evangelicals and Politics in the Third World." In *Christians and Politics Beyond the Culture Wars*, edited by David P. Gushee, 105–28. Grand Rapids: Baker, 2000.
Fuller Institute of Church Growth. "1991 Survey of Pastors." Pasadena, CA: Fuller Theological Seminary, 1991.
Gabbard, Glen O. "Psychotherapists Who Transgress Sexual Boundaries with Patients." *Bulletin of the Menninger Clinic* (Oct 1992) 1–17.
Gane, Roy *Leviticus, Numbers.* The NIV Application Commentary. Grand Rapids: Zondervan, 2004.
Garland, David E. *New American Commentary Volume 29: 2 Corinthians.* Nashville: B&H Academic, 1999.

———. and Diana R. Garland. *Flawed Families of the Bible: How God's Grace Works through Imperfect Relationships*. Grand Rapids: Brazos, 2007.

Gause, R. Hollis. *Living in the Spirit: The Way of Salvation*. Cleveland, TN: CPT, 2010.

Gemignani, Michael. *Spiritual Formation for Pastors: Feeding the Fire Within*. Valley Forge, PA: Judson, 2002.

Goff, James Rudolph, Jr. "Fields White Unto Harvest: Charles F. Parham And The Missionary Origins Of Pentecostalism." PhD diss., University of Arkansas, 1987.

Goldingay, John. *1 and 2 Samuel for Everyone*. Louisville: Westminster John Knox, 2011.

———. *Psalms Vol. 2: Psalms 42–89*, edited by Tremper Longman III. Baker Commentary on the Old Testament: Wisdom and Psalms. Grand Rapids: Baker Academic, 2007.

Goleman, Daniel. *Primal Leadership: Realizing the Power of Emotional Intelligence*. Boston: Harvard Business School, 2002.

Gondreau, Paul. "Jesus and Paul on the Meaning and Purpose of Human Sexuality." *Nova et vetera* 18.2 (2020) 484.

Gräbe, Petrus J. *The Power of God in Paul's Letters*. Tübingen, Germany: Mohr Siebeck, 2008.

Graham, Ruth. "Jerry Falwell Jr.'s Departure Brings Relief on Liberty University's Campus." *New York Times*, Aug 25, 2020. https://www.nytimes.com/2020/08/25/us/falwell-resigns-liberty-university.html.

Green, Joel B., Jeannine K. Brown, Nicholas Perrin, eds. *Dictionary of Jesus and the Gospels*. Downers Grove, IL: InterVarsity, 2013.

Gregory the Great. *Morals on the Book of Job: Volumes 1 to 3*. Translated by John Henry Parker, J. G. F., and J. Rivington. London: Oxford, 1844–45.

Gregory of Nyssa. *On Virginity*. Translated by William Moore. Philadelphia: Dalcassian, 2018.

Grenz, Stanley J. "We Dare Not Fall: Dealing with the Peril of Clergy Sexual Misconduct." *Enrichment* 9.4 (Fall 2004) 38–51.

———. and Roy D. Bell, *Betrayal of Trust: Confronting and Preventing Clergy Sexual Misconduct*. Grand Rapids: Baker, 2001.

Grey, Jacqueline. "A Prophetic Call to Repentance: David, Bathsheba and a Royal Abuse of Power." *Pneuma* 41 (2019) 9–25.

Grudem, Wayne. *Systematic Theology: An Introduction to Biblical Discipline*. Grand Rapids: Zondervan, 1994.

Guerry, Colleen. "Liberty University Responds after Lawsuit from 12 Jane Does Accusing LU of 'Enabling On-Campus Rapes' Settled." *WFXR Fox News*, May 12, 2022. https://www.wfxrtv.com/news/local-news/lynchburg-central-virginia-news/lawsuit-from-12-jane-does-accusing-liberty-university-of-enabling-on-campus-rapes-settled/.

Gunnoe, Marjorie Linder. *The Person in Psychology and Christianity: A Faith-Based Critique of Five Theories of Social Development*. Downers Grove, IL: IVP Academic, 2022.

Hägg, Henny Fiskå. "Continence and Marriage: The Concept of Enkrateia in Clement of Alexandria 1." *Symbolae Osloenses* (0039-7679), 81 (1), 126–43.

Haggard, Gayle. *Why I Stayed: The Choices I Made in My Darkest Hour*. Carol Stream, IL: Tyndale House, 2010.

Hall, M. Elizabeth Lewis. "Suffering as Formation: The Hard Road to Glory." In *The Holy Spirit and Christian Formation: Multidisciplinary Perspectives*, edited by Diane J. Chandler, 69–88. Cham, Switzerland: Palgrave MacMillan, 2016.

Hall, Todd, and John Coe. *Psychology in the Spirit: Contours of a Transformational Psychology*. Downers Grove, IL: InterVarsity, 2010.

Hands, Donald R., and Fehr, Wayne L. *Spiritual Wholeness for Clergy: A New Psychology of Intimacy with God, Self, and Others*. Lanham, MD: Rowman & Littlefield, 1994.

Harak, G. Simon. *Virtuous Passions: The Formation of Christian Character*. New York: Paulist, 1993.

Harper, Kyle. *From Shame to Sin: The Christian Transformation of Sexual Morality in Late Antiquity*. Cambridge, MA: Harvard University Press, 2013.

Harris, Josh. *Not Even a Hint: Guarding Your Heart Against Lust*. Sisters, OR: Multnomah, 2003.

Harvard University. "Serve and Return." Center on the Developing Child. http://developingchild.harvard.edu/science/key-concepts/serve-and-return/.

Hathaway, William L., and Mark A. Yarhouse. *The Integration of Psychology & Christianity: A Domain-Based Approach*. Downers Grove, IL: IVP Academic, 2021.

Hauerwas, Stanley. *A Community of Character*. Notre Dame, IN: University of Notre Dame Press, 1981.

Hawthorne, Gerald, Ralph P. Martin, Daniel G. Reid, eds. *Dictionary of Paul and His Letters*. Downers Grove, IL: InterVarsity, 1993.

Hayford, Jack. *Restoring Fallen Leaders*. Ventura, CA: Regal, 1998.

Hays, Richard B. *The Moral Vision of the New Testament: A Contemporary Introduction to New Testament Ethics*. New York: HarperCollins, 1996.

Hermas. *The Shepherd*. Edited by Philip Schaff. The Complete Ante-Nicene, Nicene, and Post-Nicene Church Fathers Collection. London: Catholic Way, 2014.

Hertzberg, Hans Wilhelm. *I & II Samuel: A Commentary*. Louisville: Westminster John Knox, 1964.

Herzog II, William R. *Jesus, Justice, and the Reign of God: A Ministry of Liberation*. Louisville: Westminster John Knox, 2000.

Heschel, Abraham. *Between God and Man: An Interpretation of Judaism*. New York: Pree Press, 1997.

Hession, Roy. *Forgotten Factors of Sexual Sin: An Aid to Deeper Resistance*. Fort Washington, PA: CLC, 2013. Kindle edition.

Hettiaratchy, Charles F. "But the Greatest of These Is Love." *The Latter Rain Evangel*, 2.8 (May 1910) 12.

Hetzendorfer, Ruth. *The Pastoral Counseling Handbook: A Guide to Helping the Hurting*. Kansas City, MO: Beacon Hill, 2009.

Hicks, Donald Q. "A Study of the Conflicts Within Churches that Lead to the Termination of Pastors Within the Southern Baptist Convention, Accompanied by a Proposal of Preventive and Interventional Solutions." PhD. diss., Liberty University, 2010.

Hildebrand, Stephen. "The Trinity in the Ante-Nicene Fathers." In *The Oxford Handbook of the Trinity*, edited by Gilles Emery and Matthew Levering, 95–108. Oxford, UK: Oxford University Press, 2011.

Hobbes, Thomas. *Leviathan (Illustrated): Premium Edition*. Rudram, 2016. Kindle edition.

Hoekema, Anthony A. *Created in God's Image*. Grand Rapids: Eerdmans, 1986.
———. "The Reformed Perspective." In *Five Views on Sanctification*, edited by Stanley N. Gundry, 59–90. Grand Rapids: Zondervan, 1987.
Hollenweger, Walter. *Pentecostalism Origins and Developments Worldwide*. Grand Rapids: Baker, 2011.
Hollinger, Dennis P. *Choosing the Good: Christian Ethics in a Complex World*. Grand Rapids: Baker, 2002.
Holmes, T. H., and R. H. Rahe. "The Social Readjustment Rating Scale." *Journal of Psychosomatic Research* 11.2 (1967) 213–21.
Horton, Stanley M. *I & II Corinthians*. Logion Press Commentary. Springfield, MO: Logion, 1999.
———. "The Pentecostal Perspective." In *Five Views on Sanctification*, edited by Stanley N. Gundry, 105–35. Grand Rapids: Zondervan, 1987.
Hughes, R. Kent, and John H. Armstrong. "Why Adulterous Pastors Should Not Be Restored." *Christianity Today* 39.4 (1995) 33–36.
Hunter, David G. "Marriage and Sexuality in Early Christianity." In *Ad Fontes: Early Christian Sources*, edited by George Kalatzis. Minneapolis, MN: Fortress, 2018. Kindle edition.
———. *Marriage, Celibacy, and Heresy in Ancient Christianity: The Jovinianist Controversy*. Oxford, UK: Oxford University Press, 2007.
Ignatius of Loyola. *Spiritual Exercises and Selected Works*, edited by S.J. George E. Ganss. New York: Paulist Press, 1991.
Irwin, B. H. "The Friendship of the World." In *Christian Witness and Advocate of Bible Holiness* (Jan 11, 1894) 2–3.
Isaac of Nineveh. "Ascetical Homilies 10." In *Ancient Christian Commentary on Scripture: Old Testament IV—Joshua, Judges, Ruth, 1-2 Samuel*, edited by J. R. Franke. Downers Grove, IL: InterVarsity, 2005.
Jackson, Christopher. "Tullian Tchividjian's Upside Down Christianity." *First Things*, Sep 5, 2019. https://www.firstthings.com/web-exclusives/2019/09/tullian-tchividjians-upside-down-christianity.
Jamieson, Robert. *Joshua–Esther*. A Commentary, Critical, Experimental, and Practical, on the Old and New Testaments. London; Glasgow: William Collins, Sons & Company, 1869.
Jennings, Timothy R. *The God-Shaped Brain: How Changing Your View of God Transforms Your Life*. Downers Grove, IL: InterVarsity, 2017.
John of the Cross. *Dark Night of the Soul*, translated by E. Allison Peers. New York: Image, Doubleday, 1959.
———. "The Sayings of Light and Love 158." In *The Collected Works of John of the Cross*. Rev. ed. Washington D.C.: Institute of Carmelite Studies, 1964.
Johns, Cheryl Bridges, and Vardaman W. White. "The Ethics of Being: Character, Community, Praxis." In *Elements of a Christian Worldview*, edited by Michael D. Palmer, 283–312. Springfield, MO: Logion, 1998.
Johnson, Alan F. *1 Corinthians*. The IVP New Testament Commentary. Westmont, IL: IVP Academic, 2004.
Johnson, Alex. "Tennessee Pastor Andy Savage Resigns Weeks after Admitting 'Sexual Incident' with Minor." NBC News, Mar 20, 2018. https://www.nbcnews.com/storyline/sexual-misconduct/tennessee-pastor-andy-savage-resigns-weeks-after-admitting-sexual-incident-n858541.

Johnson, David, and Jeff VanVonderen. *The Subtle Power Spiritual Abuse: Recognizing & Escaping Spiritual Manipulation and False Spiritual Authority Within the Church.* Bloomington, MN: Bethany House, 1991.

Johnson, Eric L., ed. *Psychology and Christianity: Five Views.* Downers Grove, IL: IVP Academic, 2010.

Jones, Emily. "'What I Did Was Wrong': A Southern Baptist Leader Apologizes for Dismissing Sexual Abuse Allegations." CBN News, Feb 15, 2019. http://www1.cbn.com/cbnnews/us/2019/february/what-i-did-was-wrong-a-southern-baptist-leader-apologizes-for-dismissing-sexual-abuse-allegations.

Jones, Mike. *I Had to Say Something: The Art of Ted Haggard's Fall.* New York: Seven Stories, 2007.

Jung, Carl G. *Man and His Symbols*, New York: Bantam, 2023.

———. *Modern Man in Search of a Soul.* New York: Harcourt, Brace & World, 1933.

Junk, Thomas. "Letter From Thomas Junk." *The Bridegroom's Messenger* 2.42 (Jul 15, 1909) 1.

Kapic, Kelly M. "Anthropology." In *Christian Dogmatics: Reformed Theology for the Church Catholic*, edited by Michael Allen and Scott R. Swain, 165–93. Grand Rapids: Baker Academic, 2016.

Kärkkäinen, Veli-Matti. *One with God: Salvation as Deification and Justification.* Collegeville, MN: Liturgical, 2004.

Katz, Edward. "Self-Esteem: The Past of an Illusion." *American Journal of Psychoanalysis* (Sep 1998) 303–15.

Keener, Craig S. *Galatians, A Commentary.* Grand Rapids: Baker Academic, 2019.

———. *Matthew.* The IVP New Testament Commentary Series. Downers Grove, IL: InterVarsity, 1997.

———. *Spirit Hermeneutics: Reading Scripture in Light of Pentecost.* Grand Rapids: Eerdmans, 2016.

Keller, Timothy. *Walking with God through Pain and Suffering.* London: Penguin, 2013.

———. and Kathy Keller. *The Meaning of Marriage: Facing the Complexities of Commitment with the Wisdom of God.* New York: Riverhead, 2011.

Kendrick, Alex, and Stephen Kendrick. *The Love Dare.* Nashville: B&H, 2013.

Kierkegaard, Søren. *Papers and Journals: A Selection*, edited and translated by Alastair Hannay. London: Penguin, 1996.

———. *The Sickness Unto Death*, translated by Alastair Hannay. London: Penguin, 1989.

Köstenberger, Andreas J. *A Theology of John's Gospel and Letters: The Word, the Christ, the Son of God.* Grand Rapids: Zondervan, 2009.

———. *John.* Baker Exegetical Commentary on the New Testament. Grand Rapids: Baker Academic, 2004.

———. *John.* Zondervan Illustrated Bible Backgrounds Commentary. Grand Rapids: Zondervan, 2002.

Kinnaman, Gary D., and Alfred H. Ells. *Leaders That Last: How Covenant Friendships Can Help Pastors Thrive.* Grand Rapids: Baker, 2003.

Kinnamon, David, and Gabe Lyons. *Good Faith: Being a Christian When Society Thinks You're Irrelevant and Extreme.* Grand Rapids: Baker, 2016.

Kolk, Bessel van der. *The Body Keeps the Score: Brain, Mind, and Body in the Healing of Trauma.* London: Penguin, 2014.

Konkel, August H. *1&2 Kings.* The NIV Application Commentary. Grand Rapids: Zondervan, 2006.

Koukl, Gregory. *Tactics: A Game Plan for Discussing Your Christian Convictions.* Grand Rapids: Zondervan, 2019.

Krejcir, Richard J. "Statistics on Pastors: What Is Going On with Pastors in America?" Francis A. Schaeffer Institute of Church Leadership Development. http://www.intothyword.org/apps/articles/default.asp?articleid=36562&columnid=3958.

Kretzschmar, Louise. "Authentic Christian Leadership and Spiritual Formation in Africa." In *Journal of Theology for Southern Africa* 113 (2002) 41–60.

———. "The Education of Prospective Ministers as an Invitation to Life: Moving From Moral Failure to Moral Excellence Through a Process of Moral Formation." *In die Skriflig*; Potchefstroom 49.1 (2015) 1–10.

Kruse, Colin G. *John.* Tyndale New Testament Commentary. Downers Grove, IL: InterVarsity, 2003.

Kumar, Anugrah. "Audio of Venue Church Pastor Tavner Smith Being Confronted Over Alleged Affair Leaked." *Christian Post*, Feb 5, 2022. https://www.christianpost.com/church-ministries/audio-leaked-of-megachurch-pastor-confronted-over-alleged-affair.html.

Laaser, Mark. *Healing the Wounds of Sexual Addiction.* Grand Rapids: Zondervan, 2009.

Ladner, Gerhart B. *The Idea of Reform: Its Impact on Christian Thought and Action in the Age of the Fathers.* Cambridge, MA: Harvard University Press, 1959.

LaHaye, Tim. *If Ministers Fall, Can They Be Restored?* Grand Rapids: Zondervan, 1990.

Lancaster, Jessilyn. "Tullian Tchividjian Marries After Emotional Plummeting from Affair." *Charisma News*, Nov 29, 2016. https://www.charismanews.com/us/61523-tullian-tchividjian-marries-after-emotional-plummeting-from-affair.

Lane, Tony. *A Concise History of Christian Thought.* Grand Rapids: Baker Academic, 2006.

Langberg, Diane. *Counseling Survivors of Sexual Abuse.* Wheaton, IL: Tyndale, 1997.

Lash, Nathaniel. "Catholic Church Clergy Sex Abuse: Read the Full Grand Jury Report." *Philadelphia Inquirer*, Aug 14, 2018. https://www.inquirer.com/philly/news/catholic-church-clergy-sex-abuse-read-the-full-grand-jury-report-20180814.html.

Lazare, Aaron. *On Apology.* Oxford, UK: Oxford University Press, 2004.

Lea, Jessica. "SBC Executive Committee Says Yes to Waiving Attorney-Client Privilege." *Church Leaders*, Oct 5, 2021. https://churchleaders.com/news/406761-sbc-executive-committee-yes-on-waiving-attorney-client-privilege.html.

Lea, Thomas D., and Hayne P. Griffin, Jr. *1, 2 Timothy, Titus.* The New American Commentary. Nashville: Broadman & Holman, 1992.

Lebacqz, Karen, and Ronald Barton. *Sex in the Parish.* Louisville: Westminster John Knox, 1991.

Lee, Morgan. "The Story of Mark Driscoll and Mars Hill Matters in 2021," *Christianity Today*, Jun 25, 2021. https://www.christianitytoday.com/ct/podcasts/quick-to-listen/rise-fall-mars-hill-mark-driscoll-podcast.html.

Lennox, Stephen J. *Psalms: A Bible Commentary in the Wesleyan Tradition.* Indianapolis: Wesleyan Publishing House, 1999.

Levine, Peter. *In an Unspoken Voice: How the Body Releases Trauma and Restores Goodness.* Berkeley, CA: North Atlantic, 2010.

BIBLIOGRAPHY

Lewis, C. S. *God in the Dock*. Grand Rapids: Eerdmans, 1970.

———. *Mere Christianity*. New York: HarperCollins, 2009.

———. *The Problem of Pain*. New York: HarperOne, 2015.

———. *The Screwtape Letters*. New York: HarperCollins, 2001.

———. *The Weight of Glory*. New York: HarperOne, 1980.

Lewis, Sinclair. *Elmer Gantry*. New York: Harcourt, Brace and Company, 1927.

Liefeld, Walter L. *1 and 2 Timothy, Titus*. The NIV Application Commentary. Grand Rapids: Zondervan, 1999.

Litfin, Bryan M. *Getting to Know the Church Fathers: An Evangelical Introduction*. Grand Rapids: Brazos, 2007.

Lincoln, Andrew T. *The Gospel According to St. John*. Black's New Testament Commentary. Grand Rapids: Baker Academic, 2005.

Loader, William. *Making Sense of Sex: Attitudes Towards Sexuality in Early Jewish and Christian Literature*. Grand Rapids: Eerdmans, 2013.

London, H.B. Jr., and Neil B. Wiseman. *Pastors at Risk: Help for Pastors, Hope for the Church*. Wheaton, IL: Victor, 1993.

———. *Pastors at Greater Risk*. Grand Rapids: Baker, 2011.

Lorin, Marti Tamm. *Emotional Abuse: The Trauma and the Treatment*. New York: Lexington; 1994.

Louw, J. P., and E. A. Nida. *Greek-English Lexicon of the New Testament Based on Semantic Domains*. New York: United Bible Societies, 1988.

Ludwig, Dean C., and Clinton O. Longenecker. "The Bathsheba Syndrome: The Ethical Failure of Successful Leaders." *Journal of Business Ethics* 12.4 (Apr 1993) 265–73.

MacArthur, John F. *The Master's Plan for the Church*. Chicago, IL: Moody, 1991.

Macchia, Frank D. *Justified in the Spirit: Creation, Redemption, and the Triune God*. Grand Rapids: Eerdmans, 2010.

MacDonald, Gordon. *Rebuilding Your Broken World*. Nashville: Thomas Nelson, 2004. Kindle edition.

Maddox, Randy L. *Responsible Grace: John Wesley's Practical Theology*. Nashville: Kingswood, 1994.

Malina, Bruce. *Christian Origins and Cultural Anthropology: Practical Models for Biblical Interpretation*. Eugene, OR: Wipf & Stock, 2010.

———. *The Social World of Jesus and the Gospels*. New York: Routledge, 1996.

Markham, Paul N. *Rewired: Exploring Religious Conversion*. Eugene, OR: Pickwick, 2007.

Martin, Ralph P. *Word Biblical Commentary Volume 40: 2 Corinthians*. Dallas: Word, 2012.

Martin, Stephanie. "After Pastor's Alleged Affair, Venue Megachurch Struggles to Survive." Church Leaders, Feb 3, 2022. https://churchleaders.com/news/416486-venue-megachurch-pastor-tavner-smith-alleged-affair.html.

———. "Televangelist Perry Stone Admits He's Not Perfect but Calls Abuse Accusations 'Demonic.'" *Church Leaders*, Dec 30, 2021. https://churchleaders.com/news/413751-televangelist-perry-stone-admits-hes-not-perfect-but-calls-abuse-accusations-demonic.html.

Massey, Wyatt. "Women in Perry Stone's Ministry Allege Sexual Misconduct, Say FBI is Investigating Televangelist." *Chattanooga Times Free Press*, Dec 25, 2021. https://www.timesfreepress.com/news/local/story/2021/dec/25/women-perry-stones-ministry-allege-sexual-mis/560366/.

May, Alistair Scott. *The Body for the Lord: Sex and Identity in 1 Corinthians 5–7*. London: T&T Clark International, 2004.

Mayo Clinic. "Symptoms and Causes." *Narcissistic Personality Disorder*, n.d. https://www.mayoclinic.org/diseases-conditions/narcissistic-personality-disorder/symptoms-causes/syc-20366662.

McCleneghan, Bromleigh. *Good Christian Sex: Why Chastity Isn't the Only Option—And Other Things the Bible Says About Sex*. New York: HarperOne, 2016.

McFadden, Robert D. "Bernard Law, Powerful Cardinal Disgraced by Priest Abuse Scandal, Dies at 86." *New York Times*, Dec 19, 2017. https://www.nytimes.com/2017/12/19/obituaries/cardinal-bernard-law-dead.html.

McGee, J. Vernon. *History of Israel (1 and 2 Samuel)*. Thru the Bible Commentary. Nashville: Thomas Nelson, 1991.

McGee, Robert S. *The Search for Significance*. Nashville: Thomas Nelson, Inc., 1998.

McKnight, George A. F. *Psalms Vol. 1.*, edited by John C. L. Gibson. In The Daily Study Bible Series. Louisville: Westminster John Knox, 1982.

McKnight, Scot. *Galatians*. The NIV Application Commentary. Grand Rapids: Zondervan, 1995.

———. and Laura McKnight Barringer. *A Church Called Tov: Forming a Goodness Culture That Resists Abuses of Power and Promotes Healing*. Carol Stream, IL: Tyndale House, 2020.

McMinn, Mark R. *Psychology, Theology, and Spirituality in Christian Counseling*. Carol Stream, IL: Tyndale House, 2012.

McQuilkin, J. Robertson. "The Keswick Perspective," In *Five Views on Sanctification*, edited by Stanley N. Gundry, 149–83. Grand Rapids: Zondervan, 1987.

Meawad, Stephen M. "Sexuality, Angelification, and Divine Indwelling: A Contemporary Ethic of Early Christian Asceticism." *Modern Theology* 36.3 (Jul 2020) 582–605.

Merton, Thomas. *The Ascent to Truth*. New York: Harvest, 1981.

———. *Thoughts in Solitude*. Boston: Shambhala Publications, 1956.

Methodius. *St. Methodius: The Symposium: A Treatise on Chastity*. In *Ancient Christian Writers*, edited by Herbert Musurillo. New York: Paulist, 1958.

Miller, Clarence H. *Erasmus and Luther: The Battle Over Free Will*. Cambridge, UK: Heckett, 2012.

Miller, Emily McFarlan. "Misconduct Allegations Against Willow Creek Founder Bill Hybels Are Credible, Independent Report Finds." *Washington Post*, Mar 1, 2019. https://www.washingtonpost.com/religion/2019/03/01/independent-report-finds-allegations-against-willow-creek-founder-bill-hybels-are-credible/.

Millgram, Hillel I. *Judges and Saviors, Deborah and Samson: Reflections of a World in Chaos*. Lanham, MD: Hamilton, 2018.

Mineo, Liz. "Harvard Study, Almost 80 Years Old, Has Proved That Embracing Community Helps Us Live Longer and Be Happier." *Harvard Gazette*. Apr 11, 2017. https://news.harvard.edu/gazette/story/2017/04/over-nearly-80-years-harvard-study-has-been-showing-how-to-live-a-healthy-and-happy-life/

Minirth, Frank B., and Paul D. Meier. *Happiness Is a Choice: A Manual on the Symptoms, Causes, and Cures of Depression*. Grand Rapids: Baker, 2007.

Mohler Jr., R. Albert. *We Cannot Be Silent: Speaking Truth to a Culture Redefining Sex, Marriage, and the Very Meaning of Right and Wrong*. Nashville: Thomas Nelson, 2015.

Moody, W. E. "Personal Purity." *Pentecostal Evangel* 950 (May 28, 1932) 6.

Morey, Ann-Janine. "Blaming Women for the Sexually Abusive Male Pastor." *Christian Century*, 1988-10, Vol. 105 (28), 866–69.

Mosgofian, Peter, and George Ohlschlager. *Sexual Misconduct in Counseling and Ministry*. Eugene, OR: Wipf and Stock, 2009.

Munsil, Tracy. "Is the Bible True? CRC Survey Shows America's Distrust of the Bible Undermines Its Worldview." Arizona Christian University, Apr 7, 2020. https://www.arizonachristian.edu/2020/04/07/is-the-bible-true-crc-survey-shows-americas-distrust-of-the-bible-undermines-its-worldview/.

Murdoch, Iris. *The Sovereignty of Good*. New York: Schocken, 1971.

Murray, Abdu. *Saving Truth: Finding Meaning and Clarity in a Post-Truth World*. Grand Rapids: Zondervan, 2018.

National Oceanic and Atmospheric Administration. "Hurricane Costs." Jan 24, 2024. https://coast.noaa.gov/states/fast-facts/hurricane-costs.html.

———. "Tsunamis." Oct 1, 2010. https://www.noaa.gov/education/resource-collections/ocean-coasts/tsunamis.

Newberg, Andrew, and Mark Robert Waldman. *Why We Believe What We Believe*. New York, NY: Free Press, 2006.

Newman, Barclay M., Jr. *A Concise Greek-English Dictionary of the New Testament*. Stuttgart, Germany: Deutsche Bibelgesellschaft; United Bible Societies, 1993.

Nichols, Michael. *The Lost Art of Listening*. New York, NY: Guilford, 1995.

Nicol, George G. "Bathsheba, A Clever Woman." *Expository Times* 99.12 (Sep 1, 1988) 360–63.

Niebuhr, Reinhold. *The Nature and Destiny of Man*. New York: Charles Scribner's Sons, 1943.

Niebuhr, H. Richard. *The Purpose of the Church and Its Ministry*. New York: Harper and Bros., 1956.

Nipkow, Karl Ernst. "Empirical Research within Practical Theology: Some General Considerations in the Context of Modernity." *Journal of Empirical Theology* 6.1 (1993) 50–63.

Nolin, Robert. "Calvary Chapel Pastor Bob Coy Resigns over 'Moral Failing.'" *South Florida Sun Sentinel*, Apr 8, 2014. https://www.sun-sentinel.com/news/fl-xpm-2014-04-08-fl-calvary-chapel-resignation-20140406-story.html.

Nouwen, Henri J. M. *In the Name of Jesus: Reflections on Christian Leadership*. Chestnut Ridge, NY: Crossroad, 1989.

———. *Making All Things New: An Invitation to the Spiritual Life*. San Francisco: HarperCollins, 2009.

———. *The Way of the Heart*. New York: Ballantine, 1981.

———. *The Wounded Healer: Ministry in Contemporary Society*. New York: Doubleday, 2013.

NRSV Cultural Backgrounds Study Bible: Bringing to Life the Ancient World of Scripture. Grand Rapids: Zondervan, 2019.

Nystrom, David. *James*. The NIV Application Commentary. Grand Rapids: Zondervan, 1997.

Oden, Thomas C. *Pastoral Counsel*. Classical Pastoral Care Series. New York: Crossroad, 1989.

Okholm, Dennis. *Dangerous Passions, Deadly Sins: Learning from the Psychology of Ancient Monks*. Grand Rapids: Brazos, 2014.

Olley, John W. *The Message of Kings: God is Present*. The Bible Speaks Today. Nottingham, UK: InterVarsity, 2011.

Origen, *Homilies on Luke*. In *The Fathers of the Church*, translated by Joseph T. Lienhard. Washington, D.C.: Catholic University of America, 1996.

Ortberg, John. "Can Neuroscience Help Us Disciple Anyone? Brain Science and the Renewal of Your Mind." *Leadership Journal* (Summer 2014) 19–22.

Osborne, Grant R. *Matthew*. Exegetical Commentary on the New Testament. Grand Rapids: Zondervan, 2010.

Osiek, Carolyn and Helmut Koester. *Shepherd of Hermas: A Commentary*. Hermeneia: A Critical and Historical Commentary on the Bible. Minneapolis: Fortress, 1999.

Out of the FOG. "Top 100 Traits of People Who Suffer From Personality Disorders." http://outofthefog.website/top-100-trait-blog/2015/11/4/emotional-abuse.

Outreach Magazine. "2015 Fastest-Growing Churches in America." Outreach 100. https://outreach100.com/fastest-growing-churches-in-america/2015.

Padilla, Art, Robert Hogan, and Robert B. Kaiser. "The Toxic Triangle: Destructive Leaders, Susceptible Followers, and Conducive Environments." *Leadership Quarterly* 18.3 (2007) 176–94.

Palmer, Michael D. *Elements of a Christian Worldview*. Springfield, MO: Gospel Publishing House, 1998.

———. "Ethical Formation: The Theological Virtues." In *The Holy Spirit and Christian Formation: Multidisciplinary Perspectives*, edited by Diane J. Chandler, 107–26. Cham, Switzerland: Palgrave MacMillan, 2016, .

Parham, Charles F. "Greeting." *Apostolic Faith* (Baxter Springs) (Dec 1912–January 1913).

Pascal, Blaise. *Pensées*, edited and translated by Roger Ariew. Indianapolis: Hackett, 2004.

Pashman, Manya Brachear, and Jeff Coen. "After Years of Inquiries, Willow Creek Pastor Denies Misconduct Allegations." *Chicago Tribune*, Mar 23, 2018. https://www.chicagotribune.com/news/breaking/ct-met-willow-creek-pastor-20171220-story.html.

Patton, John. *Pastoral Counseling: A Ministry of the Church*. Eugene, OR: Wipf and Stock, 2002.

Paulson, Steven D. *Lutheran Theology*. London: T&T Clark International, 2011. Kindle edition.

Pearcey, Nancy. *Total Truth: Liberating Christianity from Its Cultural Captivity*. Wheaton, IL: Crossway, 2004.

Pease, Joshua. "The Sin of Silence: The Epidemic of Denial about Sexual Abuse in the Evangelical Church." *Washington Post*, May 31, 2018. https://www.washingtonpost.com/news/posteverything/wp/2018/05/31/feature/the-epidemic-of-denial-about-sexual-abuse-in-the-evangelical-church/.

Pennington, Jonathan T. *Jesus the Great Philosopher: Rediscovering the Wisdom Needed for the Good Life*. Grand Rapids: Brazos, 2020.

Peterson, David. *Engaging with God: A Biblical Theology of Worship*. Downers Grove, IL: IVP Academic, 1992.

Phillips, Wade. *Quest to Restore God's House: A Theological History of the Church of God (Cleveland, Tennessee): Volume I 1886-1923, R. G. Spurling to A. J. Tomlinson, Formation-Transformation-Reformation*. Cleveland, TN: CPT, 2017. Kindle edition.

Pippert, Rebecca Manley. *Out of the Saltshaker and Into the World: Evangelism as a Way of Life (The IVP Signature Collection)*. Downers Grove, IL: InterVarsity, 2021.

Plantinga Jr., Cornelius. *Not the Way It's Supposed to Be: A Breviary of Sin*. Grand Rapids: Eerdmans, 1995.

Pop, Jennifer L. and Geoffrey W. Sutton, E. Grant Jones. "Restoring Pastors Following a Moral Failure: The Effects of Self-Interest and Group Influence." *Pastoral Psychology* 57.5 (Jan 2009) 275–84.

Porter, Stanley E. *Idioms of the Greek New Testament*. Sheffield, UK: Sheffield Academic, 1992.

Pratt, Dwight M. *The International Standard Bible Encyclopaedia (Vol. 1–5)*, edited by James Orr, et al. Chicago: Howard-Severance, 1915.

Prior, David. *The Message of 1 Corinthians: Life in the Local Church*. The Bible Speaks Today. Downers Grove, IL: InterVarsity, 1985.

Rae, Scott B. *Moral Choices: An Introduction to Ethics*. Grand Rapids: Zondervan, 2009.

Rand, Ayn. *Atlas Shrugged*. New York: Random House, 1957.

———. *For the New Intellectual*. New York: Signet, 1961.

Ratzinger, Joseph. *Jesus of Nazareth*. New York: Doubleday, 2007.

Real, Terrence. *I Don't Want to Talk About It: Overcoming the Secret Legacy of Male Depression*. New York: Scribner, 1998.

Rediger, G. Lloyd. "Clergy Moral Malfeasance." *Church Management—The Clergy Journal* (May–Jun 1991) 37–38.

———. *Fit to Be a Pastor: A Call to Physical, Mental, and Spiritual Fitness*. Louisville: Westminster John Knox, 2000.

Reid, Robert. *Four Voices of Preaching*. Grand Rapids: Brazos, 2006.

Richards, E. Randolph and Brandon J. O'Brien. *Misreading Scripture with Western Eyes: Removing Cultural Blinders to Better Understand the Bible*. Downers Grove, IL: InterVarsity, 2012.

Rieff, Philip. *The Triumph of the Therapeutic: Uses of Faith After Freud*. Chicago: University of Chicago Press, 1987.

Rifkin, Jeremy. *Algeny: A New Word—A New World*. New York: Viking, 1983.

Ripley, Jennifer S. and Everett L. Worthington, Jr. *Couple Therapy: A New Hope-Focused Approach*. Downers Grove, IL: IVP Academic, 2014.

Roberts, Robert C., and P. J. Watson. "A Christian Psychology View." In *Psychology and Christianity: Five Views*, edited by Eric L. Johnson, 149–75. Downers Grove, IL: IVP Academic, 2010.

Roose, Kevin. "The Last Temptation of Ted." *GQ*, Jan 26, 2011. https://www.gq.com/story/pastor-ted-haggard.

Roozeboom, William D. *Neuroplasticity, Performativity, and Clergy Wellness: Neighbor Love as Self-Care*. New York: Lexington, 2017.

Rosenfeld, Megan. "Swaggart Tells of Deposition by Hahn." *Washington Post*, Mar 27, 1987. https://www.washingtonpost.com/archive/lifestyle/1987/03/27/swaggart-tells-of-deposition-by-hahn/5839813d-4f28-4903-b4d5-202e1e155dd0/.

Rosner, Brian S. "Idolatry." In *New Dictionary of Biblical Theology*, edited by T. Desmond Alexander and Brian S. Rosner. Downers Grove, IL: InterVarsity, 2000.

RZIM, "An Open Letter from the International Board of Directors of RZIM on the Investigation of Ravi Zacharias." Feb 11, 2021. Accessed April 5, 2023. https://www.rzim.org/read/rzim-updates/board-statement

Savage, Timothy B. *Power Through Weakness: Paul's Understanding of the Christian Ministry in 2 Corinthians*. Cambridge, MA: Cambridge University Press, 1996.

Seamands, Stephen. *Ministry in the Image of God*. Downers Grove, IL: InterVarsity, 2005.

Scazzero, Peter. *Emotionally Healthy Spirituality: It's Impossible to Be Spiritually Mature, While Remaining Emotionally Immature*. Grand Rapids, MI: Zondervan, 2017.

Schaefer, Konrad. *Psalms*. In *Berit Olam: Studies in Hebrew Narrative and Poetry*, edited by David W. Cotter. Collegeville, MN: Liturgical, 2001.

Schaeffer, Francis. "The God Who Is There." In *The Complete Works of Francis Schaeffer*, vol. 1. Wheaton, IL: Crossway, 1982.

Schaff, Philip, ed. *The Complete Ante-Nicene, Nicene, and Post-Nicene Church Fathers Collection*. London: Catholic Way, 2014.

Scharen, Christian B. *Faith as a Way of Life*. Grand Rapids: Eerdmans, 2008.

Schaumburg, Harry. *False Intimacy: Understanding the Struggle of Sexual Addiction*. Colorado Springs, CO: NavPress, 1992.

Schenck, Kenneth. *1 & 2 Corinthians: A Commentary for Bible Students*. Wesleyan Bible Commentary Series. Indianapolis: Wesleyan Publishing House, 2006.

Siegel, Daniel J. *The Developing Mind: How Relationships and the Brain Interact to Shape Who We Are*. New York: Guilford, 2020.

Selzer, Louis Joseph. "An Integrated Mentoring Model for Developing Morally and Spiritually Strong Leaders in the Local Church." D.Min. diss., Assemblies of God Theological Seminary, 2006.

Sensing, Tim. *Qualitative Research: A Multi-Methods Approach to Projects for Doctor of Ministry Theses*. Eugene, OR: Wipf & Stock, 2015.

Shellnutt, Kate. "Willow Creek Investigation: Allegations Against Bill Hybels Are Credible." *Christianity Today*, Feb 28, 2019. https://www.christianitytoday.com/news/2019/february/willow-creek-bill-hybels-investigation-iag-report.html.

Sherman, Gabriel. "Inside Jerry Falwell Jr.'s Unlikely Rise and Precipitous Fall at Liberty University." *Vanity Fair*, Jan 24, 2022. https://www.vanityfair.com/news/2022/01/inside-jerry-falwell-jr-unlikely-rise-and-precipitous-fall.

Shipley, Cory D. "Increasing the Knowledge of Pastors and Church Leaders about Biblical Church Discipline." D.Min. diss., Oral Roberts University, 2009.

Sider, Ron. *The Scandal of the Evangelical Conscience: Why Are Christians Living Just Like the Rest of the World?* Grand Rapids: Baker, 2005.

Siemaszko, Corky. "Southern Baptist Convention: More Than 200 Ministers, Deacons and Others Have Been Found Guilty of Sex Abuse, Report Says." NBC News, Feb 11, 2019. https://www.nbcnews.com/news/us-news/over-200-baptist-ministers-deacons-others-have-been-found-guilty-n970276.

Silliman, Daniel. "Died: Marcus Lamb, Daystar Founder Who Believed TV Opened a Window for the Holy Spirit." *Christianity Today*, Dec 1, 2021. https://www.christianitytoday.com/news/2021/december/obit-marcus-lamb-daystar-tv-success-scandal.html.

———. and Kate Shellnutt. "Ravi Zacharias Hid Hundreds of Pictures of Women, Abuse During Massages, and a Rape Allegation." *Christianity Today*, Feb 11, 2021. https://www.christianitytoday.com/news/2021/february/ravi-zacharias-rzim-investigation-sexual-abuse-sexting-rape.html.

Silva, Daniella. "Memphis Pastor Admits to 'Sexual Incident' with Teen 20 Years Ago, Gets Standing Ovation." NBC News, Jan 14, 2018. https://www.nbcnews.com/

storyline/sexual-misconduct/memphis-pastor-admits-sexual-incident-teen-20-years-ago-gets-n836511.
Skinner, B. F. *Beyond Freedom and Dignity*. Indianapolis: Hackett, 2002.
Smedes, Lewis B. *The Art of Forgiveness*. Nashville: Moorings, 1996.
Smietana, Bob. "Head of SBC Executive Committee Questions Messengers' Resolution in Abuse Investigation." *Religious News Service*, Sep 13, 2021. https://religionnews.com/2021/09/13/southern-baptist-told-leaders-to-waive-attorney-client-privilege-in-abuse-investigation-its-unclear-if-they-will-do/.
———. "Liberty Sues Jerry Falwell Jr. for $10M Over Sex Scandal." *Christianity Today*, Apr 16, 2021. https://www.christianitytoday.com/news/2021/april/liberty-university-sue-jerry-falwell-jr-10m-contract-scanda.html.
Smith, Alexa. "When Mentor Becomes Molester." Advocate Web, Oct 2000. https://www.advocateweb.org/publications/articles-2/clergy/sexual-misconduct-church-mentor-becomes-molester-ministers-often-granted-immediate-trust-betray/.
Smith, Charles Ryder. *The Bible Doctrine of Sin and of the Ways of God with Sinners*. London: Epworth, 1953.
Smith, D. Moody. *John*. Abingdon New Testament Commentary. Nashville: Abingdon, 1999.
Smith, James K. A. "Redeeming the Affections: Deconstructing Augustine's Critique of Theater." In *The Spirit, the Affections, and the Christian Tradition*, edited by Dale M. Coulter and Amos Yong, 41–63. Notre Dame, IN: University of Notre Dame Press, 2016.
Smith, Jay E. "Can Fallen Leaders Be Restored to Leadership?" *Bibliotheca Sacra* 151.604 (1994) 455–80.
Smither, Edward. "Pastoral Lessons from Augustine's Theological Correspondence with Women." *Hervormde Teologiese Studies* 72.4 (2016) 1–6.
Stassen, Glen H. and David P. Gushee, *Kingdom Ethics: Following Jesus in Contemporary Context*. Downers Grove, IL: IVP Academic, 2003.
Steinfels, Peter. "The Deep Strangeness of the Catholic Church's Latest Scandal." *The Atlantic*, Aug 15, 2021. https://www.theatlantic.com/ideas/archive/2021/08/catholic-priest-jeffrey-burrill-grindr-pillar/619758/.
Stepp, Laura Sessions. "Church Defrocks Swaggart." *Washington Post*, Apr 9, 1988. https://www.washingtonpost.com/archive/lifestyle/1988/04/09/church-defrocks-swaggart/820223a3-0d78-41a1-afdc-6f12a59873b1/
Stott, John R. W. *Guard the Truth: The Message of 1 Timothy & Titus*. Downers Grove, IL: InterVarsity, 1996.
———. *The Cross of Christ*, Downers Grove, IL: InterVarsity, 2006.
———. *The Message of Galatians: Only One Way*. The Bible Speaks Today. Downers Grove, IL: InterVarsity, 1986.
Strohl, Jane E. "Luther's Spiritual Journey." In *The Cambridge Companion to Martin Luther*, ed. Donald McKim, 149–64. New York: Cambridge University Press, 2003.
Strom, Kay Marshall. *In the Name of Submission*. Portland, OR: Multnomah, 1986.
Struthers, William M. *Wired for Intimacy: How Pornography Hijacks the Male Brain*. Downers Grove, IL: InterVarsity, 2009.
Sullender, R. Scott. *Ancient Sins . . . Modern Addictions: A Fresh Look at the Seven Deadly Sins*. Eugene, OR: Cascade, 2013. Kindle edition.

Sutton, Geoffrey W., and Eloise K. Thomas. "Can Derailed Pastors be Restored? Effects of Offense and Age on Restoration." *Pastoral Psychology* 53 (2005) 583–99.

———., Kelly C. Mcleland, Katherine L. Weaks, Patricia E. Cogswell, Renee N. Miphouvieng. "Does Gender Matter? Relationship of Gender, Spousal Support, Spirituality, and Dispositional Forgiveness to Pastoral Restoration." *Pastoral Psychology* 55.5 (May 2007) 645–63.

———. and Kayla Jordan. "Evaluating Attitudes Toward Clergy Restoration: The Psychometric Properties of Two Scales." *Pastoral Psychology* 62.6 (Dec 2013) 859–71.

Swenson, Richard A. *Margin: Restoring Emotional, Physical, Financial, and Time Reserves to Overloaded Lives*. Colorado Springs, CO: NavPress, 2004.

Synan, Vinson. *The Holiness-Pentecostal Tradition*, Grand Rapids: Eerdmans, 1997.

———. and Daniel Woods, *Fire Baptized: The Many Lives and Works of Benjamin Hardin Irwin*. Lexington, KY: Emeth, 2017.

Tamber-Rosenau, Caryn. "Biblical Bathing Beauties and the Manipulation of the Male Gaze: What Judith Can Tell Us about Bathsheba and Susanna." *Journal of Feminist Studies in Religion* 33.2 (2017) 55–72.

Tan, Siang-Yang. *Counseling and Psychotherapy: A Christian Perspective*. Grand Rapids: Baker Academic, 2011.

Taylor, Charles. *A Secular Age*. Boston: Harvard University Press, 2007.

Taylor, Mark. *1 Corinthians*. The New American Commentary. Nashville: Broadman & Holman, 2014.

Tertullian. *Apology*. Edited by Philip Schaff. The Complete Ante-Nicene, Nicene, and Post-Nicene Church Fathers Collection. London: Catholic Way, 2014.

———. *On Modesty*. Edited by Philip Schaff. The Complete Ante-Nicene, Nicene, and Post-Nicene Church Fathers Collection. London: Catholic Way, 2014.

———. *To His Wife*. Edited by Philip Schaff. The Complete Ante-Nicene, Nicene, and Post-Nicene Church Fathers Collection. London: Catholic Way, 2014.

Thoburn, John W. "Predictive Factors Regarding Extra-Marital Sexual Activity Among Male Protestant Clergy." Ph.D. diss., Fuller Theological Seminary, 1991.

———. and Jack O. Balswick, "A Prevention Approach to Infidelity Among Male Protestant Clergy," *Pastoral Psychology* 42 (1993) 45–52.

———. and D. M. Whitman. "Clergy Affairs: Emotional Investment, Longevity of Relationship and Affair Partners." *Pastoral Psychology* 52 (2004) 491–506.

Thomas, Eloise K., and Geoffrey W. Sutton. "Religious Leadership Failure: Forgiveness, Apology, and Restitution." *Journal of Spirituality in Mental Health* 10 (2008) 308–27.

Thomas, Eloise K., and K. White, and Geoffrey W. Sutton. "Clergy Apologies Following Abuse: What Makes a Difference? Exploring Forgiveness, Apology, Responsibility-Taking, Gender, and Restoration." *Journal of Psychology and Christianity* 27.1 (2008) 16–29.

Thompson, Curt. *The Soul of Shame: Retelling the Stories We Believe About Ourselves*. Downers Grove, IL: InterVarsity, 2015.

Thompson, Lori Anne. "Victim Impact Statement." Feb 8, 2021. https://loriannethompson.com/2021/02/08/lori-anne-thompson-victim-impact-statement/.

Tozer, A.W. *That Incredible Christian*. Harrisburg, PA: Christian Publications, 1964.

———. *The Crucified Life*. Ventura, CA: Regal, 2011.

BIBLIOGRAPHY

Towner, Phillip H. *1–2 Timothy & Titus*. The IVP New Testament Commentary. Downers Grove, IL: InterVarsity, 2010.

Trask, Thomas E., Wayde I. Goodall, Zenas J. Bicket, eds. *The Pentecostal Pastor: A Mandate for the 21st Century*. Springfield, MO: Gospel Publishing House, 1997.

Trueman, Carl R. *The Rise and Triumph of the Modern Self: Cultural Amnesia, Expressive Individualism, and the Road to Sexual Revolution*. Wheaton, IL: Crossway, 2020.

Trull, Joe E., and James E. Carter. *Ministerial Ethics: Moral Formations for Church Leaders*. Grand Rapids: Baker Academic, 2004.

Uncredited. "The Day After Marvin Gorman Confronted Jimmy Swaggart With . . ." *United Press International*, Feb 27, 1988. https://www.upi.com/Archives/1988/02/27/The-day-after-Marvin-Gorman-confronted-Jimmy-Swaggart-with/7253572936400/.

Unger, Merrill F. *The New Unger's Bible Dictionary (Rev. and Updated)*, edited by R. K. Harrison, Howard F. Vos, and Cyril J. Barber. Chicago: Moody, 1988.

Useem, Jerry. "Power Causes Brain Damage." *The Atlantic*, Jul/Aug 2017. www.theatlantic.com/magazine/archive/2017/07/power-causes-brain-damage/528711.

Vermes, Geza. *The Religion of Jesus the Jew*. Minneapolis: Fortress, 1981.

Vine, W. E., Merrill F. Unger, and William White, Jr. *Vine's Complete Expository Dictionary of Old and New Testament Words*. Nashville: Thomas Nelson, 1996.

Vines, Matthew. *God and the Gay Christian: The Biblical Case in Support of Same-Sex Relationships*. New York: Convergent Books, 2014.

Volf, Miroslav. *Exclusion & Embrace: A Theological Exploration of Identity, Otherness, and Reconciliation*. Nashville: Abingdon, 2010.

von Rad, Gerhard. *Genesis: A Commentary*. Philadelphia: Westminster, 1961.

Walsh, K. L. et al. "Resiliency Factors in the Relation Between Childhood Sexual Abuse and Adulthood Sexual Assault in College-Age Women." *Journal of Child Sexual Abuse* 16.1 (2007) 1–17.

Walton, John H., and Kelly Lemon Vizcaino. *Job*. The NIV Application Commentary. Grand Rapids: Zondervan, 2012.

Ward, Tony, and Anthony R. Beech. "An Integrated Theory of Sexual Offending." In *Sexual Deviance: Theory, Assessment, and Treatment*, edited by D. Richard Laws and William T. O'Donohue, 21–36. New York: Guilford, 2008.

Wehr, Kathryn. "Virginity, Singleness and Celibacy: Late Fourth-Century and Recent Evangelical Visions of Unmarried Christians." *Theology & Sexuality* 17.1 (2011) 75–99.

Wells, Ken. "A Needs Assessment Regarding the Nature and Impact of Clergy Sexual Abuse Conducted by the Interfaith Sexual Trauma Institute." *Sexual Addiction and Compulsivity* 10 (2003) 201–17.

Wesley, John. "A Plain Account of Christian Perfection." In *The Essential Works of John Wesley: Selected Books, Sermons, and Other Writings*, edited by Alice Russkie, 1025–1102. Uhrichsville, OH: Barbour, 2011.

———. *A Plain Account of Genuine Christianity (Short & Rare Works Series)*. Hargreaves, 2014. Kindle edition.

———. "Sermon: Christian Perfection." In *The Essential Works of John Wesley: Selected Books, Sermons, and Other Writings*, edited by Alice Russkie, 397–414. Uhrichsville, OH: Barbour, 2011.

———. "Sermon: On Sin in Believers." In *The Essential Works of John Wesley: Selected Books, Sermons, and Other Writings*, edited by Alice Russkie, 341–352. Uhrichsville, OH: Barbour, 2011.

———. "Sermon: The End of Christ's Coming." In *The Essential Works of John Wesley: Selected Books, Sermons, and Other Writings*, edited by Alice Russkie, 367–376. Uhrichsville, OH: Barbour, 2011.

———. "Sermon: The Great Privilege of Those Who Are Born of God." In *The Essential Works of John Wesley: Selected Books, Sermons, and Other Writings*, edited by Alice Russkie, 331–341. Uhrichsville, OH: Barbour, 2011.

———. "Sermon: The Witness of Our Own Spirit." In *The Essential Works of John Wesley: Selected Books, Sermons, and Other Writings*, edited by Alice Russkie, 261–270. Uhrichsville, OH: Barbour, 2011.

———. *The Sermon on the Mount*. Edited by Clare George Weakley, Jr. Alachua, FL: Bridge-Logos, 2010.

West, Christopher. *Fill These Hearts: God, Sex, and the Universal Longing*. New York: Image, 2018

Whitney, Donald S. *Spiritual Disciplines for the Christian Life*. Colorado Springs, CO: NavPress, 2014.

Wilken, Robert Louis. "Blessed Passion of Love: The Affections, the Church Fathers, and the Christian Life." In *The Spirit, the Affections, and the Christian Tradition*, edited by Dale M. Coulter and Amos Yong, 29–40. Notre Dame, IN: University of Notre Dame Press, 2016.

Willard, Dallas. *The Divine Conspiracy: Rediscovering Our Hidden Life in God*. New York, NY: HarperCollins, 2014.

———. *Renovation of the Heart: Putting on the Character of Christ*. Colorado Springs, CO: NavPress, 2012.

———. *The Spirit of the Disciplines: Understanding How God Changes Lives*. New York, NY: HarperOne, 2009.

———., et al. *The Kingdom Life: A Practical Theology of Discipleship and Spiritual Formation*. Colorado Springs, CO: NavPress, 2014. Kindle edition.

Williams, Ernest S. "Assemblies of God Minister's Letter." Consortium of Pentecostal Archives, Dec 16, 1942. https://pentecostalarchives.org/?a=d&d=AGML19421216-01.1.3.

Williams, J. Rodman. *Renewal Theology: God, the World, and Redemption, Vol. 1*. Grand Rapids: Zondervan, 1988.

———. *Renewal Theology: Systematic Theology from a Charismatic Perspective, Vol. 2*. Grand Rapids: Zondervan, 1990.

Willimon, William H. *Calling and Character: Virtues of the Ordained Life*. Nashville: Abingdon, 2000.

———. *Pastor: The Theology and Practice of Ordained Ministry*. Nashville: Abingdon, 2016.

Willow Creek Independent Advisory Group. "Report." Feb 28, 2019. https://drive.google.com/file/d/1Aj_m_oHTG_ub1fvHfky5soRDgeyGF9oq/view.

Wilkins, Michael J. *Matthew*. The NIV Application Commentary. Grand Rapids: Zondervan, 2004.

Wilson, Michael Todd and Brad Hoffman. *Preventing Ministry Failure: A Shepherd Care Guide for Pastors, Ministers and Other Caregivers*. Downers Grove, IL: InterVarsity, 2007.

Wilson, Sandra D. *Released from Shame: Moving Beyond the Pain of the Past*. Downers Grove, IL: InterVarsity, 2002.

Wogaman, J. Philip *Christian Ethics, A Historical Introduction, Second Edition*. Louisville: Westminster John Knox, 2011.

———. and Douglas M. Strong, eds. *Readings in Christian Ethics*. Louisville: Westminster John Knox, 1996.

Wolfe, Alan. *The Transformation of American Religion: How We Actually Live Our Faith*. New York: Free, 2003.

Worley, Kyle. "Why It's Easier to Accept David as a Murderer Than a Rapist." *Christianity Today*, Oct 14, 2019. https://www.christianitytoday.com/ct/2019/october-web-only/david-bathsheba-debate-murder-rapist.html.

Wright, Archie T. *The Origin of Evil Spirits: The Reception of Genesis 6:1–4 in Early Jewish Literature*. Minneapolis: Fortress, 2015.

Wright, N. T. *Galatians*. Edited by Stephen E. Fowl, et al. Commentaries for Christian Formation. Grand Rapids: Eerdmans, 2021.

———. *Paul: A Biography*. New York: HarperCollins, 2018.

Yamauchi, Edwin M., and Marvin R. Wilson. *Dictionary of Daily Life in Biblical and Post-Biblical Antiquity Complete in One Volume, A-Z*. Peabody, MA: Hendrickson, 2017.

Yancey, Philip. *The Scandal of Forgiveness: Grace Put to the Test*. Grand Rapids: Zondervan, 2021.

Yarhouse Mark A., and Erica S. N. Tan. *Sexuality and Sex Therapy: A Comprehensive Christian Appraisal*. Downers Grove, IL: IVP Academic, 2014.

Youngblood, Ronald F., F. F. Bruce, and R. K. Harrison, eds. *Nelson's New Illustrated Bible Dictionary*. Nashville: Thomas Nelson, 1995.

Yuan, Christopher. *Holy Sexuality and the Gospel: Sex, Desire, and Relationships Shaped by God's Grand Story*. New York: Crown, 2018. Kindle edition.

Zoll, Rachel. "TV Evangelist Marcus Lamb Admits Adultery, Reveals $7.5 million Extortion Plot." *Associated Press*, Jan 12, 2019. https://www.cleveland.com/nation/2010/11/tv_evangelist_marcus_lamb_admi.html.

www.ingramcontent.com/pod-product-compliance
Lightning Source LLC
Chambersburg PA
CBHW070932150426
42814CB00024B/108